Frank Hazen, Martin J. Pritchard

The Passion of Rosamund Keith

Can Wisdom be put in a Siver Red, Or Love in a Golden Bowl

Frank Hazen, Martin J. Pritchard

The Passion of Rosamund Keith
Can Wisdom be put in a Siver Red, Or Love in a Golden Bowl

ISBN/EAN: 9783744692403

Printed in Europe, USA, Canada, Australia, Japan

Cover: Foto ©Thomas Meinert / pixelio.de

More available books at **www.hansebooks.com**

THE PASSION OF ROSAMUND KEITH

BY

MARTIN J. PRITCHARD

AUTHOR OF " WITHOUT SIN "

" Can Wisdom be put in a Silver Rod,
Or Love in a Golden Bowl ? "

—W. BLAKE

HERBERT S. STONE AND COMPANY
CHICAGO AND NEW YORK
MDCCCXCIX

TO MY FATHER AND MOTHER

You gathered wild flowers in the fields and brakes
   And worthless shells and stones along the sands;
   You brought and placed them in your parents' hands,
And they did hold them precious for your sakes.

And you were pleased.   I too by sandy lakes
   Of life, and in the mountains and lowlands,
   Have gathered this poor nosegay, and it stands
For moon and stars that my ambition takes.

In all your love you gave me all my life,
   In all my life I gave you all my love,
      And though I know my mountain flowers are wild,
And from my gift there's little to derive,
   If you would smile upon them and approve,
      I should be happy as a little child.

M. J. P.

INDEX

CHAPTER I ·

THE HUNT BALL

"WHAT a glorious day—and killed only four miles from home! Come along, uncle, we shall be back in time for quite an early tea and a good long rest."

As Rosamund Keith pulled her horse round and prepared to lead the way out of the small copse-edged field where reynard had died the death, a young man who had dismounted to give his mare a breather laid his hand on her bridle.

"I must congratulate you, Miss Keith. You deserve the brush. You rode splendidly. The way you took Shellerly brook was magnificent."

Miss Keith gave a little laugh as she leant forward and patted her horse's neck.

"I think we got rid of most of the field there, didn't we?"

Paul Carr could only nod acquiescence. His eyes, his thoughts, his whole personality were too absorbed in contemplating the figure before him to speak. Certainly it was well worth looking at, and most men would have forgiven his silent admiration.

Rosamund Keith was not of the Dresden china or pocket-Venus style of beauty. Rather was she one of that splendid type of womanhood which seems to be the essentially modern evolution of an English girl. Though more than common tall, the perfect proportions of her fine figure dispelled all accusations of ungainliness. Her greatest rivals had never dared to say she was either weedy or coarse. Her severely plain, well-cut habit showed to advantage the gracious outline of her shoulders and the delicate fulness of her round bosom. From her slender waist swelled her graceful hips in a fine amplitude. The outdoor life she loved so well had developed every budding beauty, and from constant exercise she had acquired a free swing and movement of the upper part of her body that was intensely fascinating. Now, as under Mr. Carr's restraining hand, Miss Keith's mount grew impatient and curvetted restlessly, the girl's lithe body swayed easily with every movement like a flower in the wind.

"That young woman does know how to show off her points," said Mrs. Crooksley of Crooksley Hall, ill-naturedly. To-day was the third day running that Rosamund Keith had carried off the brush from under her very nose, and she was feeling very sore about it.

"I beg your pardon, madam," said Lord Clariston, M. F. H., wheeling round sharply. "You are mistaken. I've known Miss Keith since she was as high as my saddle girth, and she couldn't show off if she tried. She's the prettiest figure and the finest seat in the county, and there's not a woman in England who can catch her when she's in the first flight."

The old gentleman made a general bow to those about him, and turned away for home. The little knot melted away, too, as mist upon a mountain side. But still Paul lingered at Miss Keith's bridle rein, until the mare danced with impatience.

"Quiet! Lady Bird, quiet now," murmured Rosamund.

Paul's eyes followed the course of her slim, well-gloved hand upon the satin chestnut skin of the creature's neck, and then almost unconsciously he laid his hand where hers had been.

"Are you going to be very fashionable to-night?" he asked. "Shall you be very late at the ball?"

"Oh! I hope not!" cried Rosamund with enthusiasm. "It's the last dance of the season. We must make the most of it. But I'm nearly sure we shall be in good time. Laura and Honor have made up their minds to a long night of it, and if they really want to do a thing Aunt Margot always gives way."

"Two against one, eh? Then you'll promise me the first two dances, will you?"

Rosamund was as far removed from a coquette as it was possible for any feminine entity to be, but she would herself have frankly pleaded guilty to a certain vague pleasure in her power as a pretty girl; so she poised her head daintily on one side and promised she would think about it.

"It's not worth thinking about, Miss Keith," said Carr, kicking at a withered tussock of grass. "If I were you, I would just say 'Yes' without thinking at all."

Miss Keith bent lower over her saddle and let a mischievous smile curl the corners of her mouth.

"If you were me, Mr. Carr, you would do just what I mean to do. Yes, uncle, I'm coming."

She flicked the chestnut mare on her hind quarters and cantered across the field, her supple body responding again to the lively movement of her steed.

So long as Mr. Carr could catch a glimpse of Miss Keith's smart billy-cock hat above the bare hedgerows, or the ring of her clear voice on the still air, he stood motionless where she had left him. When all but the memory of her had disappeared, he strode over to where a lad held his horse, swung himself into the saddle, and

jogged away in the direction of Shellerly Barracks, where
he had been staying with a friend, off and on, during the
past hunting season.

"What a glorious day we've had, dear," said Rosamund, out of sheer lightness of heart, to her uncle.
"And what a glorious evening we're going to have."

The Honourable Alban Kerquham, R.A., pulled up
his big brown horse on the brow of the swelling hill they
had been slowly ascending, and looked out from under
his shaggy brows across the finest bit of hunting country
in the world.

"Look, my child, what a wonderful effect the vague,
almost invisible verdure of early spring has. It is like a
soft brown velvet that hints at green where the light
catches it. Now see that long shaft of pale yellow
light that strikes across those fields. What an effect!
What an effect!"

Mr. Kerquham dropped the reins on his horse's neck
and arched both hands above his eyes, the better to
enframe the picture.

"It is lovely, uncle," murmured Rosamund, scarcely
above her breath.

Upright as a dart, solid as a rock, Mr. Kerquham sat
his horse and gazed at the scene before him till the pale
light of the short February day faded feebly behind a
thin veil of gauzy mist. He was an anomaly, both in
character and in society. The descendant of a long line
of Scottish peers, all of whom had been as Calvinistic as
they were blue-blooded, he had when quite a young man,
outraged the family traditions and all the proprieties by
claiming his small allowance from his uncle, the Earl of
Kilbeggie, and going abroad—not to make the "grand
tour," as befitted a young gentleman of his time, but to
take up his abode in a doubtful quarter of Paris and

plunge into the study and pursuit of "Art." The *Family*, which consisted almost exclusively of the old earl and two sisters, had pronounced him dead—both to them and their world. To their astonishment, however, Alban Kerquham emerged from the shades to which he had been formally relegated, neither a ne'er-do-well nor a returned prodigal, but as a successful artist, above whose handsome head Fame was already hovering, and at whose doors Fortune was knocking day and night.

But though the brilliant R.A. loved his work, and, as he said himself, "kept his heart in a paint-box," the hunting instincts of his race never died within him, and his quaint home, half hunting box, half old farmhouse, in Midshire, where he spent each year so many happy months, was as dear to him as his splendid house and wonderful studio on Campden Hill.

A day's run with the East Midshire hounds was an infinite delight to him, and as he once more gathered up his reins and put spurs to his horse he re-echoed his niece's sentiments.

"It's been a glorious day, Rosie." He flung one lingering glance at the fast fading landscape. "And it's been a wonderful sunset. Come on, my dear, let's take the horses in warm."

There was no time for any more words, for Mr. Kerquham set Brown Billy to a smart pace, but as they skirted the town, Rosamund waved her hand towards the main street, where already gas stars and devices were being lit and bunting run up in honour of *the* ball of the year.

"Look, dear!" she cried in her fresh young voice, "how gay it's all going to be."

     *   *   *   *   *

Rosamund was right. How gay it was that evening

in the old Town Hall, where tradition said that the polished floor was laid on carriage springs, and where the
Regimental Band of the Fiftieth Hussars, quartered at
Shellery, discoursed the merriest dance measures to
nearly five hundred of the flower of the hunting and
fashionable world.

The grey, distempered walls were covered with
emblems and trophies of the Sport of Kings, and the
tall, bare windows had been cunningly converted into
silk-lined alcoves, in which wide-spreading palms and
low-cushioned chairs encouraged—even implored—*tête-à-
têtes.* The shallow stone staircases had all been covered
with crimson cloth and fringed with white and red
camelia trees in pots. Tapestries hung before the doors,
and over all the pink-shaded lights shed a roseate glow.

"It's like fairyland!" cried Rosamund, as with her
two cousins she followed Mrs. Kerquham up the impos-
ing staircase.

"What rubbish you talk!" snapped Laura. "One
would think you'd just come out of the schoolroom
instead of having been through a London season."

Laura Kerquham was an exceedingly pretty girl in a
modish way. She was always a little in front of the
newest fashion—too much so for an unmarried girl, most
women said—and adapted what passed for her manners
to her company. An elderly admirer had once praised
her extraordinary adaptability of temperament. "You
mean she is all things to all men!" had rejoined a smart
woman.

The remark was as true as it was unkind.

"Posing for an *ingénue,* eh, dear?" sneered her
younger sister Honor. "Not quite suited to your classic
style, Rosamund."

Honor was a colourless copy of her more brilliant

sister, *plus* a sour expression and a shrewish tongue. She was practically tabooed by the young men of her mother's set, and the knowledge that this was so had not improved her temper.

But Rosamund was proof against every petty disagreeable that night. The lights, the passing of friends, the crash of music, the hum of many voices touched her fresh nature and unspoiled imagination as new wine touches men's brains. As she and her party neared the head of the stairs, and were stayed a moment by the crush of fast arriving guests, her slender feet in their satin slippers figured a subdued measure beneath her flounces, and her heart throbbed in her white bosom for very joy.

"By Jove! What a lovely girl!"

The remark came from a group of men who were hanging over the low balustrade criticising the arrivals.

Rosamund felt herself blushing for pleasure. She had longed to look her best to-night, and now a stranger had said she was lovely. How good the world was—she raised her eyes and caught Paul Carr's gaze fixed on her—how like heaven.

"Have you thought over those dances?" said Carr's voice in her ear, as he reached her side.

"I told you I never think—I do things." With a shy laugh Miss Keith slipped her white gloved hand into the hollow of Paul's pink sleeve, and side by side they swept with the crowd into the ball-room.

The salt of the earth and the chaperones were ensconced on a charmingly arranged platform, from which they could see and be seen. In the place of honour sat the Duchess of Midshire, holding, as befitted her position in the county, quite a court. She waved Mr. Kerquham to her side as he led his wife to the top of the room.

"My good sir, why on earth wouldn't you look my
way at the meet this morning? I'd fifty things to say
to you. How do, Mrs. Kerquham?"

"Hounds are like time, Duchess, they wait for no
man," said Alban Kerquham, throwing back his handsome iron-grey head and laughing at his own remark.

"And that niece of yours is like the hounds. How
that girl rides! Now take that chair; I'm full of family
news. I met Kilbeggie last week and your aunt, Lady
Charlotte Lundy, at the Glensides in Stirlingshire.
Kilbeggie was as grumpy as ever." Her Grace of Midshire, who was a large and comely person, chuckled at
the memories she had of the crusty old earl. "And
Charlotte Lundy was more starched than usual. Women
like that bring out all the vice that is in me. I always
long to shock her."

The Duchess looked over each plump shoulder to
make certain that Mrs. Kerquham was not within hearing, and then leant forward and whispered to the Hon.
Alban Kerquham, "And I did, too."

Then she went on aloud. "But that's not what I
really wanted to talk to you about. I want you to paint
my portrait when we're all back in town. Something
really nice, you know. That little French idiot, Fer-
nand, whom they make such a fuss about, made a regular
frump of me—more like a publican's wife than anything,
and I want something better than that to hand down to
posterity."

Mr. Kerquham bowed assent. The Duchess was
scarcely an ideal subject for his brush, but when a man
takes up the *rôle* of fashionable portrait painter he cannot always choose his sitters.

"Can you begin sittings after Easter?" he asked.

The Duchess nodded her marvellous tiara at him, and then in her abrupt manner changed the subject.

"I say! your niece—Keith's her name isn't it?—is quite the belle of the ball. Just look at the crowd of men round her. She certainly is extraordinarily handsome. Not at all in a modern way, though. She reminds me of some picture or statue I have seen somewhere."

"All the artists say that Rosamund is the living, breathing image of the 'Clytie.'"

"Ah, yes! to be sure. That's the bust with the *ondulé* hair and lily leaves all around her shoulders, isn't it? Well, artists are supposed to know all about that kind of thing, aren't they?" Her attention wandered once more. "By-the-bye, do find out who is that dreadful little creature with the cropped head over there. She's quite shocking; got on a high frock and a linen collar. I'm longing to know if she's an eccentric American or a New Woman."

Meanwhile Rosamund Keith was enjoying with all her heart and soul her position as belle of the best ball of the season. The rather cold statuesque manner which came so naturally to her when she was surrounded by strangers was lost to-night in the frank gaiety and unrestrained happiness of a healthy-minded, light-hearted girl. The velvety depths of her great dark eyes were stirred with merriment as a silent pool is ruffled by a summer breeze. The full bow of her rich red lips was parted in smiles that chased one another over her usually quiet face. The fascinating little droop of her head, which had always accentuated her likeness to the famous "Clytie," had given place to the upright carriage that her triumph demanded. To Paul Carr, who was never very far away from her side, she seemed that night

entirely desirable; yet, man-like, he was none too
pleased when he found some one else sharing his
opinions.

Rosamund was walking up to the top of the room to
dance in a quadrille with the Lord-Lieutenant of the
county; an antique gentleman, but one who had still an
eye for a pretty face and a pleasing if old-fashioned way
of turning a compliment.

"By Jove! how common she makes all the women
look, doesn't she?"

Paul Carr started, for the spoken words voiced his
own thoughts.

"Ah, Lord St. Ives! how are you? Didn't see you at
the meet this morning," said Paul, rather coolly.

"No. Just like my infernal luck. Had to go to town
last night, and only got back an hour ago. For the
Lord's sake, don't tell me again I've missed the best run
of the season. I've heard it fifty times already. They
say Miss Keith rode wonderfully."

Paul did not answer his lordship, but contented himself with watching the young lady mentioned. His eyes
grew dark with love as he devoured her from the top of
her delicately poised head to the pointed tip of her shoes
that peeped from beneath her gown as she paced through
the dance. She wore a white satin gown, severely plain
and moulded to the gracious curves of her swaying figure.
Light as the morning mist that hangs on the brows of
hills in summer time, about the edge of her bodice was
a frill of cobwebby lace that, as she moved, floated
indefinitely above the exquisite curves of her full white
arms and enhanced the mysterious charm of her superb
bosom and shoulders. Against the polished whiteness
of her neck, the delicate oval of her face, lit by the
glorious eyes and framed in a low-growing ripple of black

hair, glowed like a flower. Above her dark brows, which were so fine and true that a fairy might have pencilled them, and just where her hair was parted shone a big diamond star. It had been the only jewel that Rosamund's young mother had ever possessed. It had been the single legacy she had [been able to leave her new-born infant before she herself died.

Yet Paul Carr thought her eyes flashed brighter even than the gems, as when the quadrille was over he pushed his way to the dais where Rosamund was sitting between the Duchess of Midshire and her uncle.

"Miss Keith!" he cried, as with his broad pink-clad shoulders he made his way through the throng, "they're going to dance a Highland Fling. It's an extra, do give it to me."

"Bless the man!" said the Duchess in her loud, cheery voice. "Can't you let Miss Keith be quiet for one moment? You young men seem to think that no one wants to look at or speak to a pretty girl except yourselves."

"What's that, Carr?" interrupted Mr. Kerquham. "A Highland Fling, did you say? Ah! there was a time when I'd have danced it with a kitchen chair sooner than stand down. Rosamund, my dear child, you must go. But don't forget it's your last dance to-night. She dances it better than any girl in the three kingdoms, Duchess. I taught her myself."

Down again into the press and throng of the crowded ball-room, where uniforms of scarlet and blue, pink coats with gay-coloured facings, gold lace and glittering buttons made sharp contrast with snowy shoulders all framed in tender blue, rose red, soft green, dense black, and clear white, went the laughing girl and her partner.

The aged Lord-Lieutenant sank into Rosamund's

vacant chair.   He wore many medals on his breast and
a great jewel on a riband round his neck.

"Ah! ha! Duchess, we're going to see some dancing
now that will be worth looking at.   Mr. Kerquham, I
congratulate you on your niece.   She's the handsomest
young woman I've seen for years, and she's as sweet as
she's pretty."

The first notes from the pipes in the gallery above
drowned Mr. Kerquham's reply.   The centre of the big
room cleared as if by magic, and the dance began.

"Southrons are no good at it," muttered Alban
Kerquham into his beard, as by degrees the panting
dancers mingled with the watching crowd.   "One
must have it in the blood—and have been properly
taught."

"Ha! ha!   They've danced them down!   Now time
them, somebody, and see how long they can last!"

The Duchess's ringing tones were heard by half the
room, and fifty watches were pulled out.   Then Her
Grace, all a-beam with interest and smiles, rose to her
feet the better to see, and was followed by the Lord-
Lieutenant himself and all the great folk on the dais.

"Miss Keith!   They're all watching us.   Dance your
best," cried Paul Carr, as he waved the encroaching
crowd back.

Rosamund flashed a smile at him, and then with her
shapely head held high and her eyes flashing with the
joy of movement and of living, she began to dance in
earnest.   Each rounded limb and supple muscle did her
bidding well, and like some fair flower that is tossed by
the wind, she danced on among the gaudy-tinted throng.
Now one white arm and now the other curved like a sec-
tion of an ivory arch high above the dusky coils of her
wavy hair.   The jewel on her forehead twinkled like a

big star; her scarlet lips, from which came short, sharp cries, were parted and dewy as a budding rose.

"She's rippin'!"

"By Jove! As good as a play."

"Help me onto the seat so that I can see," cried a girl's shrill voice, and like weeds that grow in a night a score of women sprang, in all the gay glory of their smart frocks and jewels, onto the surrounding benches.

Rosamund laughed gleefully at the sight. The young blood that loved exercise and excitement was throbbing in every pulse.

"Tell them to play faster—faster!" she cried, intoxicated with her own movements. The pipes skirled and droned through the hot air, and Rosamund's feet scarcely seemed to touch the floor.

"Go on—a little longer."

Paúl Carr was flagging, but her words spurred him on. Rosamund had caught sight of her uncle's face on the crowded dais, and his evident delight in her triumph was as fuel to the fire of her energy. She waved one white hand to him, and the slight action, so heart whole, so unaffected, caught the fancy of the whole room.

"Bravo! Bravo!" cried the Duchess, holding her bejewelled arms high and applauding loudly.

"Bravo!" shouted Mr. Kerquham. "I'll paint her as a 'Bacchante.'"

"Bravo! Hurrah!" piped the Lord-Lieutenant. "Say rather, Mr. Kerquham, as 'Herodias's Daughter,' for she'd dance the head and the heart away from any man."

Then the whole room broke into a salvo of hand-clapping and "Hurrahs," and Rosamund, dazed at last, gave one last shrill cry, and holding out her two hands to Paul Carr, murmured between her quick-coming breaths: "Stop me now! Hold me! Take me away!"

In gracious abandon she let herself drop within the shelter of his circling arms, and with panting bosom and radiant face passed through the laughing, cheering crowd that made an easy way for her out of the room.

As the Kerquham's carriage rattled down the stone-paved sleeping street, Rosamund leaning forward caught a glimpse of the radiant ball-room windows, while on her ears throbbed the rhythmic beat of the well-known words:

> Do ye ken John Peel with his coat so gay?
> Do ye ken John Peel at the break of day?
> Do ye ken John Peel when he's far, far away?
> With his hounds and his horn in the morning.

CHAPTER II

"THE YEAR'S AT THE SPRING."

The quaintly straggling house that formed the Kerquham's country seat glowed redly in the afternoon sun. The western windows, which belonged to the "best" rooms, seemed all afire and flared like flaming beacons across the countryside.

In the long, low drawing-room the house party and some half-dozen visitors were drinking tea.

"So you are really off to-morrow?" sighed a young man from Shellerly Barracks, who had bicycled over to take a long farewell of pretty Laura Kerquham.

"Yes! Isn't it lovely to think that in twenty-four hours we shall be in town? Or, as near it as unfortunate artistic people can live. I often wonder why my father has never managed to fix up a studio in Park Lane or Piccadilly. Campden Hill is awfully out of the way."

Miss Laura pouted delightfully as she handed her swain a second cup of tea. His people had something to do with trade, she knew, but they lived in Grosvenor Square, and his mother gave a big ball every season, to which all the best set went. Besides, all the new peerages went to trade nowadays, so Laura Kerquham showed her pretty white teeth in a perpetual smile, and even forebore to snap when her mother asked her three times for fresh tea for new arrivals.

It was quite the break-up of the hunting season. Gentle rains and warm west winds had filled the whole

air with the scent of blossoms and the rustle of baby
leaves.   From London came rumours of full streets and
many gaieties.   Day after day the meets grew smaller
and the country more blind.   The Duchess of Midshire
had set the fashion by moving herself and her great
establishment up to Berkeley Square.   The opening of
Parliament closed at least a dozen good houses in the
immediate neighbourhood.   Laura had become restive
and Honor sulky.   Mr. Kerquham, too, felt that he must
get back to earnest work in the studio that only ranked
second in his affection after his beloved countryside.
So the head servants were dispatched to prepare the town
house; the stables and coach house were denuded of
everything save a rough pony and a governess cart.
Room after room was stripped of its *bibelots* and curios,
and packing up and saying good-bye began in real earnest.

To-day the afternoon tea was brought earlier than
usual into the white-panelled, chintz-covered drawing-
room, for Lady Sophia Kerquham, the maiden sister of
the Earl of Kilbeggie, was about to betake herself once
more to the grey old castle in the Highlands, amid wild
moors and gloomy pine forests that had been the cradle
of the Kerquham family.   Once a year Lady Sophia
quitted these fastnesses, and, as she considered, sacrificed herself, her opinions, and her feelings on the altar
of family duty, and came south to see that Alban and
Margot Kerquham were ordering themselves and their
family in accordance with family tradition.

As Lady Sophia sat by the wide open fireplace, where
a hundred impertinent little flames played hide and seek
among the piled beech logs and polished brass dogs, the
reddening sunlight shone full on her rugged face.   She
was of the fair, or sandy Scottish type, but the light
reddish hair, which was smoothed back under the frilled

cap of her coarse straw cottage bonnet, was plentifully
streaked with grey, and though her high cheeks were
rosy, a multitude of fine wrinkles puckered the skin about
her eyes and mouth. A long full cloak of serviceable
grey cloth hung over the back of her chair, and a little
table before her held the tea and plate of scones that
careful Mrs. Kerquham always had served during Lady
Sophia's visit.

Alban Kerquham sat by her side. The strong strain
of clannishness that is inherent in every true Scotch-
man's nature bound him in a way that was unaccount-
able, even to himself, to this hard-featured, austere
member of his house. He alone could fathom beneath
her narrow ideas, and her bigoted notions, the sound
judgment, the true honesty of her rough nature. He
knew, for he had heard it from his own father, how Aunt
Sophia had given up her girlhood to good works among
the cotters on the family estate, and how her early womanhood, the time of joy and love, had been embittered by
the death of her destined husband in the Crimea. Also
how she had sought comfort in religion, but throwing
herself on the stony bosom of the Church according to
Calvin, had only received threats and warnings as consolations.

That had hardened her nature, and the isolated life
she had led since then in the grim family mansion with
only the old earl and a handful of rough Highland servants had loosened the slight hold she had ever had on
her contemporary world. Yet Mr. Kerquham liked her,
for even her sternest dictums, her narrowest and most
ridiculous opinions came to him as a breath of moorland
air comes to a man sated with the close perfumes of
boudoirs and alcoves.

The old lady was knitting at a long coarse stocking

as she took her tea and made her valedictory remarks to her nephew.   She held it a sin to use the tongue and leave the fingers unemployed.

"The devil is ever on the lookout for folded hands," she would say, when she produced her rough work before strangers.

"Well, Alban, I shall have much to tell Kilbeggie on my return."

"Only good, I hope, Aunt Sophia.   If your visit has been as pleasant to you as to us, I trust it will be good."

"As to that, I live my own life wherever I go, nephew," said the old lady roughly.

Alban Kerquham smiled in his grizzled beard and his brown eyes twinkled beneath his bushy brows.   He was going to be lectured, he knew, just as he had been fifty years ago, when the Sundays at Kilbeggie had been passed in chronicling his baby crimes of the previous week and exhorting him in the words of sundry local deacons and elders to improvement in the approaching one.   Lady Sophia took a sip of tea, and then began to knit and talk at the same time.

"Your wife is a good woman, Alban, and sees that my rooms are such as I can sit in when I please, but this house is not the same as it used to be.   It's not the same—and you're piling up a load of sorrows for yourself, Alban Kerquham, with your indulgences and pamperings."

She shot a keen glance of stern disapprobation towards the big tea table.   Laura, with her pretty golden curls fluffing like an aureole round her *gamine's* face, was sitting with her elbows among the cups and plates and flirting with modern frankness with half a dozen young officers who, in various degrees of riding and bicycling dress, were lounging round her.

"Laura is very young," said Mr. Kerquham, following Lady Sophia's eyes.

"All the more reason she should be put under some discipline. Look at her now, sitting like a kitchen wench and laughing like a hoyden. What are you and Margot about to allow a daughter of yours to behave like that?"

"My dear aunt, to reform Laura's manners would be a Herculean [task. It would entail taking the whole of the younger generation in hand, for they learn their ways, monkey-like, from one another."

"True! true!" and the old lady nodded her head. "And from some of the older ones, too, eh, Alban? What would Kilbeggie have said if he could have seen the Duchess of Midshire romping the other night with all those lads and lassies? It's a bad world—and it will come to a bad end."

Alban Kerquham laughed.

"But, my dear aunt, a light pair of heels and a light head don't of necessity mean wickedness."

"You're blinded—along with the rest, nephew. Light heads and light heels lead to light conduct, and a heart that's so light it doesn't exist at all. When have you known your Laura do any unselfish thing, or say a kind one, except to some long-legged boy who ogles her all the evening? When does Laura ever occupy herself save when she's curling that yellow mop of hers before a glass or sticking some tulle and sham flowers on the top of it? I've no patience with a girl that cannot even put a sober, decent hat on her head."

She added irrelevantly: "I often think, Alban, it's a pity the days are gone by when the girls were whipped for frivolity and idleness. They all want it nowadays—except—"

Lady Sophia's harsh face softened a little and her voice sank to a lower key.

"Except Rosamund. Oh! don't think I approve of her altogether." And she waved the stocking bristling with bright steel needles before Mr. Kerquham's face. "She's very emancipated—as they call it now. Fifty years ago it was 'unladylike.' But at least her instincts are healthy. She'll get up in the dark of a winter's morning to ride to a meet ten miles off, but Laura plays 'slug-a-bed' till eleven. Rosamund comes in late for luncheon—a tendency that should be checked with a firm hand—but says she has been taking the dogs for a run, or fell in with a shooting party from the Towers and stayed to watch the guns beat up the Long Wood. Your Laura is lost for an afternoon, and explains—when she does condescend to reappear—that young Trevoir has been teaching her a stroke in billiards. Rubbish! Both those girls are modern. Both are impossible in my eyes—but with a difference. Laura always smells of smoke and patchouli; Rosamund carries the scent of new-turned earth and sweet, clean air in the folds of the absurdly short cloth gowns she will wear. You brought those two girls up together, Alban Kerquham; I fancy you'll find you have made a mistake with one of them. Rosamund sings like an angel in church on a Sunday morning, and plays golf all the afternoon; Laura goes to church, too, but afterwards sleeps over one of those wicked French novels till tea or a young man comes to wake her up. Neither spends the Sabbaths as I could wish, but there are degrees even in wrong-doing."

"And Honor—?"

"Is a nonentity and a shrew at that. She'll probably marry the first, though. Rosamund is a good girl at heart, and I pray that I may live to see her a happy woman."

"Amen to that, Aunt Sophia!" said Alban Kerquham.

But the sun was sinking in a sea of crimson and gold, and it was almost time for Lady Sophia Kerquham to begin the elaborate exhortations and preparations that invariably preceded her start on a journey.

Near the Manor House, where the trees grew high and close, the shades of the early spring evening were already drifting down, but out in the open country, two miles away, where a great space of rough common land lay like an ill-stretched carpet, all ups and downs, it was still broad daylight.

Silhouetted against the rosy sky were three figures. Paul Carr, stalwart and broad shouldered, looked the epitome of athletic English manhood in his easy country suit. A small lad standing at his side was gazing at him with reverence. He had just won a game of golf with a record stroke, and the caddie was proportionately impressed.

A yard or two away, on a slight elevation, stood Rosamund. She wore one of the short cloth skirts that always roused Lady Sophia's ire, and a smart little Norfolk jacket was held closely round her slender waist by a deep belt of russia leather. High boots of workmanlike make encased her feet, while as she stood, tall and straight against the sky line, she pushed her long white hands into loose gloves of pale tan kid. A tam o'shanter cap was pulled over her rebellious locks, and from it rose one brilliant scarlet quill feather. The exercise and the quickening spring breeze had whipped a delicious color into her cheeks and tipped the curled edges of her ears into the semblance of rosy shells. Little dark curls blew across her eyes from time to time, at which she alternately laughed and exclaimed.   Paul, looking up at her, thought he had never seen so fair a creature.

"Here, take Miss Keith's things up to the house," said Paul, tossing the caddie a silver piece.

The boy started off at a lumbering trot.   Rosamund laughed.

"And now that you have sent away my escort, what's to become of me?"

"I am going to see you home," answered Carr, authoritatively.

"But it's so out of your way!" said Rosamund, more to salve her conscience for taking Mr. Carr in an opposite direction from Shellerly, than for any other reason.

Paul Carr's face would have insured him a measure of popularity with the female sex, even without the golden halo of considerable wealth, which, in society's eyes, cast a pleasing radiance over his well-cut features.   His pale olive skin and fine dark eyes had been highly commended by connoisseurs of male beauty.   It was only the more thoughtful — or the envious — among his acquaintances who said that the full curves of his clean-shaven mouth were too womanly in their beauty, and that his delicate chin indicated a want of grip of character. Even his eyes, lustrous and deep, had been called too dreamy and introspective.   But no one could deny him his superb height and magnificent shoulders, nor belittle his prowess in the hunting field and on the moors.

He was a man of few words, and now he did not speak, but merely extended one hand to help the girl from her grassy elevation.   Scarcely touching his fingers, she sprang to his side, and then, taking a leaf out of his book, walked on silently.

They had gone some little distance—half across the

links—when some sudden impulse made her stop and face round towards the way she had come.

"What a shame it seems to have to leave it all, just when it is beginning to look its best," she said.

On every side the young grass was springing, covering the rough ground with a velvety carpet. The gorse bushes were outlined against the tender verdure by suggestions of golden yellow. The bramble thickets were flinging off slender shoots of transparent green, and where the sun had kissed them warmly were starred with blossom. Bluebells danced and shook in the freshening wind, and in sheltered spots mauve and yellow crocus cups were spread upon the grass as though arranged for a fairies' feast.

A group of blossoming hawthorn trees tossed their white arms and showered a scented snow of loosened petals over their knotted roots.

Rosamund lifted one hand.

"Listen! there's spring's harbinger. The cuckoo. Oh! how dreadful to have to go to town."

"But you'll like it when you're there."

There was a rough palisade before them, and he leaned his elbows on it.

"Yes!" said Rosamund rather reluctantly. "I am afraid I am one of those unstable characters who enjoy each thing as it comes."

She leaned upon the hurdles, too, so close to him that he could see the faultless grain of her pure skin and note the soft fulness of her dark eyelashes.

"I don't quite know how it is, but I seem to find pleasure in everything. I am just as happy over a piece of embroidery as I am at a dance. Golf gives me the same delicious sensation of freedom and movement as riding. I love my singing—oh! so much—but it is no disappointment to me to shut down the piano and go with Uncle Alban to the studio to hunt up things for him and set his palette. I am dreadfully afraid that I am a person of no taste. What do you think?''

- She turned her face to him and directed the level gaze of her big eyes at him.

''I can't agree with you, Miss Keith. I have always considered you as having tastes above the average.''

''Oh! please don't exalt me at the expense of my much abused sex,'' she said, parting her lips in a sunny smile. ''I am no better than any one else.''

''In my opinion,'' said Paul Carr, ''the question does not admit of argument.'' And then he looked at her with the frank, boyish admiration, which, when he was in her presence, always astonished him by conquering the more artificial side of his nature. ''I think you are quite the nicest girl in the whole world.''

''And what about the poor others?'' laughed Rosamund, taking the little compliment without any consciousness, and not changing colour in the least.

''Oh! the others don't count,'' he answered impetuously. ''They are most of them a lot of brainless dolls, and I suppose you will think me very rude for saying so, but those who do think at all, are as a rule not at all improved by the process.''

Rosamund shook back a wandering curl from her face.

''Now you think you are going to trap me into an argument and get me to say all sorts of ridiculous things to try and prove to you that every woman, merely because she is a woman, is ten thousand times better than a man, but I am not going to gratify you, Mr. Carr.'' She looked out over the fair landscape. ''It is too lovely an evening to even chop logic.''

Suddenly her eyes sparkled, and she cried:

"Look there! He knows the end of the hunting is near, or he would not be out taking an evening walk in that leisurely fashion."

She pointed to where an old dog fox was slinking along in the distance among the gorse bushes. A rabbit hung helpless, with little white dangling feet and draggled fur, from his jaws.

"I am afraid he doesn't care much whether the hunting is over or not; he has been out to get his supper. But are you not sorry," he went on, "you who are such a sportswoman and who ride so awfully straight, that the hunting is over?"

She shook her head.

"No; do you know, I don't think I am. The other morning when Uncle Alban and I were riding to the last meet it was as warm as May. In the meadows that we passed by there were a whole lot of funny little lambs bleating and skipping about, or nestling up against their mothers' warm, woolly sides. The thrushes and starlings were out in the damp ditches by the roadside, foraging for fat worms, and in the hedges we could see nests full of the queerest little creatures with gaping beaks and bald heads. Sheelah, the mare that does the work on the farm, had had a little foal that morning, and I had been to see it; it was top-heavy and absurdly knock-kneed, but it was young and just born. I suppose you will have a very bad opinion of me, but I was quite sorry that we killed that day. It seems such a shame to go out and kill creatures just when everything is springing into life. I think the spring ought to make people more merciful. It always seems to me as if the world were new and everything that is in it."

"And that is why you are glad that the hunting is over," said Paul.

She nodded her head.

"I should not go to a meet now if there were another."

She raised herself from the rough hurdles and stood upright, and he followed her example. He was half a head taller than she, and looked down upon her for a little space before they started to walk again. The tam o'shanter and her ruffled hair cast a shadow over her low brow and deep eyes. The evening light rested upon her mouth and the soft round curves of her chin. For the first time he seemed to read a different expression in her face.

"I did not think you had any sentiment about you," he said. "I have always thought one of your greatest virtues was your common sense, and that you had such a matter-of-fact way of looking at life."

"And we have been friends for over six months!" she cried in mock reproach. "And you pretend to know women well! Every one of us—the lightest-hearted and the coldest-hearted, the most selfish and the most silly, all have a streak of what you are pleased to call 'sentiment' in their natures. Of course it comes out in a different way with every one. One woman will cry over a dog and strike a child; another will shed tears at the theater and gaze dry-eyed upon the most fearful human suffering. But every woman has a soft spot somewhere."

"And yours?" he asked, questioningly.

"I think mine is for nature. I am not very fond of people. Perhaps the circumstances of my life have rather set me apart from others of my sex and age. You see, I never knew my parents, and although my uncle has been more than good to me, although my heart overflows with gratitude when I remember what he has done for me, it would be false of me to pretend that I regard him absolutely as I should have regarded my father and mother."

"But your aunt and cousins?"

Rosamund began to walk slowly on.

"Aunt Margot and the two girls," she said. "Are you trying to draw me again, Mr. Carr? You have been in the neighborhood long enough to know what they are and exactly what people think of them. Although they are my relations, I am of the same opinion as their merest acquaintances. Aunt Margot is a clever woman up to a certain point, but her nature and her upbringing have endowed her with a hardness, a lack of charity, and a quality of calculation which to me are not commendable traits in a woman. Laura has never had a chance; she has been spoiled from the beginning. She was so pretty as a child that she positively disarmed criticism, while her temper was sufficiently hot to defy control."

"She seems to have a very good time," said Paul Carr.

Rosamund looked up at him with incredulous eyes.

"Is that what men call having a good time? To be handed about in a ball-room from one man to another like a shuttlecock; to be laughed at as much as she is laughed with; to be admired one moment and stared at with astonishment the next. I suppose you men think that if a girl always has a crowd of men about her she is absolutely and supremely happy."

"I think most girls take care to give men that impression."

"Perhaps they do," retorted Rosamund. "But I have known Laura to dance and laugh and flirt all night at a ball, and then sit up and cry till dawn because the one man in the room she wanted to speak to had taken no notice of her.''

''She is a strange branch to have come from such a tree,'' said Paul.

''Yes, she is a sort of changeling, I think, for she is unsympathetic to her entire family and does not even seem to care that she is so.''

''And your other cousin?'' asked Paul.

''Oh! Honor is quite colourless except when she is put out.''

''But, Miss Keith, all the women you have met are not narrow minded like your aunt, vain like Miss Laura, or bad-tempered like Miss Honor. Surely, there must be some people whom you like.''

Rosamund's face grew suddenly sad.

''That is one of my troubles,'' she said. ''I think there must be something wanting in my own nature, for, as I told you before, I prefer dumb animals and the trees and the sky and the sound of rushing waters to my fellow beings.''

''Are you never going to make any exception?''

He stood before her in the path and looked down into her face with burning eyes. His gaze waked the consciousness that lies in every woman, and she blushed hotly all over her throat and face. She was angry with herself and more angry with him for having forced from her such a display of emotion.

''I really do not know,'' she said, rather shortly. ''I have never thought of such things.''

''But I want you to consider the subject, Miss Keith.''

''But why should I?''

For a moment he sought for an answer that was sufficiently downright to suit her straightforward nature.

"Well, to please me, Miss Keith."

That seemed to amuse her, for the sternness of her mouth relaxed into a little smile.

"And why should I try to please you, Mr. Carr?"

"I don't want you to try; I want it to come naturally to you. I want you to feel that your heart prompts you to think of me, and I want that thinking to grow to liking, and the liking to—"

She raised her hand until it almost touched his mouth. An instinctive shyness urged her to stay the words she felt were coming.

"Well, I will go as far as liking," she said, "if that will suit you."

"And you will think of me when you are in town?"

"But are you not coming to London soon yourself?" she cried, with a startled air that betrayed her.

He feigned to hesitate, and wrinkled his brows together as if he were calculating carefully time and dates.

"Well, you see, I am not quite sure. I have promised to stay down here with Jack Calverly for at least another ten days, and then I rather think I shall run up to my place in Scotland and see how the winter has treated the grouse and the deer, and whether there is such a thing as a bit of fishing to be had in my own particular stretch of water."

"You might as well acknowledge at once, Mr. Carr, that you hate the London season," said Rosamund, with some asperity in her tone. She felt a little ashamed to think that she had perhaps given herself and her feelings away to a man who was only playing with her after all.

"On the contrary, Miss Keith, I adore the London season. Town from May to July is a paradise, provided the right sort of angels are in it. You see, I am not like you, who pose for longing for a country life."

"I told you before, Mr. Carr, that I am an unstable creature, and that I like everything as it comes. If fate ever set me down in the country, and hedged me round so that I never need go to London again, I should be quite happy, and I suppose if the same thing happened as regards the town, I should be happy, too."

"Without any provision?" he asked, laughing and trying to catch an answer from her eyes.

"For the third time, Mr. Carr, I am not going to commit myself," she answered him back with a toss of her head. "Your paradise wants the right sort of angels to make it one; I desire no such qualifications."

"Perhaps you think you are angel enough to make your own heaven."

"Now that," she cried, shaking a forefinger at him, "is a compliment after the approved manner of Lord St. Ives. I don't like his lordship, I don't like his compliments, and if you imitate him I shall not like you, either."

She ran up the broad, low steps of the house and into the hall where Lady Sophia Kerquham, a weird mass of incongruous wrappings, was taking farewell of her family.

"Ah! Rosamund, you are just in time to say good-bye to your aunt," said Mr. Kerquham.

Lady Sophia looked her great-niece up and down.

"Those skirts again!" she said, shaking her head sternly. "And what a cap! It is easy to see you are not a vain woman, niece Rosamund, or you would not get yourself up like that!"

Her sharp eyes glanced from Rosamund's tall, slender figure to where Laura, all feminine frills and fripperies, lounged against the column of the mantelpiece and shed smiles upon her attendant satellites.

"All the same," said the old lady, "vanity is a sign

of an empty head, and if you will go scouring the country as you do, perhaps you show your sense in putting on clothes that will stand the wear and tear. What have you been doing?"

"Playing a round of golf with Mr. Carr," answered Rosamund, who always addressed her great-aunt with the direct bluntness the old lady used herself.

"And did you win?" queried her great-aunt.

"No, Mr. Carr beat me to-day, but I am still ahead of him on the score we have been keeping."

"You would not have Scotch blood in your veins if you let yourself be beaten by a Southerner at the game of your father's country."

Then Lady Sophia proceeded to bestow chill embraces and last words of advice on those about her. When she neared Laura, the girl with a little supercilious sneer, tilted her face up to her aunt's superior height. The old lady shook her by the hand.

"It is evident that you did not mean me to kiss you to-day, niece, or you would not have put all that stuff on your face."

"I say, how beastly rude!" drawled a satellite as Lady Sophia turned way.

"Cat!" said Laura, tossing her head and marching out of the hall into the drawing-room.

"I like to kiss a clean face, if I have to do it at all," said Lady Sophia, giving Rosamund a hearty smack on both cheeks. "Good-bye, Mr. Carr. If you will come up to Scotland and play golf there, you may be able to beat Miss Keith one day."

Then she sailed down the steps into the waiting carriage, and with her maid and her dog, her wraps and her baskets, was driven off to the station.

"She seems very fond of you," said Mr. Carr, watching the retreating carriage through the hall door.

"Yes, I think she is in her way," replied Rosamund, thoughtfully. "They are all rather afraid of her here, but I do not mind her much, though of course one never knows what she is going to do or say next."

"I think you inherit some of her downrightness."

"Do I?" queried Rosamund. "Well, I might have a worse trait than that, I suppose."

Mrs. Kerquham came to the door of the drawing-room, and her sharp voice rang across the hall.

"Rosamund, come in and have some tea. You have been out a very long time." A swift smile and a well-assumed air of astonishment came to her face as she caught sight of Paul. "Oh! I did not know Mr. Carr was with you. Won't you come in to tea?"

Paul looked beyond Mrs. Kerquham to where the room in the dusk was filled with young men and young women, laughing and chattering, whispering and giggling, over the tea and cakes. After the wild beauty of the links and the pure sweet air of the countryside, he felt that it would suffocate him to go in there. He wanted to remember Rosamund Keith as he had seen her all the afternoon, with the fresh wind blowing the little curls about her face, and her tall, shapely figure swinging and swaying to every stroke of the game she played so well. He looked at her, and seeing no invitation in her eyes, which, indeed, were veiled by her white lids and curling lashes, he answered:

"No, thank you, Mrs. Kerquham. I have to get back to Shellerly. I hope we shall meet soon in London."

"We shall be very glad if you will call," said Mrs. Kerquham, in her primmest manner.

"I shall come as soon as I reach town." He said these last words to Rosamund as he took her hand and held it for a brief space.

She watched him down the steps and across the lawns to where the thick growth of evergreens made a thick hedge between the gardens and the park.

"Are you not coming in to tea, Rosamund?" called Mrs. Kerquham again.

"I think not, thank you, aunt. I have all my things to change, you know. I will go straight upstairs," and with a thoughtful face and a tread that was a little slower than usual, Rosamund Keith went up the wide oak staircase to her room.

CHAPTER III

IN THE STUDIO

Up on Campden Hill the early June morning was delightfully fresh. The noise of the busy Kensington streets scarcely ever reached there, but yet the air was full of sound, for the birds in the shady grounds round Holland House were getting through their modicum of music before the heat of the day set in. The Kerquham's house stood alone in a garden of its own. There were lawns and terraces and great trees all round it, and on such a fair day it was like being in the heart of the country.

The Honourable Alban Kerquham had been in his studio betimes. He looked thinner than at the famous hunt ball, and seemed dragged by the heat. Rosamund Keith was with him. She wore a simple frock of pink cotton that threw a rosy glow on the whiteness of her skin. Her rippling black hair was gathered into a close knot at the back of her head, but no amount of care could keep in complete order the little rings and waves that would cast a faint shadow over her broad, low, brow and the flawless skin which was perfect even in the glare from the great north window.

"Now, uncle," she cried, brightly, as she pushed his big chair into the exact position before the easel, "can I be useful? The Duchess of Midshire does not come till half-past eleven, you know, and it has only struck half-past ten."

Mr. Kerquham knitted his brows and peered first at the picture on the easel, and then at Rosamund.

"Her hands will never do, my dear," he said, shaking his head; "they are dreadful; they have got to come out. The Duchess is not nearly as tall as you are, but her hands are large and yours are small in proportion to your height. I think you might sit for an hour, child."

Rosamund walked over to the model's throne, and as she did so rolled back the sleeves of her cotton blouse to just above her elbows.

"Now, uncle, how will you have me?" she said, seating herself in the wooden chair, and preparing to turn the way to suit him.

Mr. Kerquham went over to her and arranged her hands—such slender, white hands—in the position that he wanted.

"The Duchess will be astonished, I should fancy," laughed Rosamund, "if her own hands are so very large."

"My dear, she doesn't think her own hands are ugly," said Mr. Kerquham, with his quiet, slow smile. "All women, particularly when they are very wealthy and have every advantage that money can give them, think they are perfect."

He walked over to the easel and began to work, and Rosamund watched him with love in her eyes and respect and admiration in her heart. Her uncle had been her father, for she had known no other. That her home with her aunt and cousins had always been congenial to her, she could scarcely confess, but gratitude had ever been her leading characteristic; gratitude and sincere affection for her uncle. He had always loved the child; first, perhaps, because her rare beauty had appealed to his artistic instincts, and afterwards because he found in her the sympathy and appreciation, the loving care and

tender solicitude which neither his stern wife nor his frivolous daughters chose to give him.   His own children
never came to the studio save to bother him for money
or to pester him to intercede with their mother with
regard to some party or jaunt.   Mrs. Kerquham looked
upon her husband's workroom as anathema, although it
was there that he earned the large fortune that kept her
in extreme luxury.   But from the beginning, as soon as
she had learnt to balance herself upon her baby feet,
Rosamund, all unabashed and confiding, would pat her
fat fists upon his door and demand an entrance, and play
either quietly or noisily, according to his mood, amid
all the paraphernalia of the big studio.   And now in later
years it was she, and she only, who knew where everything was; who would find this; tidy the other; freshen
the flowers, and, if need be, venture a loving criticism
on colours and draperies.   Sometimes, as to-day, she
would sit to her uncle for her beautiful hands, or again
for a turn in her throat, or the carriage of her shoulders.
She was in the truest sense of the word sympathetic, and
Mr. Kerquham could never work so well as when his
dear Rosamund was about him.

"And what about Mrs. Toroni's reception last night?"
he said, presently.   "Was my intercession with your
aunt worth while?   Did you enjoy your first Sunday
party?"

"Laura did, I think," said Rosamund frankly.   "She
is always so light-hearted and gets the best out of everything."

Mr. Kerquham smiled a little to himself.   Although
he avoided as much as possible the "world" as London
knew it, he was not blind to his elder daughter's little
peculiarities.

"That means she had plenty of young men to talk to."

"Oh! any number, uncle. They all like her; she is great fun, you know, and she looked so pretty last night. She was wearing that blue frock; the one you always like her in."

"Yes, she looks nice in that," said Mr. Kerquham. "She looks her best in blue. Just curve your fingers a little more; that will do. And what about yourself? How did you like it?"

Rosamund laughed rather nervously.

"Uncle, I am afraid I am a very dull person; I was disappointed! You see we had always heard so much about Mrs. Toroni's Sunday parties; that all the artistic people went there, and that they were quite the most amusing things in London."

Mr. Kerquham looked up at her from under his shaggy brows. "My dear, you are not dull; I suppose the party was."

"Well, it seemed so to me, but then you see I do not care much about comic songs, and people who get up sham quarrels, and mock recitations, and bad imitations by amateurs of really clever people; and then it did not strike me that the best of the artistic world was there. It seemed a mixture of vapid-looking young men who were either actors or painters or singers, according to whether they shaved their upper lips or grew a mustache and beard. All the women had an undefinable atmosphere about them of dyed hair and too few clothes. It was all noise, and the only method of expressing pleasure or amusement was to shout loudly. I saw none of your friends, dear."

Mr. Kerquham laughed, then shook his head a little sadly. "I did not suppose you would, Rosamund; my friends are not the sort of people Mrs. Toroni cares about. They are people who work, and they have no time to sit up till four o'clock in the morning listening to comic songs.''

Rosamund ran on:

"But among the crowd, who do you think I did see? Hamish Lundy! He saw me, too, and somehow, didn't look best pleased."

Mr. Kerquham laughed quietly.

"Hamish Lundy at a Sunday party! Why, the Kerquham family are coming out in quite a new light." He glanced roguishly at Rosamund. "My child! I am afraid that your cousin's Sabbath-breaking is a crime that must be laid at your door."

"It brought it's own punishment, I fancy, dear; for he seemed afraid to speak to me, though he was within a yard of me at supper time."

"Conscience! my dear—a clear case of conscience! I expect his people didn't know he was there."

He painted for a few moments. "But surely, Rosie, there was some gleam of pleasure for you? Did you see nobody nice at all?"

"Yes," said Rosamund, slowly; "Mr. Carr took me down to supper."

"Paul Carr, you mean, do you not?"

"Yes, uncle."

"Ah, he is a very nice young fellow. I do not know much about him, but your aunt approves of him, and I hear from her that he calls here sometimes. What does he do?"

"I do not know, uncle. I think he is rich—"

"Which means, I suppose, that he does nothing?"

"Well, he is not quite a drone in the hive; he sings a great deal for charity. He told me once he wished he had been poor, and then he should have been a professional."

"Well, and what prevents him being one now, if he is good enough?"

"Oh! he is quite good enough," cried Rosamund, warmly, "but he always says that for a rich man who has no need to earn his living to go into a profession is to take bread out of some one else's mouth."

"There is something in that, of course," said Mr. Kerquham. "What other characteristics has he?"

"Well, I don't quite know. He is very quiet; rather an earnest sort of man. Uncle, I think that he is the sort of young man that you would like."

Mr. Kerquham laughed and laid down his palette.

"Do you think so, my dear? Well, bring him to see me one day, and we will have a chat together. There, I have done with you for this morning. Come and see what pretty hands the Duchess has now."

He slipped his arm round her waist as she came to his side. "Yes, my dear," he said, gently, "you must bring this young man to see me one day. There is the Duchess's carriage coming up the drive. Now, run away."

The Duchess of Midshire gave an unusually long sitting that morning, and luncheon at "The Hurst" was half over before the artist was able to join his family in the oak-lined dining-room. A wide verandah that ran round the ground floor of the house cast a pleasant shade on the polished walls and the fine old silver and cut glass that was scattered about the table in luxurious profusion. To come from the studio, with its sharp reflected north light, to the dim, scented room, which seemed to enframe with its open bay windows the gorgeous golden sunshine and riot of scarlet and yellow flower beds outside, gave the painter a thrill of artistic pleasure and an almost unconscious sense of thankfulness that his life was passed amid such satisfying surroundings.

The girls, too, looked fresh and gay in their bright summer frocks, and their faces with their clear skins and luminous eyes gleamed like cameos against the carved oak walls. The hat that crowned Laura's curly head was like a great bouquet of freshly cut roses, and made a charming splash of colour against the rich background.

"Are you very tired, dear uncle?" said Rosamund, gently, as Mr. Kerquham sank into his high-backed chair and slowly passed his hand across his eyes. "Has her grace been more than usually talkative to-day?"

"How crooked was her wig?" asked Honor, with her customary sub-acid manner.

"Good gracious, my dear!" cried light-hearted Laura, with her pretty mouth as usual wide open with laughter; "if I were a Duchess I would never care if my wig were straight or awry. I should exercise the prerogative of my undeniable position, and probably go about bald-headed, especially on a scorching day like this." She sank back in her chair, and waved her white, dimpled hand in front of her face in lieu of a fan.

"Well, old Lady Trevannion had to do that last year at Ostend for three days when her hat and *postiche* blew into the sea and were drowned," said Honor.

"I heard she looked such a guy without her front, and they say—" tittered Laura.

" 'I heard,' and 'They say'—girls! Girls, when will you curb your tendency to idle and ill-natured gossip? I do not know what your great-aunt Sophia would think of you if she heard you talking like that."

Mrs. Kerquham bent slightly forward as she addressed her daughters. She was a tall woman, and upright to the extent of ungracefulness. Her features were typically Scotch, but their natural ruggedness would not

have been unpleasing if they had not habitually worn an
expression of sourness and discontent, and if her plenti-
ful iron-grey hair had not been so uncompromisingly
dragged back over a high cushion. She always affected
an air of conscious superiority over the rest of the world.
Those who knew her best always described her as being
a very tiring woman to be with, for she seemed never to
rest herself nor to allow others to do so. No one had
ever seen her taking her ease in an arm-chair or indo-
lently lounging on a sofa. She had never been known,
even by her husband, to fritter away half an hour over
the pages of a novel or the harmless foolish columns of
a society paper. She always preached "duty," though
no one ever quite knew what that much-abused word
meant in her case, beyond the daily ordering of meals,
the examination of her household accounts, and the
strict supervision of her large and well-trained staff of
servants. Her daughters always said that she worried
over trifles. That was not exactly true, for Mrs. Kerquham was far too superior a person to worry, but she built
mountains out of mole-hills, and was too apt to regard
the smallest of her own affairs as being of universal
importance. She had bequeathed her temperament to
her second daughter, Honor, who at the age of twenty
was as carping and hypercritical as her mother had ever
been, though she had not acquired with that disposition
the finer qualities of rectitude and firmness that with
Mrs. Kerquham made for virtues.

Her inborn ignorance of the world had induced her
to give her daughters as they grew up the license
she noticed other girls enjoyed, but which in her heart she
secretly deplored, and when too late tried to check.
She was, however, too narrow and self-centred and too
sure of her family to see that Laura and Honor were

going all the wrong way, and that it would be luck and not wit that alone could save them from a more or less deplorable ending. A sharp scolding, modelled on the strictly old lines, and interlarded with many quotations from her own mother's vocabulary and with reminiscences of her own bringing up, of which the girls took no notice whatever, was her sole idea of discipline. Altogether she was a strange example of the old order on which the new had been grafted, and which had borne fruit in the guise of two of the most frivolous and selfish girls in London.

Mrs. Kerquham's reference to Lady Sophia Kerquham rather sobered Laura, who in her heart always dreaded that her mother would carry out her threat of sending her up to the north of Scotland, to be under that worthy woman's care and discipline. Still, she was not the girl to be brow-beaten, so she tossed her head till all the roses in her hat nodded as she retorted, "I should advise Aunt Sophia not to think of us at all if that process is likely to be hurtful to her."

"Besides," joined in Honor, "the old lady has disapproved of us ever since we had our hair down our backs and said 'prunes and prisms' in the schoolroom. It is true she likes Rosamund, but," with a little sneer at her cousin opposite, "Rosamund is scarcely a good specimen of a real London girl."

Laura gave her irritating titter again. The two sisters were never weary of giving little spiteful digs at their cousin. Their natures were too utterly shallow and trivial to do more than resent her infinite superiority of character over themselves. Rosamund changed colour a little at the unprovoked attack.

"They have all been very kind to me always," she said quietly, "and when I stayed with Lord Kilbeggie and the old aunts up in Scotland I got on quite well with them. But like all old people they are a little 'grovey.' "

"I wish you would not invent words," said Mrs. Kerquham, sharply, while she drew a letter out of her pocket. "I have a letter from Lady Sophia this morning to say that she means to come to London this season."

"Coming to London!"

"Not to stop?" cried Laura.

"We had a month of her in the winter at the Manor," gasped Honor.

Mrs. Kerquham turned the letter over and looked at it doubtfully. It was written on "Bath Post" paper in a fine, very close hand.

"She suggests coming here, but I think that it will be very much better for her if she goes to her sister, Lady Charlotte Lundy."

"Oh, but she must," said Laura. "We cannot possibly have the old thing here; it would be a frightful nuisance, and in the middle of the season, too. She's tiresome enough in the country."

"With her knitting and snuff and other horrors," cried Honor.

"Your great-aunt," said Mrs. Kerquham, severely, "is certainly a little old-fashioned in her ways, but I should not for a moment allow that to interfere with her proposed plans. It is her individual comfort I am thinking of."

This was scarcely the truth, and Mrs. Kerquham knew it. She was quite aware that she did not want Lady Sophia to come to Campden Hill in the middle of the London season. She would be a great drag on herself, and there would probably be a great deal of trouble between the old lady and the girls. Still, she lacked the courage to say so outright. She glanced helplessly across the table to where her husband, silent and self-absorbed, was quietly eating his luncheon.

"What is your opinion on the subject, Alban?" she said. "Can you make any suggestions as to what is best for us to do for dear Aunt Sophia's comfort and happiness?"

Womanlike, in an emergency she appealed to the man, and Mr. Kerquham, manlike, fell into the trap. He laid down his knife and fork, and pushed his plate a little to one side.

"I think, my dear, that under the circumstances, Aunt Sophia would scarcely be in her element here. It is the summer, you know, and we have so much tennis, and so many young people coming perpetually to the house, that I am afraid she might not like the noise and the bustle; then, again, there are the girls to consider. They must be taken out at night, and Rosamund told me this morning of at least half a dozen fresh invitations to dances. The girls must enjoy themselves while they are young." He smiled indulgently at the three faces before him. "And I think your first duty is to see that they get the full measure of their enjoyment. I am afraid Aunt Sophia would not approve of that."

"Aunt Sophia would be horrified," said Mrs. Kerquham, in a rather depressed voice. "She thinks the girls have too much dissipation in the country. She does not realize the rush and fluster of a season in town."

"Poor old thing," laughed Laura. "I suppose she would have a fit if she knew we went to two or three balls a night, and restaurant suppers and music halls." She put her hands before her mouth to smother her amusement. "My goodness! what would she have said if she had been at Mrs. Toroni's last night?"

Mrs. Kerquham drew her brows very close together.

"Laura," she said, severely, "you and your father persuaded me to let you go to Mrs. Toroni's house last night. I have always set my face, as you know, against going out on Sundays. You get more than your fair share of pleasure during the week. Let me never hear last night referred to again. I thought over the matter very seriously after you had left, and I have quite made up my mind that it must be the first and last Sunday party you and your sister ever attend."

Laura was quite clever enough to know when she had gone far enough with her mother, so she forced the smile from her face and looked very business-like, as putting her elbows on the table she leaned forward and re-directed the conversation towards great-aunt Sophia.

"Do you think Lady Charlotte will take her in?"

The idea once suggested had taken root in Mrs. Kerquham's mind. She folded up the closely written letter and returned it to her pocket.

"Your Aunt Charlotte should feel honoured; besides, she has a very large spare room and nothing like the social ties that I have. She has no daughters to take about. Rosamund, I should like you to go and see Lady Charlotte this afternoon, and ask her for me if she will be able to take in her sister from the tenth till the end of the month. It is impossible for me to drive up to Wimpole Street this afternoon, as I have promised to take the girls to Hurlingham."

"Rosamund was asked to go to Hurlingham, too," put in Laura, who, out of mere caprice could, when she chose, be fairly good-natured to her cousin.

"Rosamund will do as I ask her," said Mrs. Kerquham, and rose from the table. "I hope you will go soon, Rosamund. Remember that Lady Charlotte always drives at half-past four at this time of the year."

"Certainly, aunt, I will go," answered Rosamund.

As Mrs. Kerquham swept out of the dining-room, the three girls strolled out to the verandah.

"Pooh! how hot it is!" said Honor, with a little gasp. "I don't envy you having to pelt into town directly. Thank goodness, we do not start till five!"

"Well, mind you make it all right with Aunt Charlotte, or we shall all be furious with you," urged Laura. "Just remember that we won't have Aunt Sophia here, we positively won't."

"I will do my best, you may be sure," said Rosamund, brightly, as she turned into the house to get ready to start on her pilgrimage to Lady Charlotte Lundy.

CHAPTER IV

PRUNES AND PRISMS

Two hundred Wimpole Street was typical of Sir Alexander and Lady Charlotte Lundy, and they were typical of it. In the downstairs windows were wire blinds and red brocade curtains. When the windows were open there was from outside an ample view of walls painted a pale sea green and plentifully lined with yellow-faced family portraits set in cumbersome gold frames. A huge sideboard laden with heavy plate faced the windows, and a row of stiff-backed mahogany chairs covered in maroon leather stood shoulder to shoulder against the wall. A gasalier with five engraved globes swung from a florid ornament in the centre of the ceiling. On the heavily carved mantelpiece stood a marble clock which was always five minutes fast, and was flanked by a pair of candelabra, which for modelling and design were an outrage on taste. How well Rosamund knew it all, as she passed the windows, and after ringing at a loud clanging bell and knocking at a huge lion's-head knocker, was admitted into the wide, dim hall, which even on this hot afternoon struck icy cold.

"Her ladyship is in the drawing-room," said the family butler in a whisper as he led her up the staircase, where the varnished marble paper looked chill as the grave.

"Miss Rosamund Keith," announced the factotum, as he flung open the big double doors.

From the time she had been a little child, and even now, Rosamund was always conscious of a feeling of awkwardness which amounted to shy stupidity whenever she entered that vast, solemn, hideous drawing-room in Wimpole Street.   The white, watered walls, with an irritating pattern of small gold stars, were the same as she remembered nearly twenty years ago, and she always caught herself idly wondering how it was that Lady Charlotte Lundy managed to keep her drawing-room paper so clean, when everybody else she knew had to do up their rooms every three or four years.   The centre of the room was entirely bare of furniture, and gave an admirable view of the huge red bouquets of cabbage roses which were closely besprent on the green ground of the Brussels carpet.   In front of the centre window was a huge table, monstrous of foot and shiny of top, on which lay, ensconced on woollen mats (Rosamund had made some of those mats when she was a little girl), various standard works bound in calf and uniformly dull.

A case of medals, popularly supposed to have been won by Sir Alexander Lundy, stood on one table.   An Indian temple of carved ivory, and two baskets of wax fruits, all under glass shades, decorated another.   An Ormolu head of Minerva frowned severely from the top of a pink-faced china clock, and a full suite of carved rosewood furniture, upholstered in crimson damask, was ranged round the room.   A grand piano and a music-stand languished all unused in the far vista of the back drawing-room.   Some water colours, painted by Lady Charlotte and her sisters in the forties, hung on the walls. The whole apartment was symbolical of the abomination of desolation.

As the big doors closed behind Rosamund a large form loomed out of a small arm-chair near the fireplace.   The

girl advanced, for she had been well trained in the etiquette of the family, which forbade the hostess to leave
the hearthrug.

"Good afternoon, Aunt Charlotte."

"Good afternoon, my dear," said Lady Charlotte in
her very deep voice, and pressing a cold salute on Rosamund's cheek. "To what, pray, do I owe the pleasure
of seeing you?"

"I have come with a message from Aunt Margot."

"Pray sit down," said Lady Charlotte, waving her
hand towards the nearest chair. Then she rang the bell,
and a dead silence ensued until it was answered.

"Pray tell Sir Alexander that his niece, Miss Rosamund Keith, is here," she said to the servant, then turning
to Rosamund, she added: "Any message that you bring
from Margot I should like Sir Alexander to hear. You
know I make a point of taking his opinion on all questions in life."

Again there was a dead silence, and Rosamund shivered a little in her thin summer gown, not so much with
cold as with the sense of dulness and dreariness, the
stiffness and artificiality of the whole house and the people in it. She glanced at Lady Charlotte, sitting upright
in her prune-coloured silk gown with a little white frill
at the throat and the wrists, and a long gold chain looped
up with a cameo brooch on her ample bosom. She
looked, as with fresh eyes, at the hard lines on the snuff-
brown wig planted above Aunt Charlotte's aquiline features, and from that her eyes involuntarily fell to the
shiny toe-cap of a very large shoe which showed from
beneath Aunt Charlotte's plain and full skirts.

She always felt curious about Aunt Charlotte. She
had got used to the insincerities, the narrow-mindedness
and uncharitableness of her Aunt Margot, but Lady

Charlotte Lundy always baffled the girl. She never quite knew how much she was in earnest. She often wondered if she really was alive at all; if she had any heart beating under her well whale-boned bodice, and if she had such a thing, whose was the hand, and where was the voice that could touch it. Not Sir Alexander's certainly, for even as she went over the old ground again the little piping old gentleman, with his stick and his skull cap, came doddering into the room, and Lady Charlotte waved him into another chair just as she had waved Rosamund.

"Sir Alexander, our niece Kerquham has sent Rosamund to see us this afternoon. She tells me she has brought a message; I should like you to hear it."

The old paralysing nervousness that Rosamund knew so well crept over her and almost froze the tongue in her mouth.

"It is nothing very important," she began, with a nervous laugh. "It is about a message—a letter she had from great-aunt Sophia."

"Everything to do with your great-aunt Sophia must be of importance," corrected Lady Charlotte, severely. "Sir Alexander, I hope you are listening. Now, child, what is it?"

"Aunt Sophia has written to Aunt Margot."

"You gave us to understand that before," said Lady Charlotte. "It is a bad habit with young people of the present day to repeat themselves. Sir Alexander always says that young persons nowadays have no idea how to express their thought."

Sir Alexander had never said anything of the sort; he had probably never thought it, for, poor little old gentleman, he had left the greater part of his wits and all his will behind him in the Crimea, but it was Lady

Charlotte's idea of keeping up a proper discipline to quote her lord and master when he could not speak for himself.

"Tell me as clearly and as slowly and as plainly as you can, if you please," went on her ladyship, "what was the purport of the communication from your great-aunt Sophia to your Aunt Margot."

Rosamund really had to think quite hard for a moment; her whole brain was wandering under the influence of that drawing-room, and she could only wonder how long Sir Alexander's skull cap would stop on his head if he kept on shaking it about so much.

"Great-aunt Sophia," she began very slowly, and trying to weigh every word before she spoke it, "has written to say that she is thinking of coming to London in a few days."

"Sakes alive!" cried Lady Charlotte, momentarily shaken out of her usual stately repose. "Sir Alexander, did you ever hear such a thing? My dear sister Sophia talks of coming to London."

Sir Alexander waggled his head a little more, but expressed no opinion on the news either one way or the other.

"She suggested, I believe," continued Rosamund carefully, "for I have not seen the letter, that she should come and stay at Campden Hill."

At this moment Lady Charlotte assumed such a displeased air that Rosamund stopped dead short and wondered how on earth she was going to advance Mrs. Kerquham's request that Lady Sophia should go to Wimpole Street.

"To Campden Hill!" cried Lady Charlotte. "Sir Alexander, do you hear that? My dear sister can have no idea of what life at Campden Hill can be." She turned to Rosamund. "I am sure, Rosamund, that Sir Alexander feels with me that such a proposal is absolutely out of the question. My poor dear sister would be distracted in the midst of such disorder, such noise, such goings and comings as are the rule of life at 'The Hurst.' She has been accustomed to punctuality· and reasonable hours, to quietude and the correct order of a perfect gentlewoman's life. Everything, in fact, that she will not find at my niece Margot's house. Sir Alexander has frequently expressed his astonishment at the manner in which both your uncle and aunt have been pleased to bring you all up. He has even spoken in terms of the strongest disapproval of the people who visit your aunt, and of the friends she has seen fit to make since she cast in her lot with your Uncle Alban. He, unfortunate man, has been led away by his absurd craze for what he is pleased to term 'art.' He forgot his duty to his family thirty-five years ago, and both Sir Alexander and I are sorry to find how his influence has perverted and changed Margot. We both noticed this with regret while you and your cousins were still in the schoolroom. Your introduction into society made but little difference. Sir Alexander has always considered you, my dear, a well-conducted and respectable young person, but since Margot has brought out her own girls, she and her whole establishment have greatly changed. Of Laura I cannot trust myself to speak."

She gave a righteous shudder and closed her eyes for a moment as though to shut out some horrid sight. "I can only pray that she will find her just reward in the reproaches of her own conscience. Honor is evil-tongued, if better behaved than her sister, but neither Sir Alexander nor I can approve of those two young women, nor regard them with any other feelings than those of displeasure. We both consider that our niece, Margot Kerquham, has been a fool in the bringing up of her daughters. Sir Alexander, I am sure, will wish my dear sister Sophia to pass her time in London under our roof, which we trust will be more congenial to her mind and spirit than 'The Hurst' could ever hope to be.''

Lady Charlotte folded her hands over her prune silk lap. Sir Alexander waggled his head over his stick a little, and Rosamund shook herself free from the torrent of words to find that her task had been done for her; that she had no request to make, no favour to ask, and that she was free to get up and go home.

"Then what am I to tell Aunt Margot?'' she asked, advancing to the edge of Lady Charlotte's domain.

"Tell her that Sir Alexander and I wish my dear sister to come to us. I will write to her by this afternoon's post. Will you also tell her from me that I hear Laura wore a most *décolletté* gown the other night at Mrs. Benyon's. That girl is bound to end very badly indeed.''

She took Rosamund's cool, slim hand in hers and shook it.

"You are a very good girl, my dear, to do this message for your aunt,'' she said patronisingly. "She ought sometimes to wish that her daughters were like you.''

Again she leant forward to deposit an icy salute on Rosamund's cheek, when a little door at the further end of the back drawing-room was opened, and a young man entered the room. He was obviously short-sighted, for a pair of pince-nez dangled over his waistcoat. He was small like Sir Alexander Lundy, but had the pale, sandy-coloured hair and light eyes that characterised all Lady Charlotte's family. He was her only son.

He advanced slowly as far as the centre of the room,
and then seeing that a third person was present, stopped
short awkwardly.

"I beg your pardon; I did not know you were
engaged."

"Come in, my dear boy," said Lady Charlotte,
blandly. "It is only Rosamund. She has brought a
message from Margot about your Aunt Sophia."

Mr. Hamish Lundy grew pink all over his face. It
was a trick he had whenever he saw Rosamund. He
put on his glasses, and after a minute's vague staring,
fixed his gaze upon her.

"How do you do, Rosamund? Hot to-day, isn't it?
Hope you are quite well."

Rosamund was taller than he and looked down at his
nervous, shuffling figure, as she assented to his remarks.
Lady Charlotte meanwhile had also risen, and was blandly
regarding the pair.

"Very nice, very nice," she murmured softly to herself. It was the one ambition of her life that Hamish
should marry Rosamund. True that the girl had no
money, and never would have, but her family was all
right, for was she not an offshoot of *the* family, and then
she was so ladylike, so quiet and so amenable. When
she remembered what most girls of the period were like,
Lady Charlotte had an inward conviction that Rosamund
would prove easier to manage than any other young
woman of her acquaintance.

"Hamish, my son," she said, "our dear Rosamund
has come to announce the speedy arrival of Aunt Sophia
in London. She will stop here during her stay, of
course, and I hope—no—I expect," with a stately bend
of the head, "that dear Rosamund will not omit the
opportunity of frequently coming to see my sister."

The clock on the mantelpiece struck half-past four. Lady Charlotte turned to her husband:

"Sir Alexander, you will be reminding me in a moment that the carriage is here; I must go and get my bonnet."

She looked doubtfully for a moment from Rosamund to her son and her husband, then with a great effort she said:

"Rosamund, I will drive you back to 'The Hurst.' I shall have just time to do so before going to Lady Betty MacCan's to tea. Come with me, Sir Alexander."

With a benign smile at her own cleverness in leaving the two young people alone, Lady Charlotte tucked Sir Alexander under her arm and walked out of the room. Rosamund sank back into her chair again. Mr. Hamish Lundy took one at a little distance, and with his glasses on his nose proceeded to stare at her.

"How nice you look to-day, Rosamund—so cool, just as if it were not hot at all. I suppose it is that frock you have got on; it is awfully nice."

"Is it?" said Rosamund. "It is only a cotton; I do not think one could wear anything else this kind of weather."

Mr. Hamish Lundy smoothed his sandy hair on his head with both hands.

"I thought you looked very nice, too, at Mrs. Toroni's last night," he said, tentatively, and looking at her out of the corner of his eyes, "and you were not in a cotton frock then, you know."

"Of course I was not, Hamish. People do not go to evening parties in cottons."

"I say, Rosamund," said Hamish, in a low voice, and looking over his shoulder to see that the big doors behind him were tightly shut, "you have not told my mother, have you, about seeing me last night at Mrs. Toroni's? Do be a good girl, and promise you won't."

"There is no question of a promise about it, Hamish. First of all, I am not in the habit of gossiping about whom I meet or whom I do not meet at parties; and secondly, if you make a point of it, though I do not know why you should, of course I will not mention to your mother that I met you last night."

Hamish looked as ashamed of himself as anybody belonging to Lady Charlotte Lundy could do.

"You see, Rosamund," he began, "my mother has rather extraordinary ideas about Sundays. Of course I think she is quite right up to a certain point, you know. There is no doubt there is a dreadful amount of Sabbath-breaking nowadays," and he looked as sanctimonious as he could. "I think that the way people neglect their church and go on the river and play tennis and golf and things is nothing short of disgraceful; but when Mrs. Toroni asked me to go to her house last night I did not see very much why I should not go."

"Why, of course not," said Rosamund, frankly. "There is nothing in it. I did not care about the party very much, but I do not suppose it would have been any more pleasant on a Monday than on a Sunday."

"Er—umph—you see it is not exactly that. My mother would not mind where I went on Monday, or any other day in the week, but she does draw the line at Sunday going-out."

"Then why did you go?" asked Rosamund, raising her eyes and looking him full in the face.

He grew pink all over and smoothed his hair again.

"Well, you see—" Rosamund saw that he was searching for an excuse, and some little imp of mischief whispered to her to help him out of the difficulty at his own expense.

"You came to see me, I suppose," she said, laughing.

"That was it; that's exactly the whole truth of it!" he cried with a relieved air.

"But," said Rosamund, with arched eyebrows, "how did you manage to get out? I do not fancy that even my presence would justify you in doing an action which she could not approve."

He looked awkward again at once.

"No; you see I made an excuse to my mother."

"Hamish," said Rosamund, with a little smile twitching on the corners of her mouth, "may I inquire what you call an excuse?"

The unfortunate young man, goaded to desperation between his tantalisingly pretty cousin and the awful image of his severe mother, was on the point of committing himself to some quite serious statement when Lady Charlotte's voice was heard outside.

"William, take my parasol, and then help Sir Alexander into the carriage."

Then the double doors were flung wide. "Rosamund, my dear, I am quite ready. I hope you and Hamish have had a nice cousinly little chat."

Rosamund flashed an amused little smile into Hamish's sheepish face, as she shook his limp hand.

"We have got along splendidly, aunt, thank you. Hamish and I understand one another so well, you know. Good afternoon, cousin," and then with a demure face and a light step she followed her stately great-aunt down the gloomy staircase to the carriage.

CHAPTER V

A YOUNG MAN'S FANCY

It was late afternoon. Paul had been busy all the morning, for although he was a rich man, he was not of the temperament of which drones are made. His morning had been passed in reviewing reports from the factor of his little place in Scotland, in studying the estimates for the repairing and fitting out of his yacht at Southampton for a summer cruise, and in the thousand and one small affairs of social and business life which come to every man who chooses to receive them.

Now the heat and burden of the day were over. Below the open windows of his rooms in Piccadilly swept the ceaseless tide of traffic towards the Park; the pleasure of the evening, which would live through the night hours until the next day's dawn, had begun for his world, and as the weary-eyed clerks and city toilers went their way to the suburbs on the tops of omnibuses, looking forward with what anticipation they might to a few hours rest before their humble supper and bedtime came, the set that Paul lived in waked from its day's sleep and prepared to begin the life it loved best.

Twice his valet had been in to ask if he would dress for the Park, and twice Paul had said he did not know, and bade him come again in half an hour. He lit a cigarette and wandered over to the window. The flowers in the blue boxes bloomed in fine profusion; white daisies and scarlet geraniums made a goodly show all

along the line of his flat, while the scent of sweet mignon-
ette floated into his rooms and even up as far as the
next story.

He looked down at the crowded roadway and the
thronged pavements. Every turn of the wheels of
the smart carriages below brought some friend or
acquaintance within range of his vision, but as they did
not look up so high as his windows he was saved the
trouble of bowing to them. He could not see the pavement directly beneath, but he knew by the noise of the
passing feet that it was thronged with men lounging to
and from their clubs, and with pretty girls hastening
to the Park to see and be seen. On the opposite side of
the road, under the trees of the Green Park, was a different crowd altogether. Many of them were loafers,
gossiping, swearing, and spitting as they leant up against
the railings. There were a few nurse-maids and children and many business people and workmen. He
thought how strange it was that such a narrow roadway
should divide two such different streams of life as flowed
that afternoon down the north and south sides of Piccadilly.

Should he go out, or should he not go out? His valet
knocked for the third time at the door, and Paul from
force of habit turned and was walking to his dressing-
room, when by chance his eye fell on the largest and
most comfortable of his great padded arm-chairs.

"No, I will not change till dinner time," he said, and
the man left the room.

With a sigh of relief at having made up his mind,
Paul flung himself into the big chair, and for almost the
first time that day gave himself up to thoughts that
made for sweetness and happiness and all the domestic
virtues. His business was finished, his papers put aside;

no one was likely to intrude upon him, and he was surrounded by the richly reposeful colouring and beautiful
things that a man of wealth and taste is able to gather
round him. He was now going to think of Rosamund
Keith. He flung away the end of his cigarette as her
name, which signified so much sweetness and glorified
her as the rose of the world, passed through his mind
and broke from his lips. He laid back his head and
smiled as his fancy conjured her image to his side.

Paul Carr was essentially a product of modern society, though scarcely perhaps so much by natural inclination as by force of circumstances. He had been born
into it. His father and mother, at their marriage,
had been the handsomest couple of their day; both had
money, both had perfect physique and beauty, both were
worldly to the tips of their well-shaped fingers. Paul
had been their only child, and from the moment of his
arrival in the world had been looked upon as a necessary
evil; an item that was quite proper to be numbered in
the Carr family, but nevertheless one that, with childish
ailments, the necessities for education and social plac-
ing, was to be regarded as a nuisance in the absolutely
happy-go-lucky, thoughtless, selfish life of his popular
father and mother.

Paul could never remember the time that he had not
lived among perfumed laces and silken skirts, listening to
the tittle-tattle of a fashionable drawing-room, which was
varied only by the whispered stories and coarse innuendoes of maids and valets. He always seemed, even from
his babyhood, to have seen through the sham of it all.
He had never heard his parents quarrel so long as they
lived, but he had always intuitively known that they
cared nothing for one another beyond the fact that each
was the social complement of the other. He had some-

times wondered, even when quite a child, why his father and mother played at everything. It was always like being in a theater to sit with them, and as he grew a little older his instinct taught him that his father and mother's friends were no less puppets than they were themselves.

If his health had not been as perfect as it was possible for it to be, he would have become a very morbid boy, but Eton and Oxford developed every instinct of manhood that was in him, and while they never blinded him to the falseness of the social world in which fortune had set him, they enabled him as time went on to take a more lenient view of the foibles that marked his surroundings.

He was scarcely one and twenty when his father died. His was just such a taking-off as the handsome, hard-living man might have wished; a glorious day with hounds, a splendid run, a perfect horse under him, a trip, a roll over, and a broken neck. It was after that that Paul's mother astonished him for the first and the last time. She had never shown any affection for her husband, and at first she had missed him a little more perhaps than she would have missed a very good maid or a favourite lap-dog. But the very suddenness of his death seemed to take hold of her, and though she did not exactly pine after her lost lord's memory, her health failed her, and a slight chill undermined her weakened constitution. Paul travelled with her to the Riviera, but he came back to London alone, and found himself, while little more than a boy, master of a fine income, two country estates, and a house in town; amply provided for with everything that the heart of man could desire, always excepting illusions.

One thing other he possessed in common with very many young men of his class. There was a turned-down page in his life-book. It had been very black, but in his own eyes the law had whitened it. Still, it was one he rigourously avoided re-reading, and now the details had grown faint in his memory, and it was a story that nobody had ever known.

So it was without illusions that he had lived until he was eight and twenty—until he met Rosamund Keith. The first time he saw her he admired her for her physical beauty, and set her down as being no different from the other girls of her station. Then chance brought them together, and he talked with her. The first five minutes sufficed to show him that she was not clever or sharp; that she did not say specially witty things; that she aspired to the display of no particular branch of knowledge; that she had practically no affectations. But another five minutes revealed in her something that he had found wanting in all the other women he had met during his lifetime; she possessed an innate purity, an almost childlike innocence that still was not the affected ignorance of the society hack. She was not loud in speech or free in manner; she was able to talk for a quarter of an hour and express herself intelligibly without the aid of slang or quotations from music-hall songs. She had never cheapened herself or played with her sensations by falling in love with actors or running after society lions. He fathomed that, despite her warm colouring and misty dark eyes, she was cold of temperament, was not to be approached by the usual pretty compliments and coarse attentions that catch the fancy of the average girl, and that her life was not entirely bound up in a round of race-meetings and dances, skating parties and bicycling gymkhanas.

He could not discover, either from her manner or from her speech, that she had had love affairs, or had carried on clandestine correspondence with married men. Her greatest friends were the men whose youth had left them sixty years ago, and who came and spent quiet—sometimes silent—evenings in her uncle's studio. She would fill their pipes for them, and listen to such scraps of conversation as these veterans in life's battle chose to let drop in their less contemplative moments. Paul was fastidious enough to notice that she dressed well; that she was always perfectly groomed, and that without vanity she was careful to preserve all the good points with which nature had endowed her; but he also soon saw that she was not by way of changing the colour of her hair with every season that passed; of unduly curtailing her bodices or showing her pretty feet. That she was, in fact, that *rara avis* in the world, as he knew it, a really ladylike girl.

For some months he had considered her as nothing more than that, until it had gradually dawned upon him that she was a pearl laid before swine, and that the circumstances governing her daily life were uncongenial to her. He quickly saw through the shallowness of Mrs. Kerquham's religion and strictness. He knew that she would strain at a gnat and swallow a camel. She would not go herself to certain houses and certain places, but she allowed her daughters to over-persuade her, and permitted them to be seen here, there, and everywhere, under the chaperonage of the first lively young married woman whose services they were able to command. It scarcely needed his worldly knowledge to fathom the shallows of Laura's nature, or to guess that in her domestic life Honor's bad temper and sharp tongue must frequently be called into play for the benefit of her poorer cousin. When he had first realised this he got an odd fancy into his head that Rosamund was his mission in life. He had

always been looking for a mission, but his upbringing
had been against his taking anything really seriously.
Yet lately he had felt that to remove this girl from the
uncongeniality of her surroundings and set her feet in
the higher, nobler walks of life would be a fine thing to
do—and then—then almost unconsciously, he had fallen
in love with her.

He was still not quite sure how far that love would
carry him, for he had always made up his mind that he
would never link his life irrevocably with that of a woman.
But as that afternoon the thoughts of Rosamund and
love intermingled into one definite purpose, a smile of
grave happiness touched the corners of his mouth, and
so far from checking the longing for her sweet presence
that surged from heart to brain, he felt that to take her
hand in his and draw her to his side would be the doing
of a good thing; a thing that would make him happy,
and that would keep her unspotted from the world.   He
felt that his mission in life would be complete, and that
he was born for domesticity.   Not as his parents had
known it, but as he and Rosamund would make it for
themselves.   He would tell her of his love, and they
would be married and go away, and wander through all
the beautiful countries of the world, seeing God's handiwork only, and putting behind them the falseness and
sham, the lies and disappointments which man deals out
to man.   He acknowledged to himself as he sat there
dreaming that he must have loved Rosamund for quite a
long time, although he had only lately known it.

"I have been shamming to myself," he thought.   "I
have been playing at taking an interest in her when I was
in love with her; I wonder if her people will object?
Mrs. Kerquham has wanted Lord St. Ives for her.   He
would have been in her eyes a brilliant match for Rosa-

mund, for he is a man who only lives for the world and for society. With Rosamund as his wife, Laura and Honor might make sure of getting husbands. But once Rosamund and I are married, we should just go away and live our own lives, which, according to Mrs. Kerquham, would mean that we should be of no use to her daughters. I wonder how soon I dare speak to Rosamund."

And so in dreams of the future and plans for the present Paul Carr idled away the next hour. Then the late afternoon post came, and with it the usual batch of cards and letters, and little notes asking for appointments, and pressing invitations to quiet dinners in out-of-the-way places, that beset the path of the eligible bachelor as thickly as thorns in a hedge. He divided them into two packets.

"Those I shall decline," he said aloud, "for *she* does not go to those houses. These I shall accept, because we shall meet."

The last letter he opened was from Mrs. Toroni; she was full of some "Living Pictures" she was organising in aid of a charity, and wanted him to help her.

"The dear Princess," she wrote, "sent for me yesterday, and says the 'Home' is in a terribly destitute condition; she must have money for it at once, and she will patronise any form of entertainment I choose to get up. Isn't it charming of her? I want you so much to pose in some of the pictures. All our set have promised their help, and Miss Laura Kerquham, who is so clever, has got some quite splendid ideas. I had hoped Miss Rosamund Keith would have been of some use in a classical picture or two, but she has refused. What a very dull girl she is! Her aunt, however, has promised that she shall sing some songs between the pictures. I do hate a girl who requires such a lot of pressing and arranging for; don't you? Pray come to dinner to-night; I am not going out until eleven o'clock, and we can talk over and decide what pictures we will have. I am hunting my visiting list for all the pretty women I know. If we only get them nice-looking enough, who knows but that the Prince himself may come!"

Paul laid down the letter with a little laugh and a little sigh.

"Poor Rosamund! she is dull and dowdy because she won't stand half-naked before a room full of gaping snobs, who pay their guineas to say that they have been present at the same entertainment as a royal Princess. Well, I shall not try to alter her determination, but she must sing. Her singing is the loveliest thing in the world."

He hummed a little favourite air of hers as he rose and rang the bell. Then he scribbled a telegram and handed it to his man.

"Send that off at once; I will dress now."

He read Mrs. Toroni's letter again, and then tore it up.

"No, my dear lady," he thought, "I shall not dine with you to-night. Am I not going to the opera to hear 'Siegfried' and chance meeting my lady love?"

CHAPTER VI

MAN PROPOSES

THE servants at "The Hurst" were lighting up the fine suite of rooms on the ground floor, and giving the last touches to the draperies and palms which had transformed Mrs. Kerquham's luxurious rooms into positive fairyland. With much coaxing and trouble Laura and Honor had induced their mother to give a dance. On the first floor, where a long corridor ran from end to end of the large house, all was hurry and confusion; the Kerquham girls perpetually ringing and calling for their maid; Rosamund being summoned every five minutes to pronounce on the success of a coiffure or the disposition of a flower or feather; bouquets arriving for the young ladies, and all the excitement which precedes a dance in a house.

At a quarter to ten Mr. Kerquham knocked at his wife's dressing-room door.

"Come in," she said, and then catching sight of her husband's face in the looking-glass as he advanced towards her, she turned to her maid, "Parkins, you had better see if there is anything you can do for the young ladies before you go downstairs to the cloak-room. I can do without you now."

As the maid closed the door behind her, Mrs. Kerquham rose from her chair and faced round on her husband.

"Why are you not dressed yet, Alban? It is a quarter to ten, and you know that some of these people are sure to be punctual." Perhaps the weary look on his

face, as he sank into a low chair before the draped fireplace, touched her heart a little, for she added in more
gentle tones, "Is anything the matter? Are you not feeling well?"

"Nothing much is the matter, my dear," he replied
in his usual courteous way, "but I am not the thing.
I've not felt really well ever since we came to town in
the spring, and any excitement seems to tire me."

He settled himself as though the question of dressing
to receive his guests was the last thing in the world that
need trouble him, and Mrs. Kerquham, for the moment
dominated by his air, sat herself on the end of the sofa,
and did not even proceed with the putting on of her
gloves.

"I wanted to talk to you, my dear," began Mr. Kerquham, breaking the silence, "and tell you that really
after this season it will not be possible for me to live this
double life of work and pleasure. It is, as you know,
my earnest desire to earn money for you and for the
girls, so long as I have the power and the opportunity.
I want, in case anything should happen to me, to leave
you above all question of monetary difficulties. I should
like to know that the girls were not pinched for so much
as a half-penny. Then, too, there is Rosamund; she is
to me like a third daughter."

Mrs. Kerquham pursed her lips and stiffened her back
a little at the reference to her niece, but she was too wise
to interrupt by word or any other movement her husband's slow utterances.

"To do all this, my dear," he went on, "I must
work, and work hard. Do not think I am complaining
of that. I love my art, and after that my greatest happiness lies in knowing that you and the girls have all
the luxury and indulgence that money can buy."

He sighed heavily, and leaned forward with his elbows on his knees and his face in his hands. Mrs. Kerquham noticed for the first time how he had changed since the winter. "It is the so-called pleasure that tires me so. The dinners and dances; the first nights at plays, and the receptions that do not begin till after midnight and continue until the sun is up—that is where my weariness comes in. and that is what I feel I must give up."

Mrs. Kerquham began slowly to draw on one of her long gloves. "Then what is your idea?" she said, quietly.

"Well, I have been thinking it over in the studio this evening just between the lights. What I should like to do would be to let this house and go down to Midshire."

"But the girls!" burst involuntarily from Mrs. Kerquham's lips.

Even as she spoke there was a swish of silken skirts outside, and a ripple of light laughter which died away in the rooms below. Mr. Kerquham shrugged his shoulders.

"I think the girls will make themselves happy anywhere. They have had several seasons of this kind of thing, and they can have just as much pleasure, only of a different kind, at the Manor. I do not want to spoil their lives for them. I do not want to dock them of a single moment of happiness. They are young enough and light-hearted enough to be as pleased with horses and bicycles and golf and tennis as with supper parties and balls, theaters and the Row on Sunday."

Mrs. Kerquham buttoned her first long glove with a decided air. She said nothing, but her mind was filled with doubts as to the reception that Laura and Honor would give to the news that in a few short weeks their career in London society was to end, and that they were to be condemned to the country for an indefinite period.

"What do you think of my idea?" said Mr. Kerqu-ham, a little anxiously, trying to read something in his wife's cold, impassive face.

"What I think, Alban, is that you should go and dress and get ready to receive our guests. The suggestion you make is far too startling a one to be either consid-ered or discussed in the space of a few minutes. It is striking ten now. At any moment I may be wanted downstairs. We will certainly talk the matter over at some future date."

Gathering up her fan and bouquet, and submitting herself to a last inspection in the long mirror, Mrs. Ker-quham swept downstairs in all the glory of brocade and old lace, leaving her husband to walk slowly to his dress-ing-room and go through the monotonous process of getting into evening clothes.

As Mrs. Kerquham walked through her rooms and gave a last inspection all round she was outwardly quite calm, but in her heart she was more angry with her hus-band than she had ever been since the day she married him. She had been an ambitious woman for many years for him, and since his position had become assured her desires for aggrandisement had been centred on her daughters. The day that Laura was seventeen and made her *début* into society, Mrs. Kerquham had solemnly prayed to God that her girl should make a brilliant mar-riage. It was to that end she had sat up late night after night; that she had done violence to her feelings and gone to noisy suppers at the Savoy, and parties at houses where the company was as mixed as it was merry. It was for that that she had slaved through lists of afternoon calls; had lived in poky lodgings at Henley during regatta time; had joined gay parties for Ascot week, and, at the end of the season, commenced the round all over again at Homburg in August. It was for the sake of her daughters that she had known all sorts and conditions of men, and women whom she thought might influence those men.

For three years she had believed that Laura's Dresden-china beauty and piquant ways were going to win her a rich and titled husband. It had only been during the last few months that vague hints, half-formed suspicions, and fleeting doubts had assailed her as to the reasons for Laura's undoubted popularity with men. She had caught the whispers of dowagers in ball-rooms about "that fast Miss Kerquham." She had seen other women, whose daughters had married straight from the school-room, look at her rather pityingly when she went about with the three girls at her skirts. She had watched for little overt looks full of meaning, and had knowledge of double meanings in apparently innocent sentences.

The beginning of this season had almost proved to her that Laura was going to be a disappointment. She refused to believe that her girl would not marry at all, but she feared that she was going to marry badly.

After Honor's future state she had never troubled. She was quite aware that she had a *mauvaise langue*, and despite her youthful prettiness would probably grow at an early age into a sour-looking woman, but she felt sure she would marry some one—a rising professional man most likely, who would want a sharp-witted woman to push him in the world and a shrew to look after his servants.

And what of Rosamund? When she had first come into Mrs. Kerquham's calculations she had been only a stumbling-block. But her rare, stately beauty, her dignified, quiet manner, which had begun by being foils to Laura's freer manners, ended by making the latter seem merely vulgar. At first Mrs. Kerquham had been afraid that Rosamund would annex Laura's admirers, but she was constrained to admit that the girl seemed utterly oblivious of the existence of such people, and when, as had happened on more than one occasion, a young man, wounded by Miss Kerquham's arrant flirtations and hopelessly inconstant ways, had attempted to fly to the more staple and sedate Miss Keith for consolation, he had been ignored with quiet scorn.

It had not been until all the girls had been out for some two or three years that Mrs. Kerquham realised that the one of them who might help the others in the matter of marriage was Rosamund Keith, and that she would best do so by marrying well herself.

When once she had got this idea into her head and had grown accustomed to it, Mrs. Kerquham began to lay snares. Various eligible young men, who to do them justice were nothing loth, were trotted out for Miss Keith's inspection and approval; but she simply would not look at them. She had several very good proposals, but contented herself with refusing one after another, and going quietly back to her uncle's studio, where she made herself happy in cleaning his brushes and setting his palettes.

Mrs. Kerquham had at first been a little amused at what she called the "picksomeness" of her husband's niece, but as the months flew by matters grew more serious. Every fresh escapade of Laura's placed a good marriage for her further out of the question, and now here was this last blow of all. They were to go into the country. She guessed how such a scheme would turn out. It would mean Midshire in the hunting season and Scotland in the summer, where the only people they would see, except their own servants, would be a few old cronies who would come up for a fortnight's fishing when the streams were in good ply.

How was Laura to get settled in such places? It was positively ridiculous to anticipate her marriage under such hopelessly disadvantageous circumstances, and yet she dared not fight the plan too hard, for in her heart she acknowledged that her husband was ailing. Margot Kerquham was hard-headed enough to know what the death of her husband would mean to her. It would mean a critical income, a little house, no carriages and horses, no pleasures save those that were cheap or free. It would mean that the girls would have to make such frocks as they could afford to buy material for, and trim their own hats. She smiled a little grimly at the idea of idle, do-nothing Laura trimming a hat. It would mean that Honor's temper would get worse day by day, and that Laura, sooner than face the existence that a small competency entails, might kick over the traces altogether. Altogether it was a pretty quandary, and as she passed through her fine reception rooms, where already the light dresses of the girls were making bright patches of colour against the handsome hangings and dark foliage of the palms, Mrs. Kerquham's state of mind was not one to be envied.

She walked over to the great bay window of the drawing-room, and cast an eye round the verandah, which, draped with Eastern stuffs, filled with broad divans, and lit with Chinese lanterns, made a deliciously cool retreat. She looked at it with eyes that saw nothing, for she was still absorbed in finding an answer to the great conundrum—should she, or should she not, consent to leave London?

Suddenly Laura caught her by the arm and in a rather high voice said:

"Mother, what on earth does this mean? The whole of the verandah is enclosed round with netting—wire netting. Nobody can get outside and walk in the garden. Whoever had such a thing done?"

"The verandah has been netted in by my orders, Laura."

"By your orders, mother? Whatever for?" The girl looked so annoyed that Mrs. Kerquham, whose strong mind had always been subservient to her favourite daughter's petulant will, attempted to excuse herself.

"My dear, I thought the garden would be damp, and that some of you girls, in your thin shoes and low gowns, would catch cold."

"Rubbish!" said Laura, rudely. "You know it is a perfect night, as hot as possible, and here we are shut in like so many children. Why have you done it?" She stamped one satin-shod foot on the parquet floor. "You will make us the laughing-stock of the town. Already Mr. Morton and Mr. Abbotsford and Nellie Carmichael over there are calling this place the hen-coop. It is a positive disgrace."

Mrs. Kerquham plucked up some spirit in defence of her own act.

"My dear Laura, I do not approve, and I never shall approve, of young men and young women strolling about at all hours of the night in gardens and places. There is plenty of room here for your friends to sit out if they choose, but I will not have it said that the same free and easy manners prevail in my house as are customary in other people's."

Honor overheard the last few words of her mother's speech.

"Oh! you are insulting all our morals now," she said, with a spiteful flash of her eyes. "Insinuating that we are none of us able to take care of ourselves. Perhaps you would like me to tell the girls as they come in that they are not proper people, and that you imagine they can only be kept within the bounds of decent behaviour by being watched all the evening."

But Laura's temper by now had simmered down. She had a plan in her brain by which she and her particular friends could easily slip out into the garden if they chose.

"Be quiet, Honor; of course it is ridiculous, but it is no use making a fuss about it now." She drew her sister away, and as they walked over the polished floor, she bent down and whispered in her ear: "Try the smoking-room window; they will not have wired that over. Tell Nellie and Cora and the two Danvers girls, and of course we can take out anybody we like that way."

As she saw her two daughters whispering together, Mrs. Kerquham felt that all her misplaced efforts had been in vain; that she had merely made herself and her old-fashioned notions of decent, ladylike behaviour ridiculous by wiring in the verandah, and that in half an hour the moonlit gardens and its shady alleys would be full of girls and young men, laughing and kissing— "'spooning,' I think they call it," she said to herself— to the tune of the nightingales. Altogether the evening scarcely promised to be a pleasant one for Mrs. Kerquham, and as she turned from the window to take her place by the door to receive her guests, she wished that she had never acceded to Laura's wish at all, and consented to give a ball.

As she reached the doorway she caught sight of Lord St. Ives walking up the long corridor in his usual leisurely manner. He was the one man who might save the situation, and so she forced a smile to her thin, hard lips, and gave him a more than usually gracious greeting.

"I am so very glad you have come, and in such good time, too. There are so many things I wish to speak to you about. I feel you are such a friend of the family that I can say things to you that I should not care about discussing with anybody else. I should like to speak to you at supper time."

As Lord St. Ives bowed over her hand he wondered to himself what it all meant. He was of the age when a man ought to know the world; he would never see forty-five again. He had led a life that was not exactly conducive to ignorance, and in the early morning the effect of it showed a little too distinctly on his face; but he had managed to keep his figure, and being a well-bred looking man, had by night an air of distinction about him which certainly made him an ornament in any average drawing-room.

He passed on into the room, his eyes seeking everywhere for Rosamund Keith; Mrs. Kerquham knew perfectly well for whom he was looking, and she made up her mind to accept the inevitable. For months she had hoped that his frequent visits to the house would culminate in a proposal to Laura, but she had lately realised that such remnants of a heart as were left to his lordship had been laid at her niece's feet. He saw Rosamund almost at once, for her more than common height made her conspicuous even in a crowd. He did not walk straight up to her, however, but stopped to exchange words with almost every one, as he crossed the room.

"Some one is looking for you, Rosamund," said Honor, as she saw Lord St. Ives' carefully arranged head coming slowly through the swaying throng.

"I am to be found here," answered Rosamund quite quietly, and to Honor's disappointment neither blushing nor looking in the least conscious.

Presently, and as though quite by accident, Lord St. Ives stood before Rosamund.

"Ah! Good evening, Miss Keith. I trust you got my flowers." He glanced at the big bouquet which she carried in her hand; it was of white lilies, and not the one he had sent her.

"Yes, and I thank you for them," said Rosamund, simply.

"I had hoped that you would have carried them to-night."

Most girls would have prevaricated and talked about the colour of their gowns or the scent of the flowers, but Rosamund, in her calm, direct way, looked into his eyes, and said:

"Yours were very nice, Lord St. Ives, but I liked these better," and she raised the lilies and laid them against her face.

"Or the giver?" Lord St. Ives felt it was bad manners, but he could not help the words slipping from him.

"Perhaps," said Rosamund.

"How cruel you are!" he said with a laugh, trying to pass off his other remark. "How many dances are you going to give me?"

"I will dance with you with pleasure."

"Yes, but how often? Once or twice?"

"It is early in the evening, Lord St. Ives, and I have many great friends coming to-night; I cannot promise you more than one."

She passed by him, leaving him sulkily leaning against the wall.

"Commend me to that girl for pride," he muttered. "One would think she was a duchess or the daughter of a millionaire, instead of being a pauper and heaven knows who! But she does fetch me, I never saw a girl

I liked so much or wanted so badly.   She doesn't make herself cheap as the rest of them do."

He looked scornfully at the fluttering crowd of girls, all smiling and nodding and hiding their disappointments and petty jealousies, and putting bold faces on everything, all for the sake of getting a word or a dance from the young men who hung round the doors and windows in groups and laughed at them behind their backs.

Lord St. Ives flattered himself he was a good judge of women, and he certainly had had over twenty-five years' experience of them and their ways.   He watched Rosamund now as she moved about the room, much as a lover of horses watches and gloats over the points of some thoroughbred animal that has caught his fancy and is to make his fortune.   She was in black; it was something clear and soft that floated like a cloud about her and made the dazzling whiteness of her neck and arms almost too startling by contrast.   A silver belt was clasped about her waist, and as she danced her beautiful body swayed from the hips up with the absolute freedom and subtleness of healthy, perfectly-formed womanhood.   A little string of milk-white pearls was round her throat, and at the back of her neck an airy cloud of ringlets cast a faint shade.   She wore no other jewels, and had nothing but the perfect outlines of her bare shoulders and bosom, the glorious column of her full white throat, and the sweet small oval of her face to commend her. But to-night she seemed very happy; her great velvety eyes danced like stars, and her scarlet lips were parted in radiant smiles.

"I never saw her look so well," thought St. Ives. "I did not even know she had so much expression."

Then he caught sight of the man she was dancing

with. It was Paul Carr, and he wore in his coat some lilies like those that Rosamund carried in her hand.

"Damn!" muttered St. Ives to himself, and he strode down the long corridor into the refreshment room.

Mrs. Kerquham, for the moment relieved from the fatigues of reception, was sipping a cup of coffee. One glance at Lord St. Ives' face showed her that something was wrong. She put down her cup and went over to him.

"Dreadfully hot in the ball-room, I suppose?" she said. "I really had to leave it for a few moments. Won't you come into the verandah?" Still glowering, Lord St. Ives offered his hostess his arm. "It was so kind of you to come all this way to-night," she began, when once they were sitting in a lamp-lit corner. "We live so far out from what all you men call 'London.' In fact, I have often wondered lately how you could find time to come here so much."

"Your house is so attractive, Mrs. Kerquham, and the entertainment you give your guests so agreeable that one thinks nothing of a little distance," said Lord St. Ives, politely, and wondering as he spoke when that confounded valse would stop, and when that tall fellow Carr would take his arm from about Rosamund's slender waist.

"Yes, our house is nice," said Mrs. Kerquham with a carefully modulated sigh. "Our dear house! I shall be so sorry to leave it."

"Ah! where are you off to this autumn, Mrs. Kerquham?" said Lord St. Ives, indifferently, and trying to see if from where he sat he could get a peep into the ball-room. "Is it to be Homburg again, or Switzerland?"

"Neither; we are going to Scotland."

"Charming! charming!" said Lord St. Ives. "Quite the place to go to. There is nothing like it. It suits me admirably.   I wonder if you will be anywhere near where I am booked for?   But even if you are not, you always come south early in the autumn, and I do not think of staying away long this year myself.''

''We are leaving London for good,'' said Mrs. Kerquham, tragically.

''For good?   Going to give up 'The Hurst,' this awfully nice house and everything!   Why, what is that for?''

Lord St. Ives wondered whether Mr. Kerquham had been speculating, or whether the price of pictures was falling off, or what it could be that was affecting the family finances, and as he wondered he thanked his stars that his own monetary position placed him above any consideration of marrying for money.

''Mr. Kerquham says he can work in London no longer.   His health is not what it was, and so we are going to live between Scotland and Midshire.''

''But surely,'' said Lord St. Ives, ''you and your daughters and Miss Keith will be here.''

Mrs. Kerquham drew herself up, and the Puritanical expression settled down over her hard features.

''The place of a wife and children is by the side of the husband and father, Lord St. Ives.''

''Oh—er—ah—yes—I—yes, of course!   I beg your pardon,'' stammered his lordship.

''Well, Lord St. Ives,'' went on Mrs. Kerquham confidentially, ''I do not mind telling you that this plan of my husband's of leaving town is a great blow to me and''—looking at him out of the corners of her eyes and watching the effect of every word—''I think I may say that it will be a great blow to at least one of my young people.''

Lord St. Ives settled his shirt front and stroked his moustache.

"You think that Miss—?"

"Oh! no names, please!" cried Mrs. Kerquham. "I have no desire to be your confidant, Lord St. Ives, until you have something to tell me."

"Deuced clever woman that," said his lordship to himself, as Mrs. Kerquham left him to chew the cud of her discourse. "I suppose they are going away directly; I had better speak to-night, perhaps. When a family is on the move you can never get a word with any one, and Miss Keith is not the sort of girl one could ask out to a quiet luncheon and have to one's self. Thank goodness, that beastly valse is over!"

But when he got back into the ball-room he found Rosamund engaged for the next six dances, and it was not until after he had supped that he chanced to find her for a moment alone and disengaged.

"Give me the next; I want to talk to you."

Rosamund Keith did not like Lord St. Ives; she was always a little frightened of him, of his bold eyes and of the peculiar smile he had whenever he looked at her, but she knew her duty to her aunt's guests, and if she took his arm with a lack of cordiality, she acceded with sufficient politeness to his request that she would sit out the dance with him in the verandah.

They had that haven of refuge all to themselves, for the majority of the guests were supping, and only a few inveterate dancers were floating over the polished floor.

"Let me get you some cushions," said Lord St. Ives, collecting half a dozen and piling them behind her, and in so doing making such a nest for her that without absolutely rising she could not shift her place. Then he flung himself down at her side, and leaning on his elbow, began to look at her with that hateful coarse look that made her feel ashamed and hot and red all over.

"How splendid you are looking to-night!" he said presently, half under his breath. "But you have been a little cruel about the flowers, you know. I chose them so especially for you—great queenly red roses, I thought they would just suit your style of beauty. Those things," and he flicked with his gloves the lilies lying in her lap, "are so 'missish.'"

She did not answer, but merely took the bouquet in her hand and placed it on her other side.

"Now I have offended you," he cried. "Who gave you those flowers?"

"They came without any card, but I think that Mr. Carr sent them."

He looked at her with admiration.

"By heavens! you are a wonder! Any other girl would have told a lie about it."

"What for? I am not ashamed of receiving flowers from Mr. Carr."

"Oh, bother Mr. Carr!" said St. Ives, edging still a little nearer. "Let's talk about something else. Let's talk about—about you."

"I'm afraid I am not very interesting," said Rosamund, forcing a little laugh and feeling furious with herself, as against every instinct and wish of hers she grew hotly red again.

His eyes burned with admiration as he looked at her.

"Interesting?" he said. "You are the most interesting woman in all the world to me."

"Now that is a very pretty compliment, Lord St. Ives," said Rosamund, fighting hard to get the conversation back into a light, indifferent vein.

"It is not a compliment, and you know it," he said, rather roughly. "You know perfectly well, without my telling you, that I am awfully fond of you. I never was so gone on any woman before. Of course, I have always liked your sex; I think they are charming, and one could not quite get on without them, but—"

She held up her hand.

"I have no desire to hear your confidences about other women."

"Well, no; I do not suppose you have," he stammered a little awkwardly, and put off for the moment by her rather offended air. "I do not want to talk about other women, either. I only want to talk of you."

"Please don't," said Rosamund.

"Well, then, I want to talk about myself. Shall we put it that way?"

He took hold of a little piece of the stuff of her dress and began fiddling with it with his large strong hands.

"I know I am not much of a subject to talk about, but if you would only listen for a few minutes—I want to ask you—"

The thick fingers crept up from her gown until they touched her bare arm. With a little exclamation of anger she sprang up, as though a hot iron had burned her flesh.

"I beg a thousand pardons," he cried, rising, too. "I did not know you were so particular as all that."

Something in her attitude seemed to madden him; he advanced towards her and caught her two hands in his.

"I wonder if that prudish, icy way of yours is all put on just to drive me mad. I wonder if you are any better than the rest of your sex, and if you are not playing with me all the time. But I do not care whether you are or not. You are the girl I want, and the girl I will have."

He had caught her by the arms now, and strong and supple as she was, she felt herself being gradually drawn into his embrace. His burning eyes pierced hers, his hot breath was close upon her mouth.

"Miss Keith, this dance is ours!" said a voice behind them.

The words acted like ice upon Lord St. Ives. With a muttered oath he released Rosamund, caught up his hat, and strode into the house. She, with all her will gone for the moment, and all her control broken down, put out her hands to Paul Carr like a little child, and tottered towards him, crying, "I am so frightened; I am so frightened!"

For a moment Paul thought she was going to be hysterical, as she sank sobbing into his arms. Without a moment's thought he dragged aside a strip of hanging drapery, and by sheer weight forced a piece of the wire netting away from its frail fastenings.

"Come into the air," he whispered in her ear.

A moment later she was standing with Paul out in the clear, white flood of moonlight. The whole garden was bathed in it, and the nightingales were singing at the bottom of the avenue. The house before her was all lit up, and the crash of music rose and fell on the night air. They had been playing that bit of the valse a few minutes ago, when the other man had caught her by her arms and drawn her to him. With a shudder she drew her hand across her mouth. Paul Carr guessed what the action meant.

"He did not kiss you!"

She dropped her arms down to her sides again and stared straight before her. Though she was now outwardly calm, her outraged womanhood, her insulted purity, was still surging and beating at her heart and in her temples. She could almost have screamed at the memory of that moment.

"Are you feeling better?" said Paul. "How white you are, and you are shaking so! Walk a little; it will do you good."

He drew one of her arms through his and led her across the lawn to the avenue where the birds were singing. The moment she was out of the light her strained nerves gave way, and putting her two hands before her face, she began to cry.

"How that brute has frightened you!" cried Carr.

He did not try to stop her tears; some instinct told him she would be better for the shedding of them. Gradually her sobs grew quieter, and with a little shame-faced "I am very sorry," she dragged a scrap of a handkerchief out of the bosom of her gown and dried her eyes.

Presently with a long-drawn, trembling sigh she raised her face. She was composed now, though the dark fringes of her lashes sparkled with tears. Again a sobbing sigh swelled her white bosom, but she caught it in her throat and strangled it, for in the low bough that hung motionless in the warm air above her head a full-voiced nightingale burst into a mighty flood of song.

Paul, watching every expression of her face, saw the tension and the shame die out of it. He noted how her quivering lips settled once more into their calm curves, and how her gracious head fell into the tilted pose that became her so well.

As the rich, throbbing song died in the blue night Rosamund spoke:

"That music is like a message from heaven. How foolish—how idle—to be angry—or grieved at things that happen, when God sends us such compensations as that. Listen!" She lifted one slender hand. "He is going to sing again!"

A shaft of the white moon rays had pierced the thick foliage and fell on her face and throat, as she stood enraptured and all unconscious that Paul's soul was in the eyes he bent on her. She did not even know that his hand had crept to hers and held her slight, cool fingers in an ardent clasp.

It was only when for a moment the little singing bird checked his flood of melody that Rosamund started to find Paul was so close to her.

"Ah! Rosamund, you will not draw away from *me*. Dearest, let me tell you that I love you—that I adore you, reverence you, as a man worships a star or a saint."

Gently he drew her nearer to him, until, all trembling and sweet, she stood within the circle of his arms.

"My dear love, do not fear—do not tremble." Pale as a lily, yet bravely fighting all the maiden modesty of her pure nature, she raised her eyes—twin lakes of candour and truth—to his.

"I do not fear you—and if I tremble—it is with joy!"

"Then you love me!—Rosamund—you love me!"

A divine blush swept across the marble of her throat and cheeks; a delicious mist of passion grew in her dark eyes; the delicate bow of her mouth broke in a shy smile.

"I love you, Paul!"

His hands slipped from her waist to her wrists. Tenderly, slowly, he raised her white arms till their scented warmth was laid about his neck. Then, with his eyes searching the secrets of her own, and his mouth close to hers, he whispered passionately, "Kiss me—heart of my heart!"

And as she gave him her virgin lips, and with them all her troth and love, the nightingale thrilled the whole avenue with the passion of his song.

But Paul was only conscious that close above his heart, clasped in his arms, was the one woman he had ever loved, the only breathing handiwork of God he had ever desired. The faint pulsing of her slender body, the delicate perfume of her waving hair, the starry radiance of her dreamy eyes, all intoxicated him.

A laughing group of girls flitted across the brilliant whiteness of the wide lawn; the music from the ballroom wailed and sobbed in a langourous valse measure; the nightingale shook the very air, but he only heard the words, "I love you, Paul!"

By-and-by some thought crossed Rosamund's mind, and she drew herself from his embrace, and with her palms laid upon his heart, to hold him from her, murmured, plaintively, "Paul, you are not loving me out of pity, are you, because I am poor—?"

He caught her back to him with a laugh.

"You sweetest soul! I love you for yourself, and for that only. If all the world were rich and you were penniless, I would have you and you alone for my wife."

He caught sight of her serious face and grew grave too.

"Dearest—you have said you love me. Will you marry me?"

For answer she gave him her lips once more, with all the frankness of her nature.

"Paul! I love you, and I will be your wife—or no man's."

They spoke but little after that; pledged words were enough between them. But they lingered beneath the fragrant lime trees till the fiery-eyed carriages whirled away the tired dancers, till the fiddles gave their last scream, and till the faint flush of breaking day silenced the heavenly song of the nightingale.

CHAPTER VII

BETWEEN THE ACTS

A LAST word from Rosamund to Paul Carr, as he took leave of her after the Kerquham's dance, gave him warning that all the family were to be at the opera the next evening.

The longing to see and speak with his betrothed again drove him to be punctually in his stall, and from it to direct all his heart and thoughts to the big box on the grand tier. Laura was looking quite her best, like a beautiful, audaciously half-draped Dresden figure. A group of young men were round her chair, and she kept whispering to them behind a spangled fan. Even Honor was smiling, and had caught some reflected beauty from her sister. Mrs. Kerquham felt that the evening was being quite a success, and though she was inwardly dreadfully bored, and could not help wondering why such discordant noises were necessary to the expression of emotion, she managed to fix a fairly pleasant smile upon her stern face. Rosamund, who adored music, looked radiantly happy. She had flashed a little smile and the faintest of blushes down to Paul on her first entrance, and then gave herself up to whole-hearted enjoyment of the glorious flood of sound. He noticed that she wore some of the lilies that he had given her last night in her bosom, and that a little brooch he had sent her during the afternoon sparkled like a star among the thick masses of her dark hair.

After the first act Paul went upstairs, but only to find the box door wide open and a perfect flood of young men overflowing into the corridor. Laura was standing outside, but Rosamund had not left her seat, and it was quite impossible to force his way to her. Lord St. Ives was sitting close to Mrs. Kerquham and evidently persuading her to fall in with some plan of his. Paul could only smile at Miss Keith and bow to her aunt, and then there was no choice left him but to talk nonsense to Laura or to go to the smoking-room and have a cigarette.

In the second long interval the same scene was enacted over again, but he was more persistent this time and took up his stand outside the box, determined to get a word with Rosamund. Yet again he was thwarted, for as he leant idly against the wall, an arm was slipped through his and a man he knew said:

"Oh, come along with me, Carr, and have a drink. It is no use waiting about here."

They sauntered together down the corridor, Paul listening to Mr. Trevor's confidence and comments.

"Those Kerquham girls will be unbearable if they see such a lot of young men hanging round. They give themselves airs enough already, goodness knows!"

They turned into the crush-room, which was full of men who were discussing in loud voices every known subject under the sun—politics and finance, the scandal of the boudoir and the *coulisse;* smoking-room stories, rumours about so-and-so, racing tips, and gossip on every conceivable subject. Guy Trevor loosed Paul's arm the moment he got inside the door.

"Hallo! there is Tommy Coates over there; he can give me a tip about the Ascot Cup," and he dashed off into the crowd and was lost at once.

Paul leaned up against the wall. He nodded idly here

and there to the men in the crowd whose faces he knew, but he was a little vexed—he did not quite know whether with himself or with Rosamund—and he was in no mood for idle talk. In front of him stood a group of half a dozen men. Three of them were drinking, the others were talking.

"I say," drawled a gentleman whose strongly marked features and pronounced twang stamped him as one of the "Chosen People," "who the deuce is that pretty girl on the grand tier? The one with something blue in her head and not too much frock on. It is Lady Carruther's box, but her ladyship is not there herself, so they cannot be very intimate friends of hers."

A young man with a budding moustache lifted his head from his tumbler.

"Yes, I have been looking at her myself. Smart looking little bit of goods. But the girl who sits in the far corner is better looking—black hair, big eyes, and such a lovely neck and shoulders!"

"Don't care for that sort myself," said the first speaker. "The other's style is more to my taste. Wonder who they are?"

"Don't you know?" queried a third. "I can tell you." The group gathered closer together, and Paul writhed inwardly, for he guessed so well what was going to be said.

"They are the Kerquhams—the artist's people, you know."

"Fiddle-de-dee!" cried the youth. "Kerquham paints ripping pictures and all that kind of thing, but I don't mind betting you an even fiver that his women-folk are not like that. That black-haired girl looks like a swell of some sort."

"Nothing of the sort, nothing of the sort," said the

small man. "She is a poor relation, a niece or a cousin, or an adopted daughter of old Kerquham's. They say she is a very nice girl, and as straight as a die."

"She must be if St. Ives is after her, and I see he's been in the box all the evening," remarked the Jew. "He is very fond of a lark, but he means to marry all right. He told me once that he did not intend to add another shady Countess to the peerage."

"Is the girl going to have him?" asked some one. "He is scarcely the kind of a man a nice young woman would care about."

"Scarcely, but I do not suppose that she will have very much choice in the matter," said the little man, who posed for knowing all about everything. "It is a question of Mrs. K." He winked very solemnly. "She wants to get one of those girls married, and as her daughters are hanging fire a bit, she has just lately been turning her attention to the other one."

The callow youth grew pink and ferocious.

"But you cannot force a girl in these times," he said. "By Jove! it is a great shame, because you know, St. Ives is a bit too thick for any decent woman."

"Don't you frighten yourself, old chappie; St. Ives has pretty well sown his wild oats. He is getting on for fifty, you know, and he has lived every minute of his life. He will make a very good husband, you see if he don't, and an earl with thirty thousand a year is not to be sneezed at by a poor relation, you know, even although she has got a big pair of eyes and fine dark hair."

"Well, I call it an absolute shame!"

"Call it what you like, dear boy; call it what you like. Mrs. K. is a clever woman; she is Scotch and canny, and I think she has got his lordship on the hook by now. Hallo! there goes the bell; come along."

The black-coated stream, all laughing and joking, filed past Paul back into the theatre. He sat down on one of the big lounges and dropped his head into his hands. So that was the way they talked of Rosamund and her belongings—as if she were so much flesh and blood, just put up for sale; as though her purity and her innocence, her goodness and her happiness were marketable commodities that were bound to fetch a high price in the world's market. Then he became conscious that the people behind the bar were looking at him, and he got up and walked into the corridor again. As he passed Mrs. Kerquham's box, Lord St. Ives came out, holding the door ajar behind him.

"I have just been making up a little supper party for the Savoy to-night, Mr. Carr," he said, with an assumption of cordiality. "I hope you will join us there. Mrs. Kerquham says she shall not stop till the end; so will you meet us there about eleven?"

It was on the tip of Paul's tongue to refuse, when he caught sight of Rosamund through the nearly closed door. She had heard Lord St. Ives' words, and had turned her head eagerly and was looking at Paul.

"Yes, I will come," he said in a voice sufficiently loud for her to hear. Her eyes smiled at him before she again looked at the stage.

When he arrived at the Savoy none of Lord St. Ives' party had appeared yet, but a table had been reserved. He lit a cigarette and stood at the top of the steps of the courtyard. Perhaps he might get a chance of taking Rosamund's hand and whispering just one word in her ear. Presently the whole party drove up. Mrs. Kerquham and the three girls in her own carriage; half a dozen men packed into two hansoms, and Lord St. Ives last of all, with a lady, in another cab.

"By-the-bye, Mrs. Kerquham," he said in his loud voice to that lady, as she alighted from her carriage, "I met Mrs. Rivington just as we were coming out, and I brought her along with me."

Mrs. Kerquham bowed very stiffly. Mrs. Rivington was a grass-widow, whom she knew more by repute than personally. They exchanged cards once a year, but there the acquaintanceship ceased, for even the Scotch-woman's altered view of looking at things and people in general had never been able to include Mrs. Rivington within the bounds of her horizon.

"How awfully jolly!" cried Laura, shaking Mrs. Rivington's hand. She did it as much to annoy her mother as anything else, and also with an eye to secure an invitation some time or other to the grass-widow's festive Sunday luncheons, and tea-gown smoking parties, about which such quite too shocking stories were told.

With a rustle and much chatter the party filed upstairs and into the long, brilliantly-lit supper room. The theatres were over, and already the tables were filling fast. Here and there, though, in cosy little corners were tables which watchful waiters were reserving. They were for late comers, for wealthy patrons of the restaurant and of pretty actresses who had to get out of their stage clothes and put on their best diamonds and a fresh layer of powder and rouge before they could come out to supper.

With considerable noise Lord St. Ives' party settled themselves down. Courtesy demanded that Mrs. Kerquham should sit by her host's right hand, but she felt very out of it, for Mrs. Rivington was opposite, and was already indulging in asides in which doubtful jokes, innuendoes and slang held the chief part. Paul slipped into a seat next Rosamund, though to do so he had to roughly shoulder that same youth whose outspoken admiration he had listened to an hour ago in the crush-room at Covent Garden. As they drew their chairs to the table, their hands met for a moment.

"What a piece of luck, my darling! I have been wondering the whole night whether I should get a chance of·speaking to you."

"Are you not going to Mrs. Tregaskis' dance to-night?" said Rosamund. "I made sure we should meet there, and so I did not mind so much when we could not speak at the opera."

"I had not meant to go, but if you do, of course I will."

"Aunt Margot is sure to take us," said Rosamund. "You know she considers that she doesn't do her duty unless she keeps us up till four o'clock every morning. For my part, I would rather go home if—" and she smiled an adorable little smile—"if it were not for you."

"Oh, Rosamund, do look!" cried Laura, in her strident voice across the table; "there is that woman just come in whom we saw dancing the other night at the Paragon. Don't you remember—the one who really did cut it so awfully fine in the matter of clothes? Those she had on looked as if they were going to drop off," she added for the benefit of the giggling young men about her. "Why she is not a bit pretty off the stage! Such a coarse looking lump of a thing, but her diamonds are lovely. Whoever gave them to her, I wonder?"

Laura, launched on the sea of social and theatrical scandals, set to work to retail all the gossip and slanderous stories she had ever heard. She professed to know, by sight, half the notorious women who were in the room, and had something she would call "spicy" to tell

about every one of them. Now and then Mrs. Kerquham looked reproachfully in her daughter's direction,
but Laura was wound up. She had had her third glass
of champagne; she had got four young men to talk to;
she knew she looked her best, and that her shoulders
were as pretty as any other woman's; she was in the
seventh circle of her petty little heaven of delight
wherein she dwelt, until soon after midnight the party
rose from supper.

"You will give me the first dance when you arrive at
Portman Square," pleaded Paul, as he put Rosamund's
cloak about her. "You know we have not had a word
alone together yet, and I want to tell you how sweet you
are looking."

"Lord St. Ives," broke in Mrs. Kerquham's cold
voice, "will not Mrs. Rivington come with me, and perhaps you will take my niece Rosamund?"

But Mrs. Rivington, with her daringly cut gown, her
too yellow head, and her carefully bistred eyes, had for
the moment got the whip hand of Lord St. Ives' senses.

"Ha! ha! Mrs. Kerquham," he cried, with a loud
laugh. "Mrs. Rivington is under a promise to me, and
I am not going to let her off, you know. We shall meet
up at the Tregaskis' in a few minutes," and taking his
charge familiarly by the arm, Lord St. Ives turned
his now rather uncertain gait towards the outer staircase,
and drove off in a hansom with the grass-widow.

"If I can be of any use," said Paul, "my brougham
is here—"

But Mrs. Kerquham was annoyed. If Lord St. Ives
intended to make a fool of himself, she did not intend
Rosamund to give him any loop-hole of complaint.

"Thank you, Mr. Carr, but we can manage. Now,

girls, come along," and she unceremoniously hustled her charges into the carriage.

"Keep me all the dances," whispered Paul, as Rosamund passed him with downcast eyes.   Then he turned to the men:

"Now, then, to whom of you can I give a lift?"

And the procession started for Mrs. Tregaskis' ball in Portman Square.

CHAPTER VIII

WHILE HOUSES SLEEP

As two hours later the Kerquham carriage rolled away from Mrs. Tregaskis' house, Paul Carr walked slowly down the steps with his light overcoat over his arm. A small group of pale-faced, yawning footmen were lounging against the pillars and railings, and a few carriages with sleeping horses and tired coachmen were ranked close to the square railings. As he stepped onto the pavement a hoarse-voiced linkman hailed a hansom, but Paul shook his head, and turning sharply to the left vanished into the darkness. He felt that he must move, stretch his limbs, and exhale in deep breaths from his heart the mingled fumes of wine, the perfume from women's hair, and the faint, sickly smell of dying flowers. He longed to drive from his brain, through the medium of his regularly falling feet, the swinging measure of the sensuous string music, the witless talk and aimless laughter. To add to all that confusion, the rattle of cab wheels and the tinkle of a bell would be more than his excited nerves could bear. He felt that he must walk.

A moment later he was out of sight and hearing of the brilliantly lit house, where silhouetted figures glided before the shining windows, and where the long balcony was filled with whispering couples. It was the stillest hour of all the twenty-four. The short summer night still held sway, though the pallid gleam that shone brightly from such upper windows as faced the east heralded the quickly coming day.

Paul was a Londoner born and bred, but as he reached Oxford Street an overwhelming sense of desolation and loneliness swept over him. The great thoroughfare was still as the grave, and the only things that seemed to live were the endless rows of gas lamps that at an immeasurable distance met in a tiny point before fading into nothingness. Even at the coffee stall that twinkled like a constellation before the Marble Arch all was still. He felt for the moment as if he were the only waking man in the whole world.

He crossed the wide road leisurely, finding an almost childish attraction in the fact that he had not to hurry. Audley Street was deserted, but in Grosvenor Square another large party was breaking up, and he noticed how haggard and drawn the women looked beneath their powder and rouge, as they passed to their carriages, for it was only here and there that one of them had the discretion to draw a film of lace across her face as she emerged into the merciless light of the coming day. In Mount Street and Berkeley Square it was the same, and as he turned into Piccadilly and set his feet in the direction of his own rooms, he met many men in twos and threes sauntering homewards as they smoked their last cigars. Ten minutes ago he had fancied that all London was sleeping, and that idea had soothed him. Now it occurred to him that the whole city had been dancing all night, and the reflection irritated him and chased away such physical well-being as he had evolved from his walk, bringing back to him in a flood of memory all the events of the past night.

Spurred by his own thoughts, he turned round, and crossing the road, walked rapidly down St. James' Street.

An enforced energy· of thought and movement swept over him, and he felt that his rooms, with their damask curtains and Persian rugs, pillowed lounges and crowded palms, would suffocate him. He must get out into the open and breathe. He would go straight across the wide Horse Guards Parade and on to the Embankment to where the great waterway eternally ebbed and flowed.

It seemed at first almost dark on the Embankment; they had already put out the lights, and the river looked sullen and black under the cold grey sky. Involuntarily Paul slipped on his coat. He was not cold, but the impression of dreary desolation and the sad murmur of the passing waves made him shudder. On the seats were huddled shapeless masses of humanity, who had slept and wakened, cursed and slept again all the night through. Here and there some one had been lucky enough to get a seat all to himself, and lay at full length, snoring luxuriously.

Paul strolled along for a time, then, beneath the shadows of two great hotels, leaned his arms on the low parapet and stared into the rolling stream. Its dark depths revealed to him all the events of the past few hours. Again he saw the crush-room at the opera filled with men of all ages, whose talk and gossip were even more spiteful and biting than the tea-table gabble of their wives and sisters. Again he saw the long supper-room at the Savoy, with its myriad lights and scores of crowded tables. He remembered how the skirts of the lowest had flaunted past those of the highest; how men in company with the painted toy of an hour had laughed and nodded across the room at well-born, respectable women. He heard again the clink of glasses, the shrill screams of laughter, which told him that the last coarse story had been enjoyed by an eager audience.

Then his introspection narrowed, and he saw only the table at which he had sat with Rosamund. He remembered Laura's behaviour and Honor's talk and Lord St. Ives' face, flushed with wine, bent down almost to Mrs. Rivington's stripped shoulders. He recalled Guy Trevor's vapid chatter and Dick Charteris' broad innuendoes. He caught his breath at that last memory, when he saw once more, in angry fancy, the swift wave of colour that had swept over Rosamund's cheek at one of Dick's most outrageous remarks.

And then the pictures faded, and the lights and music died down, and only Rosamund's face, with its sweet mouth and great starry dark eyes gazing at him from beneath her broad, level brows, was reflected back at him from the rushing tide, which was now turning a sickly grey colour under the silvery heavens.

"My darling, my white rose, I must pluck you and take you away from all this, or even your purity will be smirched. I must see your uncle at once and ask him to announce our marriage. Then we will shake the dust and the soil of the world—*our* world—from our feet and go out and make one of our own."

His dreams were cut short by an insistent hand on his arm and an incoherent voice that babbled meaningless words in his ear. A wretched figure in flaunting rags and cheap paint, a caricature of womanhood, a stain on civilisation, stood at his side. The creature swayed a little, for she was not sober, and whined and leered. Half sick with disgust, Paul stepped aside quickly from this wretched remnant of femininity, and roughly bade her go.

"D—— you for a mean hound! I was a beauty when you were in your cradle. Twenty years ago the men ran after me. Give me sixpence for a cup of coffee."

She stretched out her hand as though to touch him. Paul, thrilling with horror, turned on his heel and moved away.

"Oh, my God! he is going to leave me to starve," shrieked the woman in a voice that rent the grey air. She made an unsteady run for the stone steps against which the tide rippled and lapped. Losing her footing she lurched and slipped with loud screams almost into the heavy stream. Paul, with every manly instinct roused, rushed after her and dragged her, soaked and shrieking, once more back to the pavement. Mad with drink and fright, she began to fight and scream, and it was all that Paul, strong man as he was, could do to hold her back.

"What are you doing here with this woman?" said a rough voice.

"Oh! good sir, he is driving me to starvation and the river."

Paul still held the struggling woman by both her arms, and turned his head to the policeman.

"Nonsense! I do not know her. She spoke to me and then tried to drown herself."

Another policeman came up, and the two looked very serious. Such odd things did happen; one never knew what steps these gentlemen would not take to get rid of a woman who was in their way.

Meantime the wretched creature was pretending to faint, and was hanging with all her weight on Paul's hands, while the water streaming from her skirts formed a pool about his feet. A few tattered, shadowy figures loomed up in the vague light and hung round and wondered audibly what "the swell had been a-doing of." Among these Paul saw a man who was better dressed than the others, though he was distinctly frayed about the wrists and ankles. He was small and had a mean sallow face, with red eyes which looked as though they never rested or slept. Paul noticed him more particularly because he pushed his way so aggressively through the throng and stood so very closely behind the two policemen. He pulled out a little book and began to scribble in it fast, looking first at Paul and then at the huddled-up, bedraggled woman.

"Here! can't you take her?" said Paul to one of the policemen. "She's only pretending to be ill. Get an ambulance."

"That's all very well, sir," replied one of the men, "but we wants to know a little more about this before we takes her off your hands." And the slowly gathering crowd of tatterdemalions applauded the law, and cried, "That's it, copper, don't you let him go!"

Paul looked at the faces of the people about him. They were all low and debased, the very scum of the earth. He knew that the very fact of his being a gentleman was against him in their eyes, and that he would get neither support nor sympathy from any of such a crew. Suddenly a voice behind him spoke, a voice whose ringing tones he seemed to know, and that brought back to him memories of the happiest years of his life.

"What! is that you again, Kate Gray? Now, you are only malingering, you know, unless you are too drunk to move. Constable, you ought to know this woman. Take her to the station at once."

The two policemen looked a little sheepish, and advancing, relieved Paul of the most unpleasant burden. Yet to show that they still had some independence, and to keep up their character with the crowd that thronged around, one of them said:

"All right, Father, we'll take your word for it, but

the gentleman must come with us and give his name and address."

As though by magic an ambulance was fetched and the wretched woman flung upon it, and then Paul found himself the center of a shuffling, ragged, evil-smelling crowd, walking up through the grey dawn to Bow Street police station. He had tried for one brief moment to slip away unobserved, but the people muttered angrily, and the man whose voice he seemed to know had touched him on the arm and said:

"Of course, you know nothing of this unfortunate creature, but you had better come."

As they left the Embankment behind them and walked up towards the Strand, Paul looked at the man who paced by his side. He was of middle height, square and sturdy in build, with a strong, plain face that was lit with kindly eyes, and a firm mouth that indicated a sense of humour. He wore the severely cut broadcloth suit of a priest, while the plain band of the Roman collar clearly indicated his form of faith. His hat was one of soft felt, and his appearance in no way remarkable. As Paul looked down from his superior height, the other looked up, and then uttered an exclamation.

"Why, you are Paul Carr!"

And Paul held out his hand and cried, "And you are Philip Steyne!"

"I was. I am Father Gregory now."

Paul looked him up and down, and the Father's stern mouth melting into a smile, said:

"Yes! I suppose it was the outcome of the Oxford movement. Do you remember how we used to argue when we were up there together? But four years ago I entered on my novitiate, and I have been a monk for nearly three now."

"Fancy you doing such a thing as that!"

The other man laughed a little.

"Ah! my friend, we never know from year to year where we may be or what we may become. When we were in the playing fields at Eton and rowing in our college eight at Oxford that last term that we were 'up,' we never thought we should meet again like this."

They were in Wellington Street now, and the great market on their left was alive with carts and the tramp of straining horses' feet and echoing the oaths of rough men lifting enormous weights, and the shrill cries of the flower girls of London, who had come to buy their daily stock. It was almost day, and under the high, sharp light that grew and quickened every moment, the trampled refuse of the vegetables, the rank mud and the toiling crowd, looked very unlovely in Paul's eyes. The people about scarcely took any notice of the little procession. At that time in the morning such things as a drunken woman, or a man hurt in a street brawl, were very common sights. Besides, they were a hard-working set, these market porters; their pay was not large, and they had to look out for a job, so beyond laughing a bit at the "swell" and exchanging a few coarse remarks about the woman on the ambulance, they took no notice.

It was almost a relief to Paul to leave that noisy, dirty crowd behind and step into the clean, whitewashed, quiet precincts of the police station. There the men on duty were all spick and span to a button, alert and civil. It was all over in a few minutes. The woman was taken to the cells, and some one at a high wooden desk wrote down Paul's name and address. As he gave it, he was again unpleasantly conscious of the sallow-faced, shabby man with the notebook. He wondered why he, out of all the crowd, had succeeded in getting into the police station, and why, when the superintendent laid down his pen, the shabby man walked up to the big book, in which the entry had just been written, and began to make notes with a very stumpy pencil on a dirty piece of paper. Paul had the uncomfortable sensation of being watched, but when Father Gregory's name was also taken and they were both told to return to the police court at half-past ten o'clock, he was free to go.

Almost unknowingly he retraced his steps back to the Embankment. The whole affair had been so disagreeable, so sudden, he had scarcely realised it, and was only conscious that he had touched something unclean. He walked rapidly on until he was again in sight of the river, and not until then was he fully aware that Father Gregory had kept pace with him and was by his side. The sun was now up, and the river danced and twinkled like a thousand diamonds in the new day. The pile of factories on the opposite side, faintly veiled on the right and left by the pale morning mist, looked as fair and as picturesque as a row of palazzi on a Venetian canal. The trees on the Embankment were rustling in the fresh morning air, and the birds singing as though it were the country. Paul unfastened his coat and flung himself on a seat. They were all empty now, these same wooden beds, for their nightly occupants had gone into the by-ways of the town to pick up the scraps and refuse that were flung out into the streets at cleaning time.

For some little while the two men sat silent. Father Gregory's short, strong fingers slipped over the beads of his rosary and his lips moved in prayer. Paul could only look about him and try and shake from his brain the effects of what seemed a hideous dream. By-and-bye, the priest let his beads fall with a little clatter at his side.

"You are taking this business very much to heart," he murmured. "It is nothing; the woman is well known to the police."

"Of course, of course," said Paul, shaking himself out of his reverie. "But it is dreadful to know that such creatures exist."

Father Gregory looked a little surprised. He had never, in days gone by, considered Paul as being more innocent or more ascetic than the average clean-minded, healthy young man.

"What do you mean?" he said. "I do not understand."

"Nor do I," said Paul. "I cannot exactly explain what I mean, but just lately I have been living in a world of my own making with another woman; a girl who is so pure, so spotless, so genuine and true, that even her own belongings and the people she moves among seem scarcely worthy of her. I was thinking of her, almost imagining she was by my side when that wretched creature came up and laid her hand upon my arm." He brushed his coat sleeve as though some stain remained there.

"You are nervous and overwrought," said Father Gregory in his quiet, kind voice. "It is not like you to get hysterical and fanciful over things, even for a woman you love."

Paul pulled himself together, and gave a little laugh.

"You are quite right, Philip. Ah! I beg your pardon; the old name will come back, you know. But this London life does not agree with me. I hate it from the bottom of my soul and so does she. When we are married we are going to live in the country."

A look of tender interest mingled with a sad wonder filled the priest's eyes, but he spoke kindly.

"So you are going to be married? Next to religion, a good wife is the best gift that God has to bestow on man."

Then they fell to talking in detached sentences, Paul asking questions, and Father Gregory recalling old times. One thing led to another, and they spoke of nothing long. It was a kind of *resumé* of their lives, which opened up much that was pleasant and good, and nothing that was regrettable and sad.

Behind them, as they sat and talked, London stirred itself and waked to full life. Heavy carts and vans thundered down the roadway, and often with their rattle drowned the low question and answer. Home-going cabs crept lazily along, and lumbering omnibuses brought their first loads of workers from the pleasant suburbs into the great seething city. With a snort and a splash, the early morning boat bustled past, and the barges that had been moored like great sleeping whales against the opposite wharfs all night slipped slowly out into the stream. Factory women, with flaunting feathers and clean white aprons, passed chattering by, and flower girls from the market, with thick shawls tied across their broad shoulders, and short, full skirts pinned up well over the tops of their rough boots, came down to the river's edge to arrange their fragrant wares and sort them out to the best advantage. With hands in pockets and cloth caps tipped on the back of their heads, office boys sauntered by. Some who had lain in bed late were eating their breakfasts as they came. Others who had much work to do were whistling shrilly the latest comic songs as they stepped out. From Big Ben eight o'clock throbbed out on the warm morning air. Across the bridge that joins Charing Cross to the Surrey side the first Continental train, with a shrill shriek, steamed slowly out. Paul pulled his coat across his evening dress once more and rose to his feet.

"It is late; I must get back."

Father Gregory rose, too.

"You will come and see me then," he said, holding out his hand. "Our meeting has been very strange, but our talk has been very pleasant. Mine is a poor place, for I live among poor people; but you will come?"

"I will indeed; I promise," said Paul.

The Father turned and walked citywards, and Paul, hailing a passing hansom, sprang into it and was driven back to his chambers in Piccadilly.

CHAPTER IX

THE MAGISTRATE DISPOSES

Mrs. Kerquham had gone with Honor and Rosamund to call on Mrs. Rivington. It had been no motive of friendship that had induced her to take this step, but rather of policy. She entirely disapproved of the lady and of her way of life, but Lord St. Ives' pointed attentions to her on the previous evening had made her think that it might be as well to make friends with the mammon of unrighteousness.

Mrs. Kerquham was quite aware of Paul's admiration for her niece, but she still clung to the hope that matters in that quarter would not come to a head. She did not disguise from herself that Paul Carr, with his good social position and his very satisfactory balance at the bankers, was a suitable match for the penniless orphan girl of whom she had had the bringing up. But like many women of even good birth, a title dazzled her, and having once realised that neither of her daughters would ever have the faintest chance of becoming Countess of St. Ives, she had seized eagerly on such indications as had pointed to his lordship's admiration for Rosamund. A few months ago she would have accepted Paul for Rosamund with gladness, but she had set her heart lately on her niece's becoming a great lady, and she meant to cling to that hope and work to that end until the very hour struck that might transform Miss Keith into Mrs. Carr.

As regards Lord St. Ives' attentions to the gay widow, Mrs. Rivington, she was not much troubled. She had seen too much of men and manners not to know their little ways, and she felt that if the lady in question had any influence over the earl at all, it was better to have it exercised for than against her cherished plan. So she had gone to call at the elaborately decorated, over-draped, semi-darkened house in Stanhope Gardens where Mrs. Rivington held her court, and to make the visit less pointed, she had taken the two girls with her.

Tea, out of fragile cups of jewelled Sèvres, accompanied by a large assortment of appetising sandwiches and cakes, had just been served. The conversation had not been of the most brilliant. Mrs. Kerquham had been all the time trying to find out exactly on what terms Mrs. Rivington was with Lord St. Ives. Rosamund, who, with her customary straightforwardness, frankly disapproved of the lady, sat with folded hands and lowered eyelids, on a high chair near the open window. Honor, filled with the disagreeable desire to find out how such a woman lived, had been too busy staring about the room and making a mental inventory of its luxurious contents to say much. Mrs. Rivington, all floating laces and pale pink ribbons, golden curls and a strong atmosphere of perfume, had been smothering her yawns and wondering why on earth such a dull set of people should come to see her.

Suddenly the door opened, and Miss Glossop, a middle-aged lady, much over-dressed and flushed with excitement, accompanied by Mr. Trevor, all mincing and mannerisms, came into the room. There were greetings all round, and then Miss Glossop cut across the conversation with a loud-voiced, "Have you heard the news?"

Mr. Trevor, looking portentously solemn, drew a half-penny evening paper from the immaculate folds of his frock-coat.

"Quite too awful, you know; could not have believed it myself; always thought Carr was the straightest fellow in the town. But there—you never know your luck."

As he slowly unfolded the paper, Miss Glossop cried eagerly: "Yes, it's quite too shocking! Really, to think that one knows a man like that; that one met him only last night! Well, it will give us all something to talk about at any rate for a few days," and she smacked her lips as though she had a dainty morsel between them.

"Mr. Carr? Why, what is the matter with him?" said Mrs. Rivington, roused into some semblance of wakefulness. "Is not he that awfully nice-looking young fellow who was supping with us last night, Mrs. Kerquham? He is a great friend of yours, isn't he? People are saying so."

Her eyes shot one little glance towards Rosamund, who still sat near the window with lowered lids and closed mouth, but who, beneath her mask of indifference, was all a-quiver to know what they meant. Mrs. Kerquham drew herself up very stiffly before she answered. There was evidently something wrong about Mr. Carr, and she did not intend to commit herself by an excessive profession of friendship before Mrs. Rivington and Miss Glossop.

"We do know Mr. Carr," she said, coldly. "But in town one comes across so many people, and life here is always such a bustle, that one has not always the time to discriminate between the good and the bad as one might wish."

"Well, just listen to this!" said Guy Trevor in his high voice.

Honor pulled her chair a little nearer into the circle. Rosamund did not move, but her fingers clenched themselves tightly in her lap. Then, amid many exclamations and interjections, with comments of his own, and remarks from the ladies round him, Mr. Trevor read out a highly-coloured report of Paul Carr's appearance at Bow Street police court that morning, when he had given evidence as to the miserable affair on the Embankment at early dawn.

"Was it attempted murder or suicide?" burst in Miss Glossop.

"Oh! I have not done yet," said Mr. Trevor, waving her to silence with his hand. Then he went on to read the magistrate's comments on the case; and on the singularity of a man of good position being on a place like the Embankment with such a wretched creature as stood in the dock, at any hour of the twenty-four. Father Gregory's few words were put aside and the surmises of the police as to the suspiciousness of the whole business were emphasised. The affair ended in Paul's being reprimanded for being mixed up in bad company, and being warned to be more careful for the future. The woman was sent to the workhouse.

Mr. Trevor dropped the paper on his knees, and looked round at his audience. He felt he had made quite a sensation. For a brief moment silence reigned, and then in high, shrill argument their voices rose. In Rosamund's ears they sounded like the waves of the sea. Her one prayer all the time was that she should not move or cry out or faint. She prayed as she had never prayed before that she might not make an exhibition of herself. She did not even dare to lean forward to catch the faint breeze that blew in at the window for fear of attracting attention, for she knew that her face was grey and her mouth drawn with agony. Presently she was able to open her eyes. The trees outside in the square swam like a green sea before her imperfect vision, but with returning consciousness came the sharpest pain of all. What was this that they were saying? That Paul, her lover, her affianced husband, was a man of the lowest tastes; that he consorted with the scum of the earth; that he had left her side, only that morning, to hold converse with the vilest outcast that man could have made of woman; that he had driven her to attempt suicide, or—that he had tried himself to make away with his shame! They went over and over the same subject, turning it this way and that, rolling it round their tongues, and savouring it in their mouths.

Rosamund would not look towards them, but she knew exactly how severe an expression Mrs. Kerquham was wearing, and how Honor's narrow, hard mouth was screwed together in shrewish delight. She caught a few of Mrs. Rivington's coarse suggestions and of Mr. Trevor's feeble excuses for the weaknesses of mankind, which were worse than the most outspoken accusations. She heard Miss Glossop, the old maid to whom nothing was sacred, tearing Paul's reputation to rags, and accusing him of every crime in the calendar. Yet she bore it all, and with it that deadly sick feeling, that awful blackness, that sound of many waters in her ears, and fought as she had never fought before to keep her senses.

It was Honor's voice—high and sneering—that pierced the armour of her self-control at last.

"Well! the knowledge that Carr is this kind of man ought to effectually put a stop to his dangling round *one* person whom we all know. That's to say, if she has a spark of pride or decency about her."

Rosamund—forgotten, or at least regarded as an

indifferent listener—started to her feet, and with ashen face and a voice shaking with passionate emotion, cried, "Honor! how can you so insult me?"

The women turned in their seats, and Mr. Trevor rising, withdrew behind the shelter of Miss Glossop's ample shoulders.

"Rosamund!" cried Mrs. Kerquham in expostulatory tones. "What do you mean?"

"You know—Aunt Margot—and so does Honor—and all of you. You all know that Mr. Carr—of whom you have been saying such shameful things, and who is not here to defend himself—loves me. Two nights ago—" her voice broke, but she went bravely on—"the other night he told me so—and asked me to be his wife."

"Miss Keith!"

"Rosamund! Be careful what you say."

"I am being careful, Aunt Margot. I only want to tell you all that I accepted Mr. Carr's offer of marriage—and that therefore I hold myself engaged to him in the face of every misfortune or shame that may come upon him. Good-bye, Mrs. Rivington. I will walk home, aunt!" She bowed coldly as she left the room.

"Good heavens!" cried Mrs. Kerquham, starting to say a hurried good-bye. "What a terrible thing."

."But Mr. Carr's very rich," drawled Mrs. Rivington, who was quite amused by such a display of emotion.

"What shall you really do about the engagement?" asked Miss Glossop, whose curiosity at times overstepped the bounds of good manners.

Mrs. Kerquham hesitated for a brief space. Precipitation might ruin everything. Lord St. Ives and Paul Carr might both be lost together.

"I shall wait and see what other people think," she said at length as she hurried from the room.

"Ha! you are always so clever," said Mr. Trevor, in his most flattering tones. But Miss Glossop rather spoiled his remark by adding sharply that "any fool could have seen that."

Downstairs on the doorstep Rosamund was standing, white and trembling.

A smile of amusement curved Honor's thin lips as she passed her cousin and got into the carriage. Mrs. Kerquham looked at her niece. She was a woman who disliked having her plans upset, neither did she approve of the girl's being seen on foot in the streets in the afternoon, but there was a look in Rosamund's eyes, a defiant misery in the poise of her head, that warned her it would be wiser for the moment to bow to the girl's expressed wish.

"My dear, if you care to walk home, do so. But do not go fast; it is still very warm. James, give Miss Keith her parasol."

Still with her brain on fire and her heart stone cold, Rosamund watched her aunt and cousin drive away, and it was only by degrees that she became conscious that the servant within the house was still holding the door open, and evidently waiting for her to walk away. Very slowly she went down the steps, having to feel for each one before she set her foot upon it. As she reached the pavement, the door was shut with a clang behind her, and she turned up the square towards the Cromwell Road.

Mrs. Kerquham was right; the afternoon was intensely hot, and the streets were empty, save for a few carriages filled with ladies paying their duty calls. She wondered what they were all talking about; whether they knew. For fear that some one should recognise her and stop her, she put up her parasol and held it closely

before her face.   As the action of walking steadied her
senses, a mad desire to know the truth came upon her.
She had only up to now heard the interrupted reading
from the newspaper, which had been so interlarded with
comments and suppositions and assertions from Miss
Glossop and Mrs. Rivington that she had gathered nothing more than that some hideous trouble had befallen
her beloved.   She would stop at the station in Glouces-
ter Road and buy a paper; then perhaps she might get
a little nearer to the truth.   Intent on doing so, she
slipped her hand into her pocket, but found she had no
purse with her.   It was a small *contretemps*, but it wrung
her over-wrought nerves, and for the first time her
mouth began to quiver and her eyes filled with tears.
She forced them back, however, and walked on, trying
to school herself into the philosophical reasoning that as
she had borne so much she could bear a little more.   Up
in the High Street the newspaper boys were flaunting
placards, across which was printed in thick, black letters: "Serious scandal in the West End.   Allegations
against a well-known gentleman."

The fighting instinct was roused in her again, even as
Honor's words had stirred it, and she could have torn
the papers to shreds.   She felt the whole thing must be
a mistake, if not a lie.   Paul, with his high-minded
notions, his particularity—nay, his fastidiousness about
women—could never have had any traffic with the
wretched creature, who, according to what Guy Trevor
had read, had appeared in the dock as a mere besotted
bundle of rags.   Nothing would ever persuade her that,
except for motives of charity or kindness, he could ever
speak to such a wreck of womanhood.   The papers
always made the worst of things, and she kept telling
herself that he would be able to explain it all away.   Yet

not to her! God forbid that she should ask for any explanation—that she should insult him with even the shadow of a doubt. But in the midst of all her personal grief, she remembered that there would be others who might not have the same faith in him that she herself held. To her it could make no difference whether he had done anything or whether he had done nothing. He must always be the best, the truest-hearted, the most noble man she had ever met. The man to whom she had given her love; the man she had promised to marry. She would have to fight his battles. She felt that, and the sense of coming war roused her a little and drove the blood into her clay-cold cheeks, and set her walking up the hill with a freer step. Yes, she would fight for him to the last, and stand by him. Nothing would change her opinion of him, and she was angry with herself that she even remembered what had been said of him, and determined to free her mind from the calumnies and insinuations that even in her half-fainting condition had crept into her ears and found lodging in her brain.

But as she rang the bell at "The Hurst" a sense of shame, as though she had done wrong, flowed over her once more. She imagined that the servant who opened the door looked sympathetically at her, and she flushed to the roots of her hair as she darted past the man and up the first flight of stairs.

Once there, she paused and hung over the low balustrade. She would ask if her aunt had returned or if her uncle were in the studio. Would it be an acknowledgment of doubt on her part if she went to them and asked their advice, or should she proudly ignore the whole subject and regard it as though it had never been? With her hands still upon the oaken rail she stood, torn again by a thousand emotions, turning hot and cold, filled with grief one moment, and proudly defiant of the world the next.

The door bell rang sharply, and a knock she knew so well followed it.   Her heart leaped to her throat, for she knew it was he.   She heard the door open and Paul's voice ask for Mr. Kerquham.   Was it fancy that she thought it was a little anxious?   Before the echo of his words had died in the hall, the door of the long library opened sharply, and she heard her aunt say in loud, clear tones:

"Will you tell Mr. Carr that Mr. Kerquham is at home, but cannot see him?"

The hall door was shut, and Rosamund, writhing as though she had been struck by the insult that had been hurled at her lover, staggered to her room.

CHAPTER X

CHARITY

PAUL CARR was scarcely surprised at what had happened at "The Hurst" that afternoon. His first astonishment at finding the events of the early morning so magnified and distorted had seemed to deaden all other feeling within him. He had vaguely wondered, through the luncheon hour at his own rooms, why the police had insinuated what they did; why Father Gregory's evidence had been put aside, and why he had been so roughly warned against consorting with bad characters. It never struck him that the facts of his being a gentleman of good birth and position were dead against him in the little republic that forms the floating population of a police court.

It was not until a man he knew brought him one of the evening papers that he realised that this affair was going to prove troublesome, and when an hour or two later notes of half insulting sympathy and insinuating condolence reached him, he awoke to the fact that he had better go and see Rosamund's uncle. That she herself would require any explanation never occurred to him, but he had all a young man's respect for the feelings of older people than himself, and he remembered that though Mr. Kerquham had lived his life in the world, he had the blood of a Puritan family in his veins, and Mrs. Kerquham, with her ineradically narrow views, at his side.

So he started for Campden Hill, where the repulse he
met showed him that already the poison had begun to
work against him.   He jumped into his cab and was
driven back to his rooms, where he sat down and wrote
two long letters, one to Rosamund and the other to Mr.
Kerquham.   After they were finished, an unusual curiosity drove him to send out for an evening paper.   What
he read there seemed to alter the situation, and he
destroyed the letters he had written.   Things were going
to be more serious than he imagined.   Of course it was
all nonsense; it would only be a nine days' wonder even
if it attained to that; but meanwhile he must write nothing hastily, and had better go down to the club and get
his dinner before going on to Lady Scarsdale's reception,
where he should meet Rosamund and where he could
better speak what he had to say.

He was dressed and running downstairs to his
brougham when a telegram was put into his hand.   It
was from Lady Scarsdale, "Regret my reception postponed."   He stuffed it into his pocket, feeling vaguely
annoyed to think that the opportunity of seeing his
betrothed that evening was gone.

He drove down to the club, and after ordering his
dinner went into the morning room.   There had been a
great deal of talk going on as he opened the door, but
a sudden silence seemed to fall on all the members as
he walked into the room.   It was still broad daylight,
and the evening sun was flinging broad beams through
the great plate-glass windows.

"By Jove!   How pale he looks," whispered one man
to another.

"No wonder; he is in a nasty hole."

Two of his friends, with much show and ostentation,
walked across the room, grasped him by the hand, and

after bidding him "buck up and face the music," abruptly went out. Three others whom he knew suddenly became deeply absorbed in their papers. Half a dozen men with whom he had no acquaintance whatever stared rather rudely. He flung himself into a chair and idly turned the pages of a magazine until he was told that his dinner was ready.

He had an uncomfortable feeling that he was being looked at and talked about all the while he ate. He tried to shake it off, for he felt he was getting self-conscious about this wretched business. But somehow the evening seemed very lonely, and although there was one of his favourite operas being given at Covent Garden, he weakly yielded to a strange reluctance to go there.

After dinner the club was nearly empty, for in the mid-season every man has some engagement or another for the evening. It was horribly dull, and Paul sat by the open window to catch the little air there was coming in from the sun-baked street, feeling unusually depressed and nervous. As the big clock behind him struck eleven, he rose impatiently out of his chair.

"I'm not in the cue for society and ordinary people to-night," he said to himself. "I will go down and see Philip—Father Gregory, as he calls himself now."

As he passed into the hall and picked up his light overcoat three or four young men in spotless attire and large button-holes were being helped into their coats.

"See you later at Lady Scarsdale's, dear boy," said one.

"Yes, I shall turn up there about one. I promised to meet some people at Princes' first. Are you going?"

"Rather!" said a third. "Lady Scarsdale's suppers are some of the best in town, and old Scarsdale always trots out such ripping cigars as one leaves."

Paul walked past them with his head in the air and a very set look on his handsome face. So Lady Scarsdale's party was not postponed. It was merely he who had been put off. It was a little thing, a mere pin prick, dealt by the hand of a frivolous woman, but it hurt him like a sword thrust.

"So things are going to take this turn," he thought, as a swift cab bore him eastward. "Is this the beginning of it? Are they all going to behave like this, and if so what is going to be the end?"

He passed through the silent city, deserted and smelling clean of freshly sprinkled water, on to where the long row of lights and stalls and hoarse cries and frowsy crowds made another world; where the people never seemed to go to bed; where the streets were alive with noise and light and music and quarrelling all the night through. Where the public houses shut their doors for a few brief hours, and where the wickedness and the misery and the poverty of a whole world of people seethed and fermented.

Paul seemed to drive for hours, and as they went further east the cabman had to ask his way. Finally he turned up a narrow street; it was unlit from end to end, and made more dark by the height of the houses on the other side. After the roar and clatter of the main road it was very quiet.

"I think this must be the place, sir," said the cabman through the trap, pulling up at a low, iron-studded door in a dead wall. A bell handle on a rough cord dangled high out of the reach of passing ragamuffins.

"I will try here," said Paul, getting out and pulling at the handle.

A distant clang woke the echoes for one moment and

then all was still again until the soft pattering of sandal--
shod feet came whispering down the long corridor.

"Is this the monastery?" said Paul to an indefinite
figure that, with a smoking lantern in its hand, stood
before him.

"Whom do you wish to see?" was the answer.

"Father Gregory; is he at home?"

The figure said "Yes," and Paul, tossing some money
to the cabman, entered under the low arch of the doorway.

It was very quiet within, and cool and even sweet
after the close, foul streets through which he had driven.
Here and there at the corners of the stone corridors
small lamps burned feebly, but it was all on a level and
Paul strode on behind the white-habited figure that
seemed to glide in front of him. Presently he was
shown into a little room; it was the parlour of the
monastery, and as bare and plain and clean as such
places are.

"I will send Father Gregory to you," said the monk,
closing the door on Paul.

One candle burned in the centre of the table; an open
window was making it gutter, and it formed what old
women in the country call a "winding-sheet." Paul
smiled bitterly as he watched the dropping tallow harden,
and thinking of the past day muttered to himself, "I
wonder if it is an omen?"

He continued to stare gloomily, without thought or
movement, at the wavering light until a cheery voice from
the doorway cried:

"Ah! you have come so soon; that is what I call
keeping a promise."

Paul turned and took his old friend by the hand.

"I can lay claim to no virtue on that score. I think I am driven to you by trouble."

Father Gregory looked grave. "So that you come to us at all, that is something. When people are happy and all the world goes well with them God is little more than a myth. It is only sorrow and pain and disappointment that make men cry out to Him. I think that is why such things are sent to us. Now, will you not come to my room and we will have a talk, and—" Then his eye fell on Paul's immaculate evening dress. "But perhaps you have no time; you are going somewhere to-night, out into society?"

Paul shrugged his shoulders. "No," he said, shaking his head. "Society does not want me just now; I have had a hint to stop away."

The feeling of childish petulance that comes to people even in their greatest sorrows made him pull out the crumpled telegram from his pocket and toss it on the table.

"Read that," he said. "It is all a lie—a sham! They think I have done something wrong; that I am mixed up with some low scandal, some vulgar intrigue. I am not fit to be in a drawing-room with decent men and women."

Father Gregory smoothed out the flimsy bit of paper and read it. Then he laid one cool, strong hand on Paul's feverish wrist.

"My son! my friend! you are taking this too much to heart. You are over-wrought, and are laying too great a stress on a mere trifle."

"Have you seen the evening papers?" said Paul. Then remembering that he was speaking to one who had relinquished the world, he checked himself and looked around. "But perhaps here you do not know these things."

Father Gregory smiled again. "Oh, yes we do! We are not a closed Order, and we are obliged to know everything that goes on outside. It is impossible to help people unless we know when and where to do it. Our work is among the poorest and the most wretched. If we were to shut our eyes and our ears to their needs and their cries, our labour would be in vain. I have seen the papers. You are paying, through them, the penalty of your position."

"But it is unjust! It is a lie!" cried Paul, hotly.

"Certainly it is," said Father Gregory. "But you must remember—you know it, in fact, as well as I do—that all the world loves a sensation, more particularly the set among which you move, for they have so few."

"You are right there," said Paul. "Dressing and dining and dancing; going to the play and racing; meeting in the Park in the morning and at the theatres at night are their amusements. What a treadmill it all is!"

"Yes, I suppose so," assented the priest. "You know my experience of it was very short. I had no leanings that way, but the little I did see of it convinced me that the reason of your world being so keen about scandalising one another is that you are hungry for a new emotion. You are starving for a new flavour to tickle your palates and your brains stagnate for want of exercise."

"Yet it is not fair," said Paul, "that I—"

Father Gregory raised his hand. "It is you to-day; it may be some one else to-morrow."

"But," cried Paul, impatient to speak, yet scarcely knowing what to say, "what would they have me do? Would they have had me let that wretched woman drown like a kitten with a stone round its neck? Heaven knows, the women of society are hard enough and bad enough and cruel enough for anything. Perhaps that would have pleased them. Bah! we talk of our civilisation, but the women nowadays who pose for virtue and go to court, and scream at the sight of a mouse, are not a whit better than those aristocrats of Rome who sat day after day in the circuses and watched their kind being done to death by every torture that man could devise."

"And yet there were good women in Rome," said Father Gregory, quietly. "And there are good women in London. I could tell you the names of scores who, once a week, lay aside their fine dresses and jewels and give up their receptions and gay assemblies and put on a plain gown and quiet bonnet, and come down here and work like angels in this hell."

"But all that," cried Paul, "only bears out your own words. They do it for *sensation*. It is a novelty for a woman who has ridden in a carriage all her life to travel in a tram. She likes to look at herself in the glass when her hair is tucked away behind her ears, and she has got on a bonnet that her own kitchen maid would not wear. It gives a new zest to their own idleness and luxury to come down here and go among these loathsome dens, and see these awful people who live and die in them. It is not true charity, and you know it isn't. It is playing at it; it is something to talk about over the dinner table when they get home and have had their perfumed baths and dressed themselves in their laces and silks. They are all amateurs together. They have no sincerity, no heart. They exercise hospitality towards those who can return it. They profess charity and good works as a means of making it up with their God. How many women are there who do not, under the name of charity, make exhibitions of themselves on stages and at bazaars;

who do not flaunt their beauty as they flaunt their wares; who do not meet together day after day and chatter and talk, and scandalise one another on the pretence of holding meetings? They are all selfish and hollow together. There is no true charity in the world I have lived in; no charity like yours. Why, Philip, I remember the time when you were the hardest rider, the hardest drinker, the gayest fellow in all our set at Oxford! What good days they were! We did not care much then for anything but a good horse under us, or a long pull on the dear old river at sunset. Fine ladies were not much in our way, and though most of us had a bit of money, I do not think that our particular set ever calculated on the social advantage it might bring. We all used to count upon having a good time shooting or fishing, and some of us have had. Poor Billy Tenterden got his quietus out in Africa after big game; he had his wish. And Reggie Fitzurse went to find the North Pole and never came back. Tim Mitford married and is a country gentleman. He is all right; his wife is the dearest little woman that ever wore shoe-leather, and you, though you have chosen a strange path, you seem all right, too. I am the only one who broke through the traditions and went into Society, and now see what Society has done for me!"

"My friend," murmured Father Gregory, laying his hand on Paul's shoulder. "You are taking this very badly, very bitterly."

"I have reason to do so; when I tell you the whole truth you will understand, I think."

"Come to my room," said Father Gregory. "I can give you an hour of my time."

Up the stone stairs they went to a narrow cell, and Paul poured out all his love for Rosamund, his fears concerning her feelings towards him at this present juncture, and what had happened at "The Hurst" that day.   Then Father Gregory spoke words of comfort and gave advice, not as a preacher or as one who teaches, but as friend to friend and man to man.   They parted with a long hand-clasp.

"Then you will come again," said Father Gregory.

"Yes, I will if I may," said Paul.   "For you have done me good.   I wish you would let me do something for you."

"That will be to come," said the monk, as he let Paul out at the low door.   "I will watch you as far as the main road; this street is unlit and sometimes dangerous at night."

As Paul stepped into the huge, wide, lively street, he caught the faint echo of the monastery door as it swung to with a clang.

CHAPTER XI

MR. KERQUHAM SPEAKS

BREAKFAST next morning at "The Hurst" was not a very lively affair, and there were few words spoken to break the song of the birds that floated in through the open window. Rosamund had, as usual, come down first and had superintended the mysteries of the teapot and coffee-urn, but she was very pale, and the tell-tale circles round her sorrowful eyes betrayed to Mrs. Kerquham's keen understanding when she entered the room that the girl had had a wakeful and a troubled night. She did not know, however, that Rosamund's deepest sorrow lay in the fact that she had as yet had no letter from Paul Carr. It was this silence, more than anything else, that grieved her. It seemed so mysterious, so strange, that in his great trouble he should not have come first to her.

Neither Laura nor Honor was ever very brilliant in the early morning, for they were girls who never at any time troubled themselves to be either agreeable or amusing in the bosom of their family. Mr. Kerquham, too, was very silent. He had heard the previous evening at the club the gossip about the "West End Scandal," as Paul's affair was called, and his heart bled for the girl of whom he was so devotedly fond, and so the meal proceeded in almost unbroken silence, and very little was eaten.

"Well, you are none of you very bright this morning," said Laura, with a loud yawn, as she rose from the table and stretched her arms lazily over her head.   "Honor, what are you going to do to-day?"

Honor shrugged her shoulders, and said acidly:

"Our amusements, my dear, will depend more than usual upon our friends.   It is quite on the cards that under the present circumstances nobody will care to come near us."

After delivering this little stab at her cousin, she slowly sauntered out with her sister on to the verandah, where on long, cushioned chairs, they prepared to dawdle away the morning hours.

Mr. Kerquham then rose from the table, pushing his chair back heavily and sighing.   Poor Rosamund, yearning for some sympathy, for a tender touch or a kind look, almost broke down as she caught sight of his sad face.

"Uncle," she said, brokenly, "may I come to you presently in the studio?"

"Certainly, my dear; you know I always like to see you there," said Mr. Kerquham, dreading a scene, and trying to put the most commonplace aspect on affairs.

Mrs. Kerquham looked from her husband to her niece. There were times when she was jealous of Rosamund's power over Alban Kerquham.   She feared that at the present juncture tears and prayers would be used, and that the girl might carry a point which she considered would be disastrous to the family fortunes.

"You can see your uncle presently, Rosamund.   I wish to speak to him for a few moments myself."

Rosamund took the hint and went with a slow, dragging step, that was quite unlike herself, out of the room. Her uncle looked after her, and his kind eyes glistened under his bushy brows.   Mrs. Kerquham moved over to his side and forced him back into his chair again.

"Now, Alban," she began, "you must listen to me. This business has got to be faced, and very firmly, too. I know exactly what Rosamund wants. You are her legal guardian, and, I firmly believe, the one person out of all her family for whom she has any affection. She means to persuade you to give our consent to her immediate marriage with this Mr. Carr. The thing is impossible. You must refuse at once, and for always."

Mr. Kerquham raised his hand.

"Why?" he asked. "If you consider the matter calmly, you will see that this young man, of whom I must confess I have formed a very high opinion, has done nothing wrong; he has committed no crime, he has outraged none of society's laws."

"Then what was he doing on the Thames Embankment at four o'clock the other morning speaking to a low woman?"

"I suppose you have read the papers," answered her husband, "and his explanation of the business."

Mrs. Kerquham tossed her iron-grey head.

"Explanation, indeed! I wonder that you, as a man of the world, do not judge your own sex better and know that they will perjure themselves through thick and thin if it suits them. Decent men go straight home to bed after a ball, and do not loaf about the streets. Rescuing people from drowning, indeed! That is not the occupation of a gentleman. There are plenty of police about, and it is their work."

"My dear! my dear!" said Mr. Kerquham. "Do not put yourself in such a state about it. Mr. Carr did what any man, gentle or simple, would have done. He stopped a wretched, half-drunken woman from self-murder. His act was one of common humanity."

Mrs. Kerquham, finding herself beaten on one point,

namely, the abuse of Paul Carr, turned womanlike to another.

"Of course, your argument is all very well, but think what the world is saying. You know what people are; they are sure to put the worst construction on such a thing." Mr. Kerquham could scarcely help smiling to himself at his wife's unconscious self-condemnation. "If you had only heard the conversation at Mrs. Rivington's yesterday afternoon, you would have known at once that Paul Carr's social position has been very seriously jeopardised."

"I am afraid, my dear, that Mr. Carr is scarcely likely to appeal to a tribunal of Mrs. Rivington's friends."

"It is all very well for you to gird at Mrs. Rivington," said Mrs. Kerquham, who, to serve her own ends, had suddenly taken up the cudgels for that most undesirable lady, "but what is said in one drawing-room is said in another, and I suppose you would not like Rosamund to go about with a black mark against her name for the rest of her days."

"Poor Rosamund," sighed Mr. Kerquham. "It would be a great shame if people made her suffer for the absolutely imaginary fault of some one else."

Mrs. Kerquham thought she had scored a point and pressed her advantage.

"Yes! That is just what I want you to see, Alban, only like all men you are so blind when it comes to the little things of life. I am sure I am very sorry for Mr. Carr, and I am quite willing, if it pleases you, to acknowledge that the whole thing is more of a misfortune than a fault, only other people—the world in general—will not be so broad-minded, and you know it. Rosamund is a very proud girl, and although she may feel giving up Mr. Carr for the moment, it would hurt her a great deal more to see him snubbed and cut and talked of as the man who was 'mixed up in the Embankment Scandal.'"

"I think, my dear Margot, that you are imagining a great deal of this social persecution. Paul Carr is young and wealthy; he has plenty of time to live down any little trouble his quixotic action may have brought upon him. I am quite ready to stake my word that this time next year the whole thing will be forgotten."

Mrs. Kerquham clutched at that saving clause as a drowning man catches at a straw.

"In a year, you say? Very well, then, let that settle it."

"Settle what? How do you mean?"

"I am convinced, Alban, that Rosamund is going to ask you to let her marry Mr. Carr at once. Tell her she must wait a year. Tell her you consider it is only fair to us and to her cousins that she should not rush into a marriage which will only revive the talk that is going on now. If she cannot trust him for twelve months, then she had better give him up altogether."

Mr. Kerquham leaned his head on his hands. Although in many of the minor details of life he differed in opinion from his wife, although his easy-going, kindly nature was often at variance with her stern common-sense, yet he felt that this time she was urging the right thing. He could not bear the idea of paining Rosamund, but still less could he face the prospect of her future unhappiness. Suppose, after all, there was something in what people were saying about Mr. Carr? Many young men had very dark corners in their lives, and many young men had tried before now, more by force than by wit, to make a clean sweep of the past before they married.

Perhaps the policy of temporising would be the wisest,

for he knew Rosamund's nature too well to dream for one moment of entirely breaking off her engagement. So as he rose for the second time, he looked at Mrs. Kerquham's hard face and said:

"I will speak to Rosamund in the studio and urge her to look upon this matter in a reasonable and temperate light. I cannot promise, however, that I shall succeed."

Mrs. Kerquham flushed with anger as she faced her husband.

"But you must insist. She is your ward; she was confided to you within a few weeks of her birth by the rest of the family. She owes everything to you, her position, the very food she eats, and the clothes she wears. Just remind her of that, and bring her to her senses."

"How cruel women can be to one another," thought Mr. Kerquham, as he left the room and walked down the long, sunny corridor to where his studio lay on the cool, northern side of the house. But Mrs. Kerquham felt that even in laying the embargo of gratitude on Rosamund's shoulders she was doing right. She was a woman who would not knowingly have committed a wrong action, but the world and its teachings had warped her narrow nature, and had led her to believe that any means were justified to win the goal of social advancement and position.

She had set her heart nearly a year ago on the capture of Lord St. Ives, and this not so much for her niece's benefit as for the advancement of her own daughters. It had been Paul Carr, and Paul Carr alone, who had upset her plans, for she had refused to see or admit that the earl might not in some respects prove acceptable to Rosamund. She had counted on that marriage coming off, and she had missed it once. Now she was going to have a second chance, for with Rosamund's engagement in abeyance, and Paul Carr forbidden the house, she relied on her own powers and the glamour of Lord St. Ives' flashy manners and coronet eventually to win the day. So she was very well pleased with her morning's work as she hurried forth on her domestic duties, for she had gained what women prize above rubies—her own way.

Rosamund, from her favourite seat on the wide upper landing, heard her uncle leave the dining-room and go slowly to the studio. He had not shut the door behind him, she knew, for the latch always rattled as it closed. That was an old signal which dated back to her nursery days, and meant that she was free to go to him, so she slipped down the stairs and a moment later was in the studio.

As she pushed open the door he feigned to be busy with a canvas and palette, but as her slow step sounded across the floor, in such different measure from the one he loved so well, he dropped his sheaf of brushes, and turning, opened wide his arms.

The tender expression of sympathy from the man who all her life had been her dear friend, her more than father, melted the icy restraint in which she had locked her sorrow during the past hours. With a little yearning cry she ran to him, and as he folded his arms about her and laid one broad, kindly hand upon her hair, she broke into a very passion of tears—tears which were laden with all the horror and anger, the love and anxiety, she had suffered dry-eyed till now.

"Hush! Rosie. Hush! my child—my poor little girl," murmured Kerquham, drawing her to a couch and rocking her there in his arms as he had done in her childhood. "There, my poor bird—my Rosie—don't cry so bitterly—not so bitterly, my child."

With fond incoherencies and soothing caresses he held her close to him till the first storm of her grief was over, and when she lay exhausted and sob-shaken on his breast he drew out his silk handkerchief and passed it over her flushed face and humid, tearful eyes.

For a time she was content to rest there, but with composure came courage and a desire for speech. Yet she did not raise her aching head as she said:

"Uncle Alban—my dear uncle—I've come to you in great trouble and in more anxiety than I can bear."

A sob of self-pity shook her frame, and drew from Mr. Kerquham another tender "Hush."

"I want you to help me—and advise me. I know you will give me the best of your sympathy and advice."

Alban Kerquham cleared his throat before he could speak.

"All I can do for you I will, my dear, but I fear—"

Rosamund raised her tear-stained face to his.

"Oh! uncle, don't doubt your own powers." She put out her hands with a piteous gesture, and then let them drop inert in her lap. "Tell me what to do. You are the only real friend I have ever had. Paul is my lover, and will be my husband, but somehow that is different from a friend. Please tell me what to do."

Her uncle took one of her hands in his. It was trembling and cold; so unlike the firm, strong hand of his dear Rosamund.

"Tell me, dear, first, what you want to know."

"Everything!" she answered. "Everything about this unfortunate affair in which Paul has been mixed up. What are people and the papers saying?"

The artist sighed. "Quixotism is not the fashion nowadays, I fear, Rosie."

Rosamund sighed, too, as she stared with heavy, unseeing eyes before her.

Alban Kerquham patted the hand he held while she was silent. He knew of what she was thinking, and was turning over in his mind the best manner in which to meet her next question.

"What should I do about my marriage, uncle? It would be only honourable of me to write to Paul and tell him I am willing to become his wife at once, or he may think that I am repenting of my promise to him."

Mr. Kerquham felt there was no help for it, and the question had got to be faced. With great deliberation and a final loving pat he laid Rosamund's hand on her knee, and very slowly walked over to an old Spanish chair that stood within the embrasure of the window. He was thinking all the time, for though he scarcely dared acknowledge it to himself, Mrs. Kerquham's words had rooted quickly and sprung up and borne fruit. He felt himself that Rosamund's marriage must be delayed. Deeply as he loved his niece, it would not be fair to his daughters to give them a cousin-in-law who had been so disagreeably talked about.

Rosamund felt the subtle change in his manner, for she, too, rose and stood with her fingers locked closely together and her great mournful eyes fixed on him.

"Dearest, in giving you counsel about this sad matter I want to advise you for the best—only for the best. Now, about your marriage with Mr. Carr—I want you to—"

"Not to break it off?" cried Rosamund passionately, while a great wave of colour flew over her white face.

"You would never wish me to do anything so mean as that. Uncle, you couldn't wish that."

"Hush! hush!" said Mr. Kerquham, coming towards her. He saw at once that if he had ever had any idea of expressing such a wish it would be absolutely useless to voice it. "You must know me better, my dear, than to imagine I should ever counsel you to do an ungenerous action." He took her hand again in his, and drawing it through his arm, made her walk with him up and down the studio. It had ever been a favourite habit of theirs. "But, dear, I want you to postpone your marriage, and to let me write to Mr. Carr in the character of your guardian and tell him that you agree with me, and that such a step is desirable."

"Postpone our marriage?" said Rosamund, arresting her steps and turning very white again. "But that would imply a doubt; it would make him think that I believed all the hateful stories that are going about."

"If he is a sensible man and if he loves you, he will trust you, and he will see that his marriage with you just now would not be to your advantage."

Rosamund would have broken in again, but he stayed her eager words with a gesture. "You are very young, my dear; you do not know the world as I do. You may not believe it, and I fear, my poor child, that I hurt you; but for some months Mr. Carr will be under a cloud, and although you may be ready to give up sunshine for his sake, it could scarcely add to his happiness to know that you were in the dark with him."

"But is not my name to be considered, too?" pleaded Rosamund. "You say that people are talking about Paul. What will they say of me, except that I am trying to find a way out of my engagement, and seeking for an excuse to break my promise?"

"Dearest child, no one knows of your engagement save some half-dozen people. And even if it were guessed at it would occasion no talk if you do not marry Mr. Carr for at least another year."

"A year!" cried Rosamund. "A whole year!"

"My dear, the time is not long, and it will be a probation for both of you. If you have any affection for Mr. Carr it will strengthen it. If he has any desire to prove himself worthy to be your husband he will so act that this unhappy business will be wiped away."

Mr. Kerquham's heart bled as he noted the white, set look that crept over the girl's sad face—and there was still one more condition that must be made. But he nerved himself to the task.

"You must understand that when I say that your marriage is not to take place for a year, I mean that Mr. Carr is not to come to this house and you are not to meet. I trust to your honour in that, Rosamund."

"Not to meet! Not to see each other! Oh! uncle, that is too hard. You are making it impossible. I am sure he will not consent to that—and I will not, unless he wishes me to do so."

She had drawn herself away from him and up to her full height, with upright head and flashing eyes. Mr. Kerquham felt a little mean as he prepared to make his last stand, but he had his wife and girls to consider, as well as his niece's happiness.

"Rosamund," he began, "I said just now I would trust to your honour; I find I must appeal to a still higher sense. You were scarcely six weeks old when you were given into my care. My sister, who was your mother, had died in giving you birth, and your father was shot in action out in India three weeks afterwards.

An *ayah* brought you to Scotland, and there was a question among the family as to who should take you, a little black-browed, dark-skinned orphan."

Rosamund covered her face with her hands. Her uncle's heart misgave him, but he had very little choice, and he honestly believed he was working for her own future good.

"Your great-aunt, Lady Charlotte Lundy, was at that time just married. Sir Alexander was even then a selfish hypochondriac, and absolutely refused to have anything to do with an infant who was not of his own flesh and blood. My uncle Kilbeggie—Rosamund, my dear, even then I did not think you would have liked to have been brought up by Kilbeggie and Aunt Sophia. So we took you, your Aunt Margot and I, and put you in the nursery with our baby Laura, and made you one of our own daughters. You have been that to me ever since— the sweetest, fondest daughter a man ever had. Perhaps your aunt has, from time to time, let her maternal affections override her sense of justice, but that you will admit is only natural. We have done everything for you—even more than your parents could have done had they lived. I now appeal to the gratitude which I know you feel, to the affection and honour which I believe you entertain for us, to be guided by me in this matter of your marriage. As your guardian I might insist, but I prefer rather to appeal to your affections, and I beg you to accept cheerfully the dictum I must lay before you and which I know will receive the approval of the rest of the family. I want you to consider your engagement to Mr. Carr in abeyance for a year; I want you to promise me not to see him and not to write to him or receive letters from him oftener than once a month; I want you to look upon yourself as an absolutely free girl once more,

and to let me write to Mr. Carr and tell him that these
are your wishes."

Poor Rosamund looked about her like some hunted
animal that has been caught in a trap. In appealing to
her honour and her gratitude, her uncle had touched
her tenderest feelings. She had a higher sense than
most women of what was due to herself and to her people, and her nature was deeply affectionate. She fully
realised what the Kerquhams had done for her, and that
without them she would have been an absolute outcast
and a pauper. She knew that she had lived in luxury,
had been well educated, and given every advantage and
amusement that the daughters of wealthy men regard as
their right. Yet in her loving heart she vaguely felt
that it had been scarcely fair of her uncle so to press
these things home to her, because she had always been
conscious of the debt she owed to him.

"I will give you twenty-four hours, if you wish, to
think the matter over," said Mr. Kerquham, his loving
tenderness asserting itself once more over the unnatural
firmness that had characterised him for the last few
minutes.

But Rosamund was stronger than he. The face she
turned to him was white and drawn, and her eyes were
dim with the passion of the soul through which she was
passing, but her voice was quite steady as she said:

"No, dear, I want no time to think. Such things, if
they must be done, are best done at once. I only ask
permission to write to-day to Paul, and tell him myself
to what I have agreed."

"Certainly, my dear, you may do that."

"After that, I have one more favour to ask, uncle.
Do not let me hear this business talked about; I will
bear it as best I can, but do not let me be tried too far."

Fearful of once more losing the self-control to which she was clinging with all the will and pride of her nature, she turned hastily and went out of the studio.

"Poor child! poor child!" said Alban Kerquham, flicking a tear from his eyelashes. "It is a bad business, and she is taking it very hardly, but, thank God! she is young, and love's wounds heal very quickly. I hope I have done for the best."

The door was flung wide open, and one of the elect, frock-coated, and with a gorgeous button-hole, was ushered into the studio. Mr. Kerquham dragged the big easel into the proper light and took up his palette and brushes. His first sitter for the day had arrived.

CHAPTER XII

ROSAMUND WRITES A LETTER

ROSAMUND wrote her letter to Paul that same evening.
"MY DEAR PAUL:

"A silence that is sad as it is strange seems to have
fallen between us. I cannot tell what motives are working within you that you have not written to me during
the last few terrible hours. Perhaps what you are doing
is for the best—and men are always said to be braver
than women—but I have not your courage, and so must
speak, though what I have to say seems to me very sad.

"But first of all, before I write a single word of our
past hopes and of our future, I want to tell you that I
love you, that I believe in you, that all my heart and all
my trust is as much yours now as it ever was. I want
no excuses or even explanations from you, for they would
insult me as much as though you doubted my faith in
you. I only want you to believe that nothing that has
happened or that can happen will ever alter my feelings
towards you.

"I do not know that I have ever been very demon-
strative of my love for you, but every time I have heard
your voice and whenever our hands have met, I have
been thrilled with a passion towards you. My life,
despite its surroundings, has been so far as affection is
concerned a very lonely one. My only friend has been
my uncle, and the first man's lips that ever touched mine
were yours, dear Paul.

"I recall all this that you may know the better, if indeed that were needful, how entirely my heart and soul have been given to you, and I want you to remember this because what I have to say is very hard and bitter. It is costing me tears of blood to write, and I know that it will grieve you deeply.

"From the moment that I heard yesterday afternoon what had befallen you I have suffered through the whole gamut of emotions, with pity and love for the dominant notes. But all through the past night the vows I made to you and the love I pledged you a few days ago remained the same. I had hoped—I had prayed—for a letter from you this morning. Not one of excuse—you must understand that—but just one little line to tell me that you depended on me and that you trusted in me. I wonder if, whether you had written me such a letter, this that I am now sending to you would have been different. I wonder if your silence is weakening my resolution. I wonder, my darling, whether we have both made a fearful mistake.

"For I have to tell you that our engagement must be for a time at an end. Do not blame me too much; I could not bear it. Do not think me weak or false or worldly, even if you are angry with me, for in your calmer moments you will reproach yourself for having so misjudged me, and I would not wish that you should have one single added pang of grief just now. The words I am writing you are not out of my own heart; they are but the echo of my uncle's wish. He has spoken to me this morning on the subject of our engagement, and has told me that if our love is what we profess it to be it can bear the probation of a year.

"Twelve long months, Paul, without even seeing one

another! It looks so cruel when it is written down that I am almost tempted to go back upon my promise to him, and fling every consideration to the winds and go straight to you. One thing only holds me back, and that is the knowledge that you yourself would not have me ungrateful or lacking in duty and honour to the man who has brought me up, who has fed me, educated and clothed me since the time I was born. My uncle has been my father. He has held me in trust for the rest of the family, and he has appealed to me to-day to help him fulfill that trust.

"Dearest, it is very hard, but what can I do? If even now, at the eleventh hour, you. lift your hand and beckon to me, if you bid me put behind me all the obedience and respect that I owe to the Kerquhams I will do so, but between us there will ever be the knowledge that I have broken faith with those who were good to me, and the time will come when you will wonder how soon I shall break faith with you. Paul, I am racked with trouble, torn with anxiety. Help me to be strong, help me to keep my word, so that when the year is over I can come to you with clean hands, and with the knowledge that I have been true to myself as well as to you.

"I believe my uncle is writing to you to say that we may send letters to one another. That at least will be something. As to any talk of our broken engagement and my consequent freedom, that is as idle as the sighing of the wind in my ears. I have pledged myself to you; I have given you my first love and my first kiss. Even if we never meet again, if you cast me off as being weak and unstable, if you forget me during the months that are to come, or find consolation in some one else, I shall always be the same to you. I am as much your wife as though the Church had joined us together, and, in my sight, nothing that can happen on earth will ever loose that bond.

"Always and ever your devoted

"ROSAMUND."

The dust danced high down the long hill of Piccadilly, and in the pleasant afternoon sun the great streams of traffic glittered like a rushing river.   It was Saturday, and crowds of smartly dressed women, with gorgeous hats and airy flower-trimmed sunshades, were being whirled down to Hurlingham and Ranelagh.

From where Paul Carr sat at his open windows, with Rosamund's letter between his nerveless fingers, the sound of their light laughter seemed to float up above the whir of wheels and the beat of horses' feet.   He had the feeling of isolation and intense personal misery that comes to all who are in trouble.   What did the world care for him?   The women he had danced with and dined with, the girls he had taken down to supper or walked beside in the Park, had no more thought of him than as of some one who had never existed.   He had made a mistake, though even to this moment he could not see the reason of his ostracism, or why an act of common charity should have been counted to him as a sin.   Yet a sin it was in the eyes of the selfish, dainty, overdressed dolls, and they had put him outside the pale, and were already speaking of him as "the man who got mixed up with some nasty business in a police court."   He laughed aloud sardonically; he knew so well how they would talk, or rather *had* talked, for he was man of the world enough to be aware that by this time he and the sordid affair were old and stale.   Why should he fret about such as they?   They had cast him out from among themselves; he would shut them out from his own sight and hearing. With nervous impatience he rose and shut down the windows of his room.

Ah! now it was quieter, and he could read her letter again. For an hour he perused and re-perused the closely written pages, exulting in her whole-hearted love, and proud of her self-sacrifice, till his mood changed, and he was almost angry with her for having yielded to any wishes but his own. But deep in his own heart he knew that Rosamund was right, and he knew that Mr. Kerquham was right, too, for he had also received a letter from that gentleman—a letter full of manly sympathy but firm determination; a letter that appealed to him by his highest sense of honour not to subject Rosamund to the social trouble that at present overshadowed his own life; a letter that urged his good feeling and his worldly wisdom to let matters take their course and allow the scandal to die down and be buried before he made Rosamund his wife.

But it was very hard. It was the last drop in the bitter cup which all the time he knew had to be drained to the bottom. He had unwittingly been mixed up in a perfectly harmless business; he had played Don Quixote, and quixotism was hopelessly out of fashion. He must suffer, and he must suffer alone.

Alone! alone! As the meaning forced itself by ceaseless iteration upon him, it seemed to strike through his brain to his heart, and he began to realise by degrees what it meant. All his life, since his baby days, he had never been alone. He had been in the world and of the world. He had been bred in it, and it in him; he inherited the love of it from his pretty, light-hearted mother, and his cheery boon companion of a father. First it had been a crowd of servants and the ladies in his mother's drawing-room, and then the sycophantic following of admiring schoolboys.   At Eton he had lived in a joyous, merry circle, an adept at every sport, a favourite with everybody in the school.   At Oxford his fortune and his *bonhommie* had made him troops of friends, and when he had blossomed out in London as an eligible young man all the world of fashion and beauty had been spread before him.

Alone! alone!   Now this was all to go.   He was to live in the middle of it and yet see it all pass him by, as a broken branch caught in the middle of a rushing stream withers and dies and is left behind by the watery world that flows around it.   How could he bear it? True, there was the country, but to him it had always meant delightful parties, with hunting and shooting by day and dancing at night with smart women and the cheeriest of good fellows.   Lately he had longed to live in the country with Rosamund, but he felt it would drive him mad to go there quite alone.

How that hateful word throbbed through every nerve in his body.   He caught himself repeating it parrot-like, and at that started up and began to pace his room, and cried aloud, "Am I going mad?"

To and fro among the luxurious surroundings of what were considered almost the smartest chambers in London Carr paced.   What use was it all now?—the splendid carpets and magnificent skins, the luxurious cosy corners and the cunningly arranged lights.   What did he care for rare old china and glistening curios, for huge palms and great banks of scented flowers?   They had been the picturesque background of Society, and now Society would come there no more, and he would have the stage all to himself.   As he stood staring with wide, haggard eyes at the broad mantelpiece, covered with little ivory and silver toys and the many bits of *bric-à-brac* that men had admired and pretty women had longed for, his eye fell on a written note. "The Monastery of St. Dominic" was printed in plain square letters across the head.

"My Dear Carr:

"Will you come here to-morrow and sing for us? Our tenor is ill, and High Mass to-morrow will be robbed of its chiefest attraction to our poor little congregation if we cannot give them some good music.

"Yours sincerely,   Gregory."

Paul took up the letter and read it again and again. So dear old Philip (he always called him that in his own mind) had remembered that he could sing, and for the sake of his poor little congregation had written to him, who was not of his faith, to come and help the modest little colony get through their Sunday service.

"Why should I not do it?" cried Paul. "No one has asked me to go on the river to-morrow; no one would come with me, I suppose, if I invited him."

He walked over to where the grand piano stood with an orderly cabinet of music by its side. Almost without thinking he pulled open drawer after drawer, looking through their contents and turning over loose leaves. By-and-bye he came upon what he wanted—a great pile of Gregorian chants, and a volume containing some of the great Masses. He opened the instrument and set the music on the rack. Then he read Father Gregory's letter once more.

"Yes, I will go. It is a selfish kindness to accept, for at least it will give me something to do."

He sent a telegram to his friend, and then, as a mere matter of form, telling his servant that he was not at home to any one, he sat down and began to sing.

CHAPTER XIII

PAUL'S ANSWER

PAUL spent the next day at the little monastery in the East End. By daylight it looked an even poorer place than he had thought, and though the day was warm and brilliant outside, the tiny chapel, with its rows of shabby, rush-bottomed seats, struck damp and cold. The congregation was very small and wretchedly poor, but the priests went through the services as though the elect of the land had been before them. To Paul it was all very new. Like most modern young men, he had not troubled himself much about church-going, except when he was in the country, when there had been no hunting or shooting on the Sabbath morning, and he had filled up the time between breakfast and luncheon by drowsing in the corner of a pew.

Into a Roman Catholic church he had scarcely ever been at all, except abroad, where he had regarded such places as more or less necessary sights to be seen. He thought the service very simple, and he remembered enough of his Latin to follow the prayers and to note that they were very earnest and heart-whole. The Mass was served by four wretched little half-starved boys out of the lowest streets in the neighbourhood, and their demeanour had struck him strangely. He could guess pretty well from the expression of their evil little countenances how they had spent their week days, but here, in this bare, cold, whitewashed place, they had assumed

a very creditable appearance of piety, with their sur-
plices, and he saw in neither look nor gesture the slightest levity or irreverence.

The Prior, Father Lawrence, a grey, sad-looking man,
asked him if he would stay to their mid-day meal.
Almost without knowing it, Paul assented, and at the
same time offered to sing again at benediction. The
dinner was very plain and well cooked of its kind. But
Paul was too interested in the conversation of Father
Lawrence and Father Gregory to take heed of what he
ate.

The long summer day was drawing to a close when
he took leave of Father Gregory and went out into the
evil-smelling street once more.

"It seems a very peaceful life," he thought, as he
walked along the wide road, where Jewesses in diamonds
and plush dresses were parading up and down, and where
round the door of every public-house seethed a foul-
mouthed, half-drunken crowd. "They must work very
hard, but they are so in earnest and so happy in the
small successes that they make down in this wretched
quarter of the town."

It was a long walk to the West End, but he was in no
mood for driving, for, like most active men, he could
think better when moving. It was quite dark when he
entered his rooms, and a dim lamp was burning in one
corner. On his table lay the pile of letters he had
received the day before. A little apart from the rest
was the one that Rosamund had sent him. As he took
it up tenderly in his fingers he was conscious of a vague
self-reproach; he had thought of her so little all the day.

"Am I so unstable as all that?" he cried aloud. "At
the first breath of novelty my trouble drops from me
like a loosened cloak, and the memory of her sweet faith

and trust fades into nothingness.   Is she the stronger of the two?   Sometimes I think she is, and that I am nothing but a poor weak fool, tossed by every wind, shaken and swayed by every passing emotion.   Yesterday my heart was hers, to-day my heart slumbers, and my thoughts and feelings have been absorbed by—''

By what?   He had been scarcely conscious himself of the impression that the few hours spent among those humble, hard-working men had made upon him.   His whole mind, although he scarcely knew it, was raw and bleeding like an open wound, and the first healing touch of sympathy and kindness soothed it.   He had been deeply impressed, more than he could say, by what he had seen and heard that day, and almost his last words to Father Gregory had been a promise of a speedy return.   Memories of the monastery and the whitewashed chapel haunted him, even while he read and reread Rosamund's letter.

Twelve months!   Twelve months of probation. Twelve months without seeing her.   She said herself how hard it would be, and how long they would seem. Why should they be long?   Why should they be hard?

A sudden fever of activity rushed over his mind and drove him to his feet.   He paced the room with short, nervous strides, like a man who is faced by a great problem, the solution of which he cannot attain.   Why should the next year of his life be passed in vain regret and idle solitude?   Why should he not do as other men had done in time of trouble?

Paul had never been an irreligious man, but it had scarcely been his habit to cultivate that easy converse with his God which so many people made a show of maintaining.   Even now, he scarcely thought of the future in that way.   He only felt he must do something—be something—that if he stagnated in these rooms of his in Piccadilly or went into the country he should go mad or take to drink, or perhaps to drugs, to dull his memory. The Continent was an open book to him; there was no consolation there, while to go to further and more deserted places seemed, so he argued to himself, to be merely a cowardly shuffling of responsibilities.

But there must be consolation in work, or why did men take to it? There must be healing power in religious exercises, or why did those in trouble flock to church?

Church! He thought of church as he knew it, with its set forms and impersonal doctrines; he thought of the suave parsons and their consolations in little set phrases—men who, even as they spoke, stretched out a greedy hand · for a donation. He thought of all the clergymen he had known—hard-riding, three-bottle men in the shires, who had a merry eye for every pretty country wench they passed, and could tell as good a story in the smoking-room as any youngster fresh from Sandhurst. He thought of comfortable bishops whose slight ailments required them to spend winters on the Riviera and summers in Scotland. He thought of the fashionable London clergymen, with a rustling, adoring congregation of lovely women, each one redolent of perfume and an admirable exponent of the latest *modes* from Paris. He thought of them at smart afternoon teas, at receptions in great houses, at theatres on first nights. He recalled their stables, their well-dressed wives and their daughters who lived only for society and husband-catching.

Then, as in a flash, his mind went back to his old Oxford friend—a first-rate oar, a capital talker, who could play billiards and shoot straight, and ride anything that ever was foaled. He thought of him in their 'Varsity days, his broad shoulders in a suit of flannels, his square plain face under a straw hat, swinging down the "High" in the old university town, equally ready for a frolic as for work, for a lazy day on the Cherwell, or a night's hard cramming for an exam. Then he thought of him as he was now—Father Gregory—with no surname and no entity, a mere atom in a hard-working body of good men, vowed to poverty and celibacy, cut off from all the joys of healthy manhood, living a round of rescue work among the lowest slums of London and of religious exercise in a wretched little whitewashed chapel.

"He at least is a man," cried Paul aloud. "He has sacrificed himself for his convictions and for the good of others. Surely, if he can do it, I can do the same. Life was as fair for him ten years ago as it was for me until the beginning of this week He did not need a tragedy to make him what he is. He simply became a priest for the benefit of his fellow men. He is of sterner stuff than I am, for I am only going to do what he has done under the pressure of shame and unhappiness."

He sat down, and drawing paper to him, began to write quickly:

"MY DEAREST LOVE,

"My silence to you was cowardly; I should have guessed that it added to your suffering. But a good Father and an old friend of mine is sending you the explanations and details that you say you will not accept from me.

"The step I am now going to take will, I hope, bring you some degree of peace. I am going to pass the twelve months of waiting and probation by trying to learn to be a better and a stronger man.

"I shall write to you from time to time, and beg that whatever you may hear, you will always keep the memory of my love and my faithfulness to you in your heart. When the time is passed, we shall meet again. God grant that neither of us will have changed towards the other. Whatever it may please you to do, I shall ever remain, in heart and in affection,

"Your husband,

"PAUL."

He sealed the letter, and then with a new energy turned up the light in his rooms, and began to move about them like a man who prepares for a journey. Warm though the night was, he lit a fire, the better to destroy such papers as he did not wish strangers to see. Others he sealed into packets and directed to his lawyers and his bankers. He had written many letters before the early dawn flung its first rays through the open window. They lay in a large pile on the table, and by them was a list of instructions to his servants as to the care of his rooms and personal belongings. He worked quite quietly, and never wavered for a moment, save when he took up Rosamund's photograph and sealed it with the letter she had sent him. For one moment he laid it among the others that were ready for the post, but it had scarcely left his fingers before he took it up again.

"I cannot part from that just yet," he murmured, and slipped it into the breast pocket of his coat.

When his man came in and by his looks expressed the astonishment he was too well trained to speak, Paul had finished his self-imposed task.

"Barker," he said, quietly, "I am going away for a year. You will find all my wishes on this piece of paper, and you will carry them out. Those letters are to go to the post, and any that come for me, you must take to my solicitors.   I should wish you and your wife to remain here in charge.   Do not let there be any talk about my departure.   I have written to the bank about money matters; everything will be all right.   Now pack me a few clothes, and bring me a cup of tea.   Then call me a hansom."

The man did as he was told, and an hour later Paul Carr went down the stairs and into the cheerful street, and setting his face towards the new risen sun, drove from the west to the east.

CHAPTER XIV

A GARDEN FANCY

THE season had gone apace. Ascot and Henley and the
society gatherings that are warranted by a couple of
smart cricket matches at Lord's were over. The grass
in the open spaces of the parks was burnt to a sickly
brown, and the poor thirsty trees, which but a few weeks
back had been radiant in their spring finery, were beginning slowly to shed the first withered rags of their once
green garments. The women were getting to look a little dragged and thin, and many of the young girls who
were in their first season had already begun surrep-
titiously to rouge their cheeks before starting out on a
long night of dances and receptions. The heat had been
intense, the season a good one, which meant that everybody had worked hard in the pursuit of pleasure, and all
the world was beginning to long for the salt freshness of
the Solent, or the clean, crisp air of the purple northern
moors.

In the shady gardens of "The Hurst" it was still
green and fresh. A perfect army of men watered the
velvety lawns at dawn and at night, and there was
neither sufficient dust nor traffic in the neighbourhood
materially to mar the full foliage of the magnificent trees.
The flower beds were in the full tide of brilliant colour,
and the roses that grew over the verandah hung like
great flags of cream and pink and deep crimson. Never
had "The Hurst" looked so pretty, and never had things
gone so badly within its richly furnished walls.

To begin with, Laura had given both her parents a great deal of trouble. The girl had grown utterly out of hand, and her insatiable desire for amusement, her reckless and uncontrollable passion for flirtation and admiration had only been satiated at the cost of all decency, propriety, and — although Mrs. Kerquham scarcely acknowledged it even to herself — reputation. She had kicked over the traces completely, and within the last few weeks had run serious risk of being mixed up in a scandal with a married man, whose wife had proved none too complacent under very trying circumstances. In vain Mr. Kerquham had commanded and Mrs. Kerquham appealed; Laura had only tossed her head and said she would have her own fun in her own way; she would not marry if she could; she would not be tied to one man even if he were ten times a millionaire and as handsome as Apollo.

"I do not know where I have got it from," she had cried, with her empty laugh, "but I am a free-lance. I am bored to extinction if I see too much of one person, and if you are at all a wise woman, mother, you will not urge me any more to get married. It would only end in a row, you know, and a scandal, and the divorce court and things. Oh! it is all very shocking, I know, but I think it is just as well to warn you. I am not quite the fool you take me for, but I will not be tied down by anybody."

And Mrs. Kerquham had set her mouth into a harder line than ever, and talked bitterly among her friends of the difficulty of keeping a girl in hand, and within the narrow limits of her heart had wondered what she had done that Providence should have laid such a scourge upon her shoulders. Honor had become engaged, and it was a strange irony of fate that the very thing that Mrs.

Kerquham would have desired with one daughter was a grief to her in connection with the other. The young man was a social nobody, a briefless barrister, without either the desire or the means of pushing himself. He and Honor would sit silent for hours together. Mr. Kerquham vowed that it drove him mad to see two such lymphatic lovers and Mrs. Kerquham felt bitterly that her girl had only accepted this most ineligible offer as a means of escaping from home.

Chiefest, however, of all Mrs. Kerquham's disappointments had been Rosamund. When her husband had told her that Rosamund had acceded to his proposition that her engagement with Paul Carr should be in abeyance, and when she had noted how the girl had borne her sorrow with dignity and quiet reticence, Mrs. Kerquham had at once jumped to the conclusion that it needed but a few weeks to heal the scratch, and that before the end of the season her niece would be making a brilliant marriage.

But Margot Kerquham, for all her Scotch acumen and all her twenty years' experience of the social world, was apt to look at things too much through her own spectacles. She desired her niece to marry well, and therefore she persuaded herself that such a thing would come to pass. She adopted the policy of never mentioning Paul Carr's name, of taking Rosamund about as much as ever, of having Lord St. Ives, who, by the way, had speedily wearied of *la belle* Rivington, perpetually at "The Hurst." Because Rosamund did not go about with red eyes and a perpetual sob in her throat, because she took as much pains in the dressing of her waving dark hair, and was as particular in the fit of her gowns as ever, because she laughed at the play, and enjoyed the opera, Mrs. Kerquham thought that the past was better than dead and buried—that it was forgotten.   Poor lady, she had never made a greater mistake in her life, and she was as ignorant of the working of Rosamund's heart as is a baby of the mechanism of the toy that pleases him.

Rosamund Keith was a proud girl and little given to talking of herself and her sensations.   The first shock of her grief and disappointment over, she set herself to fulfill with a whole heart the promise she had made to her uncle, and to go through, with what courage and self-control she could, the twelve months of probation.   She was not the type of woman who wears her heart upon her sleeve; she did not wander into her cousins' rooms at night and bewail her lost love and the romantic obstacles that barred immediate marriage.   No barrier had been raised between herself and her uncle, and when with him she would chat brightly about generalities and tell him little scraps of society gossip, or listen with all her old interest when he spoke of deeper things.   But all the time the wound in her heart was green, and her faith and love were ever springing.

She had only done what a proud woman should do— drawn a veil between her feelings and the world.   She was not going to let herself be a subject of idle jest or scornful pity.   Few outside her own family had known of her engagement while it lasted; she was not going to publish it to the world now that it was broken off.   But she suffered intensely.   The very strength of her nature gave her a greater capability of enduring agony.   She would dance all night, and then with unbound locks and bare shoulders weep and pray and wrestle with her longings till the dawn.   The very capacity that helped her to enjoy, enhanced the keenness of her pain.   She was like a great, deep lake that is only stirred and moved by

the most terrific forces of nature; the little breezes
and storms of life made no impression on her at all.
Outwardly, the only difference that was to be found in
her was a slightly increased pallor and a graver attitude,
but her aunt, hugging her own delusion that all was well
with Rosamund, would persist that the change was due
to the heat, and that it was the fatigue of the season
that sometimes made her look so tired.

Meantime Mrs. Kerquham's satisfaction with the way
that things were going gave Rosamund peace. Her aunt
was fully persuaded that before they all went to Scotland
at the end of the season Lord St. Ives would propose in
due form and the engagement would be announced.
Rosamund herself was but little impressed by the earl's
obvious intentions. She had been so used all her life to
a certain amount of admiration that a little more or less,
especially now when her whole brain and heart were
filled with one image, made no impression on her at all.
That Lord St. Ives came to lunch and tea and tennis and
dinner almost every day in the week did not seem
strange to her, because that particular season they had
had the house always full of people. He was only one
of the crowd, and he came and went, so far as regarded
herself, just as Honor's silent lover did, or the troop of
fast young men who hung like satellites round Laura's
brilliant beauty. That was another mistake that Mrs.
Kerquham made. She wanted Rosamund to get used to
Lord St. Ives, and she thought it was very clever to
treat him as one of a number and accept him as a matter
of course in the family circle. Her efforts certainly had
the result of avoiding any explosion between the girl
and herself, but further than that they were frustrated
by her niece looking upon him as a harmless if not very
agreeable appanage.

Goodwood was at hand, and the last event of the season, the Marlborough House garden party, was to take place that afternoon.   Mr. and Mrs. Kerquham and the girls had started off to attend that brilliant function. The most trivial excuse had won for Rosamund the rare privilege of an afternoon to herself.   Mrs. Kerquham had really to acknowledge that the girl was not looking quite the thing, so she graciously assented to her niece's plea that she might spend the afternoon quietly and alone in the garden.

As the carriage load drove down the long avenue, Rosamund, with a book under her arm, and a big white sunshade above her head, came slowly down the verandah steps and across the sunny lawn to where the basket chairs and hammocks with their gaudy cushions made a brilliant splash of colour under the cool trees.   With a heavy sigh she flung herself into a low chair, and closing her parasol, dropped it at her feet, where a moment later the unheeded volume, slipping from her knees, joined it.

A great oppression lay upon her soul that day, a prescience of coming evil.   Rosamund was not morbid, but her nerves were all a-tingle with the expectation of bad news.   Perhaps it was the heat that made her feel so cheerless and dejected.   She pushed her broad-leafed garden hat back from her low brow, and pressed her cool palms against her throbbing temples.   As she sat there, looking out from the shade onto the blazing lawn, where the scarlet and gold and purple of the flower beds quivered and danced in the sunshine, she was almost weak enough to wish she had gone with the others.   She had so looked forward to this afternoon alone; she had anticipated a long and happy dream of the sweet past and the beautiful future that was to come, but she could summon neither the one nor the other to her imagination; she could only sigh and cast anxious, frightened looks about her, and feel that the present was heavy with a coming grief.

"How foolish I am!" she cried almost aloud to herself. "I have no reason to feel like this. I am sure that Paul is the same as he was, and I know that I am unaltered, and yet I feel somehow as though a wall, a great invisible, insurmountable barrier had been built between us, and was growing and growing and growing, and that we shall be as far apart as though one were dead and the other left alive. Ah! it is absurd."

Angry with herself, she drew her book onto her knees again and opened it, but her eyes had scarcely travelled twenty lines before they had wandered from the page and stared unseeing once more out into the sun.

"Asleep, or only pretending?" cried a loud, clear voice from the verandah, and Lily Baumer, a girl friend of hers, all mauve muslin and faint blue ribbons, ran across the lawn and greeted Rosamund in a hearty boisterous fashion.

Miss Baumer was the daughter of a German artist, and a fine specimen of a modern maid, tall and broad-shouldered and with an opulence of physical charms that gave her the only pangs of anxiety that ever clouded her light-hearted disposition. Her skin of milk and roses, her large light-blue eyes and masses of pale yellow hair betrayed her German origin, which was further accentuated by an obvious want of taste in her dress and a tendency to untidiness.

"My dear! I was delighted when they told me you were in. It was a positive instinct that made me guess you would not go to that garden party to-day. It is sure to be a fearful crowd; not but that, of course, if I had been asked, I should have jumped at it like anything, but you see we are not on the Marlborough House list.''

She plumped herself down in a large chair, and began to pull off her gloves.

''My goodness! Rosie, how lovely it is out here! Why on earth you ever go anywhere is a mystery to me. If I had a garden like this, you would never catch me stuffing about in hot rooms and talking to the same silly people every day and every night. Oh, dear! I am glad the season is over. Do you know, I am going to Cowes with Mrs. Toroni? She has got a yacht, and no end of a jolly lot are going on it. Oh! here is tea— and strawberries—and what cream! Now this is better than all the parties in all the world.''

Rosamund, roused from her despondent mood by her friend's light chatter, busied herself in pouring out tea and giving Miss Baumer the good things she loved so well. Lily Baumer was exactly the sort of companion that suited Rosamund at that moment. She ran on with a trickle of light-hearted chatter, waiting for no answer and needing none. It was no exertion to listen to her, and her talk was not deep or abstruse enough to require great exercise of thought or very much concentration to follow. Lily passed in review their various acquaintances, asked the date of Honor's marriage, and hinted at some fresh escapade of Laura's. Suddenly she put down her cup with a little clatter, and clasped her large, elaborately ringed hands together.

''Oh! my dear! There, I was nearly forgetting it! I knew I had something to tell you. Quite a piece of news! How it has leaked out I do not know, but they were all talking about it last night at Ranelagh. You know he always used to be so great down there, what with polo and pony racing and things.''

"He? Who?" said Rosamund. Her voice was quite calm, and her face was like a mask, but a little sickening flutter stirred at her heart, and the sense of coming bad news swept over her again as a cloud sweeps across a sunny landscape.

"Why, my dear, that Mr. Carr, of course! Dear me, I always did think he was such a handsome man; I used quite to envy you girls here, who saw such a lot of him. It is quite a dreadfully sad thing."

The instinct of hiding any emotion made Rosamund lift her hand to the brim of her hat and drag it forward over her eyes.

"Mr. Carr! What has happened? Is he—?"

"Oh, you are going to say 'dead' of course. I never know why it is," chirped Miss Baumer in her cheeriest manner, "but whenever anybody mentions misfortune or bad news about anybody, people always jump to the conclusion that they are dead. I am sure I do not see why people should trouble about things like that; we have all got to die some time or other, you know. It is queer, isn't it, to make a fuss about a thing that cannot be helped?"

"What is the news?" asked Rosamund, in a low, dry voice and taking no notice of Lily's irrelevant philosophy.

"You have not heard it, then? Well, I made sure, of course, that as you had been such friends of his that you would have been among the first people to know. He has become a Roman Catholic. Just think of that! He was 'received'—I think that is the proper expression—into the Church last week. We had awful arguments last night as to whether he was to be called a convert or a pervert."

"Is that all?" murmured Rosamund, with an instinct that there was more yet to know.

"Oh, dear me, no! Why, that would not be any news. Lots of people, quite in the best set, are being made Roman Catholics nowadays. In fact, it is rather a smart thing to do, I think."

"Well, go on," said Rosamund. She was staring out at the ever-shifting colours of the flower beds, and her voice as she spoke sounded very far away. She was quite unnoticed by Lily, who was making an onslaught on a dish of sweet cakes. But her hands were locked together across her knees until the flowing of the blood was arrested in them and they grew white as marble.

"He has gone into a monastery, you know. That is the bit of news."

"A monastery," echoed Rosamund, vaguely trying to collect her memories as to what such an action might mean.

"Oh! he is not a real monk, you know," said Lily Baumer, crunching her fine white teeth into an almond cake. "He is a novice! He is serving his novitiate— that is the proper expression, I think. He can come out, of course, whenever he likes." This with a knowing air as though very proud of her knowledge. "You have to have an awfully long time of that kind of thing before you are a real monk. Of course, people are saying that he has only gone in there till that business—you know what I mean—that happened in the spring has been forgotten, and that then he will come out again and everything will be just the same as ever. It would be a pity, wouldn't it, if a handsome man like Mr. Carr really went in for being a frowsy, dull, stupid old monk?"

Rosamund did not answer. She could not, even if she had had anything to say. She was so overwhelmed with the suddenness of the news, so filled with speculation as to what it really might mean, that she could form no sentences that might express commonplace curiosity or idle wonder. Her silence attracted Miss Baumer's attention to her.

"Why, Rosie, you look awfully odd! Have I told you any bad news? Is it anything that you are upset at hearing?"

The good-hearted girl, in a fit of ill-restrained emotion, slipped out of her chair and down on to her knees by Rosamund's side. "My dear, my dear, I am so sorry. You know I would not have hurt you for the world, and I did not think—I did not know—indeed, I did not, that there had ever been anything between you and Mr. Carr. Everybody knew that he admired you very much, but then, you see, such lots of men do that that we do not think anything of it, and since he has disappeared from London you have been just the same. Oh! poor darling, how much you must have suffered, and how brave you have been, and what a brute I am to have told you this dreadful thing just by way of idle talk! I am so sorry, dear."

Rosamund pulled herself together, and looked down into her friend's flushed face. Her big, dark eyes were full of unshed tears, and her mouth was quivering like a little child's. It had been Lily's rough sympathy that had unnerved her, but in a moment she controlled herself, and laying her stone-cold hand upon her friend's, said:

"My dear, I would sooner have heard it from you than any one, for I am sure that you would not tell me a thing with any unkind intent."

Then she went on in her simple, direct way that saw no need of making a secret of her love: "Mr. Carr and I were very fond of each other, Lil. We were engaged and going to be married when that business happened.

My uncle was very good about it. According to his lights, he did the right thing. He insisted that for a year we were both to be free, and not to meet, and that things were to go on exactly as though Mr. Carr had never spoken to me. The time is going by, of course; but it has been very hard for me, and sometimes, Lil, I am very, very unhappy."

"You brave darling," sobbed Lil, her sentimental nature stirred to violent emotion, and crying all over the bosom of her muslin frock. "Fancy you going about as if nothing in the world were the matter! Mr. Carr is able to go into a monastery to pass his time, but you, you are braver than he is, for you are stopping out here in the world among all of us, who are just a lot of idle, heartless, empty-headed fools. How I hate them all, and how I despise myself when I think of what you go through without so much as a sigh."

"Hush! Lil," said Rosamund, trying to soothe the girl. "It is not as bad really as that. We have sworn to love one another, and I believe as much in Paul's affection for me as I do in mine for him. I am sure that what he has done he has done for the best. It was a shock to me just now when you told me, for it made me feel as though he had left me standing alone on a little island in the middle of a great sea. It gave me a deserted, lost feeling, and it was that that frightened me."

"Did you not know of this at all?" said Lil.

"No, dear. We are allowed to write to one another, but during the past few weeks we have exchanged no letters. You see we have promised to be true to each other—we have said we would never marry except it was one another—there was nothing else to say."

Lily Baumer scrambled to her feet, and scrubbing at her eyes, pushed her disordered hair back under her hat.

"You are the bravest, most splendid girl I have ever met. I do not think there is any one else like you in the whole wide world. Good-bye, my dearest," and she smothered Rosamund with kisses. "Mother only lent me the carriage for an hour, and I must go home again; but you promise to forgive me, don't you?"

"There is nothing to forgive, dear," said Rosamund, gently. "I have already told you that I would sooner have heard this thing from you than from any one. Good-bye, dear."

"So this was the evil that I had feared," thought Rosamund, as she gazed once more upon the lawn, over which the afternoon shades were creeping in long straight lines. "Or perhaps it is not evil; perhaps it is for the best, yet—what a strange thing to have done."

The strain of Scotch blood and the strict religious bringing up of her life dominated her for a moment.

"Fancy a Protestant becoming a Roman Catholic. I wonder why he did that? One does hear of others doing such things, but I thought that Paul was much too good a man to change his religion. In a monastery, too; they say such strange things go on in monasteries. Perhaps he will never come out again; perhaps they will influence him and keep him there. Oh! but Paul is not a child; he would never allow himself to be persuaded so much against his will—but it is very—very strange."

Then her thoughts turned inwards. "I wonder if it will make any difference between us. I wonder if his new vows are going to wipe out those he made to me. It was just here that he told me that he loved me, and asked me to be his wife.   I remember thinking then it was almost an idle thing to say, for somehow I knew it for some weeks before he spoke.   I wonder if he will write to me.''

And as the afternoon died into evening she sat on, a little shocked, a little sad, and very fearful of what the future would bring forth.

CHAPTER XV

A REASON

IF to Rosamund it had been strange that Paul Carr had voluntarily become a member of the Roman Catholic Church, it was to him little less than wonderful. He had been broken and disappointed when he had first taken to going to the little monastery in the vilest purlieus of eastern London. The quietness and the simplicity of the place, the lack of pretension and the sincerity of its few inhabitants had for a time acted like an anodyne on his overstrained nerves. It had soothed him to sing in the little chapel, and it had given him a sense of well-being to spend a few hours in Father Gregory's poor cell, but the idea of his becoming a Roman Catholic had been as far away from his thoughts as that he should himself give up his present mode of life and take on the habit and the vows of a monk.

Like most of the great things in either the world's history or the little story of an individual life, an accident had proved the lever that moved him. He and Father Gregory one afternoon were quietly discussing the great Sacraments of their respective churches. They had spoken of the Sacraments of marriage and confirmation, and then of the greatest Sacrament—that of baptism, which in all churches seals the soul to Christ and forms a palpable link between the body and a set form of religion. Father Gregory had been speaking for some moments, and then had stopped, waiting for Paul's answer. None came, and as the monk looked at the young man he saw that his whole face was diffused with a mingled look of horror and wonder.

"Of what are you thinking? Why do you look like that?" the Father asked.

"I was wondering," said Paul, in a low, introspective voice, as though he were trying to fling his memory back into the earliest days of his life, "I was wondering if I had ever been christened. While you have been speaking I have been trying to remember when I first went to church; it has only just come back to me that it was not until I was at Eton."

"But many worldly parents neglect the religious education of their children," said Father Gregory. "Because your father and mother never took you to church it does not follow that you were never christened."

Paul passed his hands before his eyes as though he were brushing aside a veil that hid the past.

"But more than that is coming back to me," he murmured, brokenly. "I seem to remember hearing some of my mother's relations argue with her on some course she had adopted as regards my religion. I can recall some one—I think it must have been my grandmother—urging her to do her duty by her only child, and then she laughed, and said the whole thing was a mockery and a farce—that no one was made either good or bad by the commission or the omission of the sprinkling of water and the consecrating to God. I remember now that my grandmother was very angry, and told my mother that she would live one day to regret the wrong she had done me. Poor women, they are both dead now. Neither will know whether the wrong has been righted or what the results of it will be. Only—it remains that I have never been christened, and that in

the accepted sense of the word I must be an outcast from
every church and from every sect. I am not a Christian.''

Paul buried his head in his hands. The priest, reaching across the narrow wooden table, laid one hand on
his shaking shoulders.

''What you tell me, my friend, is very strange, but at
least you have lived a life as good as the others of your
world.''

''A life like the others!'' cried Paul, rising to his feet.
''What kind of life do you think that is? You did well;
you left the world early, while the glamour of it was still
over you, while you still believed that all men were honourable and all women pure. I believe that even now
you have the heart of a child, and although you know
too well the misery and the sin that flows by your very
doorway here, I believe that you still think our world—
the world of educated, well-born men and women—is a
good one.''

He laughed scornfully. ''Your belief is the belief of
a child that knows no discrimination and judges everything from the mere outside. You told me once that
people of my world came down here sometimes and did
charitable things and screwed up their senses to the
bearing of disgusting spectacles and fearful sounds. I
told you then it was all sham and advertisement and
merely a mad longing for a new sensation. I tell you
now that all the world is rotten! If a good action is
done it is not for the love of Christ or for the memory
of the sprinkled water. It is for a motive. Father, I
could almost find it in my heart to thank God that I am
not a Christian.''

But as the storm spent itself a new mood took him,
and he seemed like a child lost in a dark forest, who

stretches out its hands and finds no support; who cries for help and is not heeded.

"Now I know," he said, "why I could not bear the transient trouble and passing shame of that affair in May; I had no one to turn to. The only reed in the world I had to lean on was Rosamund Keith—and I hope I am too much of a man to cast my burden on the slender shoulders of a mere girl."

"But she loved you!" said Father Gregory.

"Yes, she loved me. I feel sure she does so still, and will do so to the end, but there again—I was faced by my own weakness. If I could have believed, really and truly, in God, I should have felt sure of her. Don't you see that faith is a thing that must be trained, as every other attribute of humanity must be? If I had been taught to believe that an omnipotent Power was ever ready to help the weak and weary, I should have greater faith is mere humans like myself."

"And what will you do?" asked the monk.

"What can I do? I cannot make myself as a little child, simple and unthinking, and accepting everything just as it is told to me. Yet—neither can I live on with this knowledge that I have no right even to pray."

"But you have yet to prove that the neglect you seem to think was exercised towards you really did happen, and that you were never christened."

"I can do that in a few days."

It was over a week before the dull corridors of the little monastery resounded once more to Paul's firm, ringing step. He went straight to Father Gregory, and even before greeting him, cried aloud:

"It is as I thought. I have found out—I have proved that I was never christened."

And so it was that Paul, tossed on the sea of emotion and despair and with never an anchor to cling to, was swept by every sentiment and wish that swayed him at that time, into the bosom of the holy Church of Rome. He had so completely lost touch with every one who might have influenced him to another course, so many weeks had passed without his even hearing one word from Rosamund, that it seemed only natural he should turn to the first consolation that offered itself.

With his customary seriousness, he had taken the whole thing very much to heart, and early in his preparations for his baptism had decided upon entering a monastery. Not with a view of one day taking final vows—for the thoughts of Rosamund were very sacred and very dear to him, and he still counted the hours to the far-off end of that probationary year. But he was very weak at that time; he had been so accustomed all his life to living in a whirl and in a crowd that the effect upon him of social ostracism was very great, and resulted in an almost morbid and unhealthy dread of everything that appertained to Society.

So one afternoon, when he talked with the Prior after he had finished his day's instruction, he said he would like to go for some months into some quiet spot that God and man had combined to hedge about with sweet peace and silence and a simple, regular life; a spot where the roar of the world's ocean was never heard, and from which the tide of life seemed to have flowed away forever. The Prior told him of many places, and with Father Gregory he visited such monastic retreats as lay within easy distance of London. Some seemed to him unnecessarily lax; others, like the Passionists, aimlessly severe; Benedictines and Carmelites and Jesuits, he went among, and then last of all he was taken to a small Dominican settlement or monastery of the Black Friars, as they were called in older times.

His æsthetic tastes, which his new life had excited within him, were pleased by what he saw there. The long, low building, with two great wings stretching out through lovely terraced gardens and framed in great trees, pleased him. In the low meadowland that was spread like a verdant carpet to the grey horizon the cows grazed ankle-deep in the lush grass. Here and there the steeple of some village church, or the whirling arms of a windmill, broke the sky line, while in the north the tender sheen of a sea of silver betokened the whereabouts of one of the sleepiest of the Norfolk Broads. It was all grey and green and very quiet, with just the white-robed monks moving quietly about in twos against the background of the old walled gardens and the low, straggling house.

"I should like to come here," he had said to Father Gregory. "Here I ought to find peace and happiness; here I ought to be able to think calmly of things that are now irritation to me. When I am christened I will come to this place and be a novice here, subject to men older and wiser than myself. I will try and begin a new life, so that I may really be fit for Rosamund when the year is over."

The little settlement in the East End, which laboured so hard among such loathsome surroundings, was not astonished that the new convert should choose so fair a spot to live in. It was to them the haven of refuge, to which they retired when the storm and stress of their awful work was finished, and where sometimes one or other of them went to gain back the lost health and broken courage which had succumbed to the hideous circumstances of the daily life they had taken upon themselves.

A week before Rosamund heard the news Paul was baptised by the name he had always borne in the world, into the church he had chosen, and a few hours after the ceremony, with only a small portmanteau in his hand, he set out for Norfolk.

CHAPTER XVI

A RETREAT

THE flat, dyked country was flooded with the crimson light of the setting sun as Paul Carr stepped from the train at a little wayside Norfolk station. A lazy porter lolled on a truck in the shade, and the stout station-master, having seen the train move off again, pulled off his official coat, and rolling up his shirt sleeves, picked up a spade and resumed his interrupted occupation of gardening.

Paul gave up his ticket to a little girl who stood at the wicket gate, and picking up his bag, stepped out into the road. He remembered the way, so he did not need to ask for directions, and as there was no need to hurry, he walked away quite slowly. His steps first led him through a trim village, where the women, gossiping at their gates, drawled their words and laughed the long, deliberate laugh of the eastern counties. A windmill and a church bounded the village, and then he set his foot on the long, dyked road which was edged with pollard willow trees, that with their round, clumped heads, stood like a stiff row of sentinels between the roadway and the grassy, sunken meadows. High up in the sky that was paling from a deep blue to an opales-cent grey, a lark was singing its evensong. A distant sheep bell sounded hoarsely on the evening air now and then; a cart rumbled in the distance, and then every-thing was silent.

Paul, after the months of harassing worry and doubt,
the glare and glitter and the squalid horror of London,
felt as though he were treading the pathway to heaven.
The air was very warm, yet, coming over the flat country
straight from the sea, smacked of soft, foamy waves.
By-and-bye, a long line of red wall wandered like a
thread across the green country. It was the wall of the
monastery gardens.

With a sigh of ineffable happiness Paul rang at the
gate, which was opened from within the lodge by a
spring. As he passed through it, it shut with a heavy
crash behind him, and again he sighed, for he felt as
though behind that gate lay all the trouble and heart-
bitterness of the world. He crossed a meadow or two,
and then passing through an archway in a brick wall,
found himself in the straggling kitchen garden, and not
far from the main door of the monastery. This entrance
lay in the centre of the building, with the long wings
stretched out on either side of it. Some of the upper
windows were a little open, and he anticipated with
pleasure the coolness and freshness of the simply-fur-
nished rooms within. He pulled the iron handle of a
great bell that sounded loudly a long way off. He was
evidently expected, for long before its clanging died
away the door was flung open and a cheerful Irishman
in a white cloth cassock, and with his tonsure covered by
a small black *zuchetto*, or skull cap, opened the door in
wide welcome. He was a lay brother, and his name was
Patrick. He greeted Paul with a broad smile, and told
him that the novice master, whose duty it was to receive
and take entire charge of the novices, was waiting for
him in the parlour.

.The parlour was just within the door. It was panelled with oak that had grown dark with age. The

wooden floor of narrow pitch-pine boards shone like a mirror and gave off a scent suggestive of beeswax and infinite cleanliness. The three long windows were opened to the flower gardens, which sloped away from the house on that side down to a little stream that ran through the grounds. A picture of St. Dominic, crudely painted and set in a very simple frame, hung above the mantel-piece. Close by the door was a small wooden desk with a stool before it. On it was a tall, black crucifix with the Christ in white plaster. Two cheap glass vases, gaudily painted, held some white lilies. The table in the centre of the room was innocent of all books save a "Life of St. Dominic" and a volume of sermons. Half a dozen rush-bottomed chairs stood with formal neatness round the room.

As Paul was ushered in, a large, stout man rose from a chair in the furthest corner. He closed a little book that he had been reading and slipped it in to the pocket of his cassock. He advanced into the full light and greeted Paul kindly.

"I am Father Zadock," he said, "and I am the novice master. I trust you will be happy here and gain such consolations as you may wish from your studies and from our quiet life."

He was a kind-looking man, with a rather high voice and a weak chin. Paul, in his quick fashion, took a fancy to him at once, but read in every line of his large, fleshy face and soft fat hands that he was easy-going and of undecided character.

. "To-night," said Father Zadock, "you will sup in the guest chamber. You will see your fellow novices to-mor-row. The Prior will also receive you in the morning. Will you come this way with me?"

He walked before Paul down the long corridor, the

walls of which were distempered a French grey colour. At each angle of the walls, pictures of saints were roughly painted on the plaster. A stretch of cocoanut matting ran between two shining lines of polished boards. At the far end was the guest chamber. It was as severely plain as the parlour, but Paul, whose fastidious notions even his religious thirstings could not entirely eliminate, noticed that the napery laid upon the small table was very fine and white, and that the glass and china upon which his supper was served were good, if of simple form and decoration.

An ample meal was brought to him, well cooked and savoury, and as he ate it with some appetite, Father Zadock talked to him. A faint surprise struck Paul that the good man did not lay much stress upon the manner of his reception into the Church, nor did he express particular gratification that a son of the world should be content for a time to submit himself and the order of his life to the strict discipline of a religious order. Rather did the Father ask for news, interspersing his questions with remarks that showed he was not badly informed on the current topics of the day. Once, when Paul received some question of his with frank astonishment, Father Zadock leaned back in his chair and shook his fat sides with hearty laughter.

"You are wondering that I know about that, I suppose. Oh! please do not deny it; I can see it in your face; but you must not think we are hermits here. We read the papers, and people come and see us, and we know pretty well what is going on."

It was not until he was left alone in his room that Paul pondered over the worthy Father's words, and even then their full significance did not come to him, for he was busy spending the last hour of daylight in reviewing

his surroundings.   He had been led, after his supper, to
that wing of the monastery which was known as the
Novitiate. · Here, on three floors, were instructed, fed,
and housed the novices who came to the monastery either
to prepare for the oriesthood or to retreat some time
from the world.

Paul's room was one of many off a long corridor, distempered and painted like the one downstairs.   At the
extreme end of it was erected an altar with a triptych
above it and bearing a crucifix and a few flowers.   Behind it was a very small chapel, to which the novices
might repair at stated times for private prayer.

His own room was small.   The fast-setting sun
flooded it and showed in one flash every detail of the
apartment.   It was about ten feet square, with yellow
painted walls and a bare floor, polished like those he had
seen elsewhere in the house.   Opposite the door was the
window; it was a lattice and was set in an embrasure
that was deep enough to form a seat.   There was no
blind to the window, but a coloured cotton curtain drew
before the recess at night.   One corner of the room was
cut across by a deal board, on which was a basin, a soap
dish, and other toilet necessaries.   There was one chair,
and a small looking-glass in a common wooden frame
hung flat against the wall.   One fine piece of furniture
only broke the monotony and ugliness of the room.   It
was a small cupboard in fine old oak, black with age and
polished by centuries of use; the top sloped like a writing desk, and it suggested to Paul many happy hours of
sympathetic study.

Just inside the doorway hung a little plaster crucifix
and a shell moulded in cheap china, which held the holy
water.   A gas bracket of plain iron jutted out from the
wall not far from the bed, which was made of three

planks laid across trestles, and mitigated only to the human body by a single flock mattress, a small bolster, and a pillow. Of sheets it was quite innocent, but the two blankets and pillow slip were all of white wool, and a great counterpane covered it. Three slips of wood, held together by a worn red cord, formed the bookcase that hung on the wall.

As the door shut upon Father Zadock's portly form, Paul felt strangely lonely. Again, a self-conscious sense of astonishment that there was such small interest taken in the arrival of a wealthy English gentleman who had been a member of the best Society in London, the scion of a well-known Protestant family, swept over him and held him spellbound. But he would not permit himself to cavil at his reception. The men who lived here were above worldly considerations; it did not matter to them who a man had been; they would only consider him as he was to be. The pasts of people were shut outside in the road by the heavy wooden gate; it was only their futures that concerned the good Fathers.

He unpacked his small bag, wondering if on the morrow he would be allowed to keep the very few and simple articles that he had brought with him. "Not that it matters," he said to himself, "for I shall have many other things to think of here. I have to make up for a lifetime of ignorance and idle wrong-doing. I have to wipe out the past and prepare for a fairer future with Rosamund. Dear Rosamund, I wonder what she will say when she knows of this?"

He walked over to the window and looked out across the fields. A soft white mist was flowing up from them, and lying in light wreaths about the little round-headed trees; the sheep bell still rang hoarsely in the distance.

"I wonder," he cried to the rolling mist and the pale

sky, "if I am really such a coward; if I am afraid to tell
her? If I am afraid for myself or for her? I do not
quite know. She is so brave and true, so broad-minded,
so large-hearted, that I think in her generosity she would
not have thwarted me in my wish to find grace. I
believe in my own heart it would have been a great
grief to her to know of my parents' neglect, and yet—
and yet—if I believe all this why have I not written to
her and told her everything?" He pulled himself up.
"Paul Carr, you are a coward; you are afraid of yourself
and afraid of the woman you love, and you have all the
time intended to let her know you have done this thing
after the step has been taken. But now I must write to
her—I will write to her and ask her forgiveness. Until
I have done that I shall feel as though I had not been
quite fair to my love."

Some one, he did not see who, came in and lit the gas,
and then slipped silently out again. For a moment
Paul's instinct was to turn and say the night was yet too
young to need artificial light. Then he checked himself,
and remembered that doubtless this was the rule of the
place. But he lowered the light a little, and went back
to the window, where he mused and dreamed as he
watched the wreaths of mist rise and fall like a ghostly
sea over the low-lying fields. After what seemed but a
few minutes, but was in reality half an hour, a loud bell
rang in the corridor outside. He did not move, however, until some moments later a sharp knock came to
his door, and a voice he had not heard before said, "You
must put out your light." Silently he obeyed, and then,
by the clear radiance of the rising moon, slowly
undressed and prepared for bed.

The white woolen sheets had looked inviting enough,
but when he slipped between them he found that they

were rough and coarse, while the pillow, after his head
had been on it for a few moments, stung and burned as
though filled with nettles. He was almost despairing of
being able to rest, when he remembered that in his bag
he had a few silk handkerchiefs. Finding one, he spread
it beneath his face, which was already quite sore, and
then quickly lost himself and his doubts in dreams.

CHAPTER XVII

ROSAMUND READS A LETTER

THE first news that Rosamund received from Paul was forwarded to her in Scotland from "The Hurst." She recognised his handwriting at once, and in a queer, illogical way was almost surprised to find that it was not at all altered as she had somehow expected it might have been. The letter filled two large sheets of paper and was very closely written, the only break in the lines being made by a tiny sketch of the monastery that he had put in one corner.

"My dearest Rosamund," it began, "if you were any other woman than you are, if you were not the truest and the most loving and the most sweet natured of your sex, I should scarcely have dared to write to you after so long a silence. The summer was in its fullest beauty when we last met and when we parted, and now already autumn has set her palette with brown and purple, yellow and gold, and passes the clear, cool nights in painting the great clumps of trees, the low shrubberies, and the creepers that surround this place. When I look out of my window, at early dawn, I see the mists lying thick and white as carded wool over the dyked meadows. In a few days September will be here, and the ring of the guns shooting down the little brown birds among the fields will sound all day long outside the high red wall that makes this spot a haven from the turbulent world without.

"I wonder where you are now. Not in London, of course, though I send this letter to you there—and you would scarcely yet be settled in Midshire at the Manor. I like best to think of you as being in Scotland, pressing down the heather with your light step, in your dainty tam-o'shanter with its scarlet feather and those workmanlike short skirts of yours, in the wearing of which you have learned to move and walk as no other woman can do. That is how I picture you to myself, out in the fresh, free air, with the life-blood glowing through your fine skin and your big eyes radiant with the reflected sunshine and the clear blue light of the northern sky.

"And I have an instinct, too, Rosamund, that you think of me sometimes, yet it can only be in a vague way. You do not know where I am or what I am doing. I wonder if any one told you of the step I took last July. It was only two months ago, and yet it seems as though a whole cycle of time had passed since then. I wonder if you heard that I had been received into the Roman Catholic Church, and if so, what you thought? My dear, I was very unhappy, very broken, and very lonely. Even you were denied to me, and men are at best, with all their pride and all their vaunted brains and intelligence, such poor things that they must lean on some other but themselves. So it is that when woman, the natural support of man, is taken away, he turns to God. I only followed the instincts of human nature, and in doing so discovered that I had really no God to turn to.

"An old friend of mine helped me then, and it was his hand indirectly that led me out of the darkness into the light. Were you very shocked? I am sure that your family was, for it is difficult for people who have the ideas of centuries bred in them, suddenly to uproot or change the thing that has become a vital part of their natures. But I scarcely think you are like that. Convention, as the world knows it, has never influenced you much. You have lived a freer, less artificial life than the average woman of your order. You have never weakened your mind with foolish reading and light talk. At least I hope, if at first you were startled at the step I had taken, that your wise judgment, backed by the affection I know you bear me, has exonerated me long ago from any blame you may have been inclined to lay at my door.

"Once again, I wonder what you think of me now that you know I am in a monastery. I am half afraid that you will think I have carried my new religion too far, and that I am saving my own happiness and insuring peace for myself at your expense. This is not so, Rosamund, believe me. I have come here for peace, and I have come here to learn how to be happy, but it is only with a view of securing a more perfect life in the future for us both. What that life may be I cannot yet decide. Sometimes I think that the love of man for woman is not everything, that there are other Sacraments besides those of marriage; that more good may be done by quietly quitting one's place in the outer world and setting oneself apart to pray for the welfare of those one had left behind. But of this I am not yet sure. I desire to be convinced that these things are true, and I yet regard them with the eye of disbelief. They tell me here that as the weeks go by I shall become more firm and more set in my purpose. Of that I am not certain, either, but from time to time I will let you know if what they claim to be the true life of a Christian proves to me to be so. At present I am in a state of unrest. One hour I yearn for the world, and in the next I hate it. At dawn the chapel with the prayers and the dim light, the faint odour of sanctity, the soft music and the peace, prevail upon me to believe that here, and here only, is God to be found. In the evening, under identical circumstances, my whole manhood revolts, and my body cries out for the freedom that my soul will not permit it to snatch.

"Shall I tell you a little of the life here? Perhaps it will help you to form an opinion of my various moods just now, which even to myself are sometimes inexplicable.

"It was an August evening when I came and was received as a novice, a mere pupil in the profession of religion, by the monk who has the care and ordering of the lives of such who are as I am. This is a lovely place, and the wing that is set apart for the novices is clothed with creepers and small-leaved glistening ivy. The view from my little window is miles and miles of flat country towards a horizon which is but slightly broken by the low undulations that lie about the town of Stamford. The rooms that are on the other side of the corridor from mine look over a country road. Now and then, in the evening, a farm cart rumbles by carrying a load of weary bumpkins and supplies from the nearest village. That is all of outside life to be seen, and yet the novices whose rooms look out that way tell me that they spend hours crouching within the deep embrasures of their windows, behind the little curtain that runs across each alcove only to catch a view or an echo of strange faces and passing wheels.

"Our life is very simple, and the monotony of it sweeps away all marks of time. There is nothing here but day and night, and one so overlaps the other that each seems without end. When I first came it used to be dawn when we first rose for Matins, which are at four. Now that the nights are lengthening, it is more difficult to wake and rise from bed, and, after having lit the little taper which we all carry in our pockets, to pass quickly from one cell to another, rousing the occupant of each, and lighting the gas jets. That duty over—and it is one each novice takes in turn—one goes downstairs, and crossing the cloisters, which in these early autumn mornings are sometimes very keen, goes into the chapel. The little lamps that burn always before the statue of the Blessed Virgin are a guide to the altar where the candles are set ready to be lit. That done, one has to go to the belfry. At the foot of the stairs that lead up and away into an unseen distance there always stands a lantern ready to be lighted. There are three bells at the head of the staircase, and it is quite an art to ring them. They are started with one foot, then with the right hand and then with the left. Before the echo of the little peal has died away, one is out again in the cloisters ringing the sanctuary bell nine times. Then follows the shuffling of feet, and the novices, sleepy-eyed and yawning, come down in pairs and walk to their places in the choir of the chapel. The monks follow after in such order as best pleases them.

"When Matins are over most of us go back to bed again, but I have spent many of the fairer mornings out in the garden watching the sun rise and the silver mist float away like torn shreds of gauze over the tree tops. Morning after morning I have heard the lark's first song and watched the bees come out and the butterflies settle and feed on the dew-laden roses.

"Two hours later we all meet again in the choir for 'Prime,' and the day of study and prayer, and of such intercourse and relaxation as are permitted, begins. At 'prime' we first see the lay brothers. They are good, worthy men who have given up their pleasure and lives, as men of their class know such things, for hard work, implicit obedience, and endless service in the Church's cause. At a quarter past seven we breakfast in silence. At none of our meals are we allowed to speak, save at the great feast of St. Dominic, and on such rare occasions as the Bishop's visit to the monastery. Breakfast is the simplest of our meals. We have bread and coffee with sugar and milk; on Sunday we have butter. It is put up into very long, thin rolls, and it is quite an art so to help one's self as to get enough of it. It is strange to see how the little characteristics of selfishness and greediness come out over such a trifle, and how all the religion in the world does not seem to prevent a man from taking more than his fair share of a thing he likes to eat.

"At nine o'clock we repeat the Office of the Blessed Virgin Mary, and the time from then to mid-day is either passed in study, in private prayer, or in walking out in solemn silence in the gardens. I think that men feel better when they are alone with nature. The gardens here are very beautiful, and I never saw such roses, and it is in looking at them that one acknowledges the greatness of God. We go to the choir for a few minutes before dinner, which is at a quarter past twelve.

"The refectory, where all our meals are taken, is a large, well-lit room, with plain, distempered walls, only broken here and there by the picture of a saint or the presentment of some miracle. A great fixed seat goes all round the room and a narrow table is in front of that. The Prior sits at the head in an elbow chair and next to him is the Sub-prior. Both of them are kindly, good men, really imbued with the spirit of the religion they profess and deeply anxious that others should see things with their eyes. The Fathers and monks sit in their order of seniority all down the table on alternate sides. Then come the novices, who are placed in the order as they have entered the monastery. Such lay brothers who are not engaged in household duties, which they all take in turn, sit at the lower end of the table. We are served from the lowest to the highest, and the tables are cleared in the reverse order. In the centre of the room stands a desk, at which the monks in turn read a book, either of religious instruction or the life of one of the saints.

"You are a woman, and therefore will like details, so to please you I will tell you what we have to eat.

"The soup is made from vegetables, but sometimes we have a course of sardines or anchovies served with toast. Many kinds of fish come next. All are good and cooked to perfection, though very rarely is it fried. Quantities of vegetables are served to us, and various sorts of pastries and pies and fruit. Those who prefer preserves can have marmalade with *blanc mange*. Cheese and celery, with bread and one glass of beer, finish our meal. I have not as yet eaten other food than this, for the rules of the order ordain that no meat shall be served in the refectory, and that those who are in health shall observe the above diet.

"But near to where we dine is a small room called the meat room. Here the soup is made from meat, and joints and game are daily served. Twice a week and on Sundays all novices, unless they are in good health or desire to abstain, are obliged to dine in this room, and the Fathers themselves who are preaching or teaching, and all those who are in poor health or are engaged in a deep course of study, are allowed to go there. Conversation is permitted, and it must be very cheerful in there and bright, for I often hear loud voices and much laughter, but I mean to keep from it as long as I can, for my health is good, and the mood for companionship and conversation very seldom comes to me now.

"I do not want you, Rosamund, to think of me as being sad or in poor health; I never was stronger in my life. All my thoughts and instincts make for the best, and I know that I am happier here, where I am merely called Brother Paul, where no one knows who I really am or anything about me, than I should be outside. If I were in the world I should eat out my heart that I could not be with you, and a summer in Norway or climbing in Switzerland would seem to me merely an exile which would grow to be a purgatory.

"You see I am nearly at the end of my paper. We have to ask Father Zadock, the novice master, a good, kind soul, for writing materials. It is one of the petty rules that irks a little, for one is only given a single sheet of paper at a time and has to quibble to get another. I managed to get two to-day, and dare not ask for a third. When this letter is finished I must take it to Father Zadock unsealed, but he is a gentleman; he will not read it.

"Will you write to me and tell me of yourself and if you are angry with me or pleased? I have a feeling that you will be neither. I pray that you will regard my action as I want you to do—merely a way of finding patience and content until we may meet again. May God bless you.   PAUL."

CHAPTER XVIII

A RIVER REVERIE

PAUL's first letter was a great shock to Rosamund. Since the day when Lily Baumer had told her that her betrothed husband had, out of conviction, become a Roman Catholic, and retired into a monastery for a period of meditation and prayer, she had spent many anxious hours in viewing what even now seemed to her a most strange action. But out of her own simple faith she had persuaded herself that it had been the voice of God that had called to him to take this step. She had told the news to her uncle with bated breath and a look that her face might have worn if she had been announcing the death of a dear friend. Man of the world as he was, and viewing things from a wider ground than his niece could do, he also experienced a feeling of shock at the intelligence. He had always met Paul Carr in the hunting-field or in the ball-room, bicycling at break-neck speed down a quiet country road, or lounging in his stall at the opera. He had looked upon him as a very fair specimen of the average young English gentleman. If he had had a son of his own he would have been quite satisfied for him to be as Paul was—well-mannered, well-spoken, good-looking, and healthy-minded.

That a young man of Paul Carr's apparently unemotional temperament and quiet common-sense should suddenly give himself over—literally body and soul—to a Church which relied too much, as he thought, on outward

ceremony and sentimental show, he could not understand. He could appreciate a woman doing such a
thing—many of them who were soft and weak, nervous,
hysterical creatures who were soothed by the embroid-
eries on a vestment and exalted by a well-arranged
procession. As in duty bound he had spoken of the
matter to Margot Kerquham, and could scarcely help
echoing her heartfelt thanks that the strange step had
been taken before the rest of the family had been made
aware of the engagement between Paul and Rosamund.

"The earl would be horrified," Mrs. Kerquham had
said, "while as to the aunts, I cannot imagine what they
would say."

Rosamund, having done her duty as she felt it, did
not mention Paul's name again in the family circle, but
she thought of him often, and never resisted the temptation to pray for him every night as she might have
prayed for the soul of some one who was unregenerate,
or for a little child. And now this letter—his letter—
had followed her from London up to the Towers in Scotland, where the whole Kerquham family were assembled
together under Lord Kilbeggie's ancestral roof—enduring what Laura always called the yearly penance for
their sins.

Rosamund did not open her letter at the breakfast-
table, but slipped it into her lap, determined to wait until
she was away from all prying eyes in her favourite nook
at the head of the glen, a cool retreat where she spent
most of her time when at the Towers.

It was nothing more than a strange coincidence that
her great-uncle, the earl, who was possessed of a gaunt,
bony frame and a long, thin head fringed with scant
white hair, happened to read aloud that morning from
the day-old newspaper which came from Edinburgh,

that the son of an old friend of his had just "gone over to Rome." Lady Sophia Kerquham and Lady Charlotte Lundy, who was also on a visit to their brother, laid down their knives and forks in amazement, as the old man, after reading out the news, dashed down his fist upon the table and cried angrily:

"The power of these pestilent Priests grows every day. Fancy one of that clan being caught by their Popish mummeries."

"It will kill his mother," said Lady Sophia, shaking her head ominously over her coffee-cup. "The only comfort that she can find is that his father is dead. He was a staunch supporter of the Church of Scotland, and it would have broken his heart."

"If he had been a son of mine, I would have broken his head," cried the old earl in impotent anger.

"I would rather that my Hamish married a ballet girl than become a Roman Catholic," said Lady Charlotte, drawing herself up.

Lady Sophia shuddered at such a fearful alternative, and Lord Kilbeggie tapped his plate irritably.

"Charlotte, Charlotte, you do not know what you are saying. Heaven forfend that any one of our blood should ever do either the one or the other. The priests are bad enough, but I am not sure that those dancing women are not worse."

Mrs. Kerquham, who always carried the respect for her husband's relations to an exaggerated degree, ventured to interpose.

"It is a shocking thing, as you say, but for my part I think that for a young man to go on the turf is quite as bad."

Lord Kilbeggie looked across the table from under his white eyebrows.

"Niece Margot, you had best be holding your tongue. The world has spoilt you, or you would not talk about racing and betting and all such devil's inventions in any house of mine."

Mrs. Kerquham returned confusedly to the study of her plate. Honor, who was ready to argue with her mother on most points, varied the proceedings now by glaring at her great-uncle. Laura tittered in the aimless way she affected when the conversation was either boring her or beyond her comprehension. Rosamund felt her own bright colour fading from her cheeks. If they all said these dreadful things about a mere distant acquaintance who had changed his religion, what would they think if they knew that she had at that moment in her possession a letter dated from a monastery and written by a man who wore a monastic habit?

A girlish dread of being caught and questioned about her precious missive made her slip out of the room with her cousin Laura before the rest of the party.

"I am sorry to see Rosamund growing lax in her manners," commented Lady Charlotte, rather severely, as the girls' footsteps died away in the bare stone hall.

"Rosamund is going fishing," said Mr. Kerquham, ever ready to stand up for his favourite. "And she told Jock to be ready for her at the Water's Meet at nine o'clock."

"Manners should come before an unladylike sport," said Lady Charlotte, sternly, while the earl mumbled as he pushed his chair back from the table that such things as duty and politeness from the young to their elders had become dead letters since his day.

Out in the hall Rosamund busied herself by pulling on her tam-o'shanter and a pair of thick gloves, and seeing that her rod and flies were in order before she started. Laura sauntered over to the open doorway and stretched her arms wide.

"Heigh-ho!" she cried. "Here is another ghastly day begun."

"It is a lovely morning," said Rosamund, coming to her side and looking first down the glen where the trout stream rushed and swirled, and then up to the moors where the flying clouds still made a delicate tracery like lace above the purple heather.

"Oh! it's all very well for you," pouted Laura. "You seem to find some fun in tearing all over the place with a shock-headed gillie at your heels. What you are made of, I don't know. When you are not fishing you are clambering all over those dreadful moors with their hard stones and hateful, scrubby heather."

"Oh! Laura, how can you! It is quite lovely up there," expostulated Rosamund. "Why, yesterday evening as I was coming down the hill it all looked as though it were covered with purple plush. The sun caught it, and it shimmered with colour—and smelt—oh! so sweet."

"Well, you may like it," grumbled Laura, shrugging her shoulders. "All I know is that it scratches my shoes to pieces and makes me ache all over. One has to step like a well-trained horse, up to one's nose, to get about among the stuff."

Rosamund laughed as she looked down at Laura's slender feet, which were thrust into narrow, high-heeled slippers.

"My dear, you will walk about in such ridiculous things," she said. "Of course you get your shoes scratched and your ankles, too, when you go out in flimsy, low-cut affairs."

"Well, if you think I am going to wear great, big

horrid boots with no heels and no shape, you are mistaken," cried Laura, rudely. "I would not make such a fright of myself for anything. I would sooner sit in the house forever than be obliged to put such things on before I could go out."

Rosamund peeped down at her own sensibly shod feet.

"Of course they are not pretty," she admitted cheerfully, "but then you see one doesn't dress for effect up in the Highlands. You would be so much better, Laura, if you came out and had some air instead of always stopping in the house."

"You may think yourself lucky that I do not stay in bed, for there is nothing to get up for. Why one is obliged to come to such a hateful place as this I don't know. As to Uncle Kilbeggie and the aunts, they get more impossible every year. Did you hear what they were saying last night about the way my hair was dressed? It was positively impertinent the remarks they made."

"Of course, dear, they are not very much up in the fashions about here," said Rosamund, soothingly, "and your head was just the least little bit over-smart for a quiet family party."

"Smart or not smart, they are a lot of horrid old people, and I am sure I don't know why we are afflicted with them. Thank goodness! it is only for another week, and then we go to our own place and can have our own friends."

From within the dining-room came the sound of the pushing back of chairs and the tread of feet. Rosamund, afraid of being caught and delayed, stepped out on to the wide flight of grey stone steps.

"Well, I must be off or Jock will be tired of waiting," she cried, slinging her creel over one shoulder and putting her rod over the other. "Wish me luck, Laura!"

"Shan't do anything of the kind," said Laura. "I am sick to death of salmon."

A few yards from the house Rosamund plunged into the very heart of the glen which cleft the Highlands just there and made an evergreen wound in the deep bosom of the purple hills. Turning sharply to the left, she went up a narrow, rough path that overhung the brawling stream. It ran straight up the glen to where there was an open space among the trees and a deep trout pool famous for its fish and for the sport that could be got there. The gillie was waiting for her, and took the rod from her hands directly she came up, saying it was a perfect morning for sport and that she ought to do well to-day. But Rosamund's hand was in her pocket, and her fingers were clasped round the letter that lay there.

"I shall not fish this morning, Jock," she said. "You can go. I think Mr. Kerquham may want you. I may try a cast later on in the day; if so, I can manage by myself."

The reluctant Jock went his way down the narrow path, leaving Rosamund alone to enjoy the luxury of Paul's first letter. Like a child that has some special dainty on its plate which it keeps to the last, she teased herself with enforced deliberation. Very slowly she put her fishing basket on the ground and laid her rod beside it. Then, with the calmest deliberation, she looked about for a comfortable stone or mossy knoll, where she might sit at her ease. Just above her was a group of alders growing, and their roots, twining into the stony earth, made a natural chair. The sunshine glinted through the leaves and cast a golden pattern over the scant grass and clumps of moss. She walked towards the little knoll and carefully settled herself into it. Then she took off her hat, and pushing back the heavy hair from her forehead, drew out the letter and studied the envelope. After quite five minutes she broke the seal.

A smile was on her face as she did so, but before she unfolded the two closely written pages she compressed the corners of her mouth; for in a flash it came to her that it was no love letter that she was going to read, no honey sweet phrases of love and burning desires. It would be a chronicle of aspirations and fulfillments, a record of the doubts and hopes of a man who had taken the tremendous step of changing one religion for another in the wish to find true happiness and peace. With a face that was grave to sadness she ventured to approach such an outpouring of the soul as she felt the letter must contain.

She unfolded the sheets and began to read slowly and steadily, as though each word, however trivial, held a value of its own in her mind. When at length she had read to the last page and let the paper fall into her lap, she raised her eyes that were full of unshed tears, while her heart ached with the sense of pain and yearning that comes to those who read the words of one long lost. Two large drops fell, pattering on the paper she held in her trembling fingers. She passed her hands several times across her eyes before she could see to read the letter through a second time.

Then it was that a vague sense of disappointment mingled with her first sorrowful joy. "Why," she asked herself, "does he tell me so little in so much? He writes to me of the chapel and of the little sanctuary for private prayers, but he does not tell me of his thoughts; he does not even say whether he is happy. He only tells me that he eats so much fish and bread; he paints for me the rooms and the furniture. The three words, 'I am happy,' or 'I am content,' would have been enough for me. I only want to think of him that way.''

But after a time the sweetness of her nature and the charity of her disposition overcame her first thrill of dissatisfaction.

"He has only written what he thinks will please me best, and perhaps he is afraid of shocking me too much by advancing his own tenets and writing of his own new theories. I know he believes he gives me greater happiness by the relation of his life's daily details than if he poured out his soul's longings to me; for it is impossible that the sum of his life is bounded by such a narrow horizon as he speaks of. And he says that he will write to me again. This is only a letter to break things to me, and the next one will be different. Perhaps, too, everything is so new to him that he feels he must tell it to some one. But his faith—his doctrine—is new to me, too. I wish—ah!—I wish he had written of that!''

She sighed a little. "I suppose he remembers that I am only a woman and not supposed to understand such things. Perhaps he is right. Perhaps he has done the kindest thing. If he had sent me a letter filled with longings and the dreams and desires that must come to him in the dim chapel in the early morning, I might have been discontented and wanted to know how he slept and lived and walked. One is never quite pleased with the things one has. I am sure that out of his love for me he has done the best.''

She read the letter again in a happier spirit and found a new interest waking in her about his little cell and the big refectory he told her of, and the bare, cold corridors

with their grey painted walls. But each fresh turn of
thought carried her back to him in the chapel or at his
prayers. It was in those things that she was most interested, and it was about that part of his life that she
wanted to know.

Suddenly she cried aloud: "He asks me to write to
him. I suppose that I may. Yet I always thought that
they were so strict in monasteries. Shall I ask Uncle
Alban about it?"

She drew her brows together in thought. "He will
not know, and after what was said this morning I
scarcely like to remind him about what Paul has done.
I cannot make out why they all think it is so dreadful to
become a Roman Catholic. Aunt Charlotte said it was
like marrying a ballet girl or doing something disgraceful like that. I think I shall ask Uncle Kilbeggie one
day if he would think it awfully wicked for a Roman
Catholic to become a Presbyterian. I wonder what he
would say. I wish I understood more about such things.
It seems to me that women are not taught any religion
at all. They are just made to put on their best clothes
and go to church on Sundays, and that is the beginning
and the end of it. We are not told why we pray or why
we must believe. We are simply taught how to find our
places in our prayer-books, and when we were small
Aunt Margot liked us to read a chapter out of the Bible
every day. We didn't do it often, and when we did we
were never told what bits to read, so I don't think it can
have done us much good. I wonder if Uncle Alban would
give me some books about religion. I should like to
know something about it, and what is the real difference
between my form of faith and Paul's. If I am going to
marry a Roman Catholic it is only right that I should
understand about these things. At present I know

nothing—and I do not fancy that Aunt Sophia or Aunt Charlotte knows any more. They just do and say the things that they have been accustomed to all their lives, and they have been taught that to think differently or to use another form of worship constitutes a sin. If one comes to think it out, it is really impossible that it can be like that. It cannot matter to God whether we kneel in one place or stand up in another, or whether we say our prayers in Latin or English, so long as we say them at all."

Her face was calm—almost happy—as she folded Paul's letter and put it into her pocket. She looked at her rod and at the open book of flies that glistened in all the glory of amber, green and purple in the sun. As in a dream she picked up her hat and was about to put it on her head, when she let it fall again.

"No!" she said, with that characteristic straightforwardness of hers. "I will keep my promise to myself; I will not fish this morning. I will sit here and think of Paul."

CHAPTER XIX

A CLOISTERED LIFE

"MY DEAR ROSAMUND:

"Having broken the ice by writing to you, I cannot withstand the temptation of again sending you a letter. I hope it will not be counted to me as a sin.

"Yesterday was the occasion of my formal reception into the novitiate of this monastery and of my clothing as a Dominican novice. I will not tell you, for perhaps you would scarcely understand, of the spiritual preparation that I went through before this most important ceremony. I had not slept for two nights, passing them on my knees in the dark before the little crucifix that hangs in my room, while such time as I could spare from other studies I have been praying in the novices' private chapel or downstairs in the big chapel. Father Zadock helped me very much, and the Prior himself saw me twice and gave me much good advice and wise counsel about the step I was taking.

"The reception of a novice is very simple and yet very impressive. It woke in me the feeling that I think girls must have after they have been confirmed—it was as though part of me—my heart or my soul—had been made new again. It was the first time that I had ever been in the chapter room of the monastery. It is a fine apartment, lighted with small windows set very high in the walls, which are painted in frescoes with scenes from the lives of saints of the Dominican order. All round are seats for the monks and Fathers and novices, and the Prior's great elbow chair is in the centre. For this occasion I cast aside the heavy black cassock and leather belt which, since my arrival here, I have worn over my ordinary clothes. The dean, who is the eldest of the novices, cut my tonsure afresh, for though we are all tonsured every fortnight in the summer, my hair grows very quickly, and though it had been cut but ten days before I had it done again for the ceremony of my reception.

"Almost in the guise of a beggar I was admitted into the chapter room, and prostrated myself in supplication before the Prior, who, following the form set forth, consented to receive me into the novitiate of St. Dominic. Then I was led to the altar in the church and there clothed by the Prior's own hands in a white cloth habit, over which was placed the *scapula*, which hangs free and loose both back and front. Then I was given a round cape which just reaches my elbows, a white cowl, and the small black skull cap which both novices and monks wear. The black crucifix that hangs on my breast bears the figure of Christ on it in moulded brass, and my rosary is black, too. It is warm weather now, so I do not wear the long black cloak which we always don in winter and which earned us the name of the 'Black Friars.' After my clothing followed a long service of jubilation at my reception. The occasion was made one of great rejoicing, because it is now some months since a novice has been received here.

"I did not tell you, did I, in my last letter, of my fellow-novices? We are a strangely assorted little circle, with nothing in common between us but religion, for many of them, like myself, do not purpose taking the full vows of poverty, chastity, and obedience. The dean, who is the superior novice in point of time, is a man I do not like. He means well, and is very earnest, but he is hard and narrow, not of gentle birth, and too fond of exercising the authority which chance has given him. It is his duty to see that the lights throughout the novitiate are extinguished by half-past eight, and it is he who passes down the corridors during the night to listen if we sleep or are awake in our cells. His name is Henry, and we all fear him, for he has it in his power to get us punished, while we are helpless to refute such charges as he may bring against us.

"Next in seniority to him is a queer little soul, who was only nine months back a Protestant clergyman. He is about forty-five years old, and makes no secret of having joined the Holy Church because he was tired of being an ill-paid curate to country parsons, and utterly failed to get a living of his own. He has always struck me as being deficient in the qualities that should go to make a really good man. He is fretful and pettish, and lays great weight on small things. Before he came to live here he made it a condition with the authorities that he should be permitted to have one pipe and a glass of whisky and water every night before he went to bed. He is allowed to do this, but he partakes of his indulgences in an empty cell between the hours of eight and half-past. It seems such a solitary thing to do, to sit all by oneself and smoke and drink, but he told me that he could not do without it, and I believe that from the moment he gets up in the morning he spends the whole day in looking forward to his strange evening's relaxation.

"Brother Peter is a novice who rather interests me, for his cell is next to mine. He is a quiet, saturnine man of about my own age. Like myself he is a convert, and was until about two years ago a civil servant in the general post office. He is a little strange in his manner. I hear him muttering to himself sometimes all night long. He says that spirits visit him in his cell. He is subject sometimes to the most extraordinary outbursts of rage, and only three days ago, in an uncontrollable freak of temper, kicked the poor little ex-parson most cruelly. He is always doing penance and being punished for something or another, but he persists that he has a vocation, and that when he is ordained a priest he is going to be a great preacher among men. He has a wonderful memory, of which he is very proud, and which he cultivates to excess. He boasts that he knows nearly the whole of the Bible by heart, and indeed I believe that this is true, for often when I walk behind him in the garden I hear him saying to himself whole chapters from it. One Monday, when we novices with Father Zadock and the dean were, according to rule, strolling through the fields, this strange man, who remained at my elbow the whole time, said to himself the whole of the New Testament.

"Another of the novices used to be a Dissenter. I often wonder what train of circumstances brought him to such a change of thought and religion. He is a little, fat man, not very earnest in his professions nor at all clever. He seems to regard the services with less interest than he does his meals, for he is fond of good living, and takes every opportunity of going to the meat room. On days that he is obliged to dine in the refectory with the rest of us, he always stays behind after we have finished, and has as much of the meal as he can get served to him over again. He has a disagreeable way of smacking his lips and remarking on the food. He strikes me as being a man who until he came here never had sufficient to eat. He is already wondering how he is going to manage when Lent comes, and he dreads the Ember days that precede the Christmas feast. One day last week I caught him stealing plums in the kitchen garden. If it had been the dean that had seen him he would have had to do penance after the next monthly 'proclamation,' when, in the common room of the novitiate, the shortcomings and sins of the novices are proclaimed at full length, and punishment is meted out by the dean and the novice master.

"Nothing to my mind so shows the worldly spirit that animates even a holy community like this as this 'proclamation.' It has in it an element of pettiness and unfairness, for it seems to me unjust that men should be set to spy upon one another's little failings and report small breaches of rules. Each novice in his turn is indicted, lying during the time on his right side at full length on the floor, and forbidden by the rules of the order to deny anything or to attempt any exculpation. The whole system is governed on the lines of seniority, and I, being the youngest novice here, can be indicted by those above me, but may not in my turn, even if I would wish to do so, bring any charge against them.

"I must admit, however, that the punishments and penances, as a rule, are as petty as the crimes for which they are dealt out. A very ordinary one is to be made to kneel or to lie in the form of a cross and recite a given number of paternosters. The other day after Brother Peter had hurt Brother Henry by kicking him, he was made to kneel before him and apologise before us all for his act. As he showed temper in doing this, his first punishment was supplemented by an order to sit on the floor of the refectory during the dinner hour and eat his meals from his knees there. The greatest punishment of all, and one which is but seldom administered, obliges the delinquent, during supper time, to crawl on his knees and hands under the refectory table, kissing in turn the feet of the Fathers. Excommunication, which practically means confinement to one's cell, is also but seldom ordered, and then only under what are considered the gravest circumstances.

"Have I told you that twice a week we retire to our cells for the purpose of using the 'discipline?' The amount of pain inflicted is optional, and very different from the discomfort which arises during the weekly 'discipline' held in the common room during the Lenten fast. Then, with bared shoulders each in turn receives from the whip four strokes to each one of twenty verses of the Psalm that begins: '*Misere, mei Deus.*' That is the moment when a private quarrel or a personal dislike can be avenged; for if the lash is wielded roughly and strikes the face or breast it cuts keenly.

"Once in each year all the denizens of the monastery meet in the painted chapter room, and the Prior himself 'disciplines' us with a long, thin wand.

"The novice with whom I am most in sympathy is a young man who came here a few weeks before I did. He is known as Brother Basil, and he is a tradesman's son. He is very simple in manner, and evidently never had any knowledge of the world to lay aside when he came in. His whole soul is wrapped in religion, and his greatest ambition is to so mortify his flesh that his sacrifices shall be counted for good against the overwhelming wicked-ness of mankind. He fasts beyond the rules of the order, and wears himself out with vigils. When of an evening we are allowed to recreate ourselves in the common room of the novitiate, where a few illustrated papers, an old grand piano, and a musical box are kept, he sits

apart conning his prayers, or steals up to the private
chapel on the first floor. When we take our weekly walk
in the meadows, where we are allowed to smoke, to pluck
flowers, and to wander about as we choose in twos and
threes, he seats himself beneath a tree and tells his rosary
until it is time for us to return. During the first month
that he was here they found him one dawn in a dead
faint at the foot of the altar, and it then came out that
he had eaten no food for three days because he had at
one meal succumbed to the temptation and taken two
helpings of butter. Ordinary conversation, such talk as
we make among ourselves here, seems hateful to him,
and if one will not discuss religious subjects with him, he
goes away silent and sad to walk alone and meditate on
our sins—and perhaps his own virtues.

"Poor fellow! I am very sorry for him, for the religion that he is hugging so fondly to his breast does not
even bring him happiness and consolation. He has
transformed his God into an angry being who is to pass
all time and all eternity in dealing out terrible punishments to poor human souls. The Prior speaks with him
often, and has tried to point out to him that the Church
has consolation for those who live a higher life and die
in the odour of sanctity, but even that will not suit his
mood. He takes his religion as a child would take a
nasty medicine; believing on the one hand that it is
good for him, and yet dreading and fearing it. When he
administers self-chastisement twice a week in his cell,
he draws blood from his thin, starved body, and he
resents almost with tears the jokes that some of the
novices make about their own half-hearted administration of the 'discipline,' a whip which to the lay mind
would look like a cat-o'-five-tails. One night when
Brother Henry was saying how he had managed to stain

the lashes of his 'discipline' with a little red sealing wax, poor Brother Basil spent the night in the chapel praying for one whose soul was so lost to all true righteousness. He told me the other day he did not think he should stay here long.   He thinks no one here is earnest enough in his prayers or sufficiently severe in his mortifications.

"He went to the library the other day and borrowed some books about the Trappist monasteries which lie hidden among the fastnesses of Eastern Europe.   He told me about them in such rare moments as he ever devotes to speech, and as he spoke his pale face and haggard eyes were quite transfigured at the idea that somewhere on earth he could devote himself to a living death.

"In strange contrast to him is Brother Martin, a red-headed merry Irish lad. He is always in disgrace, and yet takes his punishments so cheerfully, and expresses such genuine regret at his shortcomings that even the Prior, before whom he has been sent several times, cannot find it in his heart to be really angry with him.   He breaks every rule that governs the community with the most extraordinary regularity.   He talks during the hours of enforced silence, whistles loudly as he runs up and down the stairs, and chatters to the lay brothers when he meets them in the garden or corridors—and this last is a most grave disobedience.   He is lax in chapel, and fidgety at choir practice.   He stares about him every time he goes into church, and if he is spoken to answers in the fresh, breezy, loud-voiced manner with which he must until a few months ago have hailed his friends across the fields.   He is altogether an undisciplined, good-hearted soul.   Why he came here I cannot make out, for his religious exercises seem to bore him consistently.   I suppose, however, being one of many sons in an old and poor Irish Catholic family, he was destined from his birth for the priesthood, and against his inclinations and his capabilities has been doomed to it.

"Are we not a strange assortment? Very much out of keeping with one another, I am afraid, and even in our religious exercises having but little in common, for we all view them from a different standpoint, and all regard them as means to a different end. I did not think when I came here that a monastery could be such an epitome of the outside world.

"I have discovered that I have quite a talent for using my fingers. We have here, on the upper floor of the Novitiate, a fine large room almost the length of the wing, where we are sent at stated times to do what is called manual labour. Here we make the tapers which we all carry in our pockets for use in the early morning when we call one another and light the chapel gas for Matins. Here, too, we make rosaries, and that is very pretty work. The small plyers and the fine brass or silver wire and the beads of different kinds are all dainty and interesting to use. Some of the novices are so devoted to the occupation that they make rosaries even during their recreation time. There is a very fine plant for bookbinding here, for two years ago one of the novices was a bookbinder, and taught the trade to several of the others. I am sorry that we are all ignorant of it now, for I think I should have liked it. As it is, we get no further than sewing the books, and when we have fastened together all the loose leaves we can find, we unpick the stitches and begin again. Some of us would like to work in the garden, but we are not allowed to do that. All other manual labour in the monastery, save the cleaning and the tidying of each cell by its occupant, is done by the lay brothers, who are a pleasant, cheery set of men.

"In such time as I have free from the daily round of prayer, study, the hours of silence, and of choir practice and the recital of offices, I read a great deal. The library here is fairly well stocked with histories and books of travel, and even story books. I am, however, most interested in works that deal with the religion I have adopted, for I feel that even now I am very ignorant on the subject. I have just finished Bishop Ullathorn's great work on God, and am going to begin a volume of Milner's 'Essays,' and Roderigue's 'Christian Perfection,' which the Prior particularly wishes me to study.

"Rosamund, when are you going to write to me? A letter from you would be the best reading of all. Tell me something of yourself, and tell me that you still think of me as you did before we parted.   Yours,

"PAUL."

CHAPTER XX

ROSAMUND'S RECORD

It took Rosamund some weeks to comply with Paul's request that she would write to him. His second letter had brought her a greater sense of disappointment and doubt than his first had done. The smallness of the details of his life struck her more keenly than before and seemed to build a great wall of reserve between him and herself. Thàt she was a thing apart from· his occupations and actions almost forced her to regard him as a stranger, and not the Paul she had known and loved.

Perhaps, too, it was the vague, superstitious regard which all women hold for religious institutions that chained her thoughts when she at length took up her pen and set paper before her to write to him. She could not free herself from the idea that it could not be right for her to comment on all the frivolous surroundings of her life to a man, who, even for a time, was set apart in a holy life. How could she tell him of the Highland meetings and the balls which followed them? How could she write to him about the number of salmon she had killed, or relate the prowess of her uncle and his friends in stalking deer? How could she retail to a man whose mind should be filled with spiritual things the foolish gossip that surrounded a quarrel Honor had had with her *fiancé?*

It would be impossible to tell him—he who was cut off from the world for the time and forbidden to see her for so many months—that Lord St. Ives was staying on a visit and again pressing his attentions upon her.   Yet these things made up the sum and parcel of her life that autumn, for Rosamund had lately grown into the habit of putting all thought behind her and of living merely for the hour and what it brought.   Almost unconsciously she was giving way to a kind of moral dram-drinking, trying by mental excitement and by physical exertion to deaden the sense of weariness that crept over her when she was alone or unoccupied.   She sometimes feared that she was weakly giving way to a bad habit, and that she was shirking the responsibilities that would have to be faced sooner or later.   She felt that she was only putting off an evil day which must inevitably come, but more than anything she realised how utterly alone she was at this time, for her uncle was shooting hard and painting hard, and his moments of leisure were very rare.

She sat for hours one morning in her room trying to frame a letter to Paul.   Her natural reserve and modesty checked any indication or any terms of endearment, pride stayed her when she longed to pour out her troubles, and a sense of incongruity between her position and his arrested all expression of mere worldly matters. The morning had gone by and she had written nothing and still was no nearer what she should write, only she grew angry with herself for being so cowardly, so undetermined, and so weak.   Then suddenly a thought came to her.   She would keep a diary, in which she would record every incident of her daily life, and which, when they met next year she would lay without reserve in Paul's hands, so that at least he should never feel that any one day of her life had been hidden from him.   Now she would merely write to him and say what she was doing, and promise to send him every now and again a little line of assurance that she was well and true to him.

She wrote the words down. They were very few, and did not fill more than the front of the sheet of paper. It looked such a tiny scrap when it was finished that she was almost ashamed to put it in an envelope and address it to him, but she felt that it was best done that way, and that she should never forgive herself if anything she said in a longer, fuller letter distracted his thoughts unduly or disturbed his life.

That done, she drew towards her a quantity of paper and began with the careful minuteness that was part of her nature to write down on it a statement of the facts that were then influencing her daily life. She fenced with nothing. She did not put anything down in extenuation or exaggeration. She did her best to make it all as truthful and as clear as possible. She tried hard to keep her own feelings and her own thoughts within what she wrote. It was only here and there that a faint note of sorrow that she now saw so little of her uncle, or an indication of the heart loneliness she was then suffering, slipped among the pages.

"The surroundings of my life," she wrote, "are imperceptibly but surely changed—or is it I who am changed and imagine a difference in others? Perhaps it is my fancy that Aunt Margot looks upon me more severely than she has ever done, and my cousins alternately slight or sneer at me. While even my dear uncle does not seem to have the leisure for my company that he used to do. Sometimes I think that they are trying to make me discontented, with a view to forcing me into some other life.

"Lord St. Ives arrived here on a visit last week. He has been out shooting almost every day with Uncle

Alban and the other men who are in the house. I have gathered from the way he speaks that his visit here is to be an indefinite one. I am sorry for this, because I cannot like him. I might perhaps get over my aversion a little if he would not always so persistently intrude himself upon my notice. But the longest days on the moors come to an end, then there are the late afternoons and dinners and the evenings, and Lord St. Ives is always at my side. He has not since that night in May ever dared to insult me again with any outspoken admiration or demonstration, but I feel instinctively that he is only here because of me. Of Honor he takes no notice. Laura he treats like a spoilt child. . . . .

"Every evening Lord St. Ives asks me to sing, and if I demur at all or excuse myself he appeals to Aunt Margot, and she commands me to do my best to make myself agreeable, and not to give myself airs. He always sits by the piano while I play, and however much I.may look at the keys or fix my eyes and my attention on the music, I always know that his eyes are wandering over my face and my throat and neck, and it makes me tingle to the tips of my fingers. For the last three nights I have made the excuse of having a cold, and have come down to dinner in a high gown. He asked me last night why I did so, and told me I had no business to cover myself up as much as all that. I wish he would go away, or, if he stays, I wish he would leave me alone. . . . .

"Another fortnight has gone by, and Lord St. Ives is still here. Twice the guests staying in the house have been changed, but he shows no signs of leaving. Laura this morning said she was sick of the sight of him, and wished I would bring matters to a head so that I might be engaged to him, and that then perhaps he would go. 'He wants you,' she said, in her blunt way, 'and mother means him to have you. You had better give in at once.' But I cannot do it; Paul has my promise for a year, and whatever happens at the end of that time I will at least hold to my word until he himself tells me that he loves me no longer. . . . .

"I had another letter from Paul yesterday. I love to see his handwriting on an envelope; it thrills me with joy to press out the folds from the sheets of paper over which his dear fingers have passed—and yet I always feel so unhappy by the time I have finished reading what he has written. Like all the others it is full of trivialities. He says the leaves are falling fast and the creepers that grow over the house hang like flaming banners of crimson silk against the grey walls. It is very cold there in the early morning, and he dreads the days when it is his turn to rise in the chill dark and rouse the monastery for Matins. He says it is so eerie to go down into the damp chapel, and by the light of a feeble taper to wander up the aisles and make ghostly sounds with his own footsteps. He tells me as a joke—that when he lit the gas one morning in Father Zadock's room and gave him the greeting of the order, '*Benedicamus Dominie,*' instead of answering '*Deo gratius,*' as he should, the Father only roared from his bed, 'Put out that gas and go to the devil!' He tells me that that unfortunate creature who was so odd when he first went there has since gone mad and tried to kill first a lay brother and then himself. Paul has been preaching his first sermon. It was at the eleven o'clock service, and only those in the monastery were present. He says it was very badly written, and he hopes he will not have to do another. He has been punished for going into the kitchen, where, it seems, he had no business, and he and the head novice, whom he calls the dean, have fallen out about the cutting of his tonsure. He has lately taken to collecting botanical specimens for a certain Father Lucius, who is something of a naturalist. Father Lucius smokes a great deal, and the novices make an excuse of going to his cell, so that their clothes should not betray them when they smoke themselves. . . . .

"The musical box in the common room of the novitiate has a broken spring, and the novices have invented a new game by which they can play the 'Dead March' in 'Saul' as fast as a galop or as slowly as a dirge, just as it pleases them. Some one was ill in the monastery the other day. Paul does not say who, but three or four of them rummaged among the old bottles of medicine which had been put aside from time immemorial in the *infirmorium*, and picking out the first thing they could find, gave it to the sick man. A monk has lately died there. Paul tells me he was a bad-tempered man and unpopular in the monastery, but was a wonderful artist. He illustrated in black and white stories for some of the magazines, and exhibited his pictures from time to time in London. Just before he died he painted a portrait of Paul. Paul says that if the portrait is like him, it shows him to have grown thinner and to have lost the colour of his eyes and lips.

"Paul is no longer the youngest novice. An Italian has come to the monastery lately. He is a man of good birth, but of strange habits and but little education. He can only speak a jargon of Italian, Latin, and English, and his habits are ultra-foreign and unclean. The others make him sing to them in the common room of an evening, and he improvises tunes to words that have no meaning. Paul says that the new novice spends most of his time praying to a hideous little Italian picture of the Virgin, and that in his cell he keeps a queer collection of fruit and dead flowers, candle ends, and such ragged bits of stuff and ribbon as he has been able to accumulate. When on Sunday the Prior goes round the monastery for *Asperges* and sprinkles every cell in turn, the visit made to Brother Lorenzo's is the briefest. A novice was severely punished the other day for picking up his habit to run faster when playing football.

"And then Paul finishes his letter by telling me he loves me and thinks of me and longs for me. What does it all mean, this chronicling of childish punishments and petty gossip—this little, narrow, sordid world in which nothing is of any moment save the looks or the speech of any of the community? There is not one word to imply that he has found the comfort he sought—or even that he has been disappointed. He only mentions the chapel as a place that is cold and filled with weird shadows and ghostly sounds in the early mornings. His preaching has given him no pleasure; his whole life at present seems to be wasted. Paul, Paul, what made you do this thing? Why did you not come to me in your great trouble, and together we might have met it and fought it? . . . .

"I wonder whether I was weak and to blame in giving way to my uncle's rule? Perhaps it has all been my fault, and I should have forgotten the duty and the gratitude and the love I owed to my family, and left them all in disobedience and in anger and gone to Paul and helped him. Now it seems to me that we have both made a fearful mistake—I, in so easily giving him up, and he in fearing his own strength and his capability to live in the world without me to help him. Each time I hear from him I grow more unhappy. I blame myself for the past, and I tremble in anticipation of what the future may bring. I have sent him another little letter to tell him I have received his. That is all I can do, and I have, even in writing that, to force myself to measure each word for fear that I should say too much.   .   .   .   .

"We all came to the Manor House three days ago from Scotland, and go to London to-morrow to buy some horses. Cubbing has already begun, and uncle is keen to start work. I don't know that I am looking forward to it. It must be myself, after all, that is changed, for this time last year I was wild at the idea of having a couple of mounts of my own, and of all the sport and fun of the winter.   .   .   .   .

"The last three weeks of our stay in Scotland were not happy ones. Aunt Margot was not well. I think she is changing very much, and I fear that among other things she is troubled about Lord St. Ives and me. He did not speak to me while we were there, but I know he did to her, and his last words before leaving were that he would be in Midshire early in December. How I dread that time! It used to be such a happy month, with Christmas for its ending, and all the good wishes and presents and kindliness that came with that day. This Christmas will be very different from last. Honor will be married and gone away on her honeymoon, and Paul will not be here. Paul's last letter tells me he has not been well, and has been ordered to eat meat. He and the dean have had more quarrels, and Paul was excommunicated for two days to his cell. His letter was very short and very hard. It seemed to me as though it were written by a man whose heart was crushed within him, or who was suffering from some terrible disappointment. I do so pray that he is not finding out that he has made a mistake.   .   .   .   .

"Honor's wedding is over, and the house is quiet again. To-morrow is Christmas Day, but we are having no party here. Aunt Margot's health grows worse, and she never comes down now until nearly luncheon time. I have not heard from Paul for three weeks. I wonder if anything is wrong. Laura has gone away for Christmas; I am glad, because the silence of this house and her mother's illness were making her so irritable and resentful against every one. She has grown to take it as a personal injury to herself when, from one cause or another, she cannot fill the house with her own friends. My grey mare, 'Silvertop,' broke her leg yesterday by jumping short over that stone wall at the top of Farmer Viner's copse. Uncle says she will have to be shot. I am so sorry; she was such a darling, and carried me beautifully. I wonder if I shall hear from Paul to-morrow or at the New Year. : . . .

"I am writing to-day with all my windows wide open. The rooks are so busy in the trees and all the little birds are making love in the shrubbery that runs under my window. The last meet will be in another fortnight, and then back to town once more we go. Aunt Margot is better, but the least thing fatigues her nowadays, and we have had very few people staying here this winter for the balls. Laura has taken to playing golf, or rather she walks round the links with Captain Fairleigh, a rather nice looking man who has for the past month been quartered at Shellerly Barracks. He is supposed to admire athletic girls, so Laura has copied the cut of my country skirts and taken to wearing a deer-stalker hat and going for long walks with the captain. Lord St. Ives is in the south of France. He was here for a while in January, but I am glad to say, left me more in peace. I have not heard from Paul since the middle of December, although I have written to him many times, beseeching him to tell me if aught is amiss with him, or if his heart is changed. In a few weeks now the time of our probation will be over, and we shall be free at least to meet—if nothing more. Does he remember this, and will he come to see me? After so long a silence on his side, it is difficult for me to write again, but yet I feel almost tempted to cast aside all reserve and pride and tell him that I am longing for the hour that is to bring us together once more. . . . .

"We are settled down again in town for the season. Uncle had hoped to let 'The Hurst,' but Aunt Margot, though very weak, has insisted on one more season for Laura. Honor and her husband are staying here. The house is full from morning till night. Aunt Margot is herself again, and we are engaged every day and evening in the week. The past year might be nothing but an evil dream if it were not that Paul is not here, but to-day three weeks, if he remembers, and if he still loves me, he ought to come."

CHAPTER XXI

YOUNG BLOOD

ONE day early in the long and bitter winter Paul wished to write another letter to Rosamund. To obtain materials to do this he had to go through the form of asking the novice master for envelope and paper. A week earlier the good Father Zadock had left for Rome, to sojourn there in one of the great Dominican monasteries for the winter. He had been replaced in his position of authority and responsibility by an austere member of the brotherhood, whose reign over the novices threatened to make their lives very different from those they had passed under the easy-going, genial rule of Father Zadock.

Father Joseph was a stern man; his early manhood had been stormy, and his repentance and retirement from the world accompanied by the upheaval of his entire nature. Like many men who had passed loose lives outside, he was a martinet in all that concerned authority, observance, and self-abasement, once he was within the pale. He was a man who fasted and prayed and used his "discipline" with a fierce satisfaction in every sting it gave him. He was anticipating the monthly "proclamation" of his pupils' shortcomings with a sardonic pleasure, and was already devising heavy punishments for their peccadilloes and petty sins. He looked sternly at Paul as he proffered his request.

"You write many letters, do you not, my son?"

"Not more than some of the others," answered Paul.

"Do not spoil that sheet of paper," said the Father.
"You will get no more from me. Father Zadock was
too lenient in such matters."

Paul took up the single sheet of paper and envelope,
and moved to leave the room.

"Mind that your letter is brought here unsealed when
it is finished," said the monk.

"I have always observed the rules about letters,"
answered Paul, rather defiantly, as he turned round in
the doorway.

Father Joseph affected not to hear, and bent again
over his book.

Paul in his letter to Rosamund laid this time but
little stress upon his own daily life. Rather did he write
of the New Year that was within measurable time and
was to bring them together once more. In a half-
hearted way—for he dared not acknowledge it even to
himself—he implied that his present life was fast becoming a weariness to him; that he had not found in it that
which he had sought, and that though he meant to hold
to his word and keep his novitiate of twelve months, he
should, after the New Year, count the days that would
make him free once more and bring him to her side.

It was not a long letter, but it was quite enough for
Father Joseph when a little later he drew it out of the
envelope, and—justified by the rules of his order—read
it from beginning to end. With the document in his
hand he went straight to the Prior, and together they
read it again and again, gathering from it that the
novice Paul had been writing to a woman the whole time
he had been in the monastery, as well as receiving letters from her. The Prior was deeply grieved, and
Father Joseph angry and outraged, but they decided that
for the moment Paul should not know his secret had

been discovered. These worthy men of God still retained enough of the leaven of the devil to know that a young man thwarted in his heart's desires is as likely as not to prove troublesome, and openly to defy all the rules of the order, and perhaps to leave the monastery in scandalous haste.

Therefore they agreed between themselves that special "novena," or prayers, should be said for him in the chapel every day, though his name should not be mentioned in them. And so Paul drifted on through the dark winter months, writing his letters to Rosamund, and wondering why none ever came from her.

As the new year grew to its second month, he wrote her, saying he was now counting the hours, as a school-boy counts the time to the holidays, to the fair morning when he should go outside the gates a free man, take train to London, and clasping her dear hands in his, claim her for his own. Whatever faint idea he might have had in the early days when he had decided to enter the monastery of feeling a vocation for a secluded life had dropped from him. The long months of rest, the monotonous passage of the hours, the repeated periods of solemn silence, during which he was free to think of what he pleased, had all tended to make him regard life from a healthier and wider point of view. He recognised that what he had thought a terrible misfortune a few months back had really been for his own good, that it had steadied him, given him a newer sense of responsibility and a more settled chance of true happiness. He still felt that he did not wish to go back to society, but he no longer endured the bitterness which had filled his heart and soul when, in the past summer, all his world had idly cut him for what he now realised was a mere whim of fancy.

He desired once more a healthy, manly life. He did not regret for one moment that he had been received into the Roman Catholic Church, for in his hour of trial he had won great comfort from its ministrations, and he still felt that it was the best and safest religion for him. But he now perceived that men can do more good out in the world, living clean lives themselves and making others happy, than by wearing out their bodies and breaking their hearts in dim, incense-perfumed chapels, or amid the four walls of a living tomb.

He longed, with all the healthy instincts of a man who has just recovered from a long illness, to live again. He wanted to hear the babble of voices, and to feel the touch of soft white hands. He wanted to feel the fresh rush of air blow past his face as he rode over the green fields. He longed for the kindly greeting, the cheery word, the whole-hearted laugh of the men of his world, and for the humanising instinct that comes from mingling with gracious women and innocent children.

As day after day went by, and winter died before the coming spring, his soul was more outside the high, red walls than within them. Day after day he was reproached for indifference at services, and reproved for breaking the rules of the order. His heart was so light that his voice and feet grew light with it, and he was in perpetual disgrace for running or shouting or singing as he passed along the straight garden paths and watched the buds bursting on the trees and the fruit blossoms gleaming like snow in the golden sunshine.

But he cared nothing for the punishments, the perpetual excommunications and enforced apologies; his only trouble was Rosamund's silence, and every day that passed brought him nearer to an explanation of that. His letters to her were all full of the future, and one

fair, warm day in mid-spring, when the life blood ran
hotly through his veins, he could not for the world's sake
restrain himself from pouring out to her all the passion
that he felt.

Father Joseph's brow, as he read that letter, grew
black as thunder. Generalities about the monastery,
foolish babblings about the spring, little messages indicative of affection or regret might be overlooked, but
a letter that breathed in every line a man's passion for a
woman which was full of virile longing and the adoration
that flesh gives to flesh, was too much.

The next day Paul was summoned before the Prior
and his accuser, the novice master, and then he learned
the secret of Rosamund's silence; learned, too, that during all these months she must have deemed him forget-
ful if not untrue. In a moment his own disappointment
and the suffering she must have endured rushed upon
him like a sea. He forgot his vows as a novice, the
schooling of the past eleven months, the restraint that
enforced obedience had placed upon him for so long; he
forgot that he was before his superiors in age, in wisdom,
and in monastical life. He only remembered that he
was a man outraged by men. With all the restrained
passion boiling to his lips he accused them of having
spied upon him, of having betrayed him. He demanded
the letters which had been sent to him and which he had
never received; he ordered them to return those that
had been written and never sent. In a very frenzy of
rage, he plucked the crucifix from his neck and the
rosary from his side and flung them at the Prior's
feet.

"I will stay in this place no longer," he cried. "Religion or no religion, vows or no vows, you have deceived
me and deceived a woman who has done you no harm—

whom you do not even know.   I break such vows as I
have made, and I leave you now and for always."

He strode to his cell, where an hour later a lay
brother brought him the clothes he had laid aside so
many months ago.   With hands that trembled with
excitement, he tossed aside everything that reminded
him of the past and resumed his own garments, feeling
that with them he assumed once more the ways and
habits of the world.   He thrust such belongings as he
had into his bag, and then made for the door.   One or
two of the novices met him on his way thither, for even
such a secret departure as Paul's becomes known in a
small community.

"Good-bye," they cried heartily; "good-bye, Brother
Paul.   We wish you well."

But one monk, a very old man, whose feet were treading gravewards fast, shook him by the hands, and said in
his piping, feeble voice:

"You are going out again, but you will come back.
Mark my words, you will come back.   Those who have
once known the peace that lies within the walls of a
monastery and the holy calm that rests within our
chapels can never stay outside."

But Paul laughed joyously in his face, and laughed
again as he almost ran down the avenue, and laughed loud-
est of all when the tall wooden gate swung behind him
and he stood out in the road with his bag in his hand,
a perfectly free man once more.   Free to go back
to London and see his friends, glean news of his love,
and pass in delicious dreams the few short days that
were to end his time of probation.

CHAPTER XXII

THE TORTURE OF TANTALUS

ROSAMUND KEITH had not been looking her best all the season, and as June set in, hot and close, with long, burning days, when the sky was like brass and the air throbbed as do heat waves from a furnace, and the nights were heavy with mist and close for want of fresh, stirring air, she faded visibly.

Although she scarcely knew it herself, Rosamund was suffering more from Paul's silence than from his absence. She had written so often to him, urging and praying for even the smallest word in reply. She only begged for an assurance that he was well, but when no answer came and the weeks of the early spring melted into the fierce summer and brought her still no news, her faith in him and in his steadfast love for her grew very faint sometimes. She herself was of so staunch and true a nature that she could not understand that a man, who should be stronger than a woman, could ever waver where he had given his word. When she had plighted her troth to Paul she had done so in no light spirit. She had given him her love and her heart freely and frankly, and it was inconceivable to her that she should ever take back such gifts, or that having once accepted them Paul should desire to return both to her.

Yet—what was she to think during all that long silence? Either he was dead or he had ceased to love her. Either alternative was terrible, but the uncertainty of not knowing which one to believe was even worse. She had no one to whom she could voice her troubles, for having given her promise to her uncle to let the matter rest for a year she felt in honour bound not to betray to him that she was anxious as to the issue. To seek for sympathy at the hands of her aunt or cousins would be mere idle waste of time. Lily Baumer had gone back to Germany to be married, and even if she had been still in London she was scarcely the kind of girl before whom Rosamund would have laid bare the secrets of her soul. A loyal friend is not always a sympathetic one, and Rosamund was too keenly jealous of her own and her lover's honour to run the risk of being the subject of light-hearted discussion over a tea-table or girlish confidence at hair-brushing time. So she had nursed her sorrow in her heart, and like all secrets it had fed upon her and sapped her energy and strength and robbed all her life of its savour.

Even when the passage of the weeks brought the end of the twelve months nearer, Rosamund found that no anticipation of happiness stirred in her bosom. She could not bring herself to believe that any good was in store for her, for although her healthy life had prevented her from acquiring a morbid turn of mind, she was just now in a sufficiently nervous, depressed condition to feel sometimes as though fate were her enemy.

Little things, too, troubled her as they had never done before. Mrs. Kerquham, for some reason of her own, had suddenly taken to having long and confidential talks with Rosamund. These interviews, which would commence with a few generalities, invariably drifted to the well-worn subject of Laura and her delinquencies. In spite of her faults, her mother was proud of her, for she was undeniably pretty and smart. But Mrs. Kerquham's pride was her own punishment, for she had always looked for Laura's advancement by marriage, and each day that went by put such a contingency more out of the question. The girl herself was growing embittered by her failure to make a good settlement, and each outbreak of temper was always the forerunner of a fresh escapade, which, as time went on, grew more and more socially flagrant.

Mrs. Kerquham, her own health shaken by her illness of the previous winter, had once gone so far as positively to weep before Laura and entreat her to moderate in some degree her outrageous conduct. Only the day before that scene Laura had been cut in the park by a very influential lady, and smarting under what she considered a gross insult, was more set than ever on defying society and all its ways, and upon making her own life and getting what fun she could out of it.

"You will never marry now, Laura," moaned Mrs. Kerquham; "or if you do, it will be some wretched boy with a few hundreds a year, and then all the world will write you down as a failure."

"I'm not likely to marry in that kind of way, mother, and you know it," snapped Laura. "But I must have my fun, and you don't take us out nearly as much as you used, so I have to go my own way."

"But, my dear child," said Mrs. Kerquham, giving way to feminine weakness and wringing her hands, "I'm not strong enough nowadays to take you out and chaperone you to good houses. You know that the doctors have forbidden me to go out at night, and these great afternoon crushes make me ill for days."

"Very well, then, don't complain if I go about with other people."

"But it will be your ruin, my dear."

"Ruin! Fiddlesticks! Why did you let Honor engage herself to that booby? She should have married well, and then she could have chaperoned me properly. Nothing gets a girl married so well as when her sister makes a good match."

"I know that; I know that, Laura," said Mrs. Kerquham. "But Honor—"

"Oh, Honor is a cat, and of course no man in his senses would have her—but there is Rosamund."

"Ah! Rosamund is a great disappointment to both your father and myself," wailed Mrs. Kerquham. "If she had married where she might have done, she could have taken you into the very best society in London, and with your face and clever ways and the money that your father will settle upon you, you might have made a brilliant match by this time."

"Then blame Rosamund and not me for it," cried Laura, as she flung out of the room.

And Rosamund was blamed accordingly, sometimes openly and sometimes by inference, when Mrs. Kerquham would retail with tears and sighs Laura's latest outrages.

Rosamund gradually grew to know what it all meant. She realised that the pressure that was being brought to bear on her to accept Lord St. Ives when next it pleased him to propose was becoming greater day by day. She had fought against it all last autumn, and had been thankful for the respite that the spring had brought her, but now in mid-season, worn out in body, sick and disappointed at heart, wearying for the love and sympathy that seemed further away than ever, it was a very hard struggle for the girl. She dreaded the time when her own strength should give way, and she should weakly yield and be forced to marry Lord St. Ives and to take

Laura under her wing for the purpose of socially white-washing her and finding her a husband. Every week her courage slipped further from her, and as the June days passed by and still no news came from Paul her last hopes of resistance died within her, and she almost made up her mind that the end was very near.

It was late afternoon in the big drawing-room at "The Hurst." A few people had been in to tea and tennis, but they had gone now. The lawns were shady, and the gardeners were watering the hot earth, which steamed and smoked after the baking it had had all day. At the end of the avenue Honor and her husband, who were spending the season at "The Hurst," were making up one of their daily quarrels. Laura had gone to her room to dress for dinner with some friends of hers. Mrs. Kerquham was lying on a sofa in the window. She was worn and aged, and her once abundant iron-grey hair looked sparse and faded where it was brushed back from her temples over a cushion. Close by the tea-table, where she had sat all the afternoon, was Rosamund. She was quite idle, and her hands, which were thinner and more transparent than they used to be, were limply crossed on her knee. Her head drooped a little over one shoulder, and the long lashes of her lowered lids swept over her pale cheeks. Alban Kerquham looked over the top of his evening paper at the girl.

"How white and tired she looks," he thought. "I wish I had held to my determination not to come to town this year. Things are going so awry here this year. The house isn't a bit like it used to be."

A sharp ring at the door bell echoed through the silent house. Mrs. Kerquham heaved a little sigh from the sofa, and Rosamund, with her neat instincts, began mechanically to separate the used from the unused tea-

cups.   Across the hall and down the long corridor came
the echo of swiftly advancing footsteps.   Some reminis-
cent ring in them struck Rosamund's ears, and she rose
slowly to her feet with her eyes fixed on the door.   A
second later and it was flung wide, and "Mr. Carr" was
announced in a loud voice by the footman.

Mr. Kerquham started up at the sound of that well
remembered name, and Mrs. Kerquham rose, frigid and
stern, from her sofa.   Rosamund swayed a little, but
uttered no cry, only a china cup she had been holding
in her fingers slipped to the floor and broke with a little
tinkle at her feet.

"Mr. Kerquham, how do you do? Mrs. Kerquham—"
Paul bowed across the room to her.   Then he advanced
with outstretched hands—"Rosamund! my darling!"

But Rosamund did not move.   She felt that the only
chance of keeping her senses at all was to cling to the
side of the table and remain silent.   But her eyes burned
like great stars in her pale face, devouring Paul's every
feature, his every attitude.

"Mr. Carr," began Mr. Kerquham, in his coldest
manner, "what does this mean? By what right do you
come here without first communicating with me?"

"The right that you yourself gave me a year ago.
You parted Rosamund from me for twelve months.   The
time is passed.   I have come back to see her now, and
to ask her once again the question she answered so
sweetly before.   Rosamund, my love, I want you for my
wife.   Will you marry me?"

A little cry came from her parted lips, a cry of
ineffable happiness and deepest love, but still she did
not move.

"My niece is scarcely at liberty to answer you," said
Mr. Kerquham.   "She owes a duty to us all—"

"Which she has paid long ago," retorted Paul.
"You only have to look at her face to see at what cost
she has discharged her debt. Have you no eyes that
you cannot see the change in her? Rosamund, my poor
love, what have they been doing to you?"

He held out his arms to her, and she, as though drawn
by some will stronger than her own, went slowly to him
and hid her face above his heart.

"Alban, are you going to allow this?" said Mrs.
Kerquham, her voice trembling with passion. "Are
you going to permit this gentleman to take Rosamund in
this fashion without one word from us, without even asking our consent, or explaining anything to us?"

"I am ready to explain everything," cried Paul, holding Rosamund in his arms, "and to ask you in due form,
as indeed I do now, for your niece's hand. But I warn
you beforehand, I will not take 'No' for an answer. I
yielded to your wishes a year ago, because I felt that,
rightly or wrongly, at that time my position might bring
some degree of trouble to Rosamund; but this time
things are different. I come to you with a perfectly
clear record. There is no reason why we should not be
married and go away and live at my own place in my
own county. I have been there for the last three weeks,
setting everything in order, and every one is waiting to
welcome me back with my bride. You have no reason
now for delaying our marriage, and it is merely as a
matter of courtesy that I ask your consent to it."

Mrs. Kerquham was about to break forth again when
her husband interposed. Paul's words had given him
time to reflect, and he had seen that in his niece's face
during the last few moments which had appealed to him
more than anything else could have done. He had seen
patience and suffering and love; and the affection that

he bore her reminded him that her future happiness was very dear to him. Turning to his wife he urged her to leave the room.

"A scene will only make you ill again," he said, kindly. "You had best go and lie down upstairs. I promise you that nothing shall be definitely settled until I have seen you again."

He led her to the door, and she, whose spirit had been broken by worry and illness, feeling that she had done her duty by making such protest as she had uttered, was not sorry to leave the burden of the fight upon her husband's broad shoulders.

"You had better come to my room; we shall not be interrupted there," said Mr. Kerquham, still with the door open in his hand, and Paul, loosing Rosamund from his embrace but still holding one of her hands in his, followed Mr. Kerquham to the studio.

"Now, Mr. Carr," said Mr. Kerquham, "let us talk this matter over quietly and without prejudice. I wish, first of all, however, to assure you that my chiefest care is for my niece's happiness. Rosamund is as dear to me as though she were my own daughter, and in addition to that I feel towards her the responsibility that must ever lie with a man who is placed in the position of trust as a guardian. It was that very sense of responsibility that urged me to act as I did a year ago, and you will have to allay that sense, as well as satisfy my affectionate solicitude for this dear child, before I can consent to your marrying her."

Paul placed Rosamund tenderly in a chair. She was looking very white and her mouth was quivering, and now and then the tears rolled from her eyes over her pale cheeks. He stood beside her as though she were a precious thing he had just regained and from which he could not be parted.

"Mr. Kerquham," began Paul, "I have merely tried to fulfil the conditions you imposed upon me. I have been living at peace with my fellowmen and out of reach of every possible temptation to which I might, in my loneliness and despair, have succumbed."

"You have been living in a monastery, have you not?"

"Yes."

"Did you go there with any idea of taking the vows in due time?"

Paul hesitated a moment before he spoke. It was a difficult question to answer.

"I was very unhappy when I determined to cut myself off from the world. I felt that, with the exception of Rosamund, I never wished to see any one again. You may say I took an exaggerated view of the case. Perhaps I did—but, Mr. Kerquham, you must forgive me if I tell you that it was your action that warped my judgment of the world. True, I was deeply wounded by the slights of an idle society and the cold shoulder of the clubs. But everything in our world is only a nine days' wonder, and I knew that the very people who did not ask me to their parties in the summer would be very pleased to come and shoot with me in the autumn. It was your action about Rosamund, and the view you took of matters, that made me regard the whole business with a distorted vision. I felt that if Rosamund was too good for me, then I was too bad for the rest of the world, and that the sooner I cut myself away from it and went somewhere where my history would be unknown and my very name changed, it would be best. But I can say with truth that when I did take up my novitiate at the monastery

I did so with the absolute intention of leaving that place at the time my novitiate expired."

"Then you have left the monastery for good?" queried Mr. Kerquham.

"Absolutely and forever.   Even if I did wish to stay they would not have me, for they found I had no vocation for a monk's life."

"And you still love Rosamund?" said Mr. Kerquham.

For all answer Paul stooped and kissed her on the mouth.

"The marriage must be a very quiet one," said Mr. Kerquham; "for though you are in every other respect a good match for my niece, the circumstances of the past year had best not be in any way raked up."

"So that you give her to me, I don't mind how she comes."

Mr. Kerquham looked at his niece.   Already there was a radiant glow in her face, and her eyes shone like jewels as she looked up at her lover.   He turned his back on the pair for a moment, and feigned to be busy at his painting table setting his brushes straight and tidying a heap of paints.   There was one question he still had to ask, and he was coward enough not to want to look at the two when he did so.

"Are you still a professing Roman Catholic?"

"Of course I am," answered Paul Carr, straightly. "I was baptised into that church; I have never had any other."

A silence fell, and Rosamund felt the blood go back from her face and lie cold about her heart.   She slipped her trembling fingers into Paul's hand and clung to him as a frightened child clings to one it trusts and loves.

"Has it ever struck you," said Mr. Kerquham, still

from the far end of the dim studio, "that your religion is likely to prove a bar to your marriage with my niece?"

Paul drew in his breath sharply before he answered.

"That did not strike me, Mr. Kerquham. I did not know—I did not think—that in these days a mere question of formula could weigh in such a matter as the marriage of two people who love each other."

The studio was almost dark, for the sun had set in the west, and only a little pale reflected light shone through the north window. Mr. Kerquham's broad figure was scarcely visible at the further end of the room, and his voice came like the voice of fate out of the clouds.

"Then, Mr. Carr, I am afraid that for the moment I can give you no definite answer on the question of your marriage with Rosamund. I owe it to her and to myself to lay the whole question before her father's family, who confided her to me twenty years ago. You must understand that they never heard of the first engagement between you. I must now write and submit the whole thing to them, and I must ask you to wait until I have their opinion before you can consider yourself bound to her."

"But, sir, this is too cruel," cried Paul, urged to expostulate by the white and drawn face at his side.

"Uncle, must this be so?" said Rosamund.

Mr. Kerquham came out of the shadows into the ring of pale light that still gleamed in the centre of the floor.

"My child, you know it must be, but I promise you I will urge them to give an unqualified consent, for I think myself that your happiness is bound up in Mr. Carr."

"But when will you write? How soon?" she cried, stretching out imploring hands to him.

"I will write to-night to the earl and to Lady Sophia, and I will call to-morrow on Lady Charlotte Lundy."

"How long will it be before you know?" asked Paul in a low, choked voice.

"Four days at the shortest, more likely a week. Until I communicate with you, Mr. Carr, I must trust to your honour as a gentleman—"

"Not to see her again?" cried Paul.

"Oh! uncle, you cannot be so cruel as that!" entreated Rosamund.

Almost Alban Kerquham yielded, but he felt that if at the very last moment the cup was to be snatched from their too eager mouths, it were best that they should not even catch the savour of it.

"I think it is best that you should not meet, and I trust you both in this matter."

"Oh, it is cruel, cruel!" cried Rosamund, leaning her face against the back of Paul's hand and letting the tears run unrestrainedly down her cheeks.

"Mr. Carr," said Mr. Kerquham in a low voice, "I trust you to give her strength, and then not to see her again until you hear from me."

He walked out of the studio, leaving them alone in the dusk to crush into the next ten minutes all the bitterness of the past, all the pain of the present, and all the sweetness of the future that they hoped for.

The moon was rising in the clear sky when Paul left the house. It flung its beams through the tall studio window and flooded with silver the old Persian rugs that covered the floor. Wider and wider its radiance grew, till it embraced within its magic circle the prone form of Rosamund, who lay, face downwards on the floor, weeping bitterly.

CHAPTER XXIII

"YES"

When Paul left "The Hurst," and by the light of the rising moon paced down the leafy roads of Campden Hill, his heart was light within him, for he could not conceive that such love as Rosamund and he bore each other could go unrequited. He could not find it in him to chide Rosamund for her tears and doubts, for he ascribed her nervous breakdown to over-excitement. That for a mere quibble of belief, a different form of worshipping the same great God, the marriage would be forbidden, seemed to him—sanguine with high hope and still thrilling at Rosamund's remembered touch and voice—little more than absurd.

In a few days all would be well, and they would be married quietly and at once. With the swinging, long stride of a happy man he threaded the crowded streets, making his way, not to his own rooms in Piccadilly, but to a small hotel in the unfashionable Bloomsbury district.

His absence from the world and the circumstances which led to it had made him rather shy of returning immediately to his old haunts, and no one knew he was in town. At times he felt strangely like a man who after an illness rises from a sick bed and essays to walk alone. He wanted some one to lean upon, some one to be always with him, some one to whom he could talk and tell all his thoughts and the disappointments he had suffered in the monastery. That some one was Rosamund. Her strong nature, he knew, would complete the healing which had already begun, and with her by his side he felt sure that mind and heart would recover their healthy elasticity. All this he had felt before he had seen her that afternoon, but now that he had touched her hand and held her in his arms, had noted the many subtle changes that had come over her, and been witness to her grief at the idea of a further separation from him, all that was best in his manhood was aroused, and he forgot his own weaknesses and personal anxieties in a mad desire to take her to him and bring the colour back to her cheeks and the light of love and happiness to her sad eyes.

Yet as his first elation and certainty of success cooled down it was scarcely strange that he should chafe a little at the fresh barrier that Mr. Kerquham's sense of responsibility to the family had raised in his path. Surely time enough had been wasted; they had lost a whole year out of their lives—a year that might have been so happy and that had been so barren of joy and empty of result. And then he fell to wondering as he walked whether the time had been really lost with him, whether the months in the monastery had been mis-spent, whether his reception into Roman Catholicism had been a mistake, a mere foolish ebullition of hysterical and ill-controlled emotion. He needed a wiser head to decide the question for him, for the past year's reliance on the judgment of others and his submission to a life ordered by strict rule had weakened his own purpose and filled him with doubt as to his own judgment on any point. He must wait five days, a week if necessary, until he saw Rosamund again.

That evening the time of waiting stretched before his impatient mind to an interminable length. But when a

few mornings later his man brought his letters from
Piccadilly and he saw her dear, well-known handwriting
among them, the past hours of anticipation seemed as
though they had been all too short.

"My Dear Paul:

"Will you come and see me to-day?

"Yours ever and ever,

"Rosamund."

The words had neither good news nor bad; they
were reticent and reserved almost to a fault. But
through the veil Paul caught the magnetism of joy and
guessed that all was well.

If he had doubted, one glance at her dear face must
have reassured him, when, later in the day, he was ushered into the studio at "The Hurst." A delicious blush,
a lovely happy smile, formed her silent greeting to her
lover, as with punctilious respect he crossed the wide
room to greet Mr. Kerquham.

The firm, long hand-clasp over, Paul was free to turn
and with outstretched arms cry to her to come to him.
Like a tired bird she crept to his embrace, trembling
with happiness, tearful with joy.

"At last! my love! at last!" he murmured, bending
his face down to her rippling tresses.

"At last! dear Paul," she whispered back to him.

"Yes! young people, you may well say 'at last!' But
it has been a hardly grudged consent, I can tell you, and
Mr. Carr, if I had been anything but well-disposed
towards you—and most anxious for my dearest ward's
happiness—I am not sure but that I could have put
another interpretation on these letters."

There were tears in Mr. Kerquham's kindly eyes as

he seated himself and pulled from the pocket of his well-worn painting jacket three letters.

"Sit down, and I will read you what is necessary." A grim smile crossed his face. "I think you had better not see the letters in entirety. They are not uniformly pleasant."

The first he spread upon his knee was written in a square, wavering hand on old-fashioned paper.

"From Lord Kilbeggie. He begins with an exordium on the merits of the Church of Scotland, and a —well a sweeping condemnation of your faith, Mr. Carr. He goes on with a lament about the wilfulness of modern girls and the lack of deference they show to their elders. He ends by saying, 'If she will marry this Papist, she will, for Rosamund has something of the family spirit in her. I will send her as a gift the Cairngorm necklace I should have given her mother had she lived—but you may tell her I never wish to see her again.'"

"Oh, uncle," cried Rosamund, "Lord Kilbeggie is very hard."

"My dear child," said Kerquham, laying aside the letter, "ten years ago you would never have won even so half-hearted a consent from him. But he is very old and breaking fast nowadays. Be content with small mercies. Lady Charlotte Lundy begins her letter less pleasantly. She considers you have deceived your cousin Hamish."

They all laughed, the clear, happy laugh of people who can afford to make merry over others' disappointments.

"I never could dissuade her," went on Mr. Kerquham, "that such a marriage was out of the question. She made up her mind to it when you were a little child, and she's a tenacious person. She quotes largely from

Sir Alexander's opinions—which are rather uncompli-
mentary—and then, like a true woman, wants to know
the date of the wedding, and who is going to make your
frock. Ah! Rosamund, your sex loves a marriage even if
it is not one they care about. By-the-bye, in a postscript
she offers to find you a staff of servants. 'Girls are so
lamentably ignorant on such points.' I think we may
take it as a consent.''

Rosamund and Paul, who had been listening with
clasped hands and smiling mouths, looked with love-
laden eyes at each other. So they might marry, what
did it matter what was said?

"My third letter is from Lady Sophia Kerquham.
She writes temperately, Rosamund, but sadly. She was
always fond of you, and bewails the barrier that must
shut you out of her life. But she sends you her blessing
and prayers that you may be very happy.''

"Poor Aunt Sophia,'' murmured Rosamund, gently.

"So you see, Mr. Carr, the family allow me to give
you my niece and ward.''

Alban Kerquham rose and came towards them. The
hands he held out to them trembled, and his voice was
veiled with emotion.

"Paul! in giving you Rosamund I am giving you the
best and dearest part of myself. That you love her loy-
ally I am sure—that you will be kind to her I believe.
Only in one thing will I charge you—never betray her.
She is the soul of truth and honour. If you, willingly
or otherwise, deceive her—if once you shake the perfect faith she has in you, you will break her heart.''

He moved towards the door. "Rosamund, dear,
come presently to the drawing-room. You aunt will like
to see you both.''

Then followed a rose-coloured week—a week of days

all pleasure and joy, and evenings all peace and love. Night after night Paul and Rosamund stood hand in hand and heart to heart in the long avenue beneath the tree where a year ago they had plighted their troth, and where now—as then—a nightingale poured out his amorous lay to the summer moon.

They wondered sometimes if it was the same bird which had hymned their betrothal and now chanted their epithalamium.

Mrs. Kerquham, forced at last to abandon her cherished dreams of Rosamund's future, had decided to make the best of what in her heart she considered a bad job. Still, things might be worse. Paul was rich and full of hospitable instincts. Under the *ægis* of himself and Rosamund, Laura might see a great deal of pleasant society, might yacht, hunt, travel, and finally pick up that long-sought-for husband. So Mrs. Kerquham, filled with hopeful anticipations, made herself as pleasant as she could to the young couple, and entered with such animation as her health permitted into preparations for a speedy wedding.

The day had been fixed and all preliminaries arranged. Rather to Laura's disgust, the affair was to be very quiet.

On that Paul had insisted, and Mr. Kerquham, who feared over-exertion for his wife, had strongly supported him.

Out in the garden, now but feebly lit by a waning moon, Rosamund was saying "good night" to Paul. Her slender hands, white and light as lily leaves, rested on his shoulders. Her pure face, radiant with love and happiness, was raised to his.

"Darling, how few more times have we to say 'good-bye!' " she whispered.

"Not many now, sweetheart! Now that our marriage day is fixed, I feel nearer, closer to you—almost as though we belonged to each other. Nothing can part us now!"

"Hush! hush!" she cried, one hand across his mouth. "You should not boast. It is tempting Providence."

"Providence! Do you not think we have been the sport of Providence long enough?"

Rosamund shivered as she drew closer to him and her face grew pale.

"One never knows!" she murmured.

"Foolish little love!" laughed Paul, kissing the colour back to her face. "Providence has given us one week of heaven—just as a taste, you know—to prepare us for more. You're trembling again, dear heart. You must go indoors. There's a cool breeze blowing up and your pretty gown is too thin. Good night. God bless you."

A moment later the echo of Paul's steps died away, and she went back into the house to the discussion of gowns and hats, shoes and coats, and all the details of a luxurious trousseau.

CHAPTER XXIV

"NO!"

As Paul strolled down the hill a neighbouring church clock struck ten. How early it was. What should he do? Music halls—the Exhibition—? No! he would pay a long-owed, long-neglected visit. He would go down to the East End and try to see Father Gregory.

It was a long distance, and clear as the streets were it was fully an hour later before he arrived at the familiar doorway in the little Whitechapel street. He was told in answer to his ring that Father Gregory was in his cell, but very ill and unable to see any one.

"But surely he will see me," Paul argued with the lay brother at the door.

"I don't think he can see any one," said the man sadly. "An hour ago he received the last offices of the Church and he is very weak."

"The last office of the Church!" cried Paul. "Is Father Gregory dying?"

"They say he cannot live through the night."

"I beg you to find out if I cannot speak to him, if it is only for a few minutes."

Moved by his agitation, and remembering the friendship that had existed between the good monk and the young man a year ago, the lay brother went to inquire if the dying father could see Paul Carr. He seemed gone for ages, and Paul, sitting in the dim corridor, which was draughty and damp even on this warm summer's night, felt the cold sense of a coming change creeping over his heart. The intense happiness of the last few days slipped from him like a garment, and as a wave sweeps away traces in the sand, so memory obliterated all that was fair in his future. He seemed merely able to remember that he had been lost to life and the world for a year past, and that he had come back again only to find a difference. Even his old friend, the pal of his school days, the chum of his college years, stood at death's threshold.

"Father Gregory will see you," said a voice in his ear. "Those who are with him say it can make very little difference now. He is sinking fast."

With a heavy heart and bent head Paul walked slowly up the familiar stairs and into the mean cell.

The narrow bed had been dragged into the middle of the room, and the window thrust open wide to admit what little air stirred in the closely built neighbourhood. A pair of candles at the bed-head shed a ghastly light over the monk's waxen countenance. Between them was a crucifix and an open book. At the foot of the bed knelt a priest praying, and a lay brother leaned with his face against the pall in the corner sobbing monotonously. Father Gregory was propped up with many pillows, but even with their aid he seemed too weak to support his head, which hung over one shoulder. His eyes were closed, but his pale lips were murmuring in prayer as his thin, worn fingers passed the beads of his rosary between them.

"My friend—Phil—what is this?" cried Paul as he entered the room, and forgetting all the present went back to the past boyhood's days.

Father Gregory opened his eyes and turned them painfully on the fresh face.

"Is it you, Paul?" he muttered in a harsh, low voice that already rattled in his throat.

"Yes, it is I.   I came to see you to-night to tell you something of my past year's life and to ask your prayers for my future."

The monk looked wistfully from his friend to his own wasted form.

"My prayers," he murmured, lifting one hand and dropping it again weakly on the sheet, "my prayers shall be for you."

He made a motion with his hand, and the priest and the lay brother crept outside the door, which they left ajar and through which the sound of their prayers and their sobs could be heard at intervals.

Paul knelt by the bed, and his old friend raised one feeble hand and laid it on Paul's head, where the fresh hair was springing up so fast and hiding the tonsure.

After a moment's pause, he said, weakly:

"So you left the monastery, my son.   You failed in your vocation there?"

"Yes, Father! I failed—and lamentably.   I recognised many months before I left that I went there in the wrong spirit—that I had no real wish to succeed."

The dying man sighed, and a few words of a prayer parted his pale lips.

"So you had no call to a higher life, my poor friend. That has been a great grief to me—I made so sure—you seemed so earnest.   But tell me for my comfort that you are still a professed Catholic."

"Now and always, Father.   I swear it."

A faint ray of joy illumined the monk's worn features.

"I held to my faith," went on Paul, "even when my love was thrown into the balance against it."

"Your love!   What love?"

"My love for the woman who loves me. Don't you remember I told you about—Rosamund Keith?"

A slow fire burned in the faded, sunken eyes.

"And it was for her sake that you left the monastery?"

Paul bowed his head yet lower beneath the light touch of his wasted hand.

"You read my heart, Father! But, oh! if you had seen how she was changed, how pale and pitiful she looked, you would not blame me. It was her love that had been almost killing her. I think I only came back in time."

"And now that you are back, what are you going to do?"

"We are going to be married—almost directly."

The dying man struggled to sit upright and his voice grew strong and loud.

"Do you not know you cannot marry Miss Keith?"

Paul started to his feet, white with astonishment and wonder.

"Not marry Rosamund! In heaven's name, what do you mean? Surely not my religion?—mixed marriages take place every day."

"It is not your religion—as you feel it. It is the religion of the Holy Church of Rome." Father Gregory raised a gaunt, lean hand. "Have you forgotten Kittie Clyde?"

Paul turned grey as the dying man before him. "Kittie Clyde!" he gasped. "My —"

"Your wife, Paul Carr! Married by you before God ten years ago when we were both lads at Oxford."

Paul thrust out his arms in expostulation. "But the law freed me a few months later. You know I divorced her."

Again the priest raised his hand. It was like the hand of a cruel Fate.

"The Catholic Church does not recognise divorce. In the eyes of the religion you swore a few moments back to hold to and profess, you are already a married man."

With a loud cry Paul fell on his knees and hid his agonised face in his hands.

Father Gregory sank back among his pillows, with the death dews starting on his pinched forehead.

"My God! my God!" moaned Paul, as a strong man moans under a crushing blow.

The monk's sight was failing fast; for him the light of the world was growing very dark, and the everlasting radiance of heaven had not yet broken. He groped feebly for Paul, and when he found what he sought, laid his hand on his shoulder.

"The cup is bitter—I know, my son—but it must be drained."

"I will not drink from it—Father—I cannot." Paul lifted his distorted face from his clenched hands. "We have borne so much—suffered so much—and now, when life and love and all that makes this world fair to man and woman is held out to us, you would dash it away from our longing lips."

"It is not I—it is your Church."

"Then," cried Paul, wildly, "we will go away together where no one need know our names or faiths. By the laws of this country we can be married."

"And by the laws of your Church you will be making the woman you love a wanton and your children bastards."

"Not that, my God! not that. Better to leave a Church that has such cruel laws," groaned Paul.

The monk's thin fingers, already clammy and cold with the sweats of approaching death, caught the young man's hands in an iron grasp as he went on in a hoarse voice:

"Are you going to let your body damn your soul? Are you going to give up the faith which you embraced with such fervour a year ago, for the sake of a woman's eyes and a woman's hair? Are you going to turn your back on your salvation and the world to come for the sake of a few short years of what men call love? Paul! Paul! when we were boys and young men together, your nature was always easy and soft. You could be played upon by every passing emotion, and you responded to every careless hand. Are you going to let your past life influence your eternal future?"

And Paul, torn by the old weaknesses, cried aloud:

"I don't know—I don't know. Tell me—teach me—show me what I am to do."

"How can I—a wreck of humanity, already prepared to appear before my God—how can I, who have dropped so early in the fight, hope to help you? In a few short hours I shall be dead, but the woman you love and your own passions will be alive. What I may say to you to-night, she can undo by a word from her lips, a touch of her hand to-morrow—for you are weak, you are unstable, you do not know whether you will serve God or man."

"You speak truly," said Paul, once more dropping his head upon his clasped hands. "You lay bare before me the things that I scarcely dare admit to myself. I am a moral coward; I have been one all along. I came to your Church because I was a coward; I went into the monastery because I was a coward; I left it, and now yearn to deny my God because I am a coward."

"Then what can I hope to do for you," sighed Father Gregory, "if you can do nothing for yourself?"

"Protect me from myself.   Make me swear here by your death-bed that I will hold to my Church and be subject to her laws."

"You took the vows at your baptism.   How have they helped you up to now?" murmured the Father. "The resolution that requires an oath to back it is as chaff before the wind.   It is blown hither and thither and is worthless.   No, my friend—my son—the time is too short with me to point out to you the temptations and the dangers that lie at your feet.   A year ago I prayed earnestly for your happiness in this world, but if it is only to be won by the committing of a sin against your Church, against the woman you love, against your unborn children, then may God guard you from it."

"Then you can do nothing for me?" said Paul, brokenly.

"I can pray for you.   I have made my own peace with God—my last moments shall be spent in intercession for you."

His head fell back, and he gasped for breath through a strained mouth.   Paul started to his feet and called for help, and the priest who had been there before entered the room, and after giving his dying comrade a cordial, knelt once more at the foot of the narrow bed and prayed for the welfare of the parting soul.

Father Gregory was past all speech, but he laid his hands once more upon Paul's head and rested them there.   All the night Paul knelt and watched the battle between the human and the Divine.   Life struggled hard, but Death fought harder.   Yet through all those awful hours Paul heard his name from time to time pass from his friend's lips.   At dawn the battle was almost over and death had nearly won another victory.

"Oh! God, help this poor man to keep his vows—help him to hold to his faith.   Give him strength to walk straight in the path in which his feet are set.   Let him not turn back for earthly things—grant that he be not hindered in his journey to Thy throne and to the life everlasting."

Heavier and heavier grew the monk's hands on Paul's bowed head, and quieter and more calm the twitching face.

"Holy Mother, I leave this erring soul to thee—in the name of the Father and of the Son and of the Holy Ghost—Amen."

With his right hand he feebly blessed him, and then with a sigh sank into the arms of triumphant Death.

CHAPTER XXV

WHOM GOD HAS JOINED

ROSAMUND was singing a happy song as she ran down the long corridor to her aunt's room.   She had been sent for, to choose some hats that a smart milliner had brought for inspection.

White and rose, amber and blue, each in turn crowned her dusky locks, and each was criticised in the same words:

"Do you think Paul will like this?"

Laura, all white muslin and azure ribbons, was lounging in a low chair, and found cheap amusement in the milliner's adulation and Rosamund's pretty anxieties.

The last airy creation of tulle and flowers had been submitted to the ordeal, when a maid, knocking at the door, said that a messenger wished to see Miss Keith at once.

"I'll come directly," said Rosamund, patting her ruffled hair into order.   "Whom is he from?"

"From Mr. Carr, miss."

The words lent additional swiftness to her light steps. In the hall stood Paul Carr's valet.   He looked troubled and strange as he handed a small sealed packet to Rosamund.

"Did Mr. Carr send any message with this parcel?" asked the girl.

"No, miss! only that you would find a letter inside."

"Thank you!   Will you tell Mr. Carr that we expect him to dinner to-night?"

The man's lips parted as though he were about to speak, but he closed them again abruptly, and as Rosamund turned away he left the house.

Rosamund with the packet in her hand and a slight smile curving her lips went into a small apartment littered with books and work, music and flowers. Since the girls had grown up, it had been called their sitting-room. It was redolent of femininity. Some one had been trimming a hat there that morning, and scraps of ribbon and lace and a few sprays of artificial flowers were littered on the floor in a broad patch of sunlight. The open piano was covered with music—Rosamund's music—and a bunch of fading roses. Some canaries in the window were twittering and fluttering and preening themselves in the hot afternoon air.

"My Darling Rosamund:

"Pity me—weep for me—forgive me out of your gracious, womanly heart, if you can, when you read the few lines I have the courage to write to you.

"Yes! dear—at last, in this most terrible crisis of our lives, I have found the courage that has failed me always before and has made shipwreck of our future. With tears of blood and passion I am forced to tell you that we—you and I—cannot be married.

"I only learned the truth last night after I left you—learned how the thoughtless, foolish act of a headstrong boy can ruin the whole happiness of a man.

"When I was a lad, just nineteen, at Oxford, my fancy was caught by a girl in the town. She was a tradesman's daughter. Her name was Kitty Clyde. I married her. God forgive me that I should say so—but my sense of honour was too great to believe she was not

worthy to be my wife.   Six months later I learned I was
her fool—her dupe—and I divorced her.

"Rosamund—I swear before God that the whole of
this wretched business had so faded from my mind that
I never even thought I was keeping a secret from you
in not telling you of it.

"Would to Heaven that the memories of others had
been as short as mine.   But last night one who had been
my friend at Oxford—who knew the story—faced me
with it—and forbade my marriage—with you or any
other woman.   I believe his soul is now with God, for
he was dying last night.

"Dearest heart, I swore by his deathbed that I would
not drag you from your purity to be, in the eyes of my
Church, my mistress.   I repeated that oath on the cross
they laid at dawn above his dead heart.

"I have sinned—in my weakness—in my cowardice—
and the most poignant pang in my agony is that you, so
stainless and so brave, must bear the load of punishment
with me.

"I said I had found courage to write this to you.
That is only another weak excuse.   I write this because
I am afraid to see you.   I dare not trust myself again
within the magic of your presence—the passion of your
grief.

"Do not write to me.   Before you read this I shall
have left London, and England a few hours later.   From
henceforth I shall be dead to the world—dead even to
you.   Forgive me—pray for me as for one who is no more.

                                                "PAUL."

The canaries twittered and fussed in the hot sunshine,
but Rosamund with an ashen face sat and trembled
as though it froze outside.   God was good to her, and

for a time her only sensation was of intense cold, and it was with shaking limbs and chattering teeth she stumbled upstairs to her room.

Then, amid the disorder of her scattered trousseau and the profusion of her wedding presents, something snapped in her brain, and she fell, a huddled mass, to the ground.

CHAPTER XXVI

LORD ST. IVES MAKES AN OFFER

"Is Mrs. Kerquham at home?"

Lord St. Ives, in irreproachable town attire, sat in his phaëton while his smart tiger asked the question of the footman at "The Hurst."

"Mrs. Kerquham is too ill to see any one, but the young ladies are out on the lawn."

Lord St. Ives left his carriage and walked into the house. It was refreshingly cool in the long corridors, where the palm trees bent their huge leaves towards each other and made pale green arches. It was a delightful contrast to the streets, where the heat was frightful. The pitch in the wood pavements was oozing and bubbling in the sun. The men looked either apoplectic or faint, and the women all washed out and dragged to death. Half way down the long corridor Lord St. Ives stopped the footman who preceded him.

"Is the family going away?" he asked, looking about him, and noting in the many rooms that opened on either hand the unmistakable signs of an immediate flitting.

"Yes, my lord. They did hope to start the day after to-morrow, and we all begun packing up last Monday, but my mistress was taken very ill yesterday afternoon, and there was three doctors here last night and a consultation this morning. Two nurses came in just before lunch, and they don't seem to know as when she will be well enough to be moved.

"I am very sorry," said Lord St. Ives.

He was a polite man, and very seldom forgot his manners, even before servants.

If within the house all was disorder and trouble, out
in the garden there was no indication that the usual life
at "The Hurst" was in any way upset.   The wide lawn
was scattered with tennis balls, and a fluffy lace sunshade had been dropped by one of the many girls who
formed a goodly group under the big beech trees.   The
usual umbrella tent, the Japanese sunshades, the ham-
mock chairs and rockers were all as Lord St. Ives had
seen them before.   The long, low table was spread for
tea and made charming by a big bowl of roses and cut
glass dishes piled high with strawberries.   A score of
young men and girls were lounging about in the shade.
Those who had just finished a set were unbecomingly
hot and were clamouring for refreshments.   The rest of
the party appeared aggravatingly cool.

"How kind of you to come," said Honor, who, as
married woman, was playing chaperone and aping her
mother's frigid little airs to perfection.   "But you are
not dressed for tennis," she added, looking at his
immaculate frock coat, silk hat, and patent boots.

"It is rather too hot to play this weather.   Besides,
I did not know you had anything of a party on.   I only
came to make a call."

"Oh! no party, I assure you," minced Honor.   "Just
a few young people in for the girls."

The phrase and manner were so ridiculously like
Mrs. Kerquham's that every one laughed.   Honor flushed
with annoyance, and Lord St. Ives, under cover of the
foolish jest, slipped round to the very back of the group
where Rosamund was seated in a wicker chair listening
to the boyish confidences of a newly caught and very
amorous swain of Laura's.

Rosamund gave the coldest nod to Lord St. Ives as he approached her. For the moment she was half afraid that he was going to take an empty chair on her right hand, but he contented himself by standing at a little distance and looking down at her as she sat there with quiet hands and immobile face, listening to the nonsensical talk of the love-sick youth.

Now and then she murmured some idle words in reply, but Lord St. Ives, watching her with his eager eyes, noted that she was absolutely inattentive to all that was going on around her.

He was a man who heard most things that went on, and he was one of the very few who knew that Paul Carr had passed two or three weeks in London a month ago. He guessed, though he had not been told so for a fact, that that young gentleman had found his way to "The Hurst" during that time. That his visits there, however, had not resulted in any settled engagement with Rosamund Keith he felt certain. Even if there had been anything of the kind proposed, he felt sure from the pallor of Rosamund's face, the droop of her proud head, and the dark rings round her velvety, dark eyes that the wooing had had no happy termination. However proud a girl may be, and however still she may keep her tongue, her face must betray her to those who choose to study it, and for the past year or two Lord St. Ives had gazed often enough at her to have learned by heart every expression that reflected her thoughts.

As he looked down at her now with the glints of sunshine playing hide-and-seek in the warm shadows of her throat and ears, he guessed by her attitude, by the listlessness of her air, from the very slackness of her open hands as they lay in her lap, that she was unhappy.

"A heart is easier caught on the rebound," he thought

to himself. "I will speak to her presently. Meanwhile, I shall try her and see if there is any sympathy between us at all."

He stood just behind her, a little out of the range of her carelessly wandering eyes, then fixed his own gaze on her so hard, and forced such a look of fiery passion to his eyes that presently he noted a hot blush creep slowly above the collar of her white gown and mount in a rosy tide right to the roots of her hair.

"How divinely she blushes. It is the most fascinating thing in the world to see a woman blush naturally."

And feeling the satisfaction that fills a schoolboy when he has tortured a helpless animal enough, he strolled over to the tea table, and as he helped to serve the strawberries and cream, whispered little scraps of gossip and flattery into Laura's greedy ears.

"And what is the matter with your mother?" he asked later on, when the shadows began to stretch themselves like long, grey fingers across the lawn and two fresh sets for tennis were made up.

"I really don't know," answered Laura, pettishly. "She has been frightfully tiresome lately, always grumbling about her health and making quite a fuss when we want her to take us anywhere."

"Just as if I could not chaperone the girls," put in Honor, "now that I'm married. She seems to think that I am a baby still and not to be trusted with them."

Lord St. Ives murmured something polite about Honor's youth and beauty making her a dangerous chaperone, at which that acid young woman bridled and looked intensely pleased—so pleased, in fact, that when a little later on Lord St. Ives addressed a request to her under his breath, she nodded and smiled at him, and said in a loud aside:

"Certainly, with the greatest pleasure. You leave it to me—I will arrange it beautifully."

Ten minutes later, whether by accident or by Honor's design, the shade of the beech trees was deserted, except for Rosamund, who sat with her chin in her hands staring at nothing, and Lord St. Ives, who under the plea of being unsuitably dressed refused to play either tennis or croquet, or to go to the paddock to see the new calf.

"Dear me!" he cried, suddenly breaking the silence, "this is quite a '*solitude à deux.*' "

Rosamund started.

"I beg your pardon," she said. "I am afraid I am very rude. I thought everybody had gone."

"Does that mean that I am nobody?" asked Lord St. Ives, pulling his chair nearer hers and tossing his cigarette into the shrubbery.

"Of course not," replied Rosamund. "Everybody is somebody, you know. Perhaps I should have said I thought I was alone."

"And believing you were alone you gave free rein to your thoughts."

He leaned suddenly forward, resting his elbows on his knees and bringing his head quite close to hers. "Whom were you thinking about, Miss Keith?"

He had expected her to flush and prevaricate. He knew the tricks of girls so well, but Rosamund disappointed him and upset his calculations, for she did neither.

"I was thinking of poor Aunt Margot. She is very ill."

"So I hear," said Lord St. Ives, carelessly. "Do you know what is the matter with her?'

"No! I don't think anybody does, only I fancy she is very worried. She has often told me so these past few months."

"Worried? Why, whatever has Mrs. Kerquham got to worry about? The money is all right here, and Kerquham is a good husband. He is not the kind of man to give a woman any anxiety."

"It is neither of those things," said Rosamund simply. "I think she is troubled a great deal about Laura. She is disappointed in Laura, you see. She doesn't marry."

"Isn't she also disappointed in some one else who does not marry?" murmured Lord St. Ives, in a very low voice.

Rosamund saw that she had fallen into a trap, and drawing herself upright, pushed her chair back a little.

"I don't—"

"You are not going to tell me that you don't know what I mean, Miss Keith?" cried Lord St. Ives, determined on pushing the slight advantage he had gained. He looked hastily around him. The tennis-players were busy with their game; the croquet party was on the farther side of the lawn; Honor would be careful that the visitors to the calf had plenty of time in which to observe the beauties of that animal.

"You are a very truthful girl. I don't think I have ever heard you tell even a white lie. Why beat about the bush now?"

Again he drew nearer to her. "Miss Keith—Rosamund—for months past I have seen that you are not happy here. I think that you feel that you are wasting your life amid these idle, foolish people. Your cousin must be uncongenial to you, and your aunt's affection is probably measured by what you can do for her. You know that I'm awfully fond of you and that I have been anxious for a long time past to make you my wife. You shall have everything that the heart of a woman can desire and as much liberty as you like. I am not the sort of man who would not trust the woman I married."

No one was looking at them, and he tried to take her hand. "Rosamund, I ask you to marry me. Tell me that you will do so, and I will go at once to your uncle and ask his consent. He is scarcely likely to make any difficulty about the matter."

He said the last words with intention, or at least she thought he did, for she sprang to her feet and faced him with scarlet cheeks and flashing eyes.

"Lord St. Ives, I have suffered your attentions too long. I neither want your love nor your title nor all the advantages and liberty you can give me. I would not marry you if you were the last man in the world."

"Not even to please your people?"

"Not if they ordered me to do so. When I marry, if ever I do, it will be to please myself and myself alone."

She swept past him and ran across the lawn, disappearing into the house. Lord St. Ives pulled at his moustache a moment.

"What a difficult fish she is to play! I admire her for it. She has got more pluck and more spirit than all the girls in town put together, but I will catch her if I can. I ought to have spoken to her people first. She is one of the obedient, dutiful sort. If they managed things properly she would give way in the long run. I will go and see Kerquham now."

He knew every inch of the place, and so with his hat in his hand and a freshly lit cigarette between his teeth he sauntered round the garden till he reached the studio window. Honor, in the paddock, quite tired of the calf and bored by the silly remarks of the young people she had with her, flattered herself that all was well.

"Thank goodness! it is settled," she thought. "Now Laura will have some one to look after her, for he is not the man to stand any nonsense when he is her cousin, and I shall get that diamond bangle he promised me if I gave him a chance to speak to Rosamund."

Mr. Kerquham was putting the finishing touches to a picture when the broad figure of Lord St. Ives flung a shadow across his work.

"Good evening," he nodded, still painting.

"Good evening, Kerquham, good evening. Hot, isn't it? But you look beautifully cool."

"Yes, it isn't bad in here. You look baked in those town clothes of yours."

Lord St. Ives laughed gaily.

"Doesn't a man put on the garments of ceremony when he comes on an important errand?"

"Tea and tennis on the lawn with the girls isn't so important, is it?" queried Kerquham.

"I have not called to see the young ladies," said Lord St. Ives. "I wanted to speak either to Mrs. Kerquham or you."

"My wife is very ill. A great pity, as we were to have left this in a day or two. We all want a little north country air, I think. Rosamund looks terribly fagged."

"I have been very sorry to notice that Miss Keith has not been looking well of late." Then after a pause he went on, "It is about your niece, Miss Keith, that I wish to see you."

Mr. Kerquham stopped painting at once and faced round on his visitor.

"It would be idle pretending, Lord St. Ives, that I do not guess the purport of your visit."

"Then that helps me out," said Lord St. Ives, with

the engaging frankness he could assume with great success when he chose. "I have come to-day to ask your formal consent to—"

He paused and wondered whether it was wise to tell Rosamund's uncle that he had already been refused by her. He decided to veil that little fact.

"I have come to ask you if you will intercede with Miss Keith on my behalf. I wish most ardently to make her my wife, and I can assure you that the provision I will make for her will more than satisfy your most affectionate desires."

Alban Kerquham laughed a little shortly.

"We have no desire to sell our niece, Lord St. Ives; and if you love her and make her a good husband and give her a comfortable home, that is all that we should ever require. Her happiness would be our first thought."

Alban Kerquham meant what he said, but Lord St. Ives, who had for a long time seen through Mrs. Kerquham's schemes, knew that that lady would consider his proposal from quite another point of view.

"Perhaps I ought not to have laid such stress upon the mere worldly advantages," he said, graciously; "but I know some people—especially women—attach great importance to that kind of thing. I am sorry that I could not myself have spoken to Mrs. Kerquham, because I should have liked to have made my intentions perfectly clear to her."

"You may trust me to let my wife know what you have said."

"And Miss Rosamund?" queried Lord St. Ives.

"After I have seen my wife, either one or both of us will speak to her. Rest assured that we shall do our best to urge her to accept an offer which I feel sure would be for her own welfare."

"Oh, by-the-bye," went on Mr. Kerquham, as Lord St. Ives, after a ceremonious leave-taking, was about to quit the studio, "has Rosamund any idea—have you spoken to her yourself on this subject?"

St. Ives assumed the embarrassment of a boy.

"Well, really, Mr. Kerquham, such words as have passed between us are perhaps too sacred to be repeated or even commented on. I am sure that Miss Keith is quite aware of my admiration for her, but you know she is cold and a little shy. It is for that reason that I think it would be best for the proposal to come from the members of her family, whom she trusts and who, she knows, love her and would only advise her for her own benefit."

"I will speak to her this evening most probably," said Mr. Kerquham, turning again to his work as Lord St. Ives left the studio.

"What an excellent thing it would be," thought the good man as he painted on. "Give her a good husband, and, please God, a lot of healthy, jolly babies, and Rosamund will forget that sad business with Carr. It breaks my heart sometimes to look at that poor child and see how bravely she bears her sufferings. But she is so sensible—and I feel sure that such a settlement would be for the best. When my time comes, as come it must some day, she will be quite alone in the world—or worse than that, she would be buried alive with Kilbeggie and the old aunts, and once they got hold of her they would force her to marry that muff, Hamish Lundy. For her own sake I must put it to her very plainly that she will be very foolish to throw away such a chance. I must tell her that it is not every girl who has nothing but her face for her fortune who is asked in marriage by one of the wealthiest men in London, and of irreproachable lineage into the bargain."

A soft tap came at the studio door, and a neatly-gowned figure, crowned with a goffered cap and endowed with very soft hands, murmured that Mrs. Kerquham had just awakened from a nice sleep and felt a little better, and would like Mr. Kerquham to come upstairs and see her.

The light was fading fast, but without a second thought Alban Kerquham laid down his brushes and palette and followed the nurse up to his wife's room. He could tell her the good news at once, he thought. She had always been so anxious about the girls' marriages. It would cheer her up and probably help her recover if she knew one of them was going to be so splendidly settled in life. So with his strong, hearty voice toned down to the silence of a sick chamber, Alban Kerquham told his wife Margot of Lord St. Ives' proposal. Her face was very sharp and bloodless from ill-health, and it looked grey and hard as stone on the white pillows.

"So now, my dear, all we have to do is to see Rosamund and ask her what she thinks of the really splendid proposal," finished up Mr. Kerquham.

"You will not do that," said Mrs. Kerquham, with a flash of her old decided manner coming back to her. "You will merely tell her that Lord St. Ives has proposed to us for her hand and that we have accepted him."

Alban Kerquham knitted his brows.

"Do you think that is quite the way to take Rosamund? You must remember that that affair with Paul Carr is still fresh in her memory."

"I trust," interrupted Mrs. Kerquham, "that Rosamund will not forget the duty and obedience she owes us and about which she has prated so often. Send for her at once."

The nurse was rung for and asked to fetch Miss Keith. Then Mrs. Kerquham, to prepare herself for what she thought might be a difficult task, but out of which she intended to come triumphant, had some fresh pillows put behind her back, and took a little beef tea to help her through the coming conversation.

Rosamund, still in her white frock and garden hat, came quickly into the room. Her light step made no sound on the floor, and in the fading light, which was only broken by a green shaded lamp, she looked, with her slender form and pale face, like a spirit.

"I hope you are better this evening, dear aunt. You must try and get your strength back again, and then we can all go up to Scotland. You know that air always suits you. Don't people say that their native air is best for everybody?"

"I thank you for your inquiries, Rosamund," said Mrs. Kerquham, "and for the affectionate solicitude you display. Whether I get well-soon and am able to go to Scotland depends very much upon you."

"Upon me?" Rosamund queried with astonished eyes, and half inclined to think that her aunt's brain was wandering. "What have I to do with it? I am not allowed in here to nurse you. I would come at once if they would let me."

"It is not lip service that I want—but heart service," muttered Mrs. Kerquham very sharply.

Her illness was of a nervous character, and the suspense and anxiety were already making her worse.

"Speak to Rosamund, Alban, at once."

Mr. Kerquham cleared his throat. The memory of Rosamund's tears and love for Paul were present with him now, and in his heart he sorrowed for the girl.

"My dear child," he began gently, "your aunt and I

have this evening received a most flattering offer of marriage on your behalf. Without wishing in any way to force your inclination, we urge you to give the matter your most careful consideration, and not to dismiss lightly or for a mere passing whim a chance which will in all probability never come to you again."

"Rosamund, if you refuse this offer, I will never forgive you, and I will never speak to you again," cried Mrs. Kerquham from her pillows.

Rosamund looked from one to the other. She almost guessed what was coming as her uncle again prepared to speak.

"Lord St. Ives has spoken to me in terms of the highest admiration of you this afternoon, and has expressed the most earnest desire—which is prompted by the highest affection—to make you his wife."

An uncontrollable scorn for the man, who having but a few moments before been refused by her and who had then resorted to the mean trick of bringing pressure upon her to change her mind, filled Rosamund's heart. An hour ago she had declared she would not marry him if he were the only man in the world. Now, she felt that she could never again look upon his face or touch his hand, even as a distant acquaintance.

"Well, my dear," said Mr. Kerquham, "what have you to say?"

"What should she say?" interposed Mrs. Kerquham. "There is but one answer to a question like that, and Rosamund must give it immediately."

"Lord St. Ives has already had my answer," replied the girl, very quietly. "I refused him an hour ago in the garden."

"Then you will reconsider your decision," said her aunt, "and to-morrow when he calls you will accept him."

"I am sorry, Aunt Margot, but I cannot please you in this matter."

"If you are sorry you can easily repent and accept his lordship."

"My dear Rosamund," put in Alban Kerquham, kindly, "there is no need to come to a hasty decision. Lord St. Ives particularly told me he would give you time."

"I want no time, thank you, uncle. My mind is quite made up. Nothing can ever change it."

"And pray why not?" asked Mrs. Kerquham. A pale red flush was rising to her face and her small eyes sparkled angrily.

"I do not love him," replied Rosamund, firmly.

Mrs. Kerquham laughed shrilly. She was fast losing all self-control, and began to beat her hands upon the bedclothes.

"Love! A nice maidenly thing to talk about. Ah! if you had been brought up in Scotland by Lady Sophia and the old earl, there would have been none of this nonsense. You would have married the man they chose for you or been put on bread and water till you came to your senses."

Alban Kerquham caught one of his wife's restless hands in his.

"My dear child, don't you see that what we are urging upon you is for your own good? Lord St. Ives is of excellent family and very wealthy. He has promised to make the most splendid settlements Think for one moment what an anxiety you will take off our minds as to your future."

"And pray remember how you can help Laura," urged Mrs. Kerquham, clinging to her fetish till the end.

"Uncle Alban," said Rosamund, "I have obeyed you

once about the disposal of my future.   Over a year ago
you persuaded me to become a coward, and to give up
Paul Carr because he was in trouble.   That act of mine
has spoiled both his life and mine.   I cannot—cannot let
you do it again.''

"Isn't an earl good enough for you, then?'' cried Mrs.
Kerquham in a voice that trembled with passion.   "Isn't
a name and a family that is as old as your own and a big
rent roll and huge estates sufficient to satisfy you?''

"I want none of these things, aunt, but I did want
the man I loved and to whom I gave my heart.   The
day I learned I could not marry Paul, I vowed I would
never marry any one else.''

"Rosamund, you will kill me with your ingratitude!''
moaned Mrs. Kerquham, who was now crimson in the
face and shaking violently from head to foot.   "Rosamund, if I die—remember it is you who will have killed
me.   Get out of my sight and never come into it again.
I shall keep my oath—I will never set eyes on you or
speak to you again so long as I live.''

"My dear!   Go at once,'' said Alban Kerquham.
"Send the nurse here directly.   Your aunt is worse.''

Sick at heart and broken in spirit, Rosamund, after
summoning the nurses, went to her room.   Why was
life so hard for her?   Why could she see no promise of
peace or rest?

By-and-bye she heard through her half-closed door one
of the nurses run downstairs and call to the footman to
drive into town and fetch the doctors.   Then the young
people who had been wandering in the twilight came
shuffling into the hall and whispered together as they put
on their coats and hats.   She heard her two cousins
come upstairs.   Laura was sobbing noisily, and Honor
was trying to comfort her.   The doctors came, and at

nine o'clock dinner was served to two of them down-stairs, while the third remained in the sick-room. Once she went to the door of her aunt's bedroom, but from within there was no sound save rustling and whispering and the moaning cry of Laura.

Too sad and wretched to remember her own trouble, she could only pace up and down the long corridor wait-ing for such scraps of news as the hurrying nurses brought out from time to time, and hoping to catch a glimpse of her uncle. But he never left the room at all. At midnight the women servants went up to bed. Their staircase ran past her own door, and she could hear them chattering in low tones and speculating as to what kind of black dresses would be given to them. At one o'clock two of the doctors drove away. "It is no use waiting," she heard them say to each other as they walked downstairs. "Henderson can see it through to the end; it cannot be long now."

"How dreadful! Her aunt was dying without a word of forgiveness or a sign of reviving remembrance of the duty which had held the place of love between them both all these years. She must go into the room, if only to wait behind the screen and to be with them all at the last. It made her feel such an outcast; it cut her so adrift from them all to stay outside.

Softly she slipped into the room and stood behind the high screen which stood between the bed and the door. All was silent, and from the sound of breathing that came from the bed it seemed as if her aunt were in a drowsy sleep. But Rosamund did not realise that the strong light, shining through the open door behind her, threw her shadow in strong relief on the opposite wall, where Mrs. Kerquham, if she opened her eyes, must see it.

The figure on the bed stirred a little.

"She is waking," said a nurse's voice. "We must get her to take something at once."

There was the tinkle of a teaspoon and the rattle of a glass. Then suddenly a loud cry rose from the bed.

"She is in the room! She is in the room!" screamed Mrs. Kerquham in a frenzy of fury. "That wicked girl has dared to come near me again. I know why she has done it. She has come to see me die. She thinks she has got her own way. She will be punished at the last for her disobedience and her stubbornness. Take her away! Take her away!"

Rosamund, cowering behind the screen, was invisible to any one in the room, and they thought that Mrs. Kerquham was again raving, but Honor, who fancied she had heard a slight sound from the door, looked round and volunteered:

"Yes, mother, you are right. Rosamund is here."

"I knew it! I knew it!" shrieked the dying woman. "May my death be upon her head!"

There was a rush of the nurses and a loud scream from Laura.

"Good God! She is dying," cried Mr. Kerquham.

"All is over," said the doctor.

And Rosamund, unheeded and sorrowful, crept like a criminal from the room.

CHAPTER XXVII

SPOILS

THE funeral was over, and "The Hurst," which for a week had been a very haven of stillness and quietude, now rang with the noise of hammers, the heavy tread of workmen, the passage of hurrying footsteps, and the flicking of impetuous housemaids' skirts. The windows, which had been shaded for so long from the glaring summer sun, had already been stripped of their blinds and dainty frilled muslin curtains and heavy silken hangings, while the verandah, which had been so gay with carpets and the scarlet cushions of luxurious lounges, was now swept and bare as is a ball-room the day after a great festivity. Out in the garden men in shirt sleeves were moving seats and tables and taking down the bright umbrellas and snowy tents under which had been held so many bright little gatherings. Men with shiny coats and doubtful linen were to be met in odd corners of the grounds and in every part of the house. They had little notebooks in their hands and stumpy bits of pencil with which they scribbled down lists of furniture and their comments thereon.

Even the peace of the studio had been invaded. The great Persian rugs that had clothed the floor with their harmonious colouring were rolled aside and made a dingy heap in one corner. Canvases and palettes, brushes and paints, had been securely packed in huge cases which, piled one upon the other, rose like a wooden

mountain in the centre of the room.   The pretty cushions and quaint pieces of pottery, the stands of old arms,
and the silver hanging lamps had all been moved from
their accustomed places, and lay about dust-covered and
forlorn.   In the drawing-room the silken furniture was
being shrouded in brown holland covers by the chattering housemaids, who seemed to enjoy the excitement
and the prospect of the compensating present which Mr.
Kerquham had promised them for such sudden dismissal
from his service.

For "The Hurst" and its contents, the silver and
china, the furniture and hangings, were all to be sold.
People who talked without thinking considered that it
was ultra-romantic that a man of Alban Kerquham's age
and calm disposition should take his wife's death sufficiently to heart to vow he would never live in the house
again or use the things which she had chosen and bought
with him in the early days of their prosperity.   His
family had argued with him on the point, his friends had
almost laughed in his face.   But he was a man of strong
feelings, and under his calm Scotch exterior there was a
deeper well of tenderness than the world had any idea
of.   His set had always regarded him as cheery and
easy-going, a man who was content to earn large sums
of money and then give them to his wife to spend or to
save.   They always imagined that the married life of
the Kerquhams had drifted into that state of friendly
indifference which characterises the majority of unions
after five-and-twenty years.

Alban Kerquham, however, was not a man who protested overmuch.   He had made no great scenes, he had
borne himself with a subdued dignity at the funeral.   He
had set about the settlement of his affairs without any
nervous breakdown, and it was only Rosamund who

even guessed how much he had suffered all the time. He had never cared particularly for society. He had been happier working in his studio or rattling across country behind a pack of hounds than lounging about in drawing-rooms or eating large dinners in uncongenial company and overheated rooms. His world had been in his home, which he had worked very hard to make, and the pivot of that home had been Margot Kerquham, with her hard face and cold eyes and her high, clear voice.

And so "The Hurst" was to go. She had furnished it, she had governed it, she had made all her social successes under its hospitable roof, and she had died there—all excellent reasons in his eyes why he should leave the place and sever all connection with it. Laura had grumbled loudly, and cried that it was a cowardly thing to do to condemn his only daughter to live in the country or to wander about just anyhow among such people as would have her to visit them. But when her first annoyance simmered down she considered matters from another point of view, and she thought perhaps it would be for the best. It would save her the responsibility and bother of housekeeping, and give her even more freedom than she had taken for herself during the last few years. So she mapped out a long series of visits, and interviewed her father on the question of her allowance with a business capacity and thoroughness worthy of her dead mother.

Rosamund had said nothing. But she had felt her aunt's death most keenly, and even the sympathy and kindness with which her uncle had tried to persuade her that Mrs. Kerquham had been unconscious when she had uttered those last fearful words could not rid her of an uneasy feeling that if she had only done what she had been expected to do, and unconditionally consented to marry Lord St. Ives, Aunt Margot would be alive now, and this great grief would never have fallen upon her uncle.

It was the belief that the whole thing had been her fault that had added a poignancy to Rosamund's natural sorrow, and that had made her since the sad event follow Mr. Kerquham about with mute lips and great miserable eyes, even as a dog that does not understand follows his master. In her heart she vowed to devote her whole life to him and try to make up in some small measure for all that he had lost. She hated herself for what now seemed the basest ingratitude, and even her broken engagement, and the fact that she knew nothing of the whereabouts of Paul Carr, faded for the time into nothingness before her new determination to be her uncle's constant companion and most faithful and obedient niece so long as he lived.

In her own room, the room where the greater part of her girlhood had been spent, where she had wept and prayed for Paul, and grieved and shuddered over the horror of her aunt's death, she was preparing to enter upon the first stage of her life's devotion to Alban Kerquham. To-morrow the whole household would be broken up, and strange men would come in and take away the things that she had seen purchased and placed with pride and care by the dead housewife.

Surrounded by large trunks and with every wardrobe wide agape, she was busy with the sorry task of going through her possessions and belongings, each one of which recalled some incident of the past or of the nearer present. Ball gowns and fête dresses, riding habits and country suits all came out from the scented shelves, and one by one were laid aside as being things that were done with. There were letters to go through, invitations and little dainty cards with glazed surfaces and fancy pencils, scribbled over with the names of men she had danced with. Each one was indicative of a triumph, and each one reminded her of some pleasant, happy evening. But they all went with the coloured frocks and the crushed flowers and tumbled ribbons. Only a very few she sorted out from the general confusion. Paul Carr had written in them, and they were sacred. She tied them up with his letters; the few notes she had had from him from time to time and those longer, disappointing missives he had written her from the monastery in Norfolk. They made but a small packet, and she smiled a little sadly as she saw what a little room they took in one of her trunks.

The few things—and they were very few—that her aunt had given her she kept, wrapping each with reverent care in silver paper, and packing it in orderly fashion. Some photographs and favourite pictures, a dozen little ornaments—most of them childishly simple and desirable only by reason of association—she put aside, purposing to give them as souvernirs to the servants she would never see again. Almost everything else might go. The costly dressing-bag that her uncle had given her on her last birthday she packed for travelling, and also two small trunks. She and Mr. Kerquham meant to go very far afield, and now that she was in such deep mourning her wants were very few, and she could always purchase what she needed in the cities they would travel through.

When she had finished she sat down and looked around her—and then for the first time it struck her that the wandering life that lay before her might mean a great deal. It had already commenced by forcing her to cut almost every link that had bound her to the luxurious past. For what use was there in keeping things that she might never want again? Amid all her grief Rosamund still retained that streak of practicality which had set her apart all her life from her cousins. Yet she felt quite a personal grief in parting from her dainty fans and scented gloves and silken hose, her lace-trimmed petticoats and smart shoes and all the thousand and one prettinesses that go to make up the toilet of a well-dressed young lady of the present day. But even that sentiment was assuaged after a few moments by the thought that, if in years to come her uncle elected to turn his face homeward and go down to the old Manor House in Midshire, and perhaps spend the evening of his days with his rod and his horses, she could easily replace such things as she might require.

So with a smile struggling forth on her sad face, she locked the two small trunks that were to travel with her, and fastened up and sealed the other that contained her letters and such things as she meant to keep. Then with a brave heart she rang the bell and ordered the servant to take everything else away. It was a hard wrench at the last, to know that when she came back into the room everything that she had enjoyed having and loved to wear would be gone. Yet she had never been a girl to flinch or to spare herself, and the tears in her eyes were hushed and the quiver of her lips brought to control as she walked down the long corridor to where, in the distance, she could hear her cousins chattering and wrangling.

They were in Mrs. Kerquham's room, the room that since the night of her death Rosamund had hated to enter. Even now, though the windows were stripped bare, the bed taken away, the carpets up, and the whole apartment littered and untidy, Rosamund could see in a flash the room as it looked that night, with the low lights casting shadows on the wall, and the drawn curtains and the screen behind which she had hidden, and the forms that bent or knelt about the bed. She stood irresolute at the door for a moment, and was about to turn away when Honor caught sight of her.

"Oh! here you are, Rosamund. What have you been doing all this morning? Packing up your own things, I suppose, instead of coming here as you promised. Now I ask you—didn't mother always say I should have that Brussels flounce? Laura sticks out that it ought to be hers, because she wore it on her presentation gown, but I know I ought to have it. Laura has taken the Venetian point and would like to put me off with the Honiton set, but I hate Honiton and want the Brussels."

Rosamund leaned against the door post and looked at her two cousins. They were gowned in the deepest and the most fashionable black, but their grief was very much on the outside, for their cheeks were scarlet and their eyes shining over the division of the spoil. To Rosamund their small white hands looked almost like claws as they dragged out their dead mother's clothes from the shelves and chests and quarrelled and haggled over every gown and cloak. · The dressing-table was piled with jewellery, the big arm-chair was filled with fans and feathers. Lengths of silks and velvet lay in shimmering heaps on the floor. Where the bed had been a huge cedar box stood wide open. The furs with which it had been filled were all tossed and disarranged, and exhaled a faint odour of the wood which had enclosed them, but to Rosamund the room seemed filled with the heavy scent of hot-house flowers, and to be dim and dark with the light of a few candles.

"Honor is a perfect pig!" cried Laura, stamping her

foot. "She thinks that just because she is a married woman she is to have everything. She seems to forget the trousseau mother gave her. I never had a trousseau, so I am entitled to take the equivalent of it now. Don't you think so, Rosamund?"

"Oh, that is like you," sneered Honor, "always selfish. I have given in to you about the diamond necklace. You know that was the best piece of jewellery mother had, and you have got it. It is only fair that I should have the Brussels lace."

Laura did not particularly want the Brussels lace. She was only bent on driving a bargain with her sister, and even as she argued with Honor, her bright eyes were travelling round and round the room in search of something that she could claim as a set off against the disputed flounce. When she had made her choice she gave in with an air of aggrieved virtue.

"Well, if you must have it, it is only on condition that I take all the sables. They are the only furs of mother's that would ever suit my complexion. Is that a bargain?"

"What a Jew you are?" cried Honor. "But I suppose you must have them." And with some sharp scissors she ripped the coveted lace off a gown and tossed it into a corner among a heap of other things. "That's all right," she said, with a sigh as of one who had fought and won a great battle.

"That's my heap of things, Rosamund, and those are Honor's," explained Laura, complacent at having got the furs she wanted, and pointing to two great piled masses of property which were heaped at either end of the room. "We neither of us want any of those gowns over there. They might come in useful to you at some time or another, if you like to take them."

Rosamund looked with quiet scorn from one cousin to the other.

"I am sure you are very kind, but I have no desire to flaunt through the world in any of my dead aunt's clothes."

Honor pulled down her mouth sourly, and Laura shrugged her shoulders.

"What a horrid way you have of putting things, Rosamund. I suppose you mean that as a dig for us, but really I do not see why we should not have our own mother's things."

"Nor do I," answered Rosamund. "You have every right to them. But is it worth while to quarrel about them?"

"I am sure I did not wish to quarrel, but Honor is so ridiculously self-willed. I was quite prepared to be most amiable about them, only of course she wanted everything that she knew would suit me."

"Well, and haven't you got them?" said Honor from her knees on the floor, where she was smoothing out and folding up a quantity of richly jewelled embroidery. "You have got your own way about it all, I am sure."

The girls were just going to begin hostilities again when a heavy footstep was heard advancing in the corridor.

Lady Charlotte Lundy, her arms full of a heterogeneous collection of articles, loomed tall through the doorway.

"What on earth have you got there?" cried Laura and Honor together.

Lady Charlotte sank heavily into an empty chair, and dropping the armful of things into her lap, drew the hem of her skirt round them, ostensibly to prevent them from slipping to the floor, but really in order that her nieces should not see what she had got.

"Just a few slight remembrances of your poor dear mother. As I came in this morning I met your father and told him there were one or two little things I should so like to have, and that really just now I was not in a position to attend the sale and buy them. He told me I could take what I liked, and so I have just been in the drawing-room—"

Honor was on her feet in a moment. All the instincts of acquisitiveness were aroused in her, and every drop of Scotch blood in her veins was on fire to do battle for what she considered as belonging either to herself or her sister.

"We have not been in the drawing-room ourselves yet, Aunt Charlotte. Father could never possibly have meant that anybody should choose anything of mother's until we had taken what we wanted ourselves."

With rude hands she pulled down Lady Charlotte's protecting skirt and revealed to the cruel light of her own and Laura's eyes a whole lapful of little curios and rare toys.

"Well, I never!" she cried; and Laura, with her greedy little hands up, added, "Oh, but you cannot have those!"

Rosamund, leaning there with her white face and quiet eyes, watched the fight begin all over again. Every scrap of silver, every quaint carved ivory, miniature jewelled watches, old daggers, and the thousand and one expensive toys that nowadays crowd the little tables of a fashionable lady's drawing-room were severally fought over. Laura wanted the enamelled *bonbonnières*, and Honor, without a word, annexed the snuff-boxes. A tiny fan, painted on chicken skin and accredited to Marie Antoinette, was almost torn into pieces between the three, who with scarlet cheeks and shrill voices

squabbled disgracefully till Rosamund's very heart grew
sick within her. Suddenly above the noise her keen ear
caught a slow, heavy footstep coming up the big staircase
and advancing towards the room where they were. She
could not mistake the sound; she knew it was her uncle,
and she would not have him see for the world this
fight and wrangle over his dead wife's possessions.
Turning swiftly, she ran down the corridor and met
him. She slipped one hand through his arm and led him
to a window.

"Where were you going, dear?"

He looked a little strangely at her. His thoughts
had been for some time busy with the memory of his dead
wife, and for the moment he could not realise who was
speaking to him.

"Oh, is it you, Rosamund, my child?" he said, after a
minute or two, looking down into her eager face. "I
was going to your aunt's room, my dear."

"Not just now, uncle," she urged. "People are in
there—the room is in disorder—a little later when it is
tidied and straight."

She looked fearfully over her shoulder as she spoke,
afraid every minute lest the sound of the women's quarrel should reach his ears.

"Come down to the studio again, won't you, with me?
Is everything finished there? Are you certain you have
packed everything? You know, uncle, I feel now that I
must really look after you. I am perfectly sure that if
I went there now I should find no end of things in the
oak cabinet and the Italian chest."

"Perhaps, my dear, perhaps," said Mr. Kerquham.

"Well, then, why not come down with me and let us
have a final search? You see it would be such a pity if
after the rest of the things have gone away to be stored

we should find that a lot had been left behind.   Won't you come?''

He looked longingly towards the far end of the corridor, but she continued talking, and insensibly to himself drew him down the stairs again.

He had altered very strangely since his wife's death. A few people who had seen him said he would never hold up his head again, for he looked old and worn beyond his years.   Others, however, and chief among them his doctor, had said that all he wanted was change—change of surroundings and hours and food.

"Go away where you have never been before," the cheery physician had cried.   "See things that you have never dreamed of and people whom you did not know to exist.   You will be back again in a year and will give us a lot of wonderful new pictures.''

Three minutes later the same cheery physician, looking a little less pleased with himself than usual, had met Rosamund in the hall.

"Your uncle has told me, my dear young lady, that you propose to be his companion during the next few months.   I advise you very strongly to get him away as soon as you can.   He has been a wonderful specimen of a fine, healthy man, but this shock has touched him very nearly.   Take him away, my dear, take him away at once.''

Since that day Rosamund's intention to be all in all to her uncle had been strengthened, and she now felt towards him as a mother feels towards her helpless baby.

Now she led him to the studio, and for an hour made a gay pretence of turning out all sorts of forgotten treasures.   She engaged him in an animated discussion as to whether he should keep or sell a box full of old costumes, and as to whether the sketches of his youth should be packed among his other drawings or incontinently destroyed as mere scribbles. In her own endeavours to keep him amused and to prevent him from carrying out his intention of going to his wife's room, she forgot much of her own trouble, and it was only when the luncheon bell rang hollow and loud through the bare house that she again thought of her cousins.

"Go into the dining-room, dear," she said to her uncle. "I must just run upstairs and wash my hands; just look how dusty they are." And she ran upstairs lightly, and once again to Mrs. Kerquham's room.

The chief combatants had left the battle-field, carrying with them the spoils of war. The place was now in possession of half a dozen maid-servants, who were picking over and sorting out what had been left by Laura and Honor. As she stole away Rosamund thought of a picture she had once seen which depicted a crowd of ghost-like, ragged, creeping creatures who come forth in the depth of night and strip to the last rag the dead bodies of those who have fallen on a battle-field.

In her own room the same thing had been going on. Everything had been swept away. As she passed down to lunch she heard the excited maids comparing notes one with the other as to how smart they would look on their next Sunday out.

CHAPTER XXVIII

A CLIMBER'S VILLAGE

NEARLY fourteen months had passed since Mr. Kerquham and Rosamund Keith had left London and their friends in search of the distraction and change of scene which the former desired so much. During all that time they had been wanderers over the face of Europe, had wintered in Italy, spent Easter in Rome, and had passed the early summer in Paris before starting on a pilgrimage which had carried them all through the picturesque old towns and great galleries of Spain and Germany. In early autumn Mr. Kerquham had the sudden revulsion of fancy which comes to people who have been long among the cities of the plain and the bustle and turmoil of the great centres where men do congregate. He had wakened one morning, and bade Rosamund pack her trunks and make ready for a flight into the mountains, and she, obedient to his slightest caprice, had done as he wished, and had gone with him up and down the highways and byways of Switzerland.

It was now the second week in September, the time when, as a rule, the stolid German and the travelling Englishman begin to turn their steps towards their respective fatherlands, and when the great bare mountain hotels dismantle their scantily furnished bedrooms, close the wooden shutters, and dismiss their armies of waiting men and women. But this year the season was marvellously late. Glorious days were succeeded by summerlike nights, during which only the frozen dew fell on the highest peaks. The steamers on the lakes were still filled with passengers, and every *gasthaus* and hotel was crowded to the door.

It was a magnificent afternoon when the little train which runs from the Visp Valley pulled up at the spruce terminus station of Zermatt, that famous hub of the mountaineers' universe. From every open window bristled alpenstocks and ice axes, and half a dozen guides who lounged over the railings behind which the omnibuses stood, smiled in their beards at the pleasing sight of the newly arrived stream of visitors.

As Rosamund helped her uncle from the carriage she asked him if he would drive or walk up to the hotel.

A year ago it would have been a strange question to put to hale, hearty Alban Kerquham, but a subtle yet sure change had come over him during his months of wandering. His still broad shoulders had lost their uprightness, while his fine chest had hollowed somewhat. His hair was now almost white, and his once ruddy face paler and loose-skinned. His fine eyes still shone with kindliness from beneath the penthouse of his heavy brows, but a net-work of little wrinkles marred their beauty. He walked with a big stick by his niece's side down the platform as he answered:

"I think we will take the omnibus, dear. It isn't far, I know, but we have had a long pull in the train from Geneva, and I feel a little tired."

Rosamund smiled sadly as she helped him into the omnibus and with grave self-possession picked out her luggage. How changed things were from the time she and her uncle left "The Hurst"! At first he had found amusement and distraction from his grief in arranging and conducting all their journeys, but as the months went by she noticed that each move from city to city interested him less. She had urged upon him the necessity of employing a courier, but he had protested with some heat that he was not yet so infirm or so ignorant of the ways of travel as to need bear-leading, like a Yankee or an old woman. Still, after a time, he had not demurred when she herself took to arranging trains, securing tickets and rooms, and he even permitted her the doubtful privilege of investigating the bills and making all the payments.

On her side she never attempted to alter any decision he might come to or to thwart any wish he might express with regard to their travels. Rather with sweet cheerfulness she made his desires her own, and it was with a sympathetic and mutual pleasure that they found themselves in the great mountain valley that lies at the foot of the mighty Matterhorn.

Rosamund was, in fact, delighted to have come here. The magnificent scenery she had just passed through, the rush of the mountain torrents, the sweet pure air blowing down from the everlasting snows, had filled her anew with that joy of living which for so long had been in abeyance within her. The lakes had been beautiful, but they were too hot and enervating for one of her active temperament. So many of the people, too, in the hotels down there were invalids, who were content to bask all day in the hot sun and to sit at night under the too luxuriant trees and watch the bats flitting out against the evening sky. She had felt suffocated in such surroundings.

As the lumbering omnibus rattled over the narrow stone road, forcing the foot passengers on to such apology for a footpath as there was, her appreciative eyes noted with delight how different everything was up here.

Although it was evening and the sun was sinking fast behind the mountains, the whole of the little village was bustle and vivacity. When the omnibus pulled up before the verandah of the Mont Cervin Hotel, Rosamund noticed at once that the roadway, which had been widened at that point, was quite taken up with a number of mules and pack horses, guides and travellers, who had all come down from the Gorner Grat and the Riffel Alp. The party consisted mainly of Americans, who were talking at the tops of their voices and arguing with the guides in a mingled *patois* of bad French and worse English on the matter of payment.

On the wide steps where she stood to watch her luggage sorted from the rest, a party of three young men were preparing to set out on a long climb. Filled with the novelty of the situation, and knowing that her uncle was within, speaking about the rooms and asking for his letters, she leaned against the low wooden balustrade and watched the preparations that the mountaineers were making.

Under ordinary circumstances, she thought, they might be good-looking, smart young Englishmen. At the present moment their appearance was anything but prepossessing. Each man had the lower part of his legs encased in the thickest and clumsiest of worsted stockings. Huge boots, which were greased and decorated with large, square nails, about half an inch in height, were bound round their ankles with heavy leathern laces. Knickerbockers and a short, thick jacket of rough tweed covered the flannel shirts and knitted Spencers, which, while they were warm, were æsthetically ugly. Their sun-bronzed throats and wrists were innocent of collars and cuffs. Soft brown felt hats, round which were tied a pair of blue glass spectacles, were pulled well down over their heads. One of them, a lithe, long lad of twenty, had pinned several bunches of *edelweiss*—that woolly mountain flower—in front of his hat. There were four guides for the party, all dressed in the strong brown clothes, the cloth for which is woven in the village by the women during the long, dark, cruel, winter months. With much laughing and talking the young men were packing the bags which each one was to carry on his back. Flannel shirts and woollen stockings, pipes, tobacco, warm slippers, and comforters were all lying on the floor of the verandah, and were thrust indiscriminately into the packs. As each was filled its mouth was drawn together by a strong rope that hissed sharply through the steel rings.

"I beg your pardon," said one of the young men, suddenly turning to Rosamund, and, stepping aside, she found that she had been standing before a heap of well used ice axes and alpenstocks, which were already deeply scored with the names of conquered mountains. Each man selected his own, while the guides slung over their shoulders long coils of strong rope and stout leather flasks holding brandy. A little crowd assembled to wish the climbers good luck and a safe return.

"When do you come back?" cried a pretty girl from a window which overlooked the verandah.

The three young men pulled their hats from their heads, and one looking up at her, answered back:

"To-day is Monday; with luck we shall be back on Friday night."

"So long as that?" pouted the young lady. "What shall we all do while you are gone?"

"Why, look forward to our return, of course, and speculate as to all the wonderful adventures we shall tell you about."

"You will have no adventures," interrupted a sun-burnt, elderly man, taking his cigar from his mouth and looking up at the quiet sky. "It will be the easiest thing in the world. This weather is marvellous."

"Yes," chimed in another, "and the glass is as steady as a rock."

"By Jove! I wish I were going with you," said a rather languishing young man in the most immaculate of clothes, who was leaning against the doorpost and sucking a cigarette.

The four guides laughed among themselves, and the eldest of the party cried:

"Müller here thinks that a good joke. You would be done up before we got to the Schwarz Zee."

But Müller, the guide, was a business-like man, and having had his laugh, thought it time to attend to work.

"We must start, gentlemen," he said in his guttural Swiss-English.

"Good-bye! Good-bye! Good luck! Hope you will have a good time!" and amid waving handkerchiefs and feminine cries of felicitation and hopes for a safe return the party started out, turning to the left as they got into the road and making for the head of the valley.

"They have left a bit late," remarked a red-faced man. "It will be quite dark before they get up to the Black Lake."

A gong rang from within the house, and the little party melted away.

"We have very nice rooms, my dear," said Mr. Kerquham at Rosamund's elbow. "I have ordered dinner in an hour. It will be pleasanter to dine quietly by ourselves after the *table d'hôte*. Besides, there are a lot of letters. Will you come upstairs?"

Mr. Kerquham was quite right; he and Rosamund

had charming rooms on either side of a little salon on the first floor and overlooking the open space in front of the hotel.

"We shall see all that goes on here, uncle, without any trouble," said Rosamund, as she closed the window, and taking off her hat, prepared to unpack such things as they would immediately require.

While she busied herself unpacking, Mr. Kerquham sat in a big chair and opened a large batch of letters which had been awaiting him for some days.

She was in her own room unfastening her dressing-bag when she heard his voice calling her.

"Rosie, dear, here is a piece of news! I have a letter from Laura."

She ran to him and stood with her head a little on one side, and the smile with which she always listened to his words curving the corners of her sweet, red lips.

"Now, uncle, I am going to try and guess what is in that letter. Your face is going to tell me. It is news that has astonished you. I can tell that. And you are a little pleased—a little disappointed, too. Now, there is only one thing that could make you look like that. Laura is going to be married."

Mr. Kerquham laughed and laid the letter on the table.

"Rosamund, you are a witch. You have guessed right at once."

"Yes, but I have not finished yet. I have only stated a bald fact. I am going into details now. Laura is going to be married to the very last man in the world whom you would have expected her to look at or to look at her."

"Right again, Rosamund. Now, are you clever enough to tell me the name?"

Rosamund put her lips together and knitted her brows in thought.

"I must first think of the sort Laura would not have married, uncle—a kind of weeding-out process, you know. He cannot be a poor man. He cannot be some one whom she can't turn round her little finger. He cannot be very handsome, because Laura would never stand divided admiration, she would want it all for herself. He is not a country man, because she adores London, and by the same inference he is not a soldier or a sailor."

She clapped her hands together. "Uncle, I believe I've guessed. For your own face has told me that he is the most unlikely man in the world, and yet he is a man who fulfils all the requirements that I know Laura must have. It is Hamish Lundy, isn't it?"

Mr. Kerquham nodded his head, and Rosamund, seeing she had amused him, exerted herself still more, and proceeded to bewail mockingly the faithlessness of one who had once worshipped at her own shrine. Then she finished by throwing up her hands and wishing them both a happy life.

Mr. Kerquham, for answer to that, pushed another letter towards her.

"That is from your great-aunt Charlotte, my dear. She seems perfectly content; says Laura has steadied down, and that all her previous faults have been merely the error of youth and superabundant spirits."

Then he sighed. "I often wonder where Laura got her disposition from, she was never a true Kerquham; she had a strain in her that was alien to all the rest of us."

Later they dined almost alone at a small table in the large *salle*. A score of waiters, who chatted among themselves in bastard German, French, or Italian, were busy cleaning the three long tables where the multitude of visitors had just been fed. Most of the lights were out, but one was left for their use, and before they had finished the soup another was switched on over the next table to their own. They spoke but little as they ate, and so Rosamund had ample leisure to study the solitary man who a few minutes later swung with a heavy stride down the long room and seated himself close by them.

He was a very big man, and would have been abnormally tall but that his great breadth was in proportion to his height. He wore the roughest of clothes, and his heavy boots were clogged with clay and mud. His face and neck and hands were burnt almost as black as the short, thick hair which grew in little tight curls all over his head. To Rosamund, who had but just arrived among the great mountains, and who had had her first glimpse of life in what is called a "climber's village," this new-comer, with his giant frame and his look of indomitable courage and strength, seemed the very epitome of the life about her. When he raised his eyes from his plate and looked about the room, she saw that they were of a light blue, yet misty and deep in expression as are the eyes of people who live much alone and spend their days in communion with nature rather than with their fellow-men.

He finished his meal before they did, and Rosamund watched his broad back disappearing down the vista of the now empty dining-room. When a little later she and her uncle moved into the drawing-room of the hotel the big man was there. He sat in a far corner, buried in a huge chair, with a paper held before his face, and very little else but his rough boots and coarse stockings and his great, strong, brown hands to be seen. But the girl noticed that all eyes in the room were perpetually being

directed towards him, and when, by-and-bye, he picked
his way out of the room, passing with a certain clumsy
politeness among the crowds of women, her keen ears
caught on all sides the echoes of the chorus of wonder
and praise and admiration that rose up the moment he
had gone.

"The most wonderful thing ever done."

"It was he who saved the guides."

"They say up here that he bears a charmed life."

"The men positively worship him in these parts."

When later on Rosamund went upstairs with her
uncle, who had been sitting during the evening over by
the wood fire and chatting with the circle grouped around
it, he said to her:

"We have quite a celebrity in the hotel."

"Have we, dear? I thought the only thing that people here talk about or appreciate is climbing up a mountain and scrambling down again. I have been amusing
myself listening to the chat this evening, and I feel as if
I have been up every mountain for miles round. Every
one has either been up or is going up. Such commonplace subjects as homes, relations, books, and newspapers
seem to be absolutely tabooed here. One little lady
to-night—the one with the fair hair who was writing
letters at the table where I was sitting—began to tell
another of the dreadful attack of whooping-cough her
baby had had last May. The other lady simply said:
'Oh! how very sad it must have been for you, but I
wonder what kind of mule I shall get to-morrow to take
me up to the Riffelberg.' And then, for fear the little
woman should say any more about her baby, the other
one proceeded to relate her exploits last week on Mont
Rosa, and how she had twice been up as far as the
Grands Mulets on Mont Blanc, but had been obliged each

time to turn back by bad weather. I should have thought that no ordinary celebrity—not even a great painter like yourself, dear—would be even allowed to live up here."

"Of course not—of course not," cried Mr. Kerquham, rather shortly, for his mood in these latter days was changeable. "We have left all that kind of nonsense and chatter about fashions and domestic life down below. We are up in the mountains now, my dear—the glorious mountains—the finest works of God—the most fascinating, beautiful things in the whole world—and it is only natural that people should talk of them and nothing else. Wait till you see the Matterhorn to-morrow with the morning sun shining on his great white sides. You will say that it is a grander sight than all the pictures we have seen in all the galleries of Europe. Celebrities as they are known to us, with their little petty successes, count for nothing in the face of such surroundings as there are here. The best man in these parts is the man who can do the biggest climb, who can conquer the peak ·that has been virgin up to now, or climb the 'chimney' that has defeated the bravest and the best. That is the sort of celebrity that you find here, and that is the sort of celebrity who is stopping here now."

"Really, uncle?" said Rosamund. "And who may he be? I have seen all sorts of famous men in my time. I should like to see a great mountaineer."

"He is a very tall man, they tell me—a fine fellow— an Englishman, of course, with the longest legs and the broadest shoulders that were ever made. He has travelled all over the world and done some splendid work in the Andes and the Himalayas. They say that he climbs these mountains here as if they were mere child's play, and the best guides of the place look upon him as a positive marvel."

"A big man, they say. I wonder—was he in the drawing-room this evening?"

"They said so," answered Mr. Kerquham, "but I did not notice. However, a very nice fellow—a General Creighton, who is here with his wife, a lady you would like to know, Rosamund—has promised to introduce Mr. Fraser to me to-morrow."

"Is that the celebrity?"

"Yes, Fraser, Hugh Fraser. They will have it that he is English, but his name smacks of Scotland, and I mean to ask him if he is any connection of the Frasers of Lochie Hall. If so, he will be a distant connection of my poor, dear wife."

For the next hour Rosamund sat and listened to her uncle's speculations about Mr. Fraser and his probable connection with her dead Aunt Margot. She always rather dreaded Mrs. Kerquham's name in the conversation, for her uncle became depressed in spirits and gloomy in thoughts when the remembrance of her death came back to him. By the time she was free to go to bed Rosamund could almost have found it in her gentle heart to hate this Mr. Fraser and all his exploits, for that he had innocently set her uncle on to a strain of thought which was bad for him and painful to her.

CHAPTER XXIX

HIGH PLACES AND PERSONS

WHATEVER sense of vexation Rosamund might have felt over night was dispelled in the morning when she was awakened by the rumbling of the guides' rough voices and the trampling of mules' feet on the gravel under her window. Springing from her bed, she ran across the polished wood floor, and peeping between the lattices of her blind uttered a little cry of delight. For fear that she should be detained by too long looking, she retreated from the window and began to dress as fast as she could. When her simple toilet was finished she crept into her uncle's room, to find him still sleeping, so she ran downstairs with a light heart and eyes that shone with eagerness to see all she could.

The big square hall, with its grey stone floor, was full of a lively crowd. Some pretty American girls, all affectation, twang, and drawl, were making much of a couple of St. Bernard dogs which lolled their tongues and swung their tails with a lordly air of indifference to the open admiration they excited. Young men with a great deal of swagger and portentously thick boots were talking loudly about their day's expedition, and betting one another bottles of champagne as to the time in which they would do such and such a walk. Trunks were being lashed together and swung across the backs of the patient mules, who knew perfectly well that they would have to toil up the valley to the Riffelberg Hotel, which stood like a little toy house, clear and white against the sky-line. Ladies in ostentatiously short skirts and ludicrously heavy boots were laughing audibly at others of their sex who were proposing to walk in French heels and lace-trimmed petticoats.

Making her way through the merry throng, Rosamund went out on to the verandah, down the few steps, and across the small open space to the main street. Opposite the hotel and on either side, in the morning sun, the shopkeepers had set out their wares on trestles and boards. Photographs and pressed mountain flowers, alpenstocks, cow bells, coarse stockings and rough boots, all basked in the sunshine together, for it was yet too early to fix up the gay shreds of cloth and cotton which during the mid-day sheltered the shops and the sellers from the blinding glare. To the right, down the street, a small glass window was filled with carved coral and tortoise-shell. The wares were Italian, and a short, beady-eyed, crop-headed Venetian stood in the doorway and grinned cheerfully as a string of mules laden with trunks passed slowly up the narrow street. Some new-comers of the night before sauntered out of the hotel and proceeded to choose alpenstocks and ice axes. The men tried on some hats, and a pretty girl masked her bright eyes behind a pair of blue spectacles. The whole party laughed, and Rosamund, out of sheer lightness of heart, laughed with them.

From the *salle* came the clatter of coffee cups, for although it was still very early, the day's excursions were already starting. Anxious fathers of families, desirous of toiling with their stout wives and bouncing daughters up to the wondrous Gorner Grat, from the edge of which great glacier they could see all the Alpine giants without the trouble of climbing them, were anxiously consulting guides and engaging mules. A fragile little lady swathed in deep black and attended by a maid was brought out of the hotel wrapped in rugs and deposited in a *chaise-à-porter*.

"Poor thing," said a sympathetic woman, as two stalwart men lifted their light burden and marched away with it up the street. "The doctors have sent her up to the Riffel, but it will be no use; she will come down in her coffin."

Rosamund sighed. Even in the midst of all this brightness and life the shadow of Death was stalking. The thought made her turn her eyes for a moment from the gay scene about her, and she looked for the first time up the valley to where the great Matterhorn reared its terrific head and shoulders against the glorious blue sky. She gave a little gasp. All through Switzerland, down on the lakes and in the busy gay streets of the sun-bathed towns, she had seen pictures of the Matterhorn, photographed in winter and in summer, draped in cloud or sharply clear. Its splendid outline had become so familiar to her that she had scarcely troubled to look at it, but now that she really saw it for the first time, its unassailable majesty and glorious grandeur thrilled her to the soul. She could not have imagined that anything so marvellous existed in the world without all that world coming to see it.

The summer had been so open and the autumn so warm and fair that all the snow had melted away from one side, which rose, a sheer black wall of rock, in sharpest contrast to the delicate white mantle that veiled the other shoulder. Not so much as a wisp of cloud lay across it. It seemed to her the most wonderful and the most beautiful work of God she had ever seen in her life, and as she looked from it to the great range that

stretched right down the valley and caught the sun
gleaming on the snowy sides, she ceased to wonder that
all this little village and the strangers who came to it
could only talk and think of mountains. No longer she
thought it strange that every morning the whole of Zermatt should rise intent on getting nearer to those vast
solitudes. She understood why at last in the drawing-
room the night before the old and the young, the men and
the women alike, could only speak of where they had been
and where they were going. Everything else seemed
small. The whole world was suddenly transformed into
great fields of ice, broken by mighty peaks, and she felt
as if she, too, had but one ambition, and that was to start
forth and go amongst them.

A party was starting, equipped like that she had seen
the previous evening, in coarse clothes with rough,
uncouth baggage strapped across their shoulders. They
said "good-bye," they and the guides, and went with a
swinging step out into the street. As they turned out of
sight she caught herself holding out her hands, and
almost fancied that she had said aloud the words that were
within her heart: "Take me with you. Let me go, too."

"Your skirts are all right for walking, but your boots
would be no good," said a man's voice close by.

Rosamund, still with the sense upon her that she had
spoken her thought aloud, flushed crimson as she turned,
and found that the big man with the broad shoulders and
the sunburnt skin was standing close by her and looking
her up and down with an amused smile in his light blue
eyes.

"You would never get along in them, you know," he
said, shaking his head and looking at her neatly-shod
feet. "Nice, useful boots for an English country road,
but no good for work."

"I am afraid that I am not going to do any work," replied Rosamund, "if by that you mean climbing."

He looked her up and down again, his critical eyes taking in every detail of her well-made, beautifully proportioned body, her deep bust and fine shoulders, her strong, lithe limbs, and the clear skin which told of perfect health. He noticed how neat was her gown of grey cloth, how closely her hair was bound about her shapely head, and how serviceable was her little hat.

"Why shouldn't you climb?" he remarked presently. "You look cut out for that kind of thing. Half the women who go in for it break down at the very beginning. That is why I never will work with ladies in a party. It spoils the whole business. But you look as if you would be different."

She flushed a little at the directness of his compliments, but with feminine quickness she had already gathered that a mountain hotel contains a community in which none can stand apart. The ordinary etiquette of life, that demands a certain amount of formality, is abandoned in the face of the marvellous surroundings of a "climbing" village. A mountain hotel is a republic. Each man is as good as another, until he has won his promotion by a mountaineering feat. Then, and then only, is he a somebody and worthy of consideration from his fellows.

Rosamund had appreciated that situation during the first five minutes she had been in the hotel. Every one spoke to every one else, for the mountains were a common bond of union between people of the most opposite natures.

"But at least if you do not climb, you will go for some walks."

"I should like to, of course. It seems to me that one's first instinct at a place like this is to get nearer to those beautiful mountains," and she nodded towards the great dentated wall of snow that filled the horizon. "But I am here with my uncle, and I do not know if he means to walk much."

"But that doesn't matter," said her companion brightly. "There is a kind of freemasonry, you know, among people of the same country when they meet in these out-of-the-way places. Any of the ladies here, I am sure, would be only too pleased to have you join their parties."

"People are very kind," answered Rosamund, "and it is probably my fault—but I never get on very well with strangers."

She did not mean to say anything rude, but Mr. Fraser, like many big men, was inordinately shy, especially of the feminine sex, and at her words the light melted out of his blue eyes, and squaring his big shoulders he made a stiff bow and walked away.

"Rosamund! Rosamund! Why, you know the celebrity. Who introduced him?"

Rosamund turned to her uncle, and by way of answer, asked him another question.

"Have you had any coffee yet? The air is fresh out here."

"No, I came to find you," he answered. "I have been speaking to a most charming woman in the *salle*. I want to introduce you to her at once. She is the most wonderful traveller—been everywhere and knows everything. She says that she can tell us of a most interesting trip for the coming winter."

Taking her arm, Mr. Kerquham led Rosamund

through the busy hall into the big dining-room, where two of the long tables were being perpetually relaid for early breakfast.

"This is my niece—Miss Sheldrake," said Mr. Kerquham, leading Rosamund up to a short, square lady, who looked at her with very piercing eyes over the top of a large piece of bread spread with honey.

"Sit down, my dear, sit down and give us some coffee," Kerquham went on. "I want you to listen carefully to what Miss Sheldrake says. Her proposition is most interesting."

The short lady smiled a large smile, and Rosamund, looking at her across the narrow table, thought she was quite the ugliest woman she had ever seen. Her hair, which was short and almost white, stood out in dishevelled, spiky locks about her round, ruddy face, which was broad and flattened to an absurd degree. Her sturdy shoulders and flat chest were loosely garbed in a red merino blouse, which was caught in round the waist by a well-worn leathern belt. In crossing the room, Rosamund had noticed that her skirt of grey frieze was narrow and exceedingly short, and that her large square feet were shod in the most approved type of mountaineering boots.

"I have been talking to your uncle, Miss Keith," began Miss Sheldrake in a loud, masculine voice. "He tells me that he doesn't like this place at all. Too many people about, and not at all the sort of thing he wants."

Rosamund turned startled eyes on her uncle. Last night he seemed perfectly pleased and contented with everything. So far as she knew he had slept well. Surely if there had been any complaint to make, it should have been to her and not to an utter stranger. Perhaps

Mr. Kerquham read her thoughts, for he began in tender apology:

"There is too much noise here, my dear—a great deal too much noise. A lot of young men and women chattering and clattering about the place. It disturbs me and gets on my nerves. I feel I shall not be able to work here. I was thinking while I dressed this morning that we must move on to some place out of the beaten track—and then I met this lady on the stairs—and she quite agrees with me, Rosamund, that this is not at all the place for me to be in. Presently she will tell you of a most charming trip that she took herself a year ago. Absolute solitude—beautiful scenery—delightful people—"

"So handsome! so picturesque!" ejaculated Miss Sheldrake, smiling till her mouth stretched across her face.

"Among whom," went on Mr. Kerquham, "we shall be very happy, my dear. Just you and I, you know, in a little world of our own with nobody to interrupt or to worry us."

He held out his hand—a hand that was thinner and whiter than it used to be—to Rosamund, and she, with the motherly instinct that all true women feel towards those they love, took his fingers in hers and stroked and patted them.

"Drink your coffee, dear, while it is hot. Then we will go outside and sit in the sun, and perhaps Miss Sheldrake will tell us of this wonderful trip."

All the morning through Rosamund sat in the verandah, staring at the immutable Matterhorn that only changed its expression with the shifting sun, and listened to Miss Sheldrake's harsh, monotonous voice. Only half her attention was fixed on what the lady said, and it was not till they went indoors again for breakfast and sat at the little table they had occupied the previous night that she at all realised what the purport of the morning's conversation had been.

"I must say, my dear," began Mr. Kerquham, "the idea pleases me very much. We had better go straight through to Budapest. We were in Vienna last autumn, and don't want to stop there again. From there we can get down quite easily, Miss Sheldrake says, to Serajevo and on through Herzegovina to Cettinje. Then we shall have left everything behind us, dear, and can do just as we please and wander through that strange, unknown country till the winter is past, when we can go over the mountains into Greece—or perhaps—Miss Sheldrake says that there are parts of Salonica which are charming and well repay a visit."

Rosamund had dropped her knife and fork.

"But, uncle, when are we going to do all this?"

"Now, directly, of course," he replied, energetically. "Bless my soul! I don't want to waste any more time here. We cannot get back to Geneva to-day, but you must pack up and we will start in the morning."

"Leave this to-morrow?"

"Certainly. Didn't I tell you that all these people with their babel and noise are making me quite ill? Surely you don't want to stop in a place that you see I don't like."

His unusual impatience hurt the girl, and her eyes filled with tears.

"Oh, uncle, you know that my desires are yours. Of course I will pack to-day and we can go to-morrow. Yet there are things I should like to have seen here."

"Miss Sheldrake says the scenery in Montenegro and Albania is far finer than anything here. You ought to be very pleased, Rosamund, to be going to a place where scarcely an Englishwoman has ever set foot. Now, my dear, I will write my letters home this afternoon, and tell Laura I am glad to hear her news. Then we will walk down to the station and find out whether it is best for us to go back to Geneva or if we can get to Vienna any shorter way."

Rosamund finished her meal in depressed silence. She was working hard to do her duty, and till lately it had been a labour of the purest love, but she was young and healthy and active, and every instinct of her nature cried aloud for more varied companionship and a more natural occupation than tending the whims of a man, who as despite her love she could not help noticing, was growing more difficult to please and cheer every month of their wandering.

When he went upstairs to write his letters, she still sat at the luncheon table with her chin in her hand, staring out of the window at the nearer pine-clad mountains and the distant snowy peaks. She had made up her mind that morning that she could be so happy here. It was all so fresh and clear after the close, hot cities in which they had lived for so long. Without wishing to make friends with any of the people about her, their bright talk and their daily movements interested her so much. She had even hoped to have gone a little nearer these unattainable summits that were now to prove to her nothing but dreams.

By-and-bye she pushed her chair back and sauntered dispiritedly out of the room. She knew her uncle was busy upstairs, so she crept back again to the corner in the verandah where she had spent the morning. The place was almost empty now. A few guides lounged in the patch of shade, but most of Zermatt was up among the mountains, for the weather was so fair and promised so well that every day saw the start of big expeditions.

At the far end of the little wooden terrace two Germans were discussing their coffee and *vermouth*. Otherwise she was alone. No, not exactly, for there was Mr. Fraser again, walking up the gravel road with his heavy stride, and in his shy, strange way taking off his cap to her. It was a sense of loneliness that drove her to speak to him. She leaned over the balustrade and said:

"You advised my taking some walks about here, and I told you I did not think I should be able to. Now I know I cannot."

"Why not? Do your boots hurt you?"

Rosamund shook her head and smiled.

"You seem to have a very bad opinion of my bootmaker, or else of me, for you persist in thinking that I am ill shod. But it is not my boots. I am going away to-morrow."

"What for?" said Mr. Fraser. He came up the steps of the verandah, and gaining her side sat down in a wicker chair, which creaked beneath his weight. ."Is the hotel uncomfortable? If so, I will just speak to the people here. They know me and will do anything I ask them."

"Our rooms are charming."

"Then what is it?"

"A lady here has been putting it into my uncle's head that it is not a very nice place, and has been advising him to take the most extraordinary journey into the most out-of-the-way part of the world."

Mr. Fraser leaned forward on his knees.

"Miss Sheldrake?" he queried.

Rosamund nodded.

"Do you know her?" she said.

"Don't I? If she were not a woman I should say she was the original wandering Jew, and the worst of her is that because she is always on the move herself, she thinks everybody else ought to be so, too. It makes her positively miserable to see people arriving at a place with a lot of trunks and bags and things and settling down for a nice comfortable stay. On what track has she sent your uncle off?"

"I scarcely know," said Rosamund, shaking her head. "I am afraid I am very ignorant, but I know we go to Budapest and then to Herzegovina and Montenegro."

"You and your uncle? That old gentleman I saw with you last night—are going on that journey alone?"

"Yes; we have no one else to go with us."

Mr. Fraser's light eyes grew dark with thought for a moment.

"I was proposing to go that way myself soon," he said. "When do you start?"

"We leave here to-morrow morning.'

"Ah! I had thought of going to-morrow, too. Will you introduce me to your uncle?"

"With pleasure," answered Rosamund; "here he is."

Mr. Kerquham came out of the hotel with some letters in his hand.

"Uncle," cried Rosamund, springing to her feet, "this gentleman has been talking to me about the journey you propose to make."

Mr. Kerquham looked up and lifted his soft felt hat from his head with old-fashioned courtesy:

"I am delighted to meet you, sir. I was hearing only last night of your exploits. You are quite a celebrity here. Your name, I think, is Fraser."

Mr. Fraser bowed.

"I wonder if by chance you are related to the Frasers of Lochie Hall."

"Certainly; my father was a second cousin of the present laird."

At that Mr. Kerquham slipped his arm into Mr. Fraser's and forgot all about Rosamund. The two men walked down the steps and across to the post office. For a moment she hesitated, and then followed them. From the post office they went down to the station, where Mr. Kerquham delved into the intricacies of Swiss time-tables and through services to Austro-Hungary. Now and then Rosamund caught a few words which induced her to think that Mr. Fraser was trying to dissuade her uncle from his projected journey. Once, indeed, he turned aside to her and murmured:

"He has a will of his own, your uncle."

Rosamund smiled gravely.

"You are very kind. I know what you are doing, but it is no use. He has made up his mind to go on this journey, and he will do so."

"Then that settles it," said Hugh Fraser, in his blunt way, and offered his arm once more to Mr. Kerquham.

When they left the station they went up the street as far as the little storm-beaten church, where in the narrow limits of the churchyard lie so many men who have died terrible deaths on the mountain sides. In the angle of a buttress Rosamund read the inscriptions on the tombs of those Englishmen whose lives were demanded in speedy sacrifice by the first conquered Matterhorn. On the other side of the church and under the lee of the little mortuary chapel, where even that afternoon a dead guide lay waiting burial, she saw the rows of graves, each with a little wooden cross at its head, and all so simple and poor. On one side of her were the hotels where the wealthy English and Americans danced and flirted and passed such hours as they had to spare between their mountain scrambles. On the other hand were the guides' cottages—wretched little wooden huts, stained by the weather to a soft, velvety brown, falling into a thousand pieces and leaning over on their worn piles into the ooze and dirt of the narrow street.

On the green hillside behind the cottages the tethered cows were being milked, and broad-faced women with small eyes and scanty hair were labouring up and down the little sheeptracks laden with heavy pails. Already the return of the day's excursionists had begun, and as she and her uncle and Mr. Fraser walked along, they were jostled and pushed by the patient mules on to the little footpath which, in its turn, was overhung almost to the edge by the stalls of the shopkeepers. What a strange mixture, she thought to herself, as she looked at the village round her, with its poverty and wealth, and then up at the mighty, frozen mountains, all flushed rose pink in the setting sun. And she remembered that this wretched place was only kept alive and for the handful of moneyed people who went there year after year and used it as a playground for a few weeks.

The two men stopped in front of the Mont Rosa Hotel, and sitting down at a little table ordered some coffee.

"And what is your real opinion of Zermatt?" said Mr. Fraser to Rosamund, as they sat together.

"I don't quite know. This morning from the hotel verandah it looked the brightest, happiest, merriest place in the world, but now, since I have gone up the street and seen the poor little church and the God's Acre full of the dead fathers and sons of the women who live here, now that I have seen their wretched homes, their awful poverty and their unspeakable dirt, I think it is a very sad place."

"They are not so poor as you think," said Fraser. "In bad years it goes hard with them, for they live for nine months out of every twelve on what is made during the tourists' season, but a splendid year like this, when from May to September Zermatt is crowded, means prosperity to the whole community."

"But why don't they make it any cleaner?" she cried a little disgustedly, as a tired pack horse stumbled through the mire, splashing her neat gown.

"To alter Zermatt would be to spoil it. I have come here ever since I was a boy, and my father came for years before me. I do not believe a cottage has been mended since I knew it, or the road even cleaned; but we old *habitués* love it best like that. It is picturesque, and it reminds us of all the good times we have had here."

"Rosamund is much too particular," remarked Mr. Kerquham, helping himself to a second glass of fine champagne. "From what Miss Sheldrake tells me, she will have a lot to put up with when we get down into Turkey."

"Then I'm afraid I shan't like it, uncle," said Rosamund, with a grave smile.

"I am afraid you will not," assented Fraser, under his breath.

CHAPTER XXX

'MID MOSQUES AND MINARETS

THE Kerquhams' journey, in which Mr. Fraser joined them, commenced under the most commonplace circumstances. It was only when they swept through the valleys and gorges of the Austrian Tyrol, and he saw the little cottages nestling among the woods, that Mr. Kerquham expressed any pleasure.

Even Budapest, the "Pearl of the Danube," with its handsome women and its fine men, had no attraction for him, and they only rested there twenty-four hours before taking train for the East.

For it was indeed the East, with its dirt and its picturesqueness, its dark-skinned men and its veiled women, into which Rosamund stepped with magic suddenness when she alighted from the train at Bosnia's border town of Brod. The porters at the dingy little station wore the fez, the embroidered jacket, and the loose trousers that mark the Turk, and as the train rumbled away, Rosamund caught sight of a veiled face peeping curiously through a latticed window. As the sun rose and a flood of pink light revealed the whole landscape to her wondering eyes, she thought for a moment that she was back in Switzerland. Great rounded hills swelled up on either side of the railway. Close to the track rushed and roared an angry little stream that leaped over stones and gurgled round boulders in a fashion that was quite familiar to her.

"Are you disappointed?" asked Fraser from his seat opposite her, when, after gazing out of the window for an hour, she leaned back and half-closed her eyes.

"A little, perhaps, but I suppose I expected too much, and yet I do not quite know what I thought I should see."

"Wait till we get to Serajevo! That is Oriental, if you like, from one end of the town to the other. It might be a bit of Persia cut out and dropped into Europe."

Mr. Kerquham looked up from among his papers.

"That is the worst of it," he said. "Serajevo is a town. My niece will have no new sensations till she finds herself in the Highlands of Albania."

Mr. Fraser faced round in his seat.

"Are you serious, Mr. Kerquham, in your determination to go so far at this time of the year?"

"This time of the year?" he repeated, sharply. "What is the matter with the time of the year?"

"It is very late, and the weather is treacherous in these southern countries."

"Nonsense! it is the most open year they have had within the memory of man. I do not mind betting you, Mr. Fraser, that they are still climbing at Zermatt."

"But Zermatt is not Albania, Mr. Kerquham. There is half a continent between the two places."

Rosamund slipped her foot from under her skirt and touched Mr. Fraser, while her big eyes implored him dumbly to change the conversation, or at any rate to cease to discuss the proposed trip.

He looked back at her now with a reassuring smile, and turning again to the window studied the landmarks and told her that within an hour she would see the white minarets of Serajevo. Until then there was plenty to look at, for as they came nearer the town the country grew full of life.

The road ran close by the railway, and country carts, laden high with field produce and driven by cross-legged Turks, were creeping along with Oriental slowness. Women, who looked mere bundles of garments, were filling water-pots from the stream. In the middle of every little cluster of cottages the minarets of white mosques gleamed like snowy marble among the still green trees. The line crossed a plain that was verdant and smooth as a lawn. It was girdled by high hills, some of them bare and stern, others clothed with foliage as a stately dame is clothed in green velvet. Suddenly Hugh Fraser leaned forward and caught Rosamund by the arm.

"Look now!" he cried. "There is Serajevo. They call it the 'Golden City.' Is it not beautiful?"

And beautiful it was to the girl whose eyes had been sated with the regularity and stateliness, the order and method which has governed the building of all the great cities of Europe. The jumble of white palaces and little hovels, the exquisite mosques towering up against the blue sky, and the flat mud-coloured houses that clustered round them, the incongruous solid red brick buildings that the Austrians had built, the babble of an unknown tongue, and the passing of an unknown people all delighted her, as she stepped from the train.

The whole city was dominated by the great citadel, and the big hotel to which they went in search of rooms was a fine specimen of western architecture. But the girl cared for neither of these, and was only perfectly happy when Hugh Fraser took her to the bazaar.

What a magically suggestive word is that! To Europeans it seems to mean so much until it is attained, and then they find it means nothing at all. Never could Rosamund have imagined such a maze of narrow streets. darkened by the overhanging roofs of the low houses, which nearly met overhead. The narrow opening that was left between the eaves was overgrown by a tangle of a climbing plant, which cast a greenish shadow over the scene beneath. The road—for there was no pavement—was ankle-deep in mud and dirt, and she found it hard to force her way between the stalls which were let down from the fronts of the houses and laden with the most strange collection of goods she could have imagined. Here a board was filled with fruit—fine plums and pumpkins—and next to that was a pile of gold embroidery worked upon crimson velvet and fine black cloth. A man sold fezes just beyond, and three half-grown lads were carefully suiting themselves with head-gear in the middle of the jostling crowd.

At the corner of one street an aroma of coffee filled the air, and opposite a Spanish Jew was vaunting in loud tones the merits of his wonderful *nargilehs*. At one little shop—it was a mere hole in the wall—Rosamund paused and bought a fine gold chain to send to Laura as a wedding present. He was a grey-bearded Turk who sold it to her, and the bargaining between himself and Mr. Fraser was long and fierce. Rosamund thought it would never end, and a dozen times urged her companion to pay the price that was asked and let them go away. But Hugh Fraser had not travelled the world for nothing, and he only smiled his quiet smile at her, squared his big shoulders, and returned to the fray with unabated vigour.

"There!" he said at last as he put the parcel into her hands, "you have only paid a quarter more than the value of the thing. I would have beaten him down to the proper price if you had let me."

She laughed. "How do the natives manage?"

She stepped aside out of the mire to let a string of donkeys laden with market produce go by. Women with long veils and heavy cloaks were driving them.

"I suppose they do not rob one another much," she went on.

"No, it is a question of degree; the Jews rob the Turks, of course, and the Greeks best the Jews. Now I am going to take you to see the great mosque here. It is pure Byzantine, and they say that the lime tree that grows in the court is the biggest in the world. It was high summer when I came here last, and of an evening, in the fountain that lies beneath its shade, there were scores of Turks bathing."

"But I thought," cried Rosamund, "that the Turks never did bathe."

"Most of them don't, but a certain amount of water enters into their religion. Apart from that they are the most frankly unwashed people that exist. You will find that out a little later as you travel further south."

"How can we get to Jajace?" asked Mr. Kerquham, when at length they returned to the hotel.

"We can go by train to the foot of the old Citadel," answered Mr. Fraser, "that wonderful monument which will keep in the memory of man forever the name of Keglevitch, who held it against all Turkey, and who, when he died, was still unconquered."

They were roused at dawn the next day by the calling of the "muezzin" to prayer. From the roof of every mosque the summons went forth, and Rosamund, leaning from her window, thought how wonderful it was that at that moment every true Mussulman in the city was sending up the same petition to his God.

They started betimes, for the trip was a long one,

among high mountains that were virgin to the foot of
man, and past valleys in which they could see the maize
crops and the pastures where the sheep fed.   When they
arrived at Jajace they fulfiled the traditions of all travellers.   They wondered at the citadel and drank coffee
in the beautiful old gateway.   They climbed the winding
streets that cut a tortuous way between the thickly
placed houses; they marvelled at the holy ramparts, and
then wended their way down the rough path to see
the great cascade which shakes the old city by day and
by night, and fills the air with an everlasting roar of
many waters.   They stood at the foot of the ravine and
watched the two rivers Plevna and Verbas meet and
mingle their floods and fling them over the side of the
great ravine into the river-bed, where huge boulders and
rocks break the waters into foam rich with a thousand iridescent colours.

Then they took a carriage—a queer little wooden
box devoid of springs or cushions, and drawn by three
rough ponies—and dashed out to Jezero, the fashionable
suburb of the older town, where there was a lake bordered with graceful villas surrounded by verandahs.

Such were Rosamund's memories of Bosnia, for within
a few hours they were again in the train, and leaving the
swelling wood-clad hills behind them, they rushed into
the bare, sun-scorched, awe-inspiring Herzegovina.

The day was not hot enough to travel in the roofless
carriages and the train was stuffy and close, while the
limestone dust which lay thick on everything choked
them.   The passes through which they sped were
broken merely by great crags and the sparsest of coarse
vegetation.   It was all very grand, very lonely, and very
terrible.   It was only when they came down into the
plain of Mosta that lines of green and patches of trees

broke the bare aspect of the country. It was growing dusk as they steamed towards the city, but there was light enough to see that Hugh Fraser's keen eyes looked troubled and grave. .

"They have had a very bad summer here," he said, drawing his head in from the open window. "The tobacco has all been burned up with the heat and there is next to no maize crop."

"Yes, but look at those lovely pomegranate bushes," cried Rosamund. "I can see their flowers like great flames through the gloom."

"I am afraid that they are no sign of fertility and a good harvest, but when we drive out to-morrow you will see what an awful climate this place has. They are burnt up for eight months out of the twelve and frozen for the other four. I would sooner live anywhere than here."

"Even in Albania?" said Rosamund, with a little laugh, for Mr. Fraser's dislike for that country had become a joke with the party.

At Mosta the hotel was good, and to Rosamund's astonishment the man who attended on them at dinner spoke a fair smattering of English. In the evening they walked out for an hour before retiring to bed. Every door and window of the houses was closed with thick shutters, only the upper stories having light green blinds, which indicated that the harem lay behind them. The housetops were flat, and here and there a head peeped above the coping and stared at the travellers below. The streets were narrow and crowded and smelt most evilly, for Mosta is more than Eastern in its dirt.

Next morning, before leaving, they went to see the famous bridge—that single arch of which the inhabitants are so proud. In the streets, which were bright and

sunny, although it was October, Rosamund's keen eyes
noticed how lazily the men lounged against the houses.
No one seemed to work, and when later on they drove
through the little fields—most of them seeming no bigger
than a tablecloth—she noticed that they were quite
deserted, and that only here and there, at rarest intervals, a brown-skinned, prematurely-aged woman
scratched the uncongenial soil. They drove across the
plain to a little village which clustered round a great
house.

"They are making wine here," said Hugh Fraser.
"It is awful stuff, but it is what they drink among themselves."

The carriage pulled up, and the whole picturesque
scene was before them. Men and women together were
working, and the red grapes, the *blatimea*, and the white
Zelenka were brought, mixed together, in rough baskets
and low wooden carts. Without being sorted or overlooked they were tossed into a low vat, and there trodden and pressed in the most primitive fashion. A number of half-naked, brown children scrambled about on
the ground among the workers. Their mouths and
faces were stained with grape juice, and though they
were extremely and unspeakably dirty, they had yet the
charm and beauty that appertains to all young things.
Rosamund, who had left the carriage, caught one of the
little creatures in her arms, and picking it up, pressed
its dimpled face against her own. A big, fat woman,
who had thrown aside her heavy cloak and was helping
to fling the grapes into the wine-press, laughed and
nodded at the English girl.

"Are you so fond of children?" said Fraser.

"Indeed I am," she answered, hugging the little kicking thing to her, and laughing at its impotent struggles

to get free. "Who could help loving such funny little beings as these? They would be nicer of course if they were washed, but they are so innocent and so young, and their brown skins are so firm and dimpled that they are quite irresistible."

She let the little one go after pressing some silver into its dirty, fat palm, and then, leaning against the carriage, began to ask questions about the wine-making and how they tended the vines. Fraser answered her at random, for all his thoughts were occupied with noting her fine physique and frank nature, her perfectly healthy mind and her exquisitely proportioned body. Surely she was destined to be a good mother to handsome children.

But she chattered on about the people and the scene. A young Turk came and stood by them and told them that the people hoped to do better with the grapes than they had with the plums that year, that there had been no rain all the summer through, and that the caterpillars had eaten the leaves and the fruit had dried up on the trees.

"The whole country lives on those kind of things," said Fraser, when he had finished translating to Rosamund. "Their tobacco and their plums are the only things they manage to sell to other countries. They drink the wine themselves, and the maize they use for bread. They could do much better if they would only allow Western invention to come to their aid a little."

But Rosamund was looking now at something else.

"Ah, see!" she cried. "She is the most typical woman I have seen yet."

The woman at whom she pointed was evidently a stranger in those parts, for all the people were looking at her. She was dressed in an immensely full pair of

black *shalvars,* or Turkish trousers, which by reason
of their fulness made her ankles look singularly slender
and her feet very small.   A little jacket of purple velvet,
edged with a narrow fringe of gold, crossed her shoulders
and opened over the bosom to show a finely pleated
chemisette of white crêpe.   On her head was a small
turban, kept in its place by large gold pins and from
beneath which her black hair hung in two long plaits
which were fastened at the ends by golden ornaments.

"She comes from the Bosnian frontier, I think," said
Fraser.   "How picturesque she is, and how well you
would look in a dress like that."

Mr. Kerquham leaned out of the carriage.

"Rosamund, when we get back to Mosta we must try
and get a costume like that for you.   I will paint you in
it."

They drove back to Mosta by the light of the setting
sun.

"How short the days are getting," sighed Rosamund,
as they turned their backs on the merry group of wine-
makers.

"Yes, it is almost the middle of October," said
Fraser.

The thought that this fast-aging old man and this
young girl were going in a few days to leave behind
them every vestige of civilisation and go alone into an
absolutely unknown country struck him again, and he
resolved to make another effort to prevent what he considered a most foolish expedition.   He called up to the
driver in Italian: "When does your winter begin here?
You must have had enough of this hot weather."

The man leaned back in his seat, letting his horses go
their own way.

"The summer has been terrible," he said in his bastard language; "but the winter will be worse."

"What do you mean by that?" asked Mr. Kerquham.

"We have had no rain all the summer, signor. The sky has been cloudless for many months, but Allah is just and makes everything equal, and what does not fall in the summer must come down in the winter."

"Then you fear the snows?"

"We get winds here and rains," said the man, "but from the mountains the workpeople are coming down fast. The Italians are hurrying home. They do not like the cold, and a brother of mine who works at Cataro says the town is crowded, for there is no money to be earned in the Highlands until the spring comes."

"Attend to your horses, my good man," cried Mr. Kerquham, sharply, for he guessed the drift that the conversation would take. Then, with the obstinacy of a man who feels that he has made a mistake in the beginning, but intends to go through with it, he turned to Rosamund and said: "If there is any chance of the weather breaking, we had better go to Cettinje at once. The sooner we get into the Highlands, the sooner we shall be in some sweet, sheltered spot in Greece."

"You think of going on to Greece?" asked Fraser.

"I am not quite sure. I shall see. Sometimes I fancy I shall make for Constantinople."

The sun had set by now, and over the plain a grey dimness had crept. Mosta, with its low houses and fair white minarets, looked like a dream city in the distance. Rosamund leaned back as well as she could in the rough carriage and sighed. It seemed a pity that Mr. Fraser should worry so about the journey into Albania. Everything had been so pleasant up till now. The people were courteous, the hotels were good, and the cities and sights were beautiful. It was to her a very pleasant way of travelling—more congenial to her by far than putting up in the huge caravanseras and spending long weary days in picture galleries and museums. She almost wished that he would not be so persistent. It would be so much better to leave things as they were, and let her uncle carry through his pet scheme.

CHAPTER XXXI

THE WIFE OF A GENTLEMAN WELL KNOWN IN THE BEST SOCIETY

THE further out of the beaten track Rosamund and her uncle travelled, the more did Mr. Kerquham's health and spirits seem to improve. The autumn days were perfectly radiant, and the scenery through which they passed was the mcst exquisite they had ever seen. The valleys which lay between the wooded hills had already been cleared of their crops of maize and rye, and the tobacco fields had almost everywhere been stripped, but it was easy to see in those low lands, which are often inundated in the spring months and where the climate is always warm and moist, that the crops had been good and that fertility was the general rule. The little villages, too, although poor and simple, were well kept, and the huts of wattle and mud were in good repair and occupied by a contented people.

At Cettinje they left the train for good and all. The evening before they left the tiny capital of Montenegro, which in the distance looked like nothing more than a handful of rocks strewed upon an arid plain, Hugh Fraser took Rosamund to the bazaar, and there made her buy one of the heavy cloaks which the country people wear during the winter. In vain she argued that she had some furs with her, a sealskin coat, and a boa of sable.

"You won't regret your purchase," he answered, "and after all, if you don't want it, you can bestow it in charity on some one who does."

The guide they engaged was called Matia. He was tall, lithe, and fair of hair, like all the Miridite tribe— Highlanders who live in the fastnesses of the Black Mountains of Montenegro and the north of Albania. He did not wear the loose, easy clothes of the Turk, or the flowing petticoats and embroidered jacket of the country, for his lower limbs were clothed in tight trousers. About his waist he carried such arms as he could afford and a *yatakhan*. Across his back was strapped the universally worn long-barrelled Martini-Peabody rifle, and the close-fitting cap on his head was bound round his brows by a twisted red shawl. He was a Skreli guide, and had passed his whole life between the ports of Cataro, San Giovanni di Medua, and the capital, and had even—so he said—been over to Italy. He spoke a language which he called Italian, but which bore a very distant resemblance to such. Neither Rosamund nor Hugh Fraser liked him, for his fine blue eyes had a queer trick of shifting from the face of the person to whom he spoke, but he pleased Mr. Kerquham with his picturesque, swaggering air and his assurances that he knew every pass that led over the Charra Dagh Mountains into Turkey. It was Matia, too, who, when Rosamund and Fraser pointed out to Mr. Kerquham the crowds of labourers, Italians, Swiss, Austrians, and Hungarians, who were trooping from the uplands towards the sea coast, laughed at the implication that they were fleeing before coming bad weather.

"They have earned their money," he cried, airily, and shrugging his fine shoulders. "They are going home to spend it."

"But I heard some of the Swiss say that the snows were falling already in the Highlands." interposed Rosamund.

"What can mademoiselle expect? It is not always summer. But a little snow should not frighten the English people."

Mr. Kerquham turned sharply on his niece.

"Rosamund, once and for all, I tell you that I will brook no interference in this matter. For some reason of your own you have set your face against this expedition. If you are afraid to go with me, say so at once, and I will arrange that you return to Scotland while I go on by myself."

Rosamund flushed a little at her uncle's words, but she answered as sweetly and as patiently as ever: "Uncle, you know I would not do such a thing, and if I dread this journey it is on your account, dear. I am only afraid that it will prove too rough and uncomfortable for you."

The artist drew himself up to his full height, and for a moment looked quite his former self.

"Pooh! my dear," he cried with a light laugh. "There is plenty of life in me yet; you need not be afraid on my account."

That night, after he had retired to rest, Rosamund, full of doubt and fearful of what the future might bring forth, slipped out of her room again and went down the narrow stairs to the general sitting-room, where they had all dined together. The hotel was a very rough one—a foretaste of what they were to find further up the country. In one corner of the room two solemn Turkish merchants were smoking their *nargilehs*. A Montenegran gentleman—one of the Prince's court—with rich embroidery and gold bosses on his red velvet gyves, a spotlessly white and stiffly kilted petticoat, a vest of scarlet covered with fine gold thread, which in its turn was partly hidden by the large silver butts of the pistols thrust into his sash, was talking to Mr. Fraser, who in his rough cloth suit and flannel shirt looked peculiarly unpicturesque among such surroundings. At sight of her the two men stopped talking. The Montenegran rose from his seat, and making a bow first to Rosamund and then to Mr. Fraser, left the room.

Rosamund looked after him.

"What splendid fellows these are."

"Yes," said Hugh Fraser, "and very good chaps to boot. I have been having a long talk with him. He is the Prince's chamberlain, and hears most things that go on in these parts."

Miss Keith laughed as she sat down in the vacant chair and leaned her elbows on the table.

"Well, and what is the local news?"

"May I smoke?" asked Hugh Fraser by way of answer.

Rosamund nodded.

"I shall probably have to take to doing it myself if we go very much farther afield. Some of the inns we have passed the last day or two did not look very inviting."

Hugh Fraser pulled two or three times at his pipe, for like all travellers he refused to be. bound down by the strictures of cigar smoking.

"Miss Keith," he began suddenly, fixing his eyes on the opposite wall and knitting his hands together in a way that Rosamund had learned to know meant a certain amount of embarrassment, "must you go on this journey?"

"You heard what my uncle said this evening, Mr.

Fraser. I have done my best to make him alter his mind, but he is not easy to influence nowadays. He suffered a great grief last year—and he often—"

"Oh! you are trying to excuse him, I know, for his whims and sharp words, but I have not minded them. He is an older man than I am, and, besides, every one is entitled to his own opinions. Still I don't like your going on this trip."

"What more can I do?" asked Rosamund.

Fraser smoked hard for a moment. Then he pulled his pipe from his mouth and laid it on the table.

"Do you think your uncle would undertake this journey quite alone?"

"I don't think he would, although he says that nothing would alter his determination."

"Why not try the experiment?" suggested Fraser. "Why not tell him to-morrow that you absolutely refuse to go on?"

"Oh! I could not do that. I have no reason," returned Rosamund, clasping her slim white hands on the rough wooden table, and looking in Mr. Fraser's face with anxious eyes.

"Make *me* the reason," said Hugh Fraser.

"You? I don't understand."

"Yes! me."

He loosed his hands and slipped one across the table until his fingers lay close to Rosamund's. "Miss Keith, will you marry me? Oh! please do not think I am asking you to be my wife out of any pity," he added in a pained voice as he saw her start. "I am not a ladies' man, I know. I have lived too rough a life and been too much by myself to have very fine manners or to know quite the kind of way in which to make up to women, but I have admired you ever since that first evening I saw you up at Zermatt, and in a very few hours admiration changed into something else, and ever since then I have only been waiting for a chance of asking you to be my wife. The chance has come now. You want a reason—we both want a reason—to stop this mad journey. Let us go to your uncle to-morrow morning and tell him we are going to be married—in Vienna, Paris, London, where you will, so long as we can get him to leave this and come west with us at once.''

From the far corner Rosamund heard the gentle gurgle of the *nargilehs* and the murmurous voices of the cross-legged Turks. From the streets there seemed to come no sounds at all. The bare room faded away, the walls melted into trees, and the flaring lamp into a white, round moon. Again she heard Paul's voice in the garden of ''The Hurst,'' telling her that he loved her and would be faithful to her forever. Again she felt the pressure of his hands and the touch of his lips against her cheek as he asked her to marry him. How long ago all that seemed! Life at ''The Hurst'' was like a dream, and Paul—Paul, for all she knew, was dead, or if he were alive, could not marry her. For sixteen months she had had no sign from him. She did not know whether he was true to her memory or whether his heart still beat.

And then the London garden faded away, and Paul's voice died in the distance, and before her lay an awful range of mountain passes and wild gorges filled with a savage people or with a solitude that was even more terrible. In her ears there rang the changed notes of her uncle's voice, the tones of a man who had lost the savour of life, and who only sought to speed the few last years by perpetual change and a feverish desire of excitement.

As in a dream her past and future melted into the present, the little room in the Montenegran inn and—

Hugh Fraser. She never for a moment doubted his sincerity, she never for one second dreamed that he would be anything but a most loving and true husband to her. She grieved within her own heart that she could not just move her hand and lay her fingers in his and tell him that she would be his wife. It was almost a prophetic instinct that made her wish that she could go away with him at once and turn her back upon all this mysterious wild East, and just wander through the world with his broad shoulders and strong arms to keep trouble and anxiety from her. But she could not even formulate the wish clearly to herself, and an invisible force locked her hands within one another so that she could not move them.

"Will you give me your answer now, or would you rather wait till the morning?" asked Fraser.

But Rosamund feared what the thoughts and temptations of the night might be, so she turned her soft eyes on him and answered him:

"I thank you, Mr. Fraser, but I cannot marry you. I am not so foolish as to believe that you are merely asking me to be your wife out of pity. I do not think you are the sort of man who would marry a woman unless you really loved her, and it is because I feel sure that you love me that I must say No. I could not give you half of myself. My heart belongs already to another man."

"And he?" whispered Fraser, leaning forward eagerly. Rosamund shook her head.

"I do not know where he is. If he is alive my heart is in his keeping. If he is dead, it is in his grave. It is not mine to give."

Hugh Fraser struck a match and lit his pipe again.

"I am sorry, Miss Keith, that I have been too late."

They both rose from the table and walked across the room to the foot of the stairs. There he held out his hand.

"Then to-night it is, I am afraid, 'Good-bye.' "

"Good-bye!" she cried, a sudden fear blanching her cheek and catching at her heart. "You are going to leave us?"

"I had a telegram to-day which forces me to return to England. I had hoped that you would have gone with me. If before dawn you think differently, give me a sign, and I will wait for you."

"You go at dawn!"

"Yes. But for you I should have gone to-night."

She took a voiceless farewell of him, simply clasping his big brown hand in her two slender ones, and then passing from his sight up the dingy staircase.

At her uncle's door Rosamund listened. Mr. Kerquham was already asleep. The future did not trouble him at all. To-morrow he was going to start for the mountains and for the life of solitude and strange scenes which he so much desired.

For an hour Rosamund paced her narrow chamber. Never for one moment did her trust and faith in Paul falter, but the physical fear that comes even to the bravest at times was heavy upon her. She had struggled so hard to prevent this journey. She was so sure in her own mind that the expedition could be of no good, that to be forced to give up the last hope of escape from it frightened her. It seemed as though the hand of Fate were dragging her somewhere against her will, as though everything were against her, and as if she were being forced into some unknown land filled with vague terrors and indefinite formless shapes which threatened evil.

All the night through she struggled with her fears,

telling herself a thousand times that other people had travelled into wild countries without undue danger or difficulties. A thousand times, too, she was tempted to devise some signal by which she could stay Mr. Fraser's going in the morning, but the hours slipped by and the black night grew grey, and she was still merely a frightened, undecided girl.

At dawn the clatter of hoofs in the street below carried her with swift feet to her window. He was going. His well-worn portmanteaux were flung across a mule's back, his rugs and sticks, tied in a rough bundle, were shouldered by a strapping porter. A moment later and he himself walked out into the roadway, wearing the rough iron-shod boots, the shabby dittoes, and the formless hat in which she had first seen him. He was smoking, but as the sun leaped over the hills and flung its first pale rays across the plain he looked up at the shuttered face of the house. At that moment Rosamund would have given her soul to have been able to cry out to him to stay or to have pushed aside the shutter and beckoned with her hand to him; but everything was dead within her except her eyes, and they, haggard and miserable, watched him, after a moment's pause, swing himself into the saddle and ride slowly down the street. At the corner he turned, and shading his eyes from the morning sun, once more looked back. As Rosamund almost found voice a heavy sob caught in her throat and a rush of tears blinded her sight. When she had dashed them away he was gone.

Too weary and heartsick even to lie on the bed, Rosamund bathed her tired eyes, and then to pass the hours till her uncle should call her, opened the bundle of letters and newspapers she had found on her arrival the previous day.

Her correspondence was meagre and uninteresting, and the papers but little better. But in idly turning the *Times* over in her listless hands her attention was caught by a paragraph—and a name!

The few lines stated that a woman of the unfortunate class had been knocked down and run over in the Strand. At the hospital, after her death, one of her own kind had identified her by the name of Kitty Clyde. Some humble folk from Oxford had also come to London and claimed the body. The woman had been at one time the wife of a gentleman well known in the best society, from whom she had been divorced. The gentleman's name did not transpire.

"Good God!" cried Rosamund, holding the paper before her pale face with hands that shook like leaves. "That was the name of Paul's wife—and she—is dead. Oh! heaven forgive me that I am thankful—for he—he is free. Paul is free as air, and there is now no bar to our marriage."

The words died on her lips, the tide of living joy froze in her throat, and a great wail broke from her.

"Paul! Paul! my beloved—do you know this thing, or are you lost to me forever? Ah! God is too unkind. He has given you to me so often, and each time—each time you have been taken away."

With trembling fingers she cut the paragraph from the paper.

"At least—at least—I have been saved from one great mistake. If I had said Yes to Hugh Fraser last night and known the truth too late, what should I have done? What should I have done? I think the irony of it would have killed me."

As she grew calmer she fell on her knees and prayed that the bitter cup might in time pass from her, and that some day—not too far off—she and Paul might meet once more as happy lovers.

Her prayers were crossed at last by her uncle's voice calling her to his room.

She went to him, thankful that the dim light hid her white face and tear-stained eyes.

"Were those our horses come already?" asked Mr. Kerquham, eagerly.

"No, uncle. It is Mr. Fraser, who has gone away."

"Well, I am not sorry," said Mr. Kerquham. "He was very interfering the last few days, and for some reason or other did all he could to put you against our expedition. But now, my dear, we are all by ourselves, and I will see that lad, Matia, this afternoon and arrange everything for our start to-morrow. Rosamund, my child, we are going to have a beautiful journey. From what people tell me, we shall see the loveliest country in the world and places that have not yet been spoilt by men and by civilisation. We are going to be face to face with Nature in her wildest and grandest moods. As you pack, dear, see that all my sketching things are handy. I expect I shall want them every mile of the road."

And Rosamund, patient and quiet, holding to the promise she had made herself to be the faithful companion of her uncle, passed the day in packing and repacking their belongings, for as yet her new-found joy was too sweetly sacred to be shared even with her only companion.

They were to take merely the barest necessities with them. Everything else was to be sent on to Athens by train.

Only once during that day did the mantle of foreboding and heaviness drop from her. Matia, the guide, brought a string of horses round to the door, from which his new employers were to choose their mounts, and Rosamund, with her old love for animals roused within her, spent an hour among them. They were all small, light of build, and obviously half-bred Arabs. Most of them were half-broken, but were young and warranted sure-footed. She was amused at the way in which they were shod, with flat plates covering the entire frog of the hoof and strangely curled up nails set all round.

"That is to give them a good grip," explained Matia in his strange Italian. "We have rough work before us."

Rosamund chose a grey mare for her uncle. She seemed a quiet creature, with large soft eyes, and nestled her head against the girl's shoulder in a most engaging way. For herself she chose a chestnut horse, a fine upstanding animal, who looked to have plenty of pace in him if he were put to it. Some mules were then brought, and wooden pack-saddles, clumsy, ill-made things, on which the luggage was to be placed. A small boy, who, according to Matia and the innkeeper, was a Miridite, but who looked to Rosamund's inexperienced eyes a very swarthy gipsy, was engaged to drive the mules. This done, Mr. Kerquham considered that he had made all necessary arrangements, and it was not until Rosamund asked him tentatively if he intended to carry any arms with him or not, that, accompanied by Matia, he wandered down to the bazaar and invested in an out-of-date pair of heavy pistols.

The news that a party of Europeans were going to start for the Albanian Highlands the next day had spread through the little town by eventide, and to celebrate the event, as well as to wring some money out of the travellers, a large party of dancers and musicians came up to the inn in the evening. With great formality the host, a truculent-looking gentleman who walked about his own house armed to the teeth, begged that the visitors would patronise the entertainment.

It was a very cold evening, and Rosamund wrapped both herself and her uncle in heavy cloaks before they went out on to the terrace, where the dancing was to take place. The moon lay low on the horizon and gave but little light, but some spluttering lanterns hung on poles lent an intermittent illumination to the strange scene. Seats were brought for the English visitors, the rest of the company either stood or sat cross-legged in a ring. Then there flitted into the centre a man and a woman, who began the national dance, with springs and bounds and arms waved high above their heads. As the dance went on they twisted their bodies when in the air, and when a couple retired exhausted another took their place. The exercise was certainly violent, and as a gymnastic entertainment not unworthy of notice, but it could scarcely be called dancing. Rosamund was better pleased with a girl who, with her legs tucked under her, began to play the *ghauzla*, a one-stringed instrument not unlike a mandolin. Some of the girls sang to it, and the music was plaintive and wild, like that of all the mountainous countries. The native audience seemed so in love with it that they stayed on the terrace half through the night, and long after Rosamund had lain down to rest she heard the wail of the monotonous, single string and the plaintive voices which seemed to sing to her of Paul.

The strange, sad music still throbbed in Rosamund's ears during the next few days, as they wandered through the beautiful Zeta valley, past old monasteries and ruined forts, and by quaint villages, where Matia and the boy cooked the food they had brought with them in the khans by the roadside. It beat in time to the horses' hoofs as they clattered over the rough highways and narrow wooden bridges. It seemed to echo back at her from the sides of the lofty Dormitor, and to wander with the wind through the forests of beech which were now a blaze of gold and crimson and were casting about their feet a brilliant carpet. It seemed to echo the mingled joy and passion in her heart when they passed whole families by the roadside, shaking with the malaria and the agues that in the autumn months sap the health of the dwellers in the valleys and plains. She hummed snatches of the strange tunes while she ate the black, gritty bread they bought in the villages, or made believe, to please her uncle, that she enjoyed the sour jam called *bestilj*.

CHAPTER XXXII

THE GANDER FIGHT

THE progress of the little caravan proved to be a very slow one, for Mr. Kerquham, on the plea of lingering among the gorgeous valleys that lay between the spurs of the Albanian Alps, never rode many miles a day. Only Rosamund, who knew every tone of his voice and expression of his face, was fearful that it was fatigue that made him, after a few hours, dismount from his high-peaked saddle and seek the shelter of some squalid wayside *khan*. But he had all the obstinacy of a man who knows his health is failing, and only answered her tender inquiries with assurances that he was quite well.

Day by day the stages that they travelled grew shorter, and day by day, although the sky was clear and the sun shone brilliantly, the winds that blew down the valleys grew more keen and the evening hours brought with them a touch of sharp frost. When they started at dawn Matia would shiver and utter strange oaths between his chattering teeth, and tie the ends of the red shawl that bound his brows under his chin. Still Mr. Kerquham persisted that no snow ever fell, even in the highest passes, until the beginning of the new year, and that long before that they would be basking amid the olive groves of Greece.

For several days they had travelled amid the wildest and most lonely scenery. All verdure was left behind them long ago, and they seemed to be locked in an endless valley formed of giant rocks and frowning crags, where only here and there a hardy pine tree had thrust its roots into some little cranny and found sustenance for its funereal foliage in the scant earth. A stream tumbled far below the road. Its waters were thick and bluish. Rosamund looked down at it one morning as they rode and said to her uncle:

"There must have been snow somewhere, uncle. That is snow water surely."

Matia, when he was questioned, shrugged his shoulders and said in his bad Italian that possibly the signorina was right.

That day there was a new sensation in the air. It was sharp and keen and almost cut the skin as it whipped across their faces. Mr. Kerquham was not in his usual bright spirits, although he would not acknowledge any illness to Rosamund. She begged him hard to stop and rest at the small *khans*, which in this lonely part of the country were merely little caves built of loose stones rolled one upon the other, but the guide urged him to go on. There was a village, he said, higher up the gorge, called Rosega. They might rest there for a day or two if they pleased, and the beasts could get some fresh food, and they might all be warmed and better fed. Rosamund joined her entreaties to his, and early in the afternoon they rounded a sharp spur in the valley and saw above them a tiny village—a mere handful of mud huts clustered close about a whitewashed mosque and tucked into the hollow of the mountain side. To Rosamund's surprise, the narrow road that lay between them and Rosega was dotted with various groups of hurrying people.

"What is going on?" she asked Matia. "Where do all these people come from, and why are they running towards the village?"

Matia grinned until he showed all his white teeth.

"There is a great feast at Rosega to-night. They are going to have a Gander Fight, and the people have come down from the hills to see it."

"But how do you know?" said Rosamund.

Matia looked at her with his fine eyes half closed in a scornful way.

"The signorina did not notice me speak to one who passed us on the way this morning. He was the herald sent out to warn the countryside of the fight that is going to take place this afternoon."

Rosamund, as she urged her weary horse up the steep slope, remembered that some hours back a rough fellow had passed them and had exchanged a nod and word with Matia as he went by. That was the reason evidently that the guide was so anxious to reach the village quickly.

But she, too, would be glad to be once more amongst people, even if it were the unwashed natives, for the loneliness of the great mountains and the awful silence that had wrapped her round for days past were weighing heavily on her nerves and spirits. Yet as they forced their horses among the filthy, ragged crowd that thronged the narrow streets of Rosega, she repented that they had come. Where could they rest that night? The squalor and dirt were something unspeakable, and she grew faint and sick when Matia drew up before the principal *khan* of the place, and helping her down, showed her into the room where they would have to eat and pass the evening. At least, out on the solitary hillside, where there were but few people save the shepherds, the lodgings they had had, though rough, had been cleaner than this. She was for mounting her weary horse again and pressing on, but a glance at her uncle's face, which was paler than its wont, was enough. At all costs they must rest there that night, so once more she helped Matia to unstrap the bedding from the wooden pack-saddles and arrange the wraps and pillows they had with them.

She was so busy in settling their belongings for her uncle's comfort that she did not notice a large crowd gathering in the open space before the *khan*. When at last her ears and her sense of smell made her realise the fact, she turned to Matia:

"What are they going to do? Why is there such a crowd?"

"It is the Gander Fight!" cried the guide. "It takes place here; come and see, signorina; come and see!"

Against her will, he seized her by the arm and dragged her through the evil-smelling crowd, which, with a certain rough politeness, made way for her, and led her into the front row of spectators. A space had been cleared, and round it were grouped a ring of men and women. The latter were born Mohammedans, but under the plea of having become Christians, they had cast aside their veils and mingled freely with the men. The first two or three rows of spectators were crouched on their knees. Behind them stood, ten deep, an excited throng. Many of the men wore the soft, spotless white skirts of the country; others had the tight, close-fitting trousers of the true mountaineers. The Mussulmans had the loose, ungraceful costume of the Turk, but the fez was universal, and every man was engirdled with a whole armoury of pistols and swords.

Amid cries of exultation and excitement, the ganders—two fine birds which had been trained to their work and fed for some weeks on a particular herb to render them fierce and pugnacious—were brought into the circle. The owners of the creatures gesticulated wildly to one another, and Rosamund guessed that they were wagering on their chances of success. Then, urged on by cries, the two birds began to fight. After a few moments Rosamund shut her eyes, for she could not force her way back through the crowd that pressed so closely behind her. She wished that Providence would close her ears too, for by the shouts and yells, the shrieks of anger and the clamour of encouragement, she could gather how the battle was going.

High above the general din rang the shrill peal of a girl's laugh. She was next to Rosamund, who had noticed her for her fair beauty, her glorious eyes and scarlet mouth. Between her bursts of laughter, Rosamund could hear her in a sneering tone speaking to those behind her, and her instinct warned her that this wild daughter of the mountains was laughing at the ultra-refinement of the English woman, who, for all the vaunted bravery of her race, turned pale at the sight of blood.

For what seemed a lifetime the riot and noise and excitement endured. She found afterwards that two hours had passed before one bird had so completely vanquished the other that there was neither pluck nor struggle left in him. When Matia touched her arm and told her that it was all over, she staggered to her feet stiffly, for she had become cramped crouched down upon her knees. She gave one hurried glance towards the spot where the fight had been. It was strewn with feathers and blood, and a wretched carcass, that once had been a bird but was now a mere mass of bleeding flesh, lay upon the ground. A fight between two men was going on at the further corner, and she hurried into the *khan* so that the sound of blows and angry words should not reach her.

She found her uncle standing at the door lighting his pipe. Matia then built the fire, and leaving it to burn went out into the village to see what he could get to eat. A moment later he returned, preceded by a tall, handsome man, splendidly dressed in the national costume.

"It is the Agha—a great man in Rosega," whispered Matia in Rosamund's ear. "He has come to bid you sup with him to-night."

It suited Matia that the invitation should be accepted by the English travellers, for it meant that he, too, would be treated as a guest in his capacity of interpreter.

The Agha stood in the doorway of the *khan*, while his invitation was translated and accepted. He dropped his hand to his knee, as though he were raising the hem of a garment, then raised it to his chest, his mouth and his forehead. It was the gesture of greeting and respect of the country, and infinitely picturesque and suggestive. Then the great Boluk-Bashi swung out of the *khan* and took his gorgeously apparelled form up the road to his own quaint home, where a feast in honour of the strangers was being organised.

"It will be dark before they eat," said Matia. "Will not the signorina go down to the well and see the women drawing water? The sun will be set in half an hour."

Anxious to get away from the horrible lodging and to breathe again a little pure air, Rosamund gladly went outside, and following the main road soon reached the rough mud wall and heavy wooden gate that formed the boundary of the town. After the noise and bustle that had accompanied the Gander Fight it soothed her to find the streets so quiet.

Only one figure broke the solitude, that of an old man, white-locked and bearded. He wore the close-fitting Miridite costume, and was crouched on a low stone with a long-barrelled Martini-Peabody rifle laid across his knees.

Rosamund thought he was a guard set at the gate, till she saw him with a savage growl spring to his feet. The door of a house a little larger and cleaner than the rest had been flung wide, and a man whom she recognised as the Agha appeared in the centre of a crowd of young men and children. They were closely followed by half a dozen Turkish *zaptiehs*.

The old man sank down on the stone as with flashing eyes and haughty mien the cavalcade swept past.

Matia's laugh sounded in Rosamund's ears.

"He's clever—is the Agha. He and the old one there started a blood feud at 'Ramazin' five year ago. Greybeard has sat at his gates ever since, but the Agha never goes out alone, and has besides asked for a guard from the State. But, signorina, here come the women from the well."

A score of women were coming through the gate. Those who were in their first youth were surpassingly beautiful, with exquisite white skins and golden hair that fell in long plaits to their knees. Their forms were lithe and supple, and their natural grace was in no way hidden by the loose trousers and short embroidered jackets that they wore. The more coquettish of the girls had bound their sashes so closely round their forms that they looked as slender as sylphs. Each carried on her head a metal water pot, which glittered in the last rays of the sinking sun.

Chief among them was the girl who had been next her at the Gander Fight. Her eyes were of a deep blue, and her hair was thick and long. Her dress was of richer material than was that of her companions, and of finer

colour.   Heavy bracelets of gold jangled on her slender
wrists as she swung the pot from her head to the well's
side, and the long, loose coat that she wore was held
together across her bosom by two huge bosses of gold
set with uncut turquoises.   Rosamund heard the others
call her Kitza, and noticed that they all paid her some
deference.   She was evidently an aristocrat among these
poverty-stricken villagers.

As Rosamund went through the gloom back to the
village and the *khan* she passed Matia, the guide.   He
was holding close converse with two dark men whose
head shawls were dragged so closely about their mouths
that the lower parts of their faces could not be seen.
They were more than common tall, and singularly
swarthy when contrasted with the fair Albanians of the
Highlands.   They were speaking, too, in a language she
had never heard before.   She would scarcely have
noticed them, perhaps, save that as she approached,
Matia laid his hands upon his lips, and the two men
slipped back among the bushes.   She thought no more
of it, however, for, arrived at the *khan*, she found her
uncle awaiting her impatiently, and Matia, who had
somehow arrived there before her, urged an immediate
start for the Agha's house.

A fire made from small trees gave them a warm welcome.   It leaped from the centre of the floor and flared
ruddily almost up to the low ceiling.   In honour of the
strangers' visit, the Agha had donned fresh clothes.
A small fez decked with an enormous blue silk tassel covered that part of his head which was shaved.   The rest
of his hair was cut very close.   Instead of his full kilt,
he wore tight-fitting trousers, seamed with heavy stripes
of gold lace.   His waistcoat of crimson velvet was com-

pletely covered with gold embroidery and rows of finely
wrought buttons. The short jacket was also stiff with
needlework, and the jack boots, which reached to his
knees, were covered with a fantastic design of gold and
silver wire. He had laid aside his *yatakhan*, but the
three heavy pistols he wore in his crimson sash had butts
of sparkling silver.

He welcomed his guests with considerable grace, and
led them to a low wooden stool, which, so far as Rosamund could see by the fitful firelight, was the only furniture in the large room. Directly they were placed
several stalwart men entered, bearing on a huge spit a
newly-killed sheep, which was set above the fire to roast.
Matia at the sight beamed with delight, for a sheep
roasted whole is the greatest honour that an Albanian
mountain chief can show to his guests. Of plates and
knives and forks the feast was innocent, but Rosamund
was hungry, and to her own astonishment was able to
eat with a certain amount of enjoyment the pieces of
meat which the Agha offered her from time to time.
Some cakes steeped in honey and a dish of sheep's kid-
neys were the next delicacies. The wine was home-
made, and tasted faintly of pears. The men drank from
a big gourd filled with fiery *raki*, which was passed round
from time to time.

When her appetite failed her, she noticed in the
shadows that the women of the house sat in the far corner spinning yarn and talking and whispering among
themselves. The yellow-haired Kitza was there, and
seemed to find infinite amusement in the English girl's
endeavours to conform with the local customs. By-and-
bye the mountaineers took to telling fortunes among
themselves from a blade bone of the sheep. They had

picked it clean and white, and held it between their faces and the brilliant firelight and read coming events in the transparent edges of the bone.   The feast lasted till midnight, when in dense cold Mr. Kerquham and Rosamund took leave of their host and, accompanied by a band of cheery mountaineers, swinging lanterns and chanting a chorus, went back to their *khan*. Matia was left behind, for the sheep was not yet finished, and there was plenty more eating and drinking to be done. Mr. Kerquham was delighted with the evening's entertainment, and a thousand times went over and over every picturesque detail and fresh touch of colour to Rosamund.

"Did I not say you should see something new?" he cried, exultingly, as she covered him with rugs. "Are not these simple, wild people, with their primitive habits and unaffected natural ways, far preferable to the toilers in cities, who scheme and plot all the time to make what they can out of you, to rob you and to back-bite you? Ah! my dear child, I shall make you acknowledge before we have finished that I did well to be so firm in fighting your wishes to give up this expedition. As to Mr. Fraser, his objections were absurd. What does a little cold matter? We have plenty of good wraps and the weather remains fair."

Then he gave her his blessing and turned over to sleep, but Rosamund sat in the doorway of the *khan* and looked up at the clear frosty sky, where the stars were dancing like Kitza's eyes, and wearily wondered how soon this journey would come to an end, and where Paul was, and why Matia had been talking to those strange, evil-looking men who had slunk away so guiltily as she had passed them.

The whole valley was asleep, for even at the Agha's

house they were gorged with mutton and *raki*, and snored round the fire beneath their blankets. The deadly silence of the clear night was only broken by the wild howling of the savage dogs that were held by strong chains before every house. They cried like wolves, and now and again Rosamund fancied that she heard on the night wind an answering howl from the far mountain sides.

CHAPTER XXXIII

FALLEN AMONG THIEVES

THE start was not early the next morning, and the guide, when he did make his appearance, looked puffy about the eyes, and was most unnecessarily fussy and apologetic in manner, but Mr. Kerquham had rested well, and Rosamund prepared for the day's journey with a light heart. At the distant head of the gorge a great grey mass had risen since early morning, and lay there heavy and solid as a rampart wall.

"Surely there were no mountains there," said Rosamund, staring up at the new appearance from under her hand.

"It is a cloud," volunteered the native boy who drove the mules and to whom she had learned to speak a little.

He was going to add something more to his words, but Matia took him by the shoulder and flung him across the road, muttering something under his breath about interfering children.

"Is not the weather going to change, Matia?" asked Rosamund, thinking in her heart that if it were they had better stop in this little squalid village than venture forth again among the mountains.

Matia shrugged his shoulders airily, and assured the signorina that it was nothing but the morning mist.

"I have never seen it look like that before," she said, still doubting his assurance.

"Things look different in the mountains," was his

curt reply, as he helped Mr. Kerquham into his saddle, and the cavalcade started out of the village.

The ascent began the moment that they left the last of the huts behind them. The air was very crisp and sharp, and the fern in the hollows, which all the way up had been looking green and fresh, was curled and brown at the edges, as though frost fingers had touched it.

Within the first hour they came upon some shepherds, wild men of the mountains, all heavily armed and shod in rough goatskin boots, driving before them their flocks. They pulled up by the roadside as they met the little party coming up, and one of them stopped Matia and said something to him, but the guide laughed in his frank, careless way, and urged on the horses. Rosamund, however, noticed that the boy hung back and spoke some minutes with the shepherds, and only came trailing reluctantly at the heels of his mules when Matia yelled to him.

"What did they say?" said Rosamund in her imperfect language to the muleteer.

The lad shook his tangled head and pointed with a bare brown arm towards the head of the gorge.

"Cold, very cold," he muttered, "the snows are coming."

Matia must have guessed the purport of the few words, for when Rosamund rode on and tried to overtake Mr. Kerquham, who was in front, the guide interposed himself between the uncle and niece and effectually prevented her from uttering her renewed fears aloud.

The gradient now became exceedingly steep, and the horses scrambled like cats and the mules struggled along the loose stones in the sharp ascent. The tumbling river below them was voiceless, for they were too far above it to catch the sound of the rush and boil of the

waters.   They seemed all alone in the world, those four.
There was not a bird in the sky or the tinkle of a sheep
bell anywhere.   Huge pinnacles of rock reared their
stern heads into the air or leaned over from beetling crags
as though the next moment they would crash into the valley beneath.   All around them vegetation had ceased,
though some distance off Rosamund's keen eyes caught
the black stain of a patch of pine trees against the universal greyness.   Among themselves they scarcely
exchanged a word, and the beat of the horses' feet and
the rattle of the loosened stones falling into the valley
by-and-bye grew so monotonous that Rosamund could
have screamed, if only to make fresh echoes.   Once she
fancied that she heard, a long way off, the same long-
drawn howl that had answered the barking dogs during
the night.   It thrilled her with a sense of vague fear,
and she cried out to Matia, "What is that?"

"A shepherd's dog," he answered back over his
shoulder.   "The signorina need not mind that."

But the native boy turned a shade paler under his
brown skin, and muttered beneath his breath, just loud
enough for her to hear:

"It is the wolves.   They smell the snow."

It was impossible to count the time, and it may have
been a few minutes after that or half an hour, when with
a sudden cry Matia flung himself down in the roadway.
Rosamund, feeling sure the man was hurt, sprang from
her saddle and rushed to his side.   He was writhing
pitifully and holding his hands across his body.

"Oh! I am ill; I am ill!   Those dogs have poisoned
me.   I shall die."

He groaned and wept with all the exaggerated emotion of a Southerner, and Rosamund, certain that something was amiss, drew her flask of brandy from her

pocket and poured some between the man's clenched teeth.

"Are you better?" she cried, anxiously, while Mr. Kerquham , too, reined his horse round and looked with pitying eyes at the wriggling form before him.

"I don't know. I feel very bad," and he howled and groaned aloud.

"See," said Rosamund, taking a sudden resolution. "I will put you on my horse. I can walk, and we will go down again to Rosega."

But at that Matia sat up in the road, and still moaning and mopping his brow vowed that he would not give the signorina such trouble, and it would be a pity if they had had the journey in vain.

"I am better," he said, dragging himself painfully to his feet. "I can go on."

"But if you are in such pain it is impossible that you should go on," said Rosamund, catching at a straw of hope that this misfortune might induce her uncle to abandon the journey, at least for the moment. "We can go down at once. You might be taken ill on the road higher up, and then what should we do?"

Matia, with his slender, graceful body ostentatiously bent in half, caught hold of Mr. Kerquham's reins and turned the horses up the gorge once more.

"I promised that I would see you to the end of your journey. Matia is not a man who goes against his word," and without more ado he resumed the march.

Rosamund stood in the road staring at him, and with a vague doubt forming in her mind. Surely he was not shamming illness—nobody could look so pale and utter such fearful cries unless he was suffering terribly, and yet now he was walking as well as before the seizure. The cure was as sudden as the attack had been   Any way, Mr. Kerquham was almost out of sight round a turn in the ever-winding road, so she sprang into her saddle again and urged her horse on.

But the few moments that she had lost in thought had taken the front part of the cavalcade beyond her vision, round a sharp rock which overhung the valley like a citadel built by human hands. As she, with the little muleteer and his patient beasts behind her, turned the corner she was astonished to see Matia and her uncle pulled up in the midst of a small gipsy encampment. A little clump of pines grew back from the road and gave some slight shelter from the piercing north wind which swept down the gorge. There was some bracken, too, and among it sat the ox-eyed, black-haired Romany women, with their babies tied to their backs and their brows and bosoms covered with gay coloured handkerchiefs. Mr. Kerquham waved joyously to her. He was off his horse and was sitting on a bundle of cut ferns. A freshly lit fire was spluttering and crackling in the brisk wind. It all looked so cheerful after the frightful loneliness that Rosamund felt her heart leap with joy.

"Come, my dear!" said her uncle, as she pulled up her horse. "These good people have asked us to stop and eat with them, and Matia is ill again, so we must stay here for a bit."

Nothing loth, the girl slipped from the saddle. She was stiff and sore and cold, and glad to cower near the fire and watch the women making broth in a big iron pot.

Presently, when they had eaten of the savoury stew, she heard the wail of a sick baby just behind her, and turning, saw a pretty young girl, evidently in weak health, trying to hush a little black-polled, swarthy-skinned infant to sleep. But the more the girl crooned and rocked it, the more the child screamed and kicked.

"Let me take it," said Rosamund in English. Then remembering that the gipsy could not understand, she merely held out her hands, and the girl, after one glance into her face, gave her the child and sank wearily into the bracken.

Rosamund quickly lulled the child to sleep, and after exchanging a few words with her uncle, who was smoking peaceably, she stepped into the road and wandered a few yards from the encampment. She was looking with troubled eyes at that great grey wall that stretched across the head of the gorge and seemed to bridge mountain peak with mountain peak. She was trying to think if it had grown thicker and higher since the morning, when her keen ear caught the sibilant tones that she had overheard yesterday afternoon by the well at Rosega. She drew back a moment into the bracken. The child was asleep on her breast and would not betray her. Yes, they were the same voices—the voices of the two dark men who had long, lank black hair and their mouths hidden with their turban shawls, and those were Matia's lighter tones, hissing and soft and treacherous as the sound of a snake. They were whispering fast to one another, and then Matia laughed a low laugh that drove the blood back cold to Rosamund's heart.

Although she could guess nothing of what they said, her instinct warned her that something was wrong.

Indeed, things were wrong, for when a few minutes later her hurrying footsteps carried her back to the camp she found the tents struck and the pack horses laden with the gipsies' scant property and all ready to start, save Matia, who once more lay groaning on the ground. She could scarcely believe her eyes. A moment ago she had heard his voice, and he seemed then to be in perfect health.

"Rosamund, my dear," said her uncle, coming up to her and laying his hand upon her arm, "this poor fellow is dreadfully ill. It is impossible he can go on, but he tells me that these good folks, who know the country well and are honest, for all their black brows and forbidding looks, are going up the gorge, and that we had better go on with them. Matia will wait behind till he is better, and then follow on by a short cut that he knows of over the mountains and join us at the monastery of Chatista, where, you know, we are to rest for two days."

Almost unconsciously Rosamund handed the sleeping child back to its mother, and then turned to her uncle.

"Uncle, you will never be so mad as to trust yourself with these people! You only need to look at them to see that they are a lawless crew, to whom neither property nor life are sacred. I beseech, I implore you, to turn back while there is yet time. We have been five hours coming here from Rosega; we can get down in two. We may meet people on the way; they are scarcely likely to molest us. For heaven's sake! do as I ask you."

Mr. Kerquham drew himself up in his stiffest manner, and looked at his niece with displeased astonishment.

"Rosamund, I never knew you were a coward before!"

She flushed as scarlet as though he had struck her, and with a sigh turned away. It was quite useless. She could not voice her fears any further than she had done. The best thing to do was to stay by her uncle and to hope that the day would come when she would laugh at herself for being so foolish.

Surrounded by the gipsy band, which numbered about thirty, and was a silent, truculent crowd, Mr. Kerquham and Rosamund set out again upon their journey. Though they were now very high up in the valley and the road was running almost along the brows of the mountains, the afternoon drew on apace, and the dusk swept quickly on. As the light failed, Rosamund noticed that the great grey wall of cloud had added many cubits to its height, that it was slowly spreading and spreading, and shutting out the pale blue sky bit by bit. It was no longer in front of them. It was creeping above them.

In the rarefied air every sound became painfully sharp. Each time a shod hoof struck a stone or a woman's high voice spoke Rosamund's nerves twanged like an overstrung instrument. The air was full of electricity, as it is before a coming storm, and the cold that had up till now been bearable, became piercing, and she was more than glad when the chief of the band pulled up short in the middle of the road, and, waving his hand towards a small recess among the beetling crags, ordered his people to make a camp there.

In a few minutes the travellers' bedding was dragged from their horses and flung upon the ground, and some bundles of cut fern were spread above that. Over a handful of sticks some broth was warmed, and each one had a cup of it. Worn out by the long day's ride and made drowsy by the cold, Mr. Kerquham, after the hot broth, was soon asleep, and Rosamund, too, wearied by her previous night's vigil, and despite her uneasiness and physical discomfort, was already closing her eyes, when light fingers that seemed to creep out of the darkness were laid on her shoulder. A woman's voice murmured something—she did not know what—in her ear, and she fancied that through the night a white hand waved and pointed down the valley. Rosamund, lifting her own hand to the face that bent above her, felt it was that of a girl, and then she knew it was the mother of the sick baby, who was trying to convey some warning or message to her. Again and again the girl whispered eagerly, urging her to some action, but Rosamund could only shake her head. She could understand nothing. Suddenly a coarse voice broke through the stillness; the gipsy girl gave a low cry, and Rosamund heard her dragged back into the tent that was pitched against the rock behind her. "She was trying to tell me something," thought the girl. "I fear there is some danger that threatens us."

At length her natural fatigue wore out her nervous watchfulness, and she slept, not quietly or restfully, but lightly and always with a sense of impending danger. Once she half rose up and thought she heard Matia's high voice and light laugh close by her, and again she half roused herself in the midst of a dream about horses that were trampling past in an endless defile. But as the night wore away she grew quieter, and might have slept for hours but that the intense cold, that increased with the growing day, woke her up, numbed and shivering.

Her senses were alive before her eyes were open, and with a cry she staggered to her feet. What had happened? Why was she out there in the open, chilled to the bone? Where was her uncle? Where were the gipsies? Her eyes wandered round her. Her uncle was there, sleeping like a child in his rugs, but every one—everything else was gone, save the handful of ashes where the fire had been lit the previous evening.

With the instinct that she must not wake Mr. Kerquham too suddenly she clasped her hands across her mouth to stifle the shriek that broke from her lips, for in a moment she guessed all. Matia had betrayed them! They were robbed and deserted! Left alone on this hideous mountain side with nothing but a cruel wind and a bare rock to watch them die. For one moment she gave way to an absolute panic, and scream after scream strangled in her throat. Then, with a great effort of her will, she curbed her fear and set all her wits to work to fight this fearful calamity.

The day was dawning, but in a cold, grey, sickly way that frightened her again. There was no sun to rise, no soft pink tints upon the frowning mountain tops. The whole world seemed wrapped in that hideous grey cloud which now hid the sky from horizon to horizon and mountain peak to mountain peak. "The days are short," she thought, despairingly. "God knows what little light there may be to-day. I must rouse him at once. Poor uncle, it seems cruel to wake him to such fearful news, but we cannot stop here. We must move on somewhere."

She shook her uncle, and then as he lazily woke, she told him in a few hurried words what had happened. He took the news better than she had expected, and, rested after a good night's sleep, he rose with vigour to his feet and prepared to go with her which way she would. She decided at once that to attempt to descend the gorge would be rushing into sure death. The gipsies would have gone that way, and if they came upon them would certainly murder them to escape the inevitable punishment that would follow their theft. They must try and make for the monastery for which they had been bound, and where they had hoped to rest for a while before going over the mountain pass down towards Greece.

"Uncle," she said presently, and forced her voice to steadiness, "think, dear, and help me. Can you tell me now, looking at them from here, under which peak the monastery lies? You know we have had it in view for the past three days, but these heavy clouds have altered things this morning, and I am not sure of the way we should make.''

"It is the Argentalia mountain," Mr. Kerquham answered. "It has a double peak. Is not that it over there?"

Rosamund nodded, while a sick feeling clutched at her heart. How far off those double peaks looked, and how cruel, striking like two jagged teeth up at the heavy sky.

"It was three days from here by road," she said, and then she sighed. How were they to walk that rough track for three days? They had no food, nothing but a little brandy. She drew the flask from her pocket and smiled bitterly to think that Matia had had the greater portion of its contents.

"Uncle, we must try some of the sheep tracks. We know the monastery is there between the peaks. We were told there is a shorter way to it that the peasants use. They get about the country so quickly. We must try and see if we can be as clever as they."

She bound one of the rugs round Mr. Kerquham's shoulders and another over her own, but the rest they had to leave behind, for she dare not overweight herself, fearing that sooner or later she would have her uncle to support. With a knife that hung at her girdle she cut from the stunted bushes two sticks, and after trimming them gave her arm to her uncle and set forth with him up the first track that branched from the beaten road towards Argentalia.

CHAPTER XXXIV

IN SNOWY ARMS

THAT day passed for Rosamund like some evil dream. All thought of Paul, all hopes of their reunion were lost in the sheer struggle for shelter and food. Their progress was so slow that sometimes she fancied her feet were tied to the earth. Now and again, when she looked behind her, she saw within range the same clump of stunted bushes or heap of frost-killed fern that she had passed hours ago. They met no one, and at times the silence of the great gorge, lying still as death under the canopy of the snow clouds, was so painful that her ears ached, and when her uncle spoke to her his quiet tones seemed to echo from rock to rock until they died away like mocking laughter in the distant fastnesses of the close-ranged mountains.

There was no sun, so she could not judge when noon arrived, for the intense cold had stopped both their watches. Luckily there was but little air stirring, for she knew that if there had been they must soon have been numbed and frozen into a speedy death. But everything was so fearfully still. All nature seemed waiting for the bursting of the great clouds that rolled like a never-ending sea over the wild mountain tops. Thicker and thicker they grew, and greyer and greyer the landscape became until on a sudden a shifting whiteness filled all the air, and Rosamund saw upon her sleeve the first fine snowflake.

She knew but little of mountain climbing, and had only gathered by hearsay a slight knowledge of the dangers that lie in a great snowstorm. She recognised in a few minutes, however, how true such travellers' tales had been, for even as she urged Mr. Kerquham to fresher exertions, the air was one dancing whirl of thick, white flakes, and not only the double-peaked Argentalia and the opposite side of the gorge, but even the very path before them became obscured.

"We must find shelter, dear," she cried, "somewhere! somehow!" She forced her voice to keep steady and clenched her fingers within her thick gloves to prevent herself from wringing her hands. "A little while ago, before the snow came, just when we turned that last curve, I thought I saw a patch of dead fern. It cannot be far. If we could get there we might rest"—she raised heavy, despairing eyes to the lowering skies—"and perhaps the storm will pass over."

Her uncle, who had stopped to listen to her words, swayed a little on his feet. His face looked strangely blue and drawn, and his breath came in heavy gasps, for with the snow had risen an icy wind that caught them by the throat and almost stopped their breathing.

"I will try, my dear," he said, setting his tired feet once more among the loose stones and leaning heavily on his rough staff. "I will try."

With encouraging words and strong, young arms, she helped her uncle a little higher up the track and found what she had hoped for—a small hole, probably scooped by some watching shepherd, in the limestone rock and overhung by a few scant bushes. Thrusting her uncle into the farthest corner of the meagre shelter, she set herself 'with all her strength to uproot such miserable vegetation as there was. It strained even her young muscles and cut her hands to pull the twigs and leaves from their foothold in the rock, but after a time she had got an armful, enough to make a rough pillow for Mr. Kerquham, who was now breathing heavily, as a man does when unconsciousness is creeping over him. They had no food with them, and there were but a few drops of brandy in the bottom of the flask. Rosamund, in her agony, cursed the lying Matia for robbing them of the only thing that was now likely to be of any use. As she held the little silver cup to her uncle's blue lips, he tried to push it aside.

"Take it yourself, Rosie. It will help you to get on to the top. Nothing can be of any use to me now; I am finished."

But with firm hands she forced him to take the spirits, telling him that he would be better soon after he had had some sleep, and that in the morning the snow would probably have stopped, and they would see the peaks of Argentalia again. But in her brave heart she knew that she lied, and when she had laid him back on the rough bed she had made for him and covered him with the rugs they had, and went to the edge of the little cave to look out upon the waste of whiteness, despair seized upon her soul, and she clasped her hands together and prayed that the end might come quickly.

By-and-bye, however, she noticed that the wind, which had risen to a shrill shrieking blast, was driving the snow into eddies and drifts. In the more sheltered places the white carpet was thickening moment by moment, but where the mountain sides were exposed at all not a flake rested. Then she prayed to God that the wind might hold, and that the track which they were following might be blown bare during the oncoming night, which was now sweeping up the valley and turning the

grey and white to one universal blackness. She tried
to guess the time and rewind her watch, which she
slipped into her bosom in the hope that the warmth of
her body might set it going again. She thought it might
be four o'clock, but the day had never been more than
a prolonged dawn, and the evening had come so soon
that she feared she was wrong in her calculations.

She stood at the mouth of the little cave, and so long
as her eyes could pierce the dense blackness she watched
to see if the mountain track remained clear of snow.
Yes! thank God! the wind still set fair for them.

It was a cruel blast that hissed and lashed and tore
and raved down the gorge. It caught the snow even in
the air, and swept it clear away in huge waves. It froze
the girl almost to a stone as she stood there, filled with
only one fear and one hope. As the pall of night fell
she heard her uncle's voice behind her. It sounded
very feeble, and he seemed to be crying, as a tired child
cries.

"Rosamund, where are you? I cannot see you. I
am so cold; come and sit by me, dear."

Feeling her way by the side of the rocks she crept to
his side, and sitting on the floor, drew the rugs closer
round him and tried to get him to sleep again, but the
poor man was filled with regrets and self-reproaches.
He repeated a thousand times how wrong he had been to
disregard Hugh Fraser's advice and the instincts of
women, who foresaw dangers before they came, and he
wished that he had been guided by her dislike to the
expedition. He cursed the Skreli guide and called down
the wrath of God upon the thieving gipsies.

After a time his brain, weakened by the cold and lack
of food, wandered a little, and he talked of his studio
at "The Hurst" and of his dead wife, Margot, and com-

plained how cold the house was, and that the doors and windows must all have been left open. Rosamund, with dry eyes and a bleeding heart, could do nothing but sit and listen. Her words of comfort and encouragement fell on deaf ears, for her uncle had drifted into the land of unconsciousness, and could only mutter about what he found there. The girl was getting numbed to the bone from sitting so long in one position, when suddenly her uncle's head dropped on her shoulder.

"I am so cold," he whispered, and then he went to sleep.

Though she was aching in every limb and sick with hunger, Rosamund remained staunch to her grand resolve of taking care of the one being in the world who had done all in his power to guard her own life. Gently and by degrees she shifted herself and the sleeping man into a more comfortable position, and then wound her arms closely round him, determined that up to the last she would give him all the best of her warmth and strength.

Full of pain and weariness as she was, she must have lost consciousness for some time, for the night seemed to slip away very quickly and the ghastly pallor of the dawn crept over the ragged mountain tops almost before she thought it was possible.

Her first waking thought concerned the mountain track. If that was lost in the snow, then they had better stay where they were and wait for the end. If it was bare, they might still struggle on, for she felt sure that sooner or later the rough path must bring them to the monastery or to some mountain village. Mr. Kerquham was sleeping heavily, though his eyes were not quite closed, but she felt that he was warmer, and she saw that the blue look had gone from about his mouth.

So set were her own limbs that she could not rise to her feet when she had laid her uncle down, but she managed painfully and slowly to drag herself on her hands to the mouth of the cave. Thank heaven! the snow had stopped falling and the track was clear. Everything else was robed in whiteness and it seemed as though Providence itself had traced the little pathway up the hills on which they might walk to shelter and safety.

The head of every mountain round was robed in sullen clouds, and at any moment the storm might recommence. There was no time to be lost, and after she had rubbed some life back to her feet and hands she roused Mr. Kerquham. He seemed less weak than he had done the night before, and he got to his feet and out into the air with more activity than she had hoped for. Again wrapping themselves in their rugs they started up the hill, though the mighty wind that roared and lashed their faces seemed to cut them to the bone.

Rosamund's watch was now going, and she timed the first part of their journey. They had walked quite briskly for nearly two hours, and had made good progress, when Mr. Kerquham, with a little cry, clutched at her arm, and then fell face downwards on the stony track.

"He has fainted from hunger," cried Rosamund aloud to the pitiless crags and frowning skies. "Good God! What am I to do now? I cannot leave him to die here."

She stopped and tried to lift him in her arms, but her own strength had left her. She wrung her hands.

"What am I to do? What am I to do? This is the worst of all. If I could only get him back to the cave, at least he would die in some shelter."

Her own frantic cries so filled her ears that she did

not hear the tinkle of a bell or the scrambling steps of an approaching horse. It was only when another voice mingled with her own that she stayed her wailing and listened with sharp up-pricked ears.

"Who is there? Is any one in trouble?"

It was a man's voice speaking in Italian.

"Yes, yes," shouted Rosamund with all her strength. "Come quickly! There is a man dying."

A moment later there stood before her in the path a small sturdy pony, trapped with a rough saddle and bearing on his back a man armed to the teeth and wearing the Albanian dress. His fez was bound to his head with the customary red shawl, which had been tied about his mouth, but which he had dragged aside to speak the clearer. He had gyves upon his legs and goatskin shoes. Over all he wore the brown *capa* of a Franciscan monk.

"Good heavens!" he cried, "who are you? How have you got here?"

But Rosamund could only point to her uncle, who still lay stretched in the track, motionless and apparently dead. All speech was strangled in her throat, for now that relief had come, hysteria had seized her and she felt that if she spoke she must scream.

With a swing of his strong arms, the sturdy fellow raised up Mr. Kerquham, and pulling from his waistband a big leather flask studded round the neck with small nails, forced some spirit between the dying man's clenched teeth. Then, still murmuring to himself a strange mixture of prayers and objurgations, he handed the bottle to the girl, while he began to chafe Mr. Kerquham's icy hands.

"So, so," he said presently, looking from one to the other of the travellers, "you have had an adventure up here."

Rosamund could still only nod. She was past all speech, though the ardent spirit she had taken was beginning to thaw her freezing limbs and stir her poor numbed brain to activity once more. Presently the monk—for such he was, despite his strangely incongruous attire—rose from his knees by Mr. Kerquham. He looked at Rosamund, at the horse, and at the unconscious man on the ground.

"Can you walk?" he asked her.

Rosamund said, "Yes." She felt as if new life were thrilling through her, and as though, now that help was so near at hand, she could struggle on for hours.

"Well, so can I," said the good Franciscan, "and the poor signor shall have the horse, for he is past everything, I think."

He lifted Mr. Kerquham into the saddle, and turned the horse's head up the steep track again, holding the unconscious, swaying figure between the high wooden peaks with one sunburnt hand. Slowly as the horse went, slipping and sliding at every step, Rosamund was so weak that she had great difficulty in keeping pace with it, but now and then in the course of the wearisome progress the monk flung a question or a word of encouragement to her over his shoulder. By-and-bye her brain grew sufficiently active to ask where they were going.

"To the monastery of Chatista," was the answer.

"That is where we were bound for," said Rosamund. "We should have been there yesterday, I suppose, only some gipsies robbed us of our horses and our luggage and left us by the roadside."

The monk shook his head.

"They are the curse of the country—those vile brigands." He significantly touched the gleaming barrels of the pistols in his girdle. "We are always prepared to account for some of them."

Rosamund, looking at his kindly face and twinkling little eyes, could not help wondering at the strangeness of a country which forced the men of God to go about armed against their fellows.

"Are we far from the monastery now?" gasped Rosamund as she felt herself growing weaker and weaker and her footsteps more uncertain.

"If it were not so black, you could see the peaks of Argentalia high above our heads," said the monk. "The monastery lies on a terrace of the nearer one, but it is another hour's scramble."

Suddenly he stopped his horse before a sharp turn out of the track which wandered away to the left round the foot of a low hill and was lost in the snows.

"We go this way, to the right," he said, gently, leading the animal round the sharp curve, and beginning a steeper ascent than they had yet compassed. "That other path leads to the Chatista valley and the village that lies in it."

For one moment Rosamund stopped to take fresh breath and cast a look about her. Down below, that hideous Valley of Death from which Providence had rescued her was already hidden in lowering masses of driving clouds. To the left wandered the little track, and as she thought that she might have followed that unknowingly and been lost forever in the wide snow-filled valley that lay beyond, she shuddered.

On the right was a steep, stony path, bordered with rocks and furrowed by the course of heavy rains. At the juncture of the rough roads where she stood was reared a huge black wood cross. It was so high that it appeared to dominate the whole landscape round, and its great arms, finished at either end with the trefoil that is emblematical of the Trinity, seemed flung abroad more in menace than in blessing.   For one moment as she stood there the sun broke through a ragged rent in the scurrying clouds and the shadow of the cross was cast at Rosamund's feet.   After the whiteness which had blinded her eyes for so many hours, the sharp denseness of the shadow looked like a rift in the ground.   She did not know why, but as she started up the mountain once more she carefully stepped over the shadow, as she would have set her foot across a little brook.

She had no breath now for speech, for it took all her thoughts and strength and will to enable her to struggle through the next hour.   Long as the time seemed, she was startled when suddenly a great wall loomed before her, and a moment later the monk was standing at the top of a wide flight of stone steps and knocking with a huge iron hammer at a heavily-nailed door.

"Where is this place?" said Mr. Kerquham, roused from his torpor by the heavy strokes of the hammer.

"It is the monastery, dear," Rosamund said through her sobbing breath.   "The monastery of Chatista."

The door opened, and the monk came down again and helped them in.   Mr. Kerquham trembled and shivered.

"What a dreadful looking place," he murmured as he painfully descended from the horse and, bent nearly double, slowly crept up the stone steps.

CHAPTER XXXV

THE PRISONER OF GOD

ROSAMUND, aching in every limb and with her strength spent, followed her uncle and the monk under the wide archway, above which hung the magnificent antlers of a red deer. As they set foot across the threshold a great peal of bells rang forth through the thick, snow-laden air. It was the customary welcome that was given to all travellers.

They slowly crossed a great square court, surrounded by cloisters on three sides and overlooked by narrow windows, in which small panes were set in herring-bone pattern. From the far corner of the cloisters, where a faint light showed the bottom of a wide wooden staircase, a tall monk, clad like their escort and carrying a bunch of heavy keys jangling among the barrels of his pistols, appeared. His face was rugged and worn, but he gave Mr. Kerquham and Rosamund a kindly greeting in Italian, and telling them he was steward of the monastery, bade them follow him into the building.

Mr. Kerquham was too exhausted even to thank the father, but Rosamund murmured a few words between her dried lips. As they walked slowly through the cloisters they passed many monks, all dark-eyed and swarthy, and each sheltered from the piercing cold by the heavy brown monk's habit which looked so incongruous above the truculent and gaudy national dress. On reaching the staircase in the corner, Rosamund herself had to help her uncle up the wide shallow steps. The steps were of stone, but the balustrade was of a dark oak, richly carved, and even in the midst of her weariness and physical suffering the girl noticed the beauty of the lintel and sideposts of the doorway through which they passed when they reached the first floor.

Here the gallery was warm and comfortable. The windows were so small and set in such thick walls that the outer cold did not seem to penetrate at all. Coarsely woven carpets, that yet were thick and warm, were strewn over the polished boards, and the low ceiling of oaken beams gave an air of extreme comfort. They were ushered at once into a small room, where, on a wide hearth, set with small red bricks in a florid Oriental pattern, a young monk was blowing into life a large fire of logs. Wooden settles were placed all round the wall, and the steward led Mr. Kerquham to one of them. A moment later a couple of tawny-skinned, stalwart youths entered, carrying with them a ponderous high-backed chair built of black oak and covered in well-worn tapestry. They set it on the hearth, which spread far into the room, and supported Mr. Kerquham to its cosy depths.

All this time Rosamund was gazing with apathetic eyes at the bustling preparations. She was roused from her reverie by the steward's question:

"Are you this gentleman's daughter?"

"I am his niece," answered Rosamund. "We were travelling to your monastery, and meant, after asking your hospitality, to go over the pass into Greece, but now I fear my uncle is too ill."

The monk followed her eyes from the huddled up form of Mr. Kerquham to the narrow window, across which a few light, airy flakes were slowly floating.

"You cannot move at present," said he, in his deep voice. "I will send you some food at once, and then ask the Abbot to receive you."

Wine and bread and a dish of stewed meat were soon brought into the room, and Rosamund dragged herself over to the table and the fire and tried to get her uncle to take some food. She herself felt sick and faint, but the wine, rough as it was, in some measure restored her, so that she was able to eat a little of the savoury stew and the coarse brown bread. She was grieved that beyond taking a few sips of the wine, Mr. Kerquham could swallow nothing. As the warmth of the pleasant fire crept over her, the buoyancy of youth asserted itself and her courage came back once more.

"A few days here," she thought, "and uncle will be quite well again. It is no good forcing him to eat, he is too worn out just now."

But Rosamund's hopes were fathers to her thoughts, for as the hours stole by and the short day dwindled into night, Mr. Kerquham sank into an apathetic, unconscious state. The good monks, who had some rough knowledge of medicine, carried him gently to the next room and laid him in the bed. From time to time they forced some spirits between his lips, but nothing roused him, and it seemed at one time as if he had died in his sleep.

The monks were too humane to ask Rosamund to leave her uncle, and so the Abbot came himself to her. He was the wreck of a fine man, with a long grey beard and bent shoulders. Instead of the Albanian fez, which the other monks wore, his white hair was covered with a small black skull cap. Unlike the other whom Rosamund had seen, he did not seem a pure-bred Italian. There was a dreamy look in his large soft eyes and a certain immobility about his strongly-marked features that pointed to an Oriental descent, though he spoke the soft Southern language very well.

The few words that he said to the unhappy girl were full of sympathy and genuine sorrow. All that could be done should be done, he promised, and he and the community would offer up special prayers for the life of her uncle and for the comfort of herself in the chapel.

For three days Mr. Kerquham lay in the low-canopied bedstead like one who is dead. For three days Rosamund sat scarcely conscious of her own weariness, only eating and drinking when the monks forced food upon her, and realising nothing but that once more she was face to face with Death. On the morning of the fourth day her uncle gave a sigh and died quite quietly, utterly unconscious that he was surrounded by kindly hands and friendly faces.

Too stunned for outward grief, Rosamund submitted to be led away into another room that the steward told her had been prepared for her. It seemed a long way off, along corridors and through many carved doorways and up and down little flights of steps, the purpose of which she did not divine.

"You had better rest here," they said. "The rooms have been prepared for you. We will let you know when all is ready."

For the first time for many days Rosamund was left alone. At first the sensation of solitude brought peace with it, but by-and-bye remembrance touched her with a rude hand, and she wept long and bitterly for the loss of her dead and dearest friend. Yet that night, worn out with weary watching, she slept well, and with the morning the solemn tolling of a muffled bell woke her with both brain and body well refreshened. She felt able once more to face life again and set her foot on the path that lay before her.

It was the steward's voice that spoke to her half an hour later through the door.

"The signor is lying in the chapel," he said. "Though you are not of our Church, we feel sure you will not resent a few prayers being said for the peace of his soul. If you will follow me, I will take you there."

And so Mr. Kerquham's life ended, as so many lives do, with a strange irony. He who had been born and brought up in the hard faith of Calvin, and who, despite his worldly knowledge and big heart, had shunned the forms and ceremonies and professions of the Catholic Church, now lay in death, a poor shrunken body, on a hand bier in a monastic chapel. Rosamund's tears at first took an added bitterness from the thought, as she knelt by the black and silver pall that covered the remains of the courtly gentleman and successful artist and heard from behind the heavy curtains of the choir the deep voices chanting a Requiem Mass. But even as she wept, reason came to her, and she knew that the Father had been right. A Christian should have a Christian burial, whatever the outward forms might be.

A sweet silence reigned for some time, and Rosamund in sacred solitude took farewell of her dead. Then at the end of the Mass four stalwart monks took the bier with its light burden and bore it from her sight. The brotherhood, with bent heads, their cowls completely shrouding their faces, formed behind in a solemn procession and passed out of the chapel.

Rosamund lost all count of time as she crouched on the flagged floor with hidden face and sob-shaken frame. She was only roused by a light touch upon her shoulder.

"We feared the cold might have caused you to sleep,

you were so still," said the monk at her side. She recognised him as having been her saviour on the mountain side. "Death happens that way sometimes when we have these fearful storms."

As she rose stiffly to her feet, catching at the low bench in front of her for support, he added:

"You have knelt here too long. The Abbot would like to see you if you can come to him. He would like to speak with you."

Brushing the tears from her lashes, Rosamund followed the monk. This time she was taken through many rooms, all panelled with oak, and many of them hung with rich, gold Venetian leathers. On every wide-throated hearth roaring fires blazed on dogs of quaintly beaten iron. Here and there a dim corner was glorified by a tall cabinet of ebony and ivory, a vase of polished metal, or a settle of oak that from age and use shone like bronze in the firelight. The sound of footsteps struck no echo from the cross-beamed ceiling, for the carpets that lay upon the floors were very thick. Before each door curtains of old tapestry or leather hung in ample folds, and the whole atmosphere breathed of warmth and refined comfort.

At the end of the long suite her pilot paused, and after knocking at a door entered for a moment, leaving her outside. She heard a few words exchanged. They were not in Italian, but in the bastard language that many of the monks of mixed nationalities speak among themselves. Then the door opened and the Abbot's voice bade her enter.

She found herself in a long, low room, the five windows of which looked from under the shadow of the cloisters into the courtyard. Sacred pictures hung on the walls, and the high mantel-shelf was graced with some old bronze candlesticks of rare beauty. A long table, black with age and with a deep carved edge, was littered with papers and books. Before the fire were arm-chairs, high-backed and deep-seated. The Abbot motioned her to one of them kindly, and then spoke a few words of respectful sympathy for the loss she had suffered. Rosamund, with clasped hands and her white face standing out like an ivory carving against the dark walls, thanked the Abbot for his kindness, and then with a sigh added:

"I will ask you to be good enough to put me on the road to get to some town. Perhaps you will tell me where I should go, for I feel lost. My uncle knew the road he meant to follow, but he never confided his entire plans to me."

"All plans are useless, my daughter," said the Abbot, "for you can go nowhere. You cannot leave this place."

Rosamund turned her tear-laden eyes from the burning logs and looked in the Abbot's face.

"Cannot go!" she exclaimed. "I don't understand. I am quite rested now—or at least I shall be in another day or two. If I may have an escort to the nearest village, I am sure I can manage for myself."

"It is not the question of escort or of your own courage, my daughter. God for His own purpose has so arranged it that you must stay here. Though it is against the rules of our order that other than a sick woman shall lie beneath our roof, Providence has decreed it otherwise. If by keeping you here we break those rules, at least we are fulfilling the first laws of Christianity, which ordain that all must succour one another."

"But I wish to go," cried Rosamund, starting to her

feet with an unknown fear knocking at her heart. "I cannot stop here."

"We cannot burden our souls with the crime of murder by letting you go."

"Murder? Letting me go! Am I in any danger?"

The Abbot looked at her for a moment with his large Eastern eyes.

"Is it possible," he said in his soft, thick voice, "that your sorrow has blinded you to what has happened during these last three days? Ah! I see that it has. The snows have fallen, and no one can leave this place and hope to live until the spring comes."

"The snows? Are we snowed up?"

"The snows lie so thick about us that neither man nor beast nor any living creature, save a bird, can come to this place or leave it till many months are passed. To drive you from our doors would be to send you to certain death."

Rosamund sank back into the deep chair with a little cry.

The Abbot rose from his seat, and crossing over to her, laid his hand upon her head.

"The prospect is a strange one to you at first. I can quite understand that you are filled with grief and dismay, but it is our mission in life to minister to the unhappy, and to do what we can to reconcile them to life. Everything will be done for your comfort, and so far as is in our power and we are permitted by the rules of our order, we will grant you every consideration. Even now they are arranging rooms for you."

A mad idea seized her that she was being made a prisoner. Tales of people who had disappeared mysteriously, ransoms, tortures, and a score of other horrors filled her brain. She started wildly from her chair.

"I only want to go," she cried, stretching out pleading hands to him. "For heaven's sake, let me go. I would rather die out there in the snow than stop here. The loneliness would drive me mad. Don't think I am ungrateful—but I should do nothing but think and think and think until I should not be able to bear it."

"I know, I know," said the Abbot, soothingly. "Your thoughts can be none too happy just now, my poor child."

"The monk who brought us here told me there was a village in the valley. Let me go there. The snows will melt there sooner, and then I can get away."

"I would sooner see you dead than set your foot towards that village. They are a wild and lawless set down there. They are still sunk in Mohammedanism, and are superstitious and savage. It would not be safe for you to go among them."

"But there must be some other way down," she persisted.

"There is no way, my daughter. For six months in every twelve this monastery is a living tomb. We are cut off from everything. Even the bears and the wolves that haunt these mountains do not come here."

Rosamund sank back in her chair, her whole face and attitude bespeaking the mental collapse which was overtaking her. The Abbot seated himself, and leaning his head on his hands gazed into the fire. Presently he said:

"My daughter, the manner of your coming and your enforced stay here are so extraordinary that I cannot but believe that Providence is working to some end. I will do for you what has never been done for another woman, and if there is any sin in it I will confess it and bear the punishment. You shall go each day to the library. We have one that is well stocked here, for

most of us read· much at these times.   The good Father
who is custodian of our books shall find for you such as
he may think fit for your reading.   Come to the chapel
every day.   Oh! do not think that we are going to try
to convert you.   If it is decreed that you are to become
of our faith, God will move your heart towards us in his
own good time.   Meanwhile, to pray and to listen to the
beautiful music which was made by great men for all
religions may help and soothe you.   Do not always keep
to your own rooms; walk in the corridor that lies outside
them and in the one that runs beyond that again.   There
is a screen there which lies between the monastic quarters and those that are set apart by the rules of our
order for the visitors that come to us.   In that way you
will get change and the benefit of exercise.''

The Abbot paused and looked keenly at the girl's
face.   Her habits of self-control and reserve had helped
her to conquer the emotion that had so shaken her a
while back.   Now with drooping head, set mouth, and
veiled eyes she was as immobile as a statue.

''We have in our brotherhood a countryman of yours.
I will see him and bid him sometimes talk with you.
You must eat by yourself in your own room.   Our order
is particular about that rule.''

''I thank you for your consideration.''

A rolling sound, like the beat of a drum, suddenly
echoed along the dim cloisters, and Rosamund, turning
her head, saw a monk in the quadrangle, holding in his
left hand a narrow piece of wood about ten feet long,
and in his right hand a small hammer.   He was striking
the wood in rhythmical, regular manner, walking slowly
in a circle as the sound grew and increased in intensity.
Finally he struck the lathe one sharp, hard blow, and
ended the roll-call abruptly.

"It is the hour of Compline, and I must leave you, my daughter; but we will pray for you in the chapel this evening, and I trust that you will be happiér when you have more occupation. Father Antonio shall come to you to-morrow and take you to the library. He is a good man and very learned. He will help you in your choice of books and he will talk with you, if you so wish it."

He raised his hand in a blessing, and so left Rosamund, soothed by his quiet voice and kindly words. On quitting the Abbot's room she was taken up another staircase from the one she had come down. It was winding and steep, and it led into a narrow corridor which looked as though it were seldom used. Kindly hands, however, had lit the usual wood fire, and her guide told her that in an hour or so carpets would be placed there and curtains hung before the doors.

The brilliant reflected light that is drawn up from the snow at once attracted her attention, and she guessed that the windows were in the outer wall of the building. Now she could see for herself if what the Abbot had told her was true, for she could not conceive that in three days such snow should fall as to isolate and cut off a whole community. She ran to the first window, only to draw back appalled. The whole world seemed levelled by the snow. Rifts and rocks, even the few scant pines, had been wiped out. It was no longer like living among mountains, but like being set in the midst of a vast plain, for as far as she could see down the valley it was one great drift.

For a moment a childish fear tore at her heart that the snows might fall and fall until the feathery masses overtopped the monastery and transformed what was already a tomb for the living into a veritable grave for the dead.   The strange terror died as it was born, for her quick eyes had caught sight of a narrow path scarcely wide enough to let two people pass.   It had evidently been cut from a small doorway through the white mass which hedged it on either side with icy walls ten feet high.   It was but a few yards long, and led to what looked like a little billow among the general flatness, pierced by a door in which an iron grille had been set.

"What is that path?" she cried to her guide.   "Where does it lead?"

The Father crossed himself reverently and in a low voice said:

"That is our morgue.   Here there is not earth enough to bury those who have not the right to lie in the vaults beneath our chapel, and so—"

"My uncle lies there?" asked Rosamund.

The monk bowed his head.

"Yes.   His tomb is of snow and ice."

She shuddered as she thought of her poor uncle lying in the little building which the snows had wrapped round with an icy mantle.   The cold had killed him and the cold would hold him forever.

The monk saw her tremble, and said:

"This side of the house is cold.   We do not see many women here, and it is two years since a traveller of your sex has lain in these rooms."

Then he opened a door, and as she entered her apartments he shut it behind her, and she was alone in her own domain.

The view from the windows was quite different from that seen from the corridor.   The rooms were comfortably furnished, and the hearths were wide and cheerful looking.   On the high mantel-shelves were quaint candlesticks and vases like those she had noticed in the

Abbot's room. A heavy oak table filled the centre of one room, and she guessed that it was there she was to eat and to live. The room beyond was smaller still, and was half filled by a splendid canopied bedstead of carved walnut, inlaid with ebony and hung with damask curtains of deep crimson and gold. Between the two windows was a praying chair, and on the dark wall hung a delicately sculptored ivory Christ. A picture of the Virgin was let into the panel over the fireplace. The face was very sweet and womanly, and Rosamund felt almost as if a friend were there waiting to greet her. At the foot of the bed a settle had been placed, and two chairs and a table, above which hung an old glass set in a quaint frame of Italian metal work. A cedar chest, with wrought silver handles, filled the other end of the room, and before the windows hung ample curtains of the crimson damask.

She walked from one room to the other, noting with her artistic eye the rare beauty of her surroundings. Then she went back to the sitting-room, and kneeling on the hearth, where the red bricks gave forth such a cheerful heat, she busied herself for a time deciphering the design on the great iron fire plate. It was Biblical and quaint, and distracted her until the short day died and the fire grew low. She made it up again from the large baskets of logs which stood in either room. As she moved about once more, she remembered that she had never looked out from her windows. It was too late now to see anything, for the pallid night had fallen and nothing was visible but the strange gleam of the snow. She tried to open one of the lattices, but it was still stiff and would not yield for some time. At length it gave way and she thrust her hand out into the air, but drew it back sharply with a cry of pain. It was like plunging it into boiling water, and her skin tingled and ached afterwards. She fastened the window quickly and drew the curtains, and with a wax taper that she found lit the roughly made candles and set them on the table. Scarcely had she done so when a voice told her that her supper was ready, and would she take it in.

She stepped into the corridor, but there must have been some hidden door there, for whoever had spoken had disappeared. On a low table was spread her meal of steaming soup and bread, a piece of mutton, some cheese made from goat's milk, and a flask of wine. She carried the tray into her room, and when she had supped set the remains of her meal outside again.

Then she prayed, staying on her knees until weariness overcame her, and she crept to her bed.

During the night, from time to time, she heard the bells peal out from the little pointed roof of the chapel, which stood at the far end of the quadrangle, and guessed that the monks were praying. It comforted her in a vague way, and gave her a sense of companionship and peace.

CHAPTER XXXVI

FOOTSTEPS TO HEAVEN

WITH the first promise of day Rosamund rose and went to her window. The view was so different from what she had expected that a cry of astonishment broke from her. Neither courtyard, walls, nor mountain path were to be seen. She looked straight out across the wide waste of a snow-wrapped valley which lay nearly one thousand feet below the vast crag on which the monastery—grey and bird-like—was perched. Her window overhung a precipice so sheer that instinctively her hands clutched at the broad ledge as though to save herself from falling when she pressed her face closer to the small panes in an effort to pierce the depths below.

Across the valley, and right opposite her windows, a giant range of mountains, magnificent and awful in their white winter robes, reared rugged heads against the pale sky. From right to left they swept—a lordly chain the ends of which were lost in pearly vapours.

From their silent summits her eyes dropped again to the valley. She caught her breath, and a warm colour dyed her pale cheeks. Set in a basin, which seemed as if it had been scooped out by a giant hand below the level of the rest of the valley, was a village, clustering about a small, white-domed mosque.

She knew it was a large group of houses, for although the broad-eaved roofs were covered with many feet of snow, faint wisps of smoke drifted over them through the clear air, and she could distinguish narrow ways cut from house to ʼhouse, and now and then a tiny black figure moving against the white background. For a brief moment the shock of finding that she was doomed to imprisonment while living within so short a distance of a village teeming with life, freedom, and activity, made her senses reel. She rebelled furiously against the declared necessity that she must stay where she was, until in a flash of memory she saw again the gaunt Black Cross and the dividing tracks. The narrow road which she had noticed as she came up had trended to the left until it was lost behind the low hill, must be the only approach to the village in the valley below. That road would now be lost beneath many feet of snow. With a sigh she realised at last that though the monastery and the hamlet were within view of one another, they were as sundered as the poles.

With every moment the morning brightened, and the faint clouds, caught by the wind, were wafted from the head of the valley into nothingness. By looking to the right Rosamund could see as far as where the crowding mountains shut in the gorge. There it was that her eye caught a long bright thread of falling water that gleamed like silver in the sun. Behind this solitary moving thing stretched a smooth, white plain. "That must be a frozen lake," thought Rosamund to herself. "And that shaft of lonely, falling water must flow from it and feed a stream that runs down the valley."

She strained her eyes to trace the river's course, but failing, promised herself that she would inquire from the next monk whom she saw whether her conjectures were correct.

Meanwhile she was content to stand at her window and try to imagine what the prospect looked like in the fair spring days and the fulness of summer time. But at last that relaxation palled. Memories of the shires in soft April mornings, and the fair "Hurst" gardens in their full summer beauty, rushed to her mind and blurred the landscape before her with hot, unshed tears. She turned from the window with a sigh, and stared aimlessly about the room for something to do. Everything was neat and tidy, for she had nothing that could get out of place. With clasped hands and her face set she paced the floor, fighting wildly against the flood of recollections that threatened to overwhelm every barrier of self-control that she could raise.

Suffocating with suppressed sobs, she flung wide the door of her room and ran into the corridor outside. Still the passion of recollection and grief raged within her, and she pressed her locked fingers against her mouth till they scored rosy lines across her white skin. For a moment her ears were filled with the surging of her own blood; then, as the roar died down and courage came back to her again, she remembered she had permission to go to the chapel when she pleased.

"Perhaps I shall be able to pray," she thought, stealing softly down the stone stairs she had traversed the previous day.

With timid hands a moment later she pushed open the heavy padded doors that shut the chapel off from the monastery. One glance showed her the place was empty. Slowly she moved to the front row of seats and fell on her knees. The heavy curtain that generally hid the chancel and the brotherhood from view was pulled back, and the high altar, rich in gilt marble, silver vessels and fine lace, closed with a blaze of gorgeous colour the dim vista of the rarely carved oak stalls.

Mass had not long been over, and a faint cloud of

perfumed incense still floated in ghostly wreaths round
a pair of chased metal lamps which swung on silver
chains from the painted roof.   Down either side of the
church were deep alcoves, filled with side altars of many
coloured marbles and lit by narrow pointed windows of
wonderful stained glass.   Above one altar, guarded by
glass and resting in a narrow recess, was a jewelled cas-
ket, holding, so the words beneath it said, rare relics of
St. Francis. Pictures of saints, set in deep carved frames,
hung above the others.   Over the high altar was a deep-
toned picture of the Crucifixion, with the Mother of
many Sorrows weeping at the foot of the cross.

Close by Rosamund was the pulpit, decorated with
panels bearing on the life and death of the patron saint
of the order.   Near the door was the font.   It was of
roughly-hewed stone, but crowned with a carved cover
fine as lacework.   Near the chancel steps stood a coffin-
shaped box, the four black sides painted in white with
skulls   and   cross-bones.   It   bore   an   inscription,
"*Aujourd'hui à moi, demain à Toi.*"

The roof was high and dim, but as a shaft of brilliant
sunshine pierced the rose window above the high altar
it lit the richly-tinted paintings that were set there in
florid borderings of gilt plaster work.   In the shifting
light the whole place glowed like a multi-coloured gem,
and the silver lamps and carven wood, the marbles of
rose and orange, malachite green and polished black,
and the embroidered hangings of the altars mingled
their separate gorgeousness into one glittering, exquisite
whole.

Rosamund, with all her nervous fears and longing
doubts soothed by her fair surroundings, covered her
face and began to pray.

"Oh! Mother of God, intercede for me! Oh! Son of

God, grant me strength! The cup Thou still holdest to my lips is bitter as gall. Grant in Thy mercy that it may soon pass from me."

Who was that who spoke? Whose prayers crossed her own? Still with covered eyes Rosamund knelt on, but her straining ears, her throbbing senses, told her that some one was praying aloud in the shadow of the high altar.

"Forgive me, Mary, Most Merciful, for my sin against my love. Forgive me that in blind ignorance I took her troth and pledged her mine. Forgive me that I was the cause of such grief—such sorrow as she has endured—and ah! Holy Mother—Immaculate of all save divine Passion—forgive me that I love her still. Forgive! Forgive! and when my full pardon is accomplished—"

With a muffled cry Rosamund struggled to her feet. Her senses reeled as she staggered up the chancel steps. The praying monk, roused by the flutter of a sigh, the faint fall of an unknown step, rose, too, and advanced, gaunt and tall, into the full flood of light that bathed the altar.

"Paul!"

With weakly outstretched hands and steps that tottered, she advanced towards the silent figure.

"Rosamund!"

At the sound of his voice her strength failed her, and she would have crashed to the marble pavement but that he caught her in his arms and drew her to his heart.

"You live! You are not a beautiful dream!"

She could not speak—but for answer she lifted one of his hands and passed it tenderly over her smooth cheek.

"How did you come here?"

She paused before answering, and when she spoke it was in a low, awe-struck voice.

"Paul! It was the hand of God that led me back to you."

Then a wave of recollection swept over her, and she cried, "But oh! the price—the price I have paid."

Paul passed his hand before his eyes.

"Your uncle? Was he the traveller who died here a few days back—and were you with him?"

She mutely assented, for tears choked her voice.

"I only heard vaguely of it—I have been ill and in my cell for some time."

"You are changed!" she said, raising her swimming eyes to his face.

"Changed! my poor love—by sorrow and repentance. Ah! Rosamund, when I remember all the wrong I did you, my grief has been beyond words. When I think that even now I am dragging your life into the ruin I have made of my own, I see that my sin is unpardonable. Even if you forgive me—I can never forgive myself."

Shaken with emotion, he bowed his head upon her shoulder.

"And now that we meet again," he went on, "by a freak of fate—or by God's good guidance—your presence—your voice—your very faithfulness are like new lashes on an ever-open wound. Truly, this should be the end—for my punishment is greater than I can bear."

With outstretched, trembling hands he turned to the high altar.

"Christ—help me! Guide me! I am lost in sorrow!"

Softly her hand slipped round his throat, warm and sweet between his flesh and the coarse habit; gently her voice whispered in his ear until his grief died down.

"Paul—dearest Paul—God has helped you—God has been very good to us both. We have been tried; *He* knows how much—but our probation is overpast, and we are together once more."

Paul lifted his worn face to hers.

"But the bar—I cannot—dare not—overlook that."

Rosamund laid her face close against his.

"Dearest—I told you God had been good to us. She who was your wife is dead. You are a free man in the sight of heaven and earth."

"Free! Free!"

"I only knew it myself a little while back. How little I thought I should ever meet you—when I read the few words that told me the news."

With the love-light growing in his eyes he rose and took her in his arms.

"My love! My wife!"

He bent his mouth close to hers, but she, with a quick movement, slipped her hand between them across his lips.

"Not here, Paul! Not in this sacred place!"

"All shall be as you ordain," he answered humbly, loosing her from his arms. "You have given me back love, freedom, life—you shall do with me as you please."

She placed her hand in his.

"Paul, let us kneel here and pray for—her soul!"

As they sank together on their knees he murmured,

"And for our own—and for our happy future."

CHAPTER XXXVII

THE MONK'S STORY

THE violent emotions of the morning had their revenge on Rosamund, and left her for the time being almost incapable of consecutive thought, and merely the weak victim of thrills and physical emotions.

She was glad, therefore, when, after her simple mid-day meal, a voice outside her door apprised her that Father Antonio was ready to show her to the library. He proved to be a round, jolly-looking little man, who had sufficient fat on his bones to keep even the cold of that fearful climate out of them. He talked in a chirrupy voice. When in the course of conversation he learned that she knew his beloved Italy by heart, his round face beamed with delight, and so far as his vows permitted he became at once her humble slave.

The library was a fine square room with windows on two sides of it. One set overlooked the cloisters and quadrangle; the other had the same view down that sheer, awful precipice into the mountain valley that Rosamund could see from her own room. Bookcases, protected with wire screens, surrounded the entire room. They were beautifully ornamented along the top with carved figures of saints, while the doorways were edged with religious symbols and surmounted by groups of cherubs' heads. The big fire that burnt on the brass dogs had drawn out a pleasant, warm smell of leather, and was striking a thousand twinkling stars from the shining wires.

"I am the librarian," said Father Antonio, proudly, as he drew from his girdle a bunch of little keys, "and you have only to tell me what books you would like to read and you shall have them."

With a growing sense of calm happiness and well-being Rosamund strolled leisurely round the room, peeping through the crossway bars of wire at the backs of the books. The titles of many of them were undecipherable to her, for there were works in Russian and Turkish and sundry offshoots of the Slav tongue, but to make up for that there were many famous books in French and Italian, and tucked away in one corner some old favourites of hers in German. There were histories of the Church, its rise and its struggles and its success in Bulgaria and the Balkan peninsula. There were books, too, about the very country she was in, Albania, and records of that wonderful spot, Mount Athos, which is dotted with monasteries, and where the foot of anything that is created female has never been permitted to fall.

"You may read here in the morning and afternoon," said the father, as he unlocked the case she indicated and drew her down some books. "And our good Abbot gave leave for you to take some reading to your rooms with you. He fears your health might suffer if you give too much time to thought."

Rosamund took an armful of books and drew a big chair up to the casement that gave on to the air and on to the mountains. Father Antonio, doubtless by virtue of his office, remained in the library, softly moving about in his goatskin shoes, rearranging the contents of some glass-covered tables of curios and old coins or fluttering the pages of a book. All was peace in the warm, comfortable room, yet Rosamund read but little. The change of scene and atmosphere, the knowledge that this new ground was to be almost as her own territory, were all pleasant to her. She was content to lay the books upon her knee and fold her hands over them, and look about her at the carved saints above the bookcases and at the rude picture of the holy St. Francis that hung above the high mantel-shelf.

A great peace had fallen on her—peace and happiness so completely satisfying, so intense, that she did not even seek to examine or recall their origin. She lulled herself with the mere consciousness that all was well with *him* and with herself, and for the moment that was enough.

Yet after a time it grew upon her senses that the librarian was very restless. He heaved big sighs, unlocked and opened with considerable noise glass case after glass case, re-arranged and disarranged their contents, muttered to himself, and behaved like a person who is desirous of opening a conversation.

"Perhaps he wants to talk to me," thought Rosamund. She thrust her formless dreams aside with her books, and rising looked from the window out on to the wintry world.

"What a strange place this is! It seems wonderful that, with so many fairer spots in the world, people should ever have thought of living here."

Father Antonio bustled to her side. His face beamed with delight, and in his hands were several worn old copies and shapeless pieces of metal.

"Ah!" he cried gaily, "the signorina speaks as do all strangers who have ever set foot in this wild spot. It is indeed past understanding, but to us—to all the Church, indeed—this is a sacred spot, bound up with the earliest history of our faith and consecrated by the blood of many martyrs.''

The monk looked quite eagerly at Rosamund.

''Shall I tell you something of the story of the famous monastery of Chatista? For it is famous, alike in Christian and pagan annals.''

''I shall be pleased if you will,'' answered the girl, sweetly.

Father Antonio motioned her back to her chair, and drew one close to it for himself.

''Chatista's monastery was not the first building that man's hands hung on the lip of this terrific precipice. In that brilliant era when Greek art and arms ruled so much of the Eastern world, a great general, in honour of a victory won in the valley below over a horde of savage people, raised here a small temple to the God of war. It was at once a place of worship and a watch tower, for here in my glass cases are fragments of pottery utensils and arms which tell us that a camp was pitched close here.

''Here, too, have been found coins and votive tablets of a later date and Roman make. Think what a fight must have raged up here, with what a crash the dead and dying must have fallen into the valley below before the Romans wrested the pass from the Greeks. The temple of Mars was destroyed as well, and on virgin ground— the spot where the morgue now stands (indeed, that is built from some of the self-same stones)—the conquering legions of Rome built a temple to Jupiter.

''The Romans subjugated the wild people of the mountains better than the Greeks had done—for among my treasures here, and mingled with the remains of the Romans, are many rough-hewn offerings brought to the temple as propitiatory sacrifices against the avalanches and floods which from the world's beginning have from time to time devastated these mountain valleys.''

Father Antonio dropped his handful of rough coins into Rosamund's lap.

"See! here are moneys and tokens of the time of the great Alexander, Lysimachus and Mithridates, Juba, two of the Ptolemys, the beautiful Cleopatra, Julius Cæsar, Dionysius—a score of mighty rulers.''

He opened, without rising, a case at his elbow.

"Look at these rings—those of gold—and these armlets are of metal the mixture of which we do not know. That is an altar lamp—this is part of a necklace; the beads are of glass. Here is a hand—cast in bronze, and the snake that twines about the ring finger is pure gold. Those statuettes are bronze.''

He locked down the glass cover again.

"They made a road—those fine Roman fellows—a road that centuries later, when Jupiter's little temple was crumbling to ruins, many of the Crusaders from the centre of Europe travelled on their way to Palestine. Then was a shelter first built here for those same warriors, and then began the period of bloodshed and fire which, through the Middle Ages, won for Argentalia the name of the Death Mountain.''

The monk shook his head mournfully.

"It was in the time of that most Christian monarch, Charlemagne of France, that His Holiness Pope Adrian I. granted permission for a retreat and house of refuge. The tribes—a furious people—took umbrage, and the first members of the brotherhood were burnt with their house. Under the protection of arms another small monastery was built, only to meet a century later with the same fate. But at that time God worked out his 'own vengeance. Over a thousand men and women, with their herds and huts, were destroyed by a mighty flood.''

"A flood!" said Rosamund.

The monk pointed from the window to the right, where the silver thread of falling water emerged from the silent, level plain of snow. "Up there, where the snow lies so smoothly, is a lake. It is fair and blue as the skies in summer, and the stream that flows from it waters the whole valley.

"Records that have been preserved through all the vicissitudes of the monastery relate that once, where the lake now lies, only a narrow torrent raced between the spurs of the mountains. It was so rapid that it had never been known to freeze altogether. But during the winter that followed the outrages on God's ordained servants, a glacier—the Black Glacier, as it is called—which lies on the other side of the double peaks, flung, week by week, huge masses of ice down into the gorge. With unceasing regularity they fell, crashing with a hideous sound upon the rocks, and by the force of their own weight building an impenetrable wall across the bed of the stream. Held back by the barrier, the prisoned waters rose and grew to an enormous lake, which, when the spring came and fed it with streams of melting snow and avalanches and heavy rains, swelled to a vast size, till one night the mighty wall, weakened by the weight of water, gave way, and the enormous lake surged through the valley, carrying trees and rocks, houses and cattle upon its broad bosom. The torrent destroyed many villages, and even Rosega, which you know, was annihilated.''

Father Antonio nodded.

"After that the tribes, wild men from the steppes and

wandering bands of lawless people from Hungary and
the Carpathians, left the good monks in peace, save
once, when a bishop and his suite were murdered on the
spot where the Black Cross now stands. A splendid
church was built here, and the Pope sent delegates to
consecrate it. It became a treasure house, filled with
gold and silver and many fair things. Then Turkey—
ever greedy and rapacious—and seeking everywhere the
wherewithal to pay her vast armies—cast eyes this way,
and again the flames licked the skies and the red blood
of martyred men flowed down the mountain side."

"How cruel!"

"It was a cruelty that lasted until the State gave
reluctant consent to Christians to make abiding places
and to convert. You know, however, that only the
Catholic Church is tolerated. The Greek Church is
tabooed, and no Mussulman—if he would live at peace
with his neighbours and the State—may join it."

"And lately the monastery has flourished?"

Father Antonio shrugged his shoulders.

"Yes! thanks be to God. But we never leave our
door unless we carry arms. The gipsies are a lawless
and a savage crew—and the villagers in these mountains,
though they take our charity, and, when it suits them,
are baptised and worship in the chapel here, are treacherous."

The loud drumming summons to Compline sounded.
Father Antonio, fussily jingling his keys, began to lock
away his treasures and books.

"Which book may I take with me?" asked Rosamund.

"Whichever you like," he answered, nodding cheerfully at her.

She looked at the three or four she held.

"It shall be this, I think," and she selected a work on Rome, which, though it was little more than an historical guide-book, she knew would revive pleasant memories of the past.

"A good book, a good book," chirruped Father Antonio. "You do well to read it." Then as he put away the others and locked them up he said, "Are you going to High Mass to-morrow morning?"

"Is to-morrow Sunday?" queried Rosamund.

"Yes, it is. You have been here almost a week."

"How quickly the time has gone," murmured Rosamund, thoughtfully, "and yet it seems ages since—"

Father Antonio assumed a sympathetic expression.

"God is very merciful. He puts a great sorrow a very long way off in a few days. But shall I fetch you in time for High Mass?"

"If you please. I should like to go and hear the music."

The little monk rubbed his hands.

"Ah! the music is beautiful here. We are nearly all Italians in this place. We cannot help but sing, we sons of Italy, and your countryman, too, has a rare voice. I will fetch you in good time, but you must wear a warm cloak, for the chapel is cold these days. Can you find your way back to your rooms?"

"Yes, thank you," said Rosamund, and with her book under her arm and a brighter expression in her pale face, she walked through the corridors in the direction of her own rooms.

As she went she remembered that the Abbot had told her that she might take exercise in the gallery beyond the one outside her door. Every one was in the chapel now; she could almost fancy she heard the organ pealing. The monastery was as quiet as the tomb it really was. Feeling sure that she would meet no one, she ran with fleet steps into the corridor that was at right angles to her own. She found that its windows overlooked the cloisters, and she was standing at one of them looking down into the courtyard, where the snow was piled high against the pediments of the supporting pillars, when she remembered what Father Antonio had said about the windows in the library.

"I must try to remember not to look out here," she said to herself. "I must keep faith with them, for they are being so good and so kind to me."

She walked on till she found her way barred by a tall, carved screen, reaching from the floor nearly to the raftered ceiling. It was of olive wood and the colour and texture of gold satin. It was delicately wrought with leaves and flowers and little figures of animals and people. Two centuries ago a dreamy monk had conceived it and had carved it. A scroll was woven through the branches of the mimic trees, and on it was graven "Paradiso."

Rosamund knew then that beyond it lay the monks' quarters in the monastery, and the carved legend set her wondering if the maker had labelled the monastical side with the name of Paradise, or whether he had intended the word as a description of that part of the building which was free to all comers as the air itself.

She leaned against the screen for some time, tracing with the tip of one slender finger the quaintly designed animals, the many graceful olive leaves, and the beautiful pomegranate flowers which were mingled so incongruously.

As she stood with a happy smile flitting now and then across her face, the sweet wail of a tenderly touched violin floated like a spirit sigh through the barren silence. It thrilled her with intensest joy, and she pressed closer to the screen and turned her head that she might catch every throb of sound.

"It is Paul! Ah! how good God has been to bring us together once more—to let us meet in a house devoted to his worship and praise."

She did not voice her gratitude, but it welled higher and higher in her heart and winged heavenwards in the breath of the music.

How sweet it all was—an impassioned melody of Gounod's—a plain, solemn chant by Palestrina—an intricate passage by Bach—a grand phrase from Beethoven—all like pearls strung together on a golden chain of delicious modulations and exquisite cadences.

When silence fell once more she still leaned by the carven screen and was filled with a great content. By-and-bye she heard in the distance footsteps and voices. The monks were leaving the chapel and going to their cells. She, too, made for her own rooms, meeting as she went Father Antonio. As he greeted her he glanced from the corridor window and remarked in his garrulous fashion:

"It is going to be a fearful winter, and there is some more snow to come." He pointed up to the patch of sky which hung over the quadrangle. "That silvery look which seems as if the sky had drawn a veil across her blue face always means snow. The heavens will be dark grey by sundown, and to-night the snows will fall again."

His words brought back to Rosamund all the terrors of her fearful journey. With her heart full of thankfulness that this time at least when the snows came she would be safely housed, warmed, and with good friends, she bade the monk good evening and entered her room.

CHAPTER XXXVIII

IN THE LIBRARY

FOR the next three days, although Rosamund went to the chapel and the library, she did not see Paul. Yet she was not disappointed or unhappy. She had endured so many weary months of heart pain after she knew her marriage with him was impossible, she had been for so long schooling herself to believe him dead to her and his love nothing but a sad memory, that the certainty of his welfare and whereabouts were enough joy for her.

Already he had been assured of his freedom and of her faithfulness—and in her trusting mind a few speeches more or less could make no difference. During the many hours she now devoted to thought she came to the conclusion that Paul, too, might see matters from the same standpoint. She was the more surprised therefore when, on the afternoon of the fourth day, he came quietly into the library.

She was sitting in the place she had established for herself near the window that overlooked the valley. Though all the view was monotonously white, and frequently the whole landscape was blurred with blinding snow-storms, it gave her almost a sense of physical freedom and exercise to travel with her eyes the great gorge that fell so gradually from where the lake lay in icy silence to the low round hill which marked the track to Rosega and the great Cross.

As usual her eyes were staring more at the scene than

at the volume on her knee when she heard Paul's voice addressing Father Antonio. She tried hard to keep calm as he presently came over to her and in Italian asked after her health and inquired what book she was reading. But the love-light would shine in her dewy eyes and a faint flush flare for a moment on her cheeks.

After a moment's pause he drew a chair close to hers. "It has been such a struggle to keep from you the last few days, but I thought it best. It has given us both time to think. Tell me, dearest, that you are not angry with me."

She replied, as he had spoken, low and in English.

"I have known that you were here. That has sufficed."

"Trusting and faithful as ever, dear heart."

"Have I not been rewarded, Paul? But see, here is what I promised to show you. Please read it, and then never let us speak of her again."

Paul read twice or thrice the scrap of paper Rosamund had cut from the *Times*.

"That is done with, thank God!" He crumpled the paper between his fingers. "Let us talk, dear, of yourself. My story you know. Tell me yours."

So that afternoon she unveiled the past to him, not dwelling on her own grief at his loss, and passing over with but a few words Lord St. Ives' proposal and her aunt's death. Rather did she talk of her travels and the sights she had seen. She told him, too, with honest eyes and unfaltering lips, of Hugh Fraser's devotion.

"I like to tell you that," she said, simply. "He was a good man."

"Who could help being good to you?" was all Paul said.

Then she spoke of Matia and his betrayal, of the

awful night on the mountain side, of her terrors and fears. She grew so pale at the recollection that Paul stayed her words.

"Dearest, you must forget these things. Look forward and not back."

She smiled faintly at him through the tears of self-pity her own words had brought to her eyes.

"I am hopeful, dear, but they say the winter will be very long."

Father Antonio, who had been drowsing by the fire, drew near them, and Paul, to cover Rosamund's confusion, cried lightly to the good man:

"The signorina is grieving that the winter will be so long."

"Then, Brother Paul, we must devise means to pass the days for her."

With his head on one side he regarded her with twinkling, beady eyes.

"The signorina should study. She speaks Italian so well—and French, I dare say—that the trick of languages should be easy to her. Why not learn Turkish? When the spring comes and the signorina leaves us, she will find it useful on her travels."

"Will you be my master, good Father?" asked Rosamund.

The fat monk shrugged his shoulders.

"My own language, with French and Latin for my prayers, have ever been enough for me, but there is a fine Turkish scholar here—rough-mannered, perhaps—but you will learn quickly from him."

"Do you mean Father Ludovic?" queried Paul.

"Yes, brother, the same. He is a strange man—but good at heart, good at heart."

Father Antonio returned to the fire and his doze.

"That is a good idea, dearest," said Paul. "Above all things you must have occupation here. Last winter I should have gone mad if it had not been for my music."

Rosamund smiled at him.

"It *was* you, then, playing the violin the other afternoon. My heart told me so."

"You heard me! Why, where were you?"

"Close—very close to the screen of olive wood."

Paul nodded his head.

"Ah! that saved another man. All the beautiful things you see here—the carvings and tooled leathers, the paintings and the rugs, have all been made by men who found in their work more consolation than in their God. The long periods of isolation—sometimes even worse—that befall the dwellers in these mountain monasteries render even religious exercises a mental torture, and physical enjoyment is necessary to the health, or the sanity, of many who come here. Yes! last year my violin and a little carving saved me. This year I have—*you!*"

"But you will not desert your music? It sounds so sweet among these picturesque old surroundings."

"If it pleases you—I shall play every day."

"And to please you—and so that you may know I am not drifting into idleness—I shall try and learn Turkish."

"But your fingers must work, too. I will speak to our steward. He is a most kindly man. You used to work so much in those dear Midshire days. Would you not like to make yourself a cloak and gown?"

With the prettiest blush of confusion Rosamund looked down at herself and carefully considered her appearance. Her cloth skirt, which had been cut short to a nicety for walking and climbing, now seemed in her eyes ridiculously curtailed. Already the edges of the sleeves of her coat were worn, and she had a rent in one elbow that she had acquired during those last few hours on the mountain. The warm woollen waistcoat that she had donned for the last stages of her journey she had managed to wash in her own room, but her efforts on her linen collar had proved quite fruitless, and she had supplied its absence by a knotted handkerchief.

"I'm very shabby, I'm afraid."

Paul smiled.

"You are as true a woman in little things as in greater ones. But you will be warmer in a woollen gown, and you need some goatskin shoes instead of those thick boots."

He cast a look at Father Antonio, quietly snoring in the red glow of the hearth. Then he leaned forward and took her hand in his.

"Darling—you will so soon now be all my own that I feel I must care for you as I would for myself."

The call to the chapel sounded.

"Farewell for to-day. In an hour you will hear me playing to you."

CHAPTER XXXIX

THE BLOOD FEUD

WHEN next Rosamund went to the library she looked as fair as one of Mary's own lilies. She had sewn for herself a straight falling gown of the white woollen stuff the peasants make for their own use. A long hooded cloak of the same material hung from her shoulders. Her feet were shod in soft, white buskins, and her hair rippled and waved into a heavy coil at the back of her neck.

"Santa Madonna! but she is beautiful!" ejaculated Father Antonio.

In Paul's eyes she looked like a queen or a saint.

A third monk was present that day—Father Ludovic, the Turkish scholar. He was a gaunt, ascetic-looking man, and the sparseness of his figure was enhanced by the folds of his coarse habit that looked as though it were hanging on a mere skeleton. The bones of the forehead and the cheeks were painfully sharp, and the eyes that glittered in the sunken sockets were like live coals.

For a moment Rosamund allowed the Father's looks to dominate her feelings, but Paul had said he was a good-hearted though strange man, and she conquered herself and smiled sweetly into his dark, stern face.

"Father Ludovic is glad to have a pupil," said Paul.

"You will find you have set yourself a very difficult task," said the grim father. "It really takes years to

413

understand the language. You will get but a smattering of it during the time that you are here."

"At least it will pass the time for me. My reading till now has been very purposeless, and I find the evenings are long."

"The signorina does well to make use of the hours," murmured the dark monk, taking down some books from an upper shelf and bringing them to a table near the fire.

They made a strange group in the glow of the logs, round-faced Father Antonio, drowsing over a small case of his favourite coins, the swarthy Ludovic, with his fierce eyes and guttural voice, Paul, with a smile flitting from time to time across his handsome face and a neglected book in his hand. And amidst these brown-frocked monks sat Rosamund, with her white draperies falling about her and her delicate brows crinkled with anxiety and attention.

All was quiet and peaceful in the room. Only Father Antonio breathed heavily now and again, and the logs crackled and spluttered on the hearth.

Suddenly, through the intense stillness, the sharp ring of a shot tore the air. The monks knew what had happened, but Rosamund was ignorant even of whence the sound had come till she caught sight of a tiny puff of blue smoke floating lazily across the street of the village below. Some one had fired a shot down there. She leaned a little forward, pressing her forehead against the icy cold window. Another and another puff of smoke floated out, followed a second later by the hiss of a shot. Against the universal whiteness she caught sight of two or three figures running in mad haste across the village street. A door was flung wide, and a man who by his gait she guessed to be old and slow of movement, staggered out into the road. Once more a shot was fired, and the old man, flinging up his arms, fell forward on his face, a dark figure silhouetted against the spotless ground. For a moment Rosamund could scarcely realise what had happened. It was all so far away, although yet within sight, that she felt as though she had been watching a scene in a play. But a moment or two later she drew back with a sharp cry from the window, for from beneath the black shadow of the body, something that was red crept and slipped like a snake over the white snow.

"Ah! they have shot him!" she cried, speaking English in her excitement.

"It is the Blood Feud," said Father Ludovic. "It has broken out again. Now they will fight all the winter through."

"The Blood Feud," repeated Rosamund, drawing back from the embrasure of the window that she might no longer see that fearful thing down below. "Do they kill each other? What does it mean?"

"Have you not already heard of that custom of this country during the afternoons you have spent here?"

"Father Antonio has never told me of anything so dreadful," answered Rosamund.

"They do not call it dreadful," said the monk, looking towards the village, where once again all seemed peace, and the only thing that moved was that long, red, thin line creeping over the snow. "You are disturbed to-day. Come back to the fire and we will tell you of the custom."

Paul, with a twisted piece of iron, stirred the embers into a blaze. He flung on some fresh logs which crackled cheerily and sent bright shafts of light into the furthest corners of the dim room.

Father Ludovic alone of the party did not sit.   He seemed to glory in his great height, for he drew himself up to his tallest as he leaned against a bookcase and looked down at the others.

"The history of Albania," began the Father, "is so wrapped in legend, superstition, and mystery that no man knows when the Blood Feud first commenced, or whose hand it was that inaugurated the series of violent deaths which have carried off the flower of the country from century to century.   We Italians and Austrians—I am an Austrian"—he interpolated—"have been told that since all time this fierce feud has existed.   The tradition is this: If you kill a man, you owe his family a debt of blood which only your own death can wipe out.   The man who claims his family's debt from you is himself a creditor to the head of your own family, and so it goes on descending from father to son, from brother to brother.   Sometimes, as has happened to-day, it is an old man who falls, but as often as not it is a child, some-times even an infant.   I think I know the man down there.   If so, he has been hiding in this village here, and he fled to it from Rosega, far down the valley.   He and his sons had a feud which was bequeathed to them for five generations, and in Rosega he used to sit with a loaded rifle watching by day and by night till he who owed him blood should emerge alone from his door."

"I saw the man myself," cried Rosamund.   "Our guide told me that he waited for the Agha.   I did not understand then."

"The debt must have been paid, or the old man would not have fled up here.   He doubtless thought he would be safe during the winter, but some one must have followed him. Perhaps before the snows fell his enemy came here and has waited for his chance."

"And what will happen now that he is dead? Is it all finished?"

The monk shook his head.

"Did I not tell you that he had three sons in Rosega? When the snows melt and the paths are clear again and the news is known down there, the Blood Feud will begin again, and hide how he will, or be guarded how he may, one day the murderer will pay his debt."

"But is no man ever tried for murder in this country?"

The monk smiled.

"In the towns the Turkish *zaptiehs* make matters worse by trying to interfere, but the people of these mountains, this great Clementi tribe, and those who like them live in wild fastnesses and gorges where the foot of no Lowlander can find a hold, know no laws but their own. We, who have been called to a higher life, try from time to time to heal those breaches and to urge that 'Bessa,' the peace of forgiveness, should be established among them."

He shrugged his shoulders expressively, till the sharp bones stood out beneath the folds of his habit. "But what will you? During the summer months when we pass among them they keep peace, except perhaps during the fast of 'Ramazin.' But in the winter, when we in these mountain monasteries are held prisoners by nature's hands, what can we do? Down in the villages they pass the winter in drinking and idleness. No man can work, be he ever so willing, for their idleness is forced upon them by God; so they get quarrelsome, and the old trouble breaks out again. I have passed seventeen years here, and I shall stay here till I die. Every summer we get these wild men to consent to the 'Bessa,' and every winter the Martini-Peabodys echo round the hills and the red blood stains the white snow, and there are fewer mouths to feed in the cottages.''

"But it is hateful; it is frightful!" cried Rosamund. "They do not look such cruel people as all that. Those whom I saw at Rosega seemed kindly and hospitable; not as if they had blood upon their hands."

"The signorina should not have come to travel in these wild parts," Father Antonio said, suavely. "'There are few men who have not some blood debt upon their souls. Why, the lay brother who takes you your food is himself a refugee. When the spring comes and he sets foot upon the mountain side again, he will fall where he stands."

"The man who brings me my meals," said Rosamund, "a tall, fair man, who walks like one accustomed to much exercise. I saw many of the same type at Rosega."

"So you have seen him?" said the monk.

"Yes. I happened to open my door one day before he had left the gallery. Does he owe a blood debt?"

"Yes, and his history is a strange one. He killed a child."

Paul instinctively moved nearer to her as she turned pale and wrung her hands.

"Oh, how fearful! How dreadful! A poor little child. Oh, that could not be fair, if there is any fairness in such a fearful custom."

"The child's father had killed his father, and has never been seen since; so the debt came to the child."

"And that man killed it?"

"Yes, down there in the village street, three days before the snow fell."

Rosamund shuddered, for she pictured the tall, fair

man, with the easy, swinging walk, stained with innocent baby blood.

"He was a coward, too," interposed Father Ludovic, "for when he had shot down the little one, he ran for asylum to the mother's house, and flung himself on his knees and prayed that she would grant him the 'Bessa.' By their strange customs the woman was obliged to give him the oath of protection. When the rest of the family came to the door and cried to him to come out and pay the debt, she herself went out to them and said she had granted him 'Bessa' until noon. Then she hid him up in the mountains and told him to escape. The murderer, who is a cur, for all his fine shoulders and yellow hair, fled from house to house, hiding now here, now there, in the cellars, the balconies, even under the eaves. They hunted him out and fired at him a score of times, but the darkness veiled him. Their rifles are bad, their powder is large-grained and inferior, and they cannot aim without a rest, so he escaped. At dawn he took to the mountains and arrived here for sanctuary at the midday. Our Abbot, who is most charitable and good, took him in and clothed him—and out of gratitude the man— his name is Hassan, and he is at heart a Mussulman—was baptised into our Church, and is called Brother Gabriel. He is a menial, and no one likes him here. I fear that when the spring comes and the path is open he will find himself forced to go down to the village."

"It is a fearful story," said Rosamund, rising and drawing her cloak round her. "Poor man, how he must have suffered. Surely no one will drive him from the sanctuary of this place?"

Father Antonio shrugged his round shoulders.

"There is humanity even in a monastery, signorina."

Then Father Ludovic set her a lesson for the next day,

and with friendly farewells they parted. As she passed down the corridor she saw that the snow was beginning to fall again, not in a light and whirling shower, but in huge soft flakes like feathers, which lay where they fell, and piled themselves higher and higher in an ever-thickening sheet of whiteness.

CHAPTER XL

A WHITE SHROUD

THE lamp in Paul's cell began to burn sickly yellow in the growing dawn. Prayers in the winter were not until half-past five, and were said in the refectory for warmth's sake. High Mass in the chapel had also been over for some time. He had snatched a cup of coffee and hot milk and a morsel of black bread and cheese, and had then come up to his cell. With almost feminine particularity he made all tidy before sitting down to study his part in the Mass that was to be sung on the following Sunday.

Rosamund had been many weeks in the monastery of Chatista, and it was of her and not of the music spread open before him that Paul was thinking that morning. His violin was tuned, his bow held in position, but no sound rose from them. With dreamy eyes he stared at the notes, but it was her face only that he saw. Her face, with the tender, bowed mouth, the white-lidded eyes, the pensive droop, all enframed in waved masses of dusky hair.

As her image dominated his thoughts, his hands relaxed, and the violin slipped to his knees.

"How like a saint she is in this sad piace," he murmured to himself. "Even love's passion dies at one glance from her pure eyes. And yet— and yet—will the time never pass? The days shorten, and sometimes it seems as though an everlasting night were going to fall."

He stretched out his arms longingly.

"Ah! for the spring and the fair countryside at home—and you—my darling. You, who have been, who are, my good angel. Angel, indeed, for you brought me the news of my release, and you are giving me strength to wait with patience."

The dying lamp flared and smoked, and he put it out. A feeble sun-ray pierced through the small double window, which was in a deep recess opposite the door. It shone upon his face and hands, and he, in the pale radiance, leaned back in his wide-armed black oak chair and rested his head against the faded rose-coloured brocade with which it was upholstered.

The cell was of fair proportions, and like all the rest of the monastery, warmed during the awful winter months by heated air. A small wood fire also burned on the red brick hearth, for in that climate, cold meant death. An old piano helped to fill the wall opposite the curtained bed. It was flanked by a bookcase and a narrow writing desk. At the bed-head was a *prie dieu*. Paul had carved it himself during his first winter there. Above it hung a rare crucifix of ivory and silver—one of the many splendid gifts that from time to time wealthy patrons or grateful travellers had lavished on the community. Rugs and mats of deer and wolf skin lay upon the floor. Music and books were neatly piled on the piano top. The panelled walls were almost hidden with sacred pictures. Many were crude and poorly drawn, but they gave an air of comfort and colour to the place. A leather curtain hung before the door, near which was fixed a heart-shaped white *bénitier*. On a small table were toilet necessaries and two or three photographs. One, by the costume, was quite thirty years old. It represented Paul's mother, holding him as an infant in her arms.

Amid such surroundings Paul had passed more than eighteen months. He had taken two years' vows, and dedicated himself to the higher life and the order of St. Francis. But in the spring he would be free, and when the mountain track that led back to the world—to happiness—to her, was open, his feet would travel it.

Paul, the Franciscan brother, vowed to austerity and abnegation, was still Paul, the man of easy life and weak temperament, and his heart turned readily to dreams of a brighter future. He remembered—and a smile broke the weary lines of his mouth—that during their frequent interviews Rosamund had never spoken of his obligations, had never asked him when his freedom would be complete.

"Ah, how proud, how modest she is—how full of faith and trust! All her strong nature turns to lean on me—and I am so unworthy!"

No music sounded that morning from Brother Paul's cell, and he was paler than usual when after the mid-day meal he entered the library, and by his coming caused a slight stir among those assembled there.

Nursing the fire were Father Antonio and Father Nicholas, a countryman of the first named, who from *ennui* had lately developed a taste for numismatics. Their ruddy, round faces glowed like full moons in the hot blaze, as they argued and gesticulated like the Italians they were.

At a small table drawn close to the window sat Rosamund and her tutor. Father Ludovic was intent on his task, but Rosamund's mouth and eyes warned Paul that something was amiss.

"How does your pupil progress, Father?" he asked. Father Ludovic lifted his hollow eyes from the page before him.

"The signorina is apt and very quick.   Her progress is extraordinary—but to-day—"

"Father Ludovic has just told me that one of your brotherhood is very ill," interrupted Rosamund.   "It seems so sad that any one should be ill here—isolated from home and friends."   She thought of her uncle and sighed.   "I hope it is but a passing indisposition, and that he will be well again soon."

"Illnesses do not pass here, my daughter," said Father Ludovic.   "Once the sands of life run low in this climate it is the soul that passes."

The air of the room was hot and heavy with the pungent odour of leather-bound books.   There was more snow, too, in the sullen, grey sky, and an air of lassitude dominated the apartment.   Now and again Rosamund shot a glance at Paul, but she felt little desire to speak with him.   Their life streams were running so·tranquilly just now that there seemed no need to stir their depths. They were together so often in the chapel and the library that they had small need of words.   And then every day, as the light died and night dropped her dark mantle over the white world, he played to her and poured out all the love and passion he could not speak.

In her present mood—a time of recovery from much mental suffering and nervous trial—that intercourse was sufficient for her.   Peace and the assurance of his love were all she needed.   Yet her very tranquillity could bear but little ruffling, and when at the break of the next dawn she was awakened from her slumber by the doleful, monotonous throbbing of a single bell, she sorrowed deeply.   The snow was falling through the thick air and the sound was muffled, but each note struck proclaimed the news that a member of the brotherhood—made one by isolation—had passed away in the night.

That afternoon out of respect she did not go to the library, but only left her room for half an hour to pace up and down the long corridor outside it. It was while she was there that she heard the shuffling of feet on the stone pavement of the cloisters below and the droning of a funeral hymn. She crept to one of the windows and looked down upon the sad procession of monks with their brown cowls pulled over their bent heads and the beads hanging from hands that were crossed upon their breasts. Four of them carried the bier. The sight brought a pang of sorrow to her heart, for it reminded her acutely that she was learning to forget the memory of her dear uncle whom she had lost.

As the melancholy procession passed very slowly by and was swallowed up in the dimness of an angle of the cloisters, Rosamund's eyes, sharpened by love, pierced through the awkwardly cut, rough garments and discovered Paul in the dismal ranks.

When the last of the procession, which was closed by a group of lay brothers, had passed away, she still leaned against the window. The courtyard of the monastery was almost new ground to her, and she looked curiously at the long rows of small leaded panes, the carved mullions, the old iron water-spouts, wrought into a hundred different heads of griffins and devils, each of which now wore a long beard of ice. On the wall that faced south a hardy creeper grew. It had straggled between the close-set windows right up to the roof, and had flung one long branch round a low chimney stack. It was covered with snow, which had frozen hard and looked like a frosted silver pattern against the grey walls of the old house. Then she looked downwards to where, in the centre of the courtyard, the snow lay in an ever-growing heap, for the cloisters were swept clean each day, and the white expanse was a miniature mountain range of ups and downs.

A dreary sound rent the silence. It was the mournful funeral chant that pierced the walls and floated like a dismal wail round the desolate quadrangle. It sounded inexpressibly sad in the gloom of the dying afternoon. It was dusk before the sound of footsteps passing again over the flagged walk told her that the service was ended, and that yet another monk had been laid to his long rest in the vault beneath the chancel.

As she stood there, oblivious of darkness and cold, she fell to wondering whether many of them died like that during these terrible winters. She knew so little of those who dwelt with her inside these thick grey walls, and save for the chance words let drop by Paul from time to time, the habit of their lives was almost a sealed book to her. She recalled how changed Paul was, and how she had been told by Mr. Fraser that the Italians and other Southern-bred men who exiled themselves, either for political, family, or religious reasons, in these desolate mountain monasteries, were always regarded and spoken of by their friends as being dead men.

"Dead!" she cried to the darkness. "Shall we— Paul and I—ever leave this place alive?"

With a new doubt—a growing horror—added to the monotony of her days, she went slowly back to her rooms. That evening Paul did not play to her, and she was very sad.

CHAPTER XLI

THE LEGEND OF THE RED DEER

THE Advent fasts and Christmas feasts were past. To Rosamund they had only served as a mark in the passage of time. She fancied that a depression and anxiety filled the air. Father Ludovic grew more lean and silent, Paul looked ill and sad, and even Father Antonio's unquenchable Southern temperament seemed dim and subdued.

She wondered at the gradual change, and one day she knew the truth.

She was sitting alone in the library. A Turkish book was in her hands, and she was diligently reading it, and as she went, carefully translating each sentence.

"Rosamund!" said Paul's voice over her shoulder. She did not start. It seemed quite natural to have him there.

"Give me your attention for a moment, dearest." A graver cadence than usual in his voice made her turn sharply in her chair, letting the volume fall all unheeded among the folds of her white gown.

"Is there any trouble, Paul? How pale and anxious you look."

She put out a loving, tender hand to him.

"You seem so tired—so worn. Ah! Paul, now that I have come so far and braved such dangers to be near you—you must not fail me."

He caught her fingers between his two palms, but only the ghost of a smile flickered over his face.

"Dearest, we must each help the other now.   To-day I am the Abbot's messenger to you."

"The Abbot has sent me a message?   He wants me to help him?"

"He wants you to be brave.   That is the help we all have to give each other now."

Paul pulled one of the heavy carved chairs to her side and sat down.

"Listen, dear, to what he says.   God, for His own good purposes, has made you one of our community, and the Abbot looks upon it merely as an act of justice that you should know how matters stand with us, who are by the will of that same God prisoners here now.   The winter through which we are passing is the most terrible that has ever been known, even in these wild parts.   We have much sickness in the house, and one already of our community has been called from earth to heaven.   Now we find ourselves almost at the end of our stores and food.   The Abbot wishes you to know this, that you may not think that you are treated with any lack of hospitality if from to-day your fare is of the roughest.   All of us will feed alike until it pleases Providence to send us flesh or fowl."

Rosamund smiled in Paul's face.

"Dearest, as you fare so am I content to do."

Paul gazed at her, so brave in her youth and strength, so fair and simple in her white woollen gown.

"You are of the stuff that once made martyrs and saints.   But perhaps there will be compensation in the scales of justice.   When the weather is very bitter among the passes and the snow lies thick for many weeks on the ground, the wild red deer, which herd in the pine forests and in the more sheltered gorges, grow quite tame, and come here—the only habitation of man on all Argentalia's rugged sides—for food. Those of long experience here say that the deer must now be on the verge of starvation, and yesterday two lay brothers scattered some hay a few yards from the entrance. This morning it was gone."

"Oh! Paul," cried Rosamund, "they are going to trap the poor, pretty creatures."

"My dearest, we owe it to our Maker to preserve the lives He gave us. Yes! Each night now the great gates will be set open and the courtyard strewn with sweet hay."

He caught sight of her distressed face.

"Dear, tender heart, we but fulfil the laws of nature. Ah! I have hurt you."

To distract her thoughts he picked up her dropped book.

"What a linguist you will be, Rosamund, by the time you leave here. Father Ludovic is a good master."

"He is most patient and most kind," answered the girl, anxious to interest herself in other subjects. "But, Paul, how strangely he looks sometimes—half sad, half fierce. Has he a history?"

"Yes. He is that social anomaly—an anarchist. He escaped from justice to these fastnesses seventeen years ago. For months half a regiment of the Albanian Guard scoured the mountains for him. The Abbot gave him sanctuary, and found out later that he, in his youth, had been acquainted with Ludovic's family. It was that bond that made him keep him here. Now all his strong will and fierce passions have turned to religion. He flagellates himself at night in his cell until the walls are splashed with his own blood. He fasts and prays till he faints on the altar steps. I think now he only tastes of peace when he is with you."

"Poor man! If my presence brings any happiness to him I am glad."

But for the next few weeks there was little happiness and much anxiety in the monastery. So unusually early had the winter begun that the store of birds and mutton and venison, which is made in these mountain valleys with the idea that it will last through the winter months, had almost given out. Nothing but black bread, coarse and gritty as ashes, and goats' milk cheese was served at every meal. Often, as Rosamund sat at her books or needlework, her head swam and her sight grew dim, yet she bore the trial better than some, who became more shadowy and wan as the long January weeks crept by.

The red deer picked shyly at the scattered hay sometimes, but, as the monks said, were not yet tame enough to venture within the heavy gates.

But at last a morning came when Rosamund was startled from her sleep by shouts and cries and shots. Dragging on her gown and cloak, she ran to her door. Scattered outside was her daily supply of fire-logs. Hassan, the Albanian lay brother, had evidently been disturbed at his work of neatly piling them. Half fearful, half curious, the girl ran to the corridor window that overlooked the quadrangle.

The sight that met her eyes filled her with mingled wonder and horror. During the night a herd of red deer, driven at last from the mountains by storms, cold, and the ravages of the wolves, had rushed into the trap set for them. The piled snow in the quadrangle had been trodden in every direction by their futile efforts to escape. In the cloisters were all the monks and the denizens of the monastery. The Abbot himself was leaning from a window. His long beard was blown over one shoulder and his arms were waving directions to those below.

"Not too fast!   Not too fast, my children!" he cried, as a shot "pinged" from the long barrel of a Martini-Peabody and another lordly creature fell.   "Above all, spare the does—spare the does."

And Ludovic, from the angle by the chapel door, shouted: "Kill only three!   They will suffice for the present."

An hour later Hassan knocked at Rosamund's door. He was smiling broadly all over his fair, handsome face, and bore some steaming stew upon a platter.

"The good God has sent us some food," he cried in his strange language.   "There is no need now to eat dry bread or starve."

With all her natural longing for the food, Rosamund endured a moment of revulsion.   She had seen the pretty animals shot out there, and even now their blood was staining the snow.   Although her hands went out for the plate she shook her head at the Albanian.

"Do you know the legend, signorina, that you fear to eat?   The mountain folk vow that ill-luck follows the killing of a wild red deer."   He shrugged his broad shoulders expressively as he thrust the food into her reluctant hands.   "But you, signorina, are English—and a Christian lady.   You would not believe such idle talk.   Neither do I.   It is only for dogs of Mussulmans."

And the recently converted son of Islam hastened down the corridor intent on his own dinner.

CHAPTER XLII

THE VALLEY OF THE DEAD

FEBRUARY had set in and the Lenten fasts were close at hand. Although the days were longer, the monastery, with its narrow, lead-surrounded windows and black oaken walls, was very dark and gloomy. The sun had for days been hidden by ragged clouds, which poured a never-ceasing stream of mingled snow and rain upon the countryside. The cold became more difficult to bear, for the air was laden with damp and mist. So bad was the weather that the red does that had lived comfortably in the courtyard during the extreme frost were now stabled with the horses and mules.

Rosamund often visited them in their warm, steamy shelter, and made a playmate of a baby fawn that was there. She had to struggle hard in those days against a nervous depression, which when she was alone almost killed the strong spirit within her. The many months of close confinement to the house, the monotony of the hours, the sameness of her surroundings, told even on her equable nature. Then, too, as the days crept by she could not help speculating on the future.

In their daily intercourse—which, even when they met alone, she and Paul by unspoken consent held in the leashes of self-restraint and emotional suppression—the coming of spring and its consequences were now never mentioned. But in her solitary hours Rosamund's imagination won compensating sway, and she built a thousand castles, refuted hundreds of arguments, and dreamed endless dreams.

Of her own release—directly it should be safe for her to leave the monastery—she had no doubt. The Abbot .himself had spoken of it, and promised her assistance. Of money she would have plenty for her journey, for the Fathers held for her the pocket-book found on her uncle.

But Paul—what of him?

Her very uncertainty as to Paul's future stayed her from speaking to him of it. That his two years' vow was drawing to a close she knew, but suppose pressure— force were brought to bear upon him, and he should stay in the monastery? She longed to ask him if the brother-hood would be willing to let him go. She knew herself to be a coward, she despised herself for postponing the question. But she loved him so dearly, she dreaded so much the thought of going back alone to a world that for her held nothing but empty memories, that she lacked the courage to meet the worst.

Her chiefest happiness she now found in the chapel. Among the pictured saints and silver swinging lamps, the brilliant gilding, the statues, waxen flowers, and coloured marbles, surrounded by everything she had been taught to abjure, her soul found peace and her heart patience.

She had prayed a long time one day before the altar of the Blessed Virgin. A calm-eyed, sweet-faced picture hung above the candles and the dried flowers. After she had finished praying she knelt on, gazing at the tender features till they seemed to pulsate with life.

Suddenly with a cry she held out her hands to the picture. "Ah! Mother of God, grant me courage if thou canst not give me happiness."

Then as though impelled by an invisible hand, she

leaned forward and kissed the pierced feet of the ivory Christ that stood upon the altar. As she did so a dull roar rolled through the heavy air and muttered and echoed in the chapel roof.

She rose to her feet quickly.

"That sound again! What can it be? I heard it sleeping and waking in the night."

A little later she entered the library. Of the three brown-habited monks present, Ludovic and Paul were seated by the fire, while Father Antonio was with a magnifying glass examining a coin by the window.

The room was so warm, and the occupants, who might have looked strange in fresh eyes, but to whom she had grown accustomed, looked so cheerful and contented that much of her own depression fled at the sight of them.

Father Antonio called her as she entered.

"See here, signorina! Here's quite a new coin for you to-day. I found a leather pouch last week in an old chest that stands in the refectory, and this was in it. The first Russian money that was ever struck."

He expatiated on it for some moments before turning away to seek a place for it in the already over-full glass cases.

Rosamund looked from the window. Huge masses of cloud were lying all along the mountain tops, and the valley beneath the leaden canopy looked inexpressibly mournful. She shivered at the prospect, but with idle eyes stared on.

Father Antonio was now by the fire, round which the conversation by degrees took on quite a genial tone. The monks having dined well and being warmed by the cheerful flames, told stories among themselves and laughed and gesticulated. Even Father Ludovic unbent a little, and Rosamund heard his harsh voice from time to time raised in quite animated controversy above Paul's full, clear tones and the chirrup of Father Antonio.

"Is not the signorina cold over there? The wind comes down the valley at this season and strikes upon the windows that overlook the village," said Father Ludovic after a time.

"I am not cold, thank you," said Rosamund. "I have my cloak," and she pulled the warm, white garment still closer about her shoulders.

"Is there any new interest in the landscape to-day?" said Paul. "There are not many features left by this awful snow."

Rosamund leaned one shoulder against the window-frame and turned her face towards the group by the fire.

"I have not seen the valley for the clouds for some days, and now this afternoon I seem to miss a familiar object. It all seems different, and yet it is still white, just as it has been ever since I came here. Yet to-day it looks dead, as though something that had lived and illuminated the whole scene had gone out of it."

Father Ludovic lifted his gaunt height from the elbow chair and came over to her side, looking with curious eyes right up the gorge. Paul followed him to the window.

After a minute or two Paul touched Ludovic on the arm.

"The water has ceased to fall from the lake up there, has it not, Father Ludovic?"

Ludovic nodded his lean, brown head.

"Yes. It is as the signorina says—the light and the life have gone out of the valley, and it looks one dead waste."

Father Antonio thrust himself into the group. "A valley of the dead," he murmured to himself. "I shall not be surprised if that is what it will prove to be."

A warning look passed between the two Fathers, and in deep and whispered conversation they presently left the room together.

Paul still stood looking from the window up towards the frozen lake. Rosamund with a sigh was turning towards the fire, when once again a fearful roar, followed by a splitting, crashing sound tore the sullen silence.

The suddenness of the sound, acting on her over-wrought nerves, startled her, and she gave a slight scream.

"Paul!" she cried, her carefully guarded self-restraint breaking down before the instinct that drives a woman in danger to the man she loves.

As a spark fires fuel, her plaintive cry, her trembling outstretched hands made him, too, forget.

"My darling—my sweet—come to me."

He caught her in his arms, and as the magic of her eyes drew his will— his soul from him, he kissed her on the mouth.

Ah! the heaven of that kiss! The rare fulfilment of a starved desire.

It thrilled her, too, with rapture, and drove the blood madly through her veins. But it also roused memory and honour. She drew herself from his embrace.

"Paul! Let us not have one thought—one word to reproach ourselves with in the future."

"The future! Rosamund, it grows nearer every hour."

She crept close to him again, but only laid a hand upon his arm, He smiled as he saw it there, resting upon the coarse brown habit, as a white rose-leaf lies on the bare ground.

"Paul, you speak hopefully of the future. Dear, that gives me courage. Is there to be a future for us— together?"

"Dearest—there is! There must be. God's hand has ruled our destinies from the first. Ah! if you could only know how I tried to kill myself and my love and my memory for you. A thousand times when I first came here I prayed to heaven that I might die. Last winter I lay at death's door for weeks, and they told me when I was well again that my restoration to health was a sign from the Almighty that I was destined for other things than to be thrust into a coffin and buried away out of sight. I thought in my foolishness that some day I might be a great preacher or reformer among men; that I might go out among these poor heathens here and reclaim some of them and bring them to the true God. But now I know that I was not saved for that. I know that I was saved for you, and you only. It must be that, or why did Providence bring you to these doors when there was the whole of Europe for you to wander over, and thousands of monasteries could shelter you?"

He took her hand and led her over to the fire. "Don't shake your head, my dear love, and don't look so sad. Don't you see that we are in God's hands— that we cannot help ourselves, you and I? We were meant for one another from the first. I myself, by the folly of my youth, by the ill-considered actions of my manhood, raised between us the greatest barriers that man knows of. But love has triumphed and destiny has won, Rosamund, and we are going away from here—not, perhaps, back to the world, but to some sweet, quiet spot where we can thank Providence for its goodness, and be happy till the real time of our inevitable separation comes.''

Rosamund raised her eyes questioningly to his.

"Back to the world, Paul? Ah! would that we were there now. But we are prisoners here."

"Yes, dearest, prisoners for the moment, but not forever. The spring is coming, and with the spring, deliverance. When the snows melt and the paths are free again they will send you with an escort down the mountain, and you can wait for me in some safe refuge till I come to you.''

A few weak tears welled in her eyes.

"When will that be, dear? Paul, it is such a terror to me to think that we must be parted, even for a little while. Cannot we leave together?''

"Perhaps. The two years for which I took my vows are nearly over. It may be that the same day will set us both free; and even if we cannot go together, be sure that my feet will tread the paths that yours will have touched, and once I am with you, darling, we shall never be parted again.''

He wiped the tears gently from her pale cheeks and drew her head down to his shoulder.

"Why, you used to be so brave, Rosamund. I always looked to you and leaned upon you, and now it is I who am the stronger.'' ·

"I am afraid," she said at length. "I am so afraid up here. They have all been good and kind to me, and I am sure that they will let me go in the springtime, but there are many weeks till that time comes.''

A loud roll, sullen and muffled, shook the earth. She trembled and clung to him.

"Rosamund, Rosamund, you must not give way to such idle fears. Look what we have lived through, you and I. As to that noise, it is but the first snows slipping from the steeper peaks to the valley. If the clouds did not lie so low, you could watch the avalanches. When the sun shines on them they are like falls of molten silver. Why, dearest, they are the harbingers of spring. Now you know that, I expect you to count each one as a friend."

"But that strange, crackling noise—there it is again—that can't be snow."

"Avalanches often carry rocks in their fall. I must go. It is just the hour for vespers."

She caught a fold of his habit in her hand.

"Paul, at what time do you all pray in the evening?"

"At nine o'clock, dear, in the refectory. We spend our hour of recreation there also, after we've finished supper."

"At nine. Paul, remember to-night that at the same hour I shall be praying, too."

She glided softly out of the room. When he was alone, he ran quickly to the window and strained his eyes in vain to pierce the heavy clouds that lay like a pall over the upper end of the valley.

"Almost I could fancy that those noises were thunder, save that the Fathers looked so grave."

The summons to vespers sounded. With a pale, thoughtful face he took his way to the chapel.

CHAPTER XLIII

THE HEADMAN'S HOUSE

In the Headman's house down in the village of Chatista the wood fire burnt low, and the lazy smoke scarcely reached the ceiling, but hung in blue wreaths among the low rafters. It was at the end of the day, and the women of the house were busy in a dark corner preparing the evening meal. Nearer to the brazier of charcoal sat the Headman himself, a powerful giant, with a blue-tasselled fez upon his head and a red shawl bound tightly round his throat. He was addressing, in low, measured terms, a group of about twenty neighbours, half of whom squatted cross-legged on the mud floor, while the others either leaned against the wooden walls or paced to and fro just within the open door. That some trouble was afoot it was easy to see, for the faces of the men, dark and heavily moustached as they were, all betrayed anxiety or anger.

"Catanio's son is dead," said the Headman, shaking his head at his friends. That is the third child he has lost this winter, and it is the twentieth youth whom death has claimed since the snows fell."

Several of the men on the floor raised their hands with a gesture of sorrow.

"The times are surely bad," went on the Headman, "when the village sees the flower and pride of its manhood dying like sheep."

One who was dressed as a Mahomedan spoke next, taking his long pipe from his mouth.

"And what of the women?" he said. "My wife Aisha is no more, and the wife of my neighbour Ali is dead. Tell us where we are to get new women to tend our huts and draw the water."

The Albanian flashed a scornful look at the Turk. He had been born of a Christian mother and a Mahomedan father, and his upbringing had been a mingling of both religions, and had made him neither a follower of God nor of His Prophet. Though he had married a Turkish girl, it had been in the Albanian fashion, taking her from the priest's house. He had the scorn of a healthy living man for the more sensual and idle Turks, who, however poor they were, kept their wives in strict seclusion, and though they treated them little better than animals, looked upon them as absolute necessities to their existence.

"I think there is a curse upon this place," cried a swarthy mountaineer from the background. "Never since the time of my grandfather — peace be to his soul!—have we had such snows."

"And never has death been so rife among us," said another.

"And never have we starved so long," put in a short man with a wide, animal mouth.

One who was leaning against the door, nis brown head crowned with a white felt skull cap and his straight lower limbs outlined by the tight-fitting pantaloons of the true Albanian mountaineer, stepped forward into the circle.

"You *think* there is a curse upon this place," he said. "I *know* there is."

"What do you know, Agar?" asked Nikleka, the Headman, fiercely.

"Perhaps one of the younger monks who lives in that

eagle's nest above us proves he is still a man and has cast eyes on that new slave of yours that you brought up from Rosega last autumn.   A woman of the village said she was beautiful.''

"Silence there!" thundered the other.   "The girl is dead.   Dead of the same strange, mysterious disease that has killed so many during the last few weeks, and as to that, Selim, I would like to see one of them dare set so much as an eye upon one of my women."   He tossed his head back and laughed.   "They do not want our women.''

A thrill ran through the group gathered in the shadows cast by the fire.   All these men—Albanians and Turks, Mussulmans and Christians—whatever they said among themselves from time to time about the saintly priesthood that lived year in and year out on the crags above them, in their hearts had always felt that grudging admiration which brave men grant to brave men.   Living as they did themselves in the comparative shelter of the valley, even their hardy natures could never withhold a tribute of wonder to these, most of whom they knew came from softer climes than their own, who voluntarily exiled themselves to the bleakest and most exposed spot on the mountains for many miles round. Their hard-working efforts in the summer months, their privations during the long winter, the stoicism with which they bore isolation and desolation had always wrung from these rough mountaineers a certain measure of respect.   Above all, those who were Mahomedans, and absolutely free in their domestic relations, had always been struck with the fact that these strange Christian men had voluntarily deprived themselves of one of the joys of life—the companionship of women. They laughed in their beards sometimes and called them fools; they made coarse jokes among themselves, and yet every man believed secretly that by what they deemed this chiefest sacrifice these Christian men were laying up for themselves a certain future of beatitude. Those among them who had from time to time left the mountains and been down to the great cities had told them of pious Mussulmans who had deprived themselves also of all the joys of life, and they could appreciate and admire, though they never wished to follow, the example of such an existence.

"Ah! but they kill—and eat—the red deer," cried Selim. "They have hung the bare bones and antlers of a red deer's head above their doorway. That in itself is a defiance to us."

"Never mind the red deer. That is an old wife's tale," sneered Nikleka. "God is angry with us or with them.ˋ You all know there is a God, whether it is He to whom they pray or our own, and this region has been blasted by His fury."

"*Ala who akbar; la Ala il ala!*" muttered a grey-bearded Turk, crouching near the brazier. "Sickness and starvation and cold have come upon us, and we are helpless."

"Nikleka is right!" cried two or three voices, as the Albanian finished, while an old woman, in a far corner began to croon a dirge about punishment and sin, and in strange rhythmical lines urged on the men to remove the stain from the village.

"Silence there!" shouted Nikleka, noticing how in a few minutes the droning words had fired the men and how they were muttering threats and curses among themselves.

"What matters it if I am silent?" called back the hag. "A sin once committed cries aloud for punish-

ment.   Wine that is spilt must be wiped up, or it leaves
a stain forever.   A sin has been committed.   Let those
who have done it meet with the just reward."

The shadowy figure sank again to the floor and the
long, withered hands of the old woman began again to
knead the coarse maize bread.

Nikleka looked round him.   He was a fair-minded
man, though stern and strict in the administration of
justice in the village.   He was born of a savage people,
and had been brought up amid savage surroundings.
The laws he administered were almost all those of his
own making, and were governed by the crudest sense of
right and wrong.   Still, in his rough way, he had always
entertained a sympathy for those men who lived out their
voluntary exile so far above his head, and if he felt anything at the vague hint that they had fallen from the
pedestal on which he had placed them, it was a sense of
disappointment more than of anger.   But the men about
him, his neighbours in the village—and some were
almost as powerful and as rich in flocks and herds as
himself—would not be easy to manage, he felt, if in the
spring a collision occurred between his own people
and the monks.   Leaning his head upon his hand, he
stared into the embers, while the men about him whispered together, and Agar, standing again by the door,
was addressing in angry tones the two or three who had
followed him.

Suddenly a great roar resounded through the air.   It
was followed by a heavy crash that shook the whole village.   It reverberated back in thunderous waves from
mountain top to mountain top, and bellowed hoarsely in
the slumbrous, snow-bound valleys.   Every man started
to his feet and made for the narrow doorway, rushing

pell-mell into the street and standing with wide eyes and open mouth staring about him. But as the sound died away a dead silence followed, and all was still and at peace again, save that here and there some of the sleepy peasants peered from their doorways, and then crept back to their blankets by their firesides.

"The Black Glacier is moving fast to-night," said Nikleka. He cast his eyes up the valley, but in the darkness nothing was to be seen. "I have never heard so great a fall."

A trembling Mahomedan on the outskirts of the group looked up at the monastery.

"I thought it was an explosion, and that Allah had wiped out the Christian dogs and the building that they have made."

Selim spoke next.

"Say rather that Allah is wiping us out. Listen! They are wailing down at Selza's hut. That means his child is dead. The little one was only taken ill three hours ago. I feared it would not live."

He spoke truly, for the howl of the mourning women pierced the quiet night air and made each man draw shudderingly nearer to his neighbour. Truly it was a fearful and a deadly sickness that walked their village street and entered at their doors, and no one knew who might be stricken next. Then each man grasped another by the arm, for a second and then a third crash sounded from the head of the gorge.

"How the ice comes down," said one to his neighbour. "Surely the glacier is not going to topple over altogether," he cried. He had jested before, and he now made a feeble attempt to be merry again. "It will be a fine sight if it does."

"Stop thy foolish tongue," said Nikleka, sharply. Then he raised his hand again above his eyes and tried to pierce the dense darkness.

"Would it were not so dark a night, that we might see what is going on up there. The Black Glacier has been moving fast for the last few weeks, and much ice has fallen since the new year. I cannot make it out."

Agar shrugged his shoulders.

"Another trouble."

Nikleka turned his fierce eyes on the pessimist.

"There may be more trouble than you think, friend Agar. I mind me of a story that I heard when I was yet a little child. It is an old tale—almost a legend—that has lived through the centuries. My father told it to me. It bodes no good when the Black Glacier stirs in its bed."

"Is it truly a portent?" cried one.

"Was the story an evil one?" said another.

Nikleka shook his head.

"I cannot tell till dawn, and even then the snows lie so thick that I doubt if we can get beyond the village, but you must sleep now, good friends, for there may be work before us."

But the group, still reluctant to part and bound together by an unknown fear, clustered closely in the narrow street. The wail of the women in the house where the child had just died had sunk for a moment into nothingness. The silence could almost be felt. Suddenly every man's head turned, and over every man's face, in the dim light that shone from the open door of Nikleka's hut, a strange look, half of expectation, half of astonishment, crept. A tiny, faint, trickling sound cut through the darkness. It was very soft and very sharp at the same time. It was the sound of trickling water, falling and dropping from a rock. Nikleka raised his hand.

"Friends, the snows are melting; the spring is at hand. We must try in a few days to get up the gorge and see what the great glacier is doing. Now, good night."

As each went down the white silent street to his own hut once more the great ice river stirred in its bed, and once more the roar and crash of the falling of tons of splintered ice pierced the night. As Agar reached his own hovel he turned and stared in the direction of the distant beetling crag with its crown of buildings. He shook his fist fiercely towards the silent mass before entering his own dark hut and shutting the tiny door behind him.

CHAPTER XLIV

THE BLACK GLACIER

The days were slowly lengthening and the weeks well set in the second quarter of the year when one day the Abbot sent for Rosamund to come to his room and told her that she might now walk, if she so pleased, upon the narrow terrace that overhung the cliff. She heard his words with astonishment, and could not keep her eyes from travelling to the window, from which nothing was to be seen but a great waste of pure white snow. The good Father smiled at the look of incredulity that came into her face.

"You think there is no change out there," he said. "It is not so. It is within these thick walls that there is no change. Once the biting colds and damps of the winter make their way in here it takes many weeks of sunshine and pure air to drive them out. But I beg you to put on your cloak to-day and walk on the terrace. Directly you set foot there you will understand why I advised you to go."

And when a few minutes later Rosamund, with her big white *capa* drawn about her and the cowl pulled over her dark locks, stepped on to the clean swept flags of the narrow promenade, she knew that the Abbot had been right. True that the snows were still thick on all sides, and that the skies here and there were veiled with a grey gauze that circled round the mountains and stretched like scarfs between the hills. But the keen cruelty had died from the air, and when she placed her hand upon the glistening snow that lay upon the parapet

she drew it back all wet, for the sun was shining and a
west wind was blowing and the snows were beginning to
melt.

A strange exultation filled her heart at the idea, and
yet for all her growing happiness she felt guilty of
ingratitude to those who had saved her from a lingering
death, and out of their own meagre store had fed and
clothed her all the winter through. She pressed her
hands over her eyes and stood with her face covered for
a moment. As she dropped them again she saw Paul
standing before her.

"You here! You and the spring together. Oh! Paul,
is this really the beginning of the end? Are we soon
going to be free?"

"The beginning of the end!" he cried. "No, it is the
beginning of the beginning. The Abbot has already been
considering how soon it will be safe to send you down
to Rosega and who are to be your escort."

"How kind he is," said Rosamund, her eyes filling
with tears at the delicious prospect that opened up
before her.

"Yes, he is a good man," Paul sighed. "It is the
thought that in leaving this place I shall grieve him that
is my one sorrow. But he is human; he is a man; and
I think when I go to him and tell him that I cannot
renew my vows—when he hears the story of our ill-
starred love—I think that he will be the first to bid me
go and to wish me, 'God-speed.'"

"Paul, when will that be? How soon shall I be able
to go, and how soon will you be able to follow me?"

"The spring comes in quickly in these parts, but the
path down the mountains will not be safe for some time
yet. Not till next month."

"Another month—only another month! Paul, it

seems too good to be true after this long imprisonment. And you—you will come at once?"

"As quickly as I can, dear love. You will not be more impatient for my coming than I shall be to join you. You must wait for me at Rosega, and together we will go to San Giovanni di Medua on the coast. From there we can take ship to Trieste, and once in Italy we shall be married before the Consul."

Rosamund, with her heart on her lips and all her love shining in her eyes, slipped her hand for one brief moment into Paul's.

"Dearest," she murmured, "our happiness will be all the greater then, for being so long deferred."

"It is a fair and promising day, is it not, signorina?" murmured a voice behind them.

Father Ludovic stood within a pace of Rosamund's shoulder. She, startled for a moment out of her self-possession, uttered a slight scream as she sprang back against the low parapet. Like lightning the monk's lean hand caught her arm.

"Be careful," he cried, warningly. "The wall is very low; you nearly fell over. And it would be a pity if you fell down there just now," continued Father Ludovic, advancing between the two, and himself leaning over the parapet. "There has been some trouble in the village the last few days, and I do not think they would take kindly to strangers just now."

Almost mechanically Rosamund's eyes followed his thin, pointing finger. Down below, the narrow village street seemed full of people. There was much hurrying to and fro, but by-and-bye the men detached themselves from the women and children and set forth, about a hundred of them, up the winding road that led from the village to the head of the gorge.

"The thaw is more advanced down there," said Father Ludovic. "The road is almost clear. See, they walk with comparative ease."

The watchers on the terrace saw that his words were true, for although the snow still lay all round the village, it was undoubtedly soft and turning to water, for every footprint left a great brown mark on the hitherto virgin ground.

"They carry picks and implements of labour, good Father," remarked Paul. "Yet it is not seed time. The fields are still wrapped in snow."

The priest nodded his head gravely.

"They dread a harvest of another kind, I fear. Watch and you will see."

A black and straggling procession amid the whiteness, the villagers toiled ankle-deep in slush and water up the narrow path. After a time they stopped, and those from above could see that they gathered together in a knot, talking and gesticulating and pointing at something that seemed to bar their progress.

"What are they doing?" asked Rosamund, with curiosity.

"The signorina's eyes are not used to gazing at the snows, or she would see amid the universal whiteness that those men are stopped, not by snow, but by ice."

"Is that where the Black Glacier has been flinging down so much ice the last few weeks?" said Rosamund, remembering the crashing sounds that had sounded day and night through the valley for so long.

"Yes," replied Father Ludovic. "God has built a wall there that man is not going to break down in a hurry."

Presently they saw two figures, with picks and axes and long iron-shod poles, slowly begin to climb the vast dam formed from the thousands of tons of ice that had accumulated right across the bed of the stream. For over an hour they scrambled and slipped, pulling themselves up by the aid of their picks, and always exhorted to further efforts by the cries and shouts of the men below. Father Ludovic brushed some of the soft snow from the top of the parapet and leaned his elbows on the wet coping-stone.

"They will have hard work to get to the top," he said. "That wall is at least four hundred and fifty feet high. I cannot think how such simple folk—unlearned as they are in science or mechanics—are going to avert the danger that their untaught instinct warns them is threatening them."

"Danger?" echoed Rosamund.

Father Ludovic turned his head and looked up into her inquiring face.

"Has no one ever told you the story of the great flood that centuries ago devastated these valleys? It is written in the history of the monastery, and is a legend with the people down there."

Suddenly he started to his full height.

"Ah, the news is bad! Watch how these two, perched on that giddy height, wring their hands and shout and sign to their friends. See how those below run about like frightened ants."

And indeed in the far distance the little dark figures, alternately crowding together and then separating amid the surrounding whiteness, looked like terrified insects. In desperate haste, the two men who had scaled the ice barrier descended once more to the ground, and then there was evidently a consultation and a drawing up of plans. One, who from his superior height and better dress, seemed to be the Headman, began to harangue the others, who pressed round him. They were a motley crowd. Some wore the pleated white kirtle and the richly embroidered vest; others the loose, baggy Turkish trousers and the scarlet fez; others again—and they were by far the finest and hardiest men—the tight pantaloons and close fitting vests that, even on a working day, were of velvet covered with embroidery.

In her eagerness to catch each action of the throng, Rosamund leaned far over the parapet, unconscious that the rough, warm wind had blown back the cowl from her head and that she stood betrayed for what she was, a woman. Suddenly those below caught sight of her and her companions. A tall man sprang before the others and with menacing finger pointed up at her.

His fierce gestures were evidently accompanied by fiercer words, for the other men surrounded him, some following his waving hand, and others endeavouring to soothe him.

Father Ludovic, who had grown strangely grey under his brown skin, thrust his head further and further over the parapet as though straining to catch the words that accompanied the all-expressive gestures.

By-and-bye he spoke, but without moving:

"The signorina had best go within."

As Paul made to follow her he caught him by the habit and signed to him to remain where he was. For a while Father Ludovic was silent, and when he spoke it was in grave, low tones.

"I am sorry they saw the signorina. They are a savage, undisciplined people, and this threatened danger"—he waved his hand towards the ice dam—"may inflame their superstitious dislike to our community."

"But do they really hate us?" asked Paul.

"No! But they do that which is akin to hate; they

fear us. In the summer, when the roads are open, they beg from us maize for their fields and physic for their sick. But in their eyes we are men who by reason of our ascetic lives and our abstention from all that makes existence dear to them, command a respect that borders on fear. I am afraid that now they have seen a woman's face and form within our walls, that respect and that fear will turn to the dangerous fanatical hatred with which a heathen people ever regard those of a different faith.''

''You think, then, that some ill may come of this?''

Father Ludovic did not answer, for he was ever a man of few words. He was gazing down into the valley again. The Headman was appealing—and not in vain—to the villagers, to consider the present danger that menaced them. With agitated gestures he pointed to the great ice wall, and seemed to be urging some immediate action. One by one the people turned again to him, leaving the tall man who had first seen Rosamund to himself. The Headman now addressed his people. Presently he snatched a pick from a bystander, and dashing at the vast barrier attacked it with fury. A score more followed him. For a few moments all seemed mere confusion to the watchers on the terrace. But by degrees they saw that a certain order had been arranged among the workers, and as each body grew weary another shift was ready to take up the task.

''They have a plan—their Headman, Nikleka, was ever an able, quick-witted fellow. Brother Paul, if, as I think, they have set themselves the enormous task of tunnelling that vast wall, they will have work that will keep them busy for many days. They will have no time to think of us or of the signorina.''

Late in the afternoon the two monks repaired again to the terrace.

"It is as I fancied," cried Father Ludovic. "They mean to try and cut a tunnel, through which the dammed up waters of the lake may escape gradually. See how they have marked out with their picks the width and height. The idea is worthy of a cleverer head even than Nikleka, but the task will be a long one and a dangerous."

The low rumble of an avalanche cut across his words. He shook his head.

"The snows are sliding fast, and help to feed the dammed up lake, while every warm day now makes the mountain sides alive with little rivulets that all flow to the same spot."

"How much water do you think is there now?"

"The basin that the barrier has formed is nearly seven thousand feet in length, and the depth varies from sixty feet to two hundred. Remember, too, that every hour the fast-melting snows are added to the volume of the prisoned water."

"No wonder they work so hard," said Paul.

A number of women were dragging up the rough road, now trodden to a watery mire, two huge iron braziers. Others were laden with fuel and torches made from pine staves.

"They mean to work all night," he added, as through the gathering dusk the braziers were lit. Bravely they flared and smoked by the side of the miry road, while a score of torches flung a lurid light on the ever-shifting crowd. Now and then a sharp puff from the warm west wind drove heavy wreaths of smoke across the scene, but by-and-bye some dusky figures dragged the fire-baskets further under the lee of the frozen barrier, and the obscuring curtain trailed raggedly away.

All during that April month and far into May did the villagers of Chatista work by day and night, while from time to time the Black Glacier heaped fresh tons of ice upon the lofty wall, and the melting snows slipped and trickled into the lake that grew with every hour. The men worked now in the very heart of the icy mass, and were only seen as they went in and came out of the tunnel. At night the braziers and torches shone like giant rubies through the hundreds of feet of clear blue ice. And Rosamund, watching the strange scene from her window, thought how beautiful it was, and promised herself to carry every detail of it back to England in her memory.

CHAPTER XLV

THE SIN OF SEX

THE first half of May was lost in the lap of time when Rosamund, leaving the terrace walk in the dusk of the spring afternoon, was summoned to the Abbot's presence.

The long winter had tried him severely, but he rose to his feet as she entered the dim room.

"My daughter!" he began in a kindly voice that trembled as he spoke, "I have sent for you to say 'farewell.'"

"Farewell! Then I may go?"

The brilliant colour leaped to her cheeks, and her eyes sparkled like twin stars.

The Abbot smiled back at her a little sadly, and bowed his head in mute assent.

At his gesture all that was tender and womanly rose within her. She drew near him and held out a pleading hand.

"I pray you, forgive me for my hasty expression of joy. Gratitude and sincere thankfulness should have sprung first from my lips."

The old man took her hand in his.

"My child, your natural delight pleases me, for it shows me that your spirits have not suffered during your long imprisonment. Of gratitude—pay none to us, but rather to the good God, who set your feet in the path to this place. We have but done our duty, and in so doing we find our reward."

He moved over to the table.

"Here is the pocketbook that belonged to your uncle. To-morrow at dawn the lay brother, Gabriel, who quits our roof, will be your escort down the mountain side."

"Brother Gabriel—he is Hassan—the Albanian, is he not?"

"The same! He will take you on the road so far as the great Cross. He knows the track well, and will be a sure guide."

"But I thought," said Rosamund, pausing an instant, "that a price was set upon his head down there—that he dare not be seen in the village."

"I did not say he would go to the village. I told you he would take you down to where the roads meet," answered the Abbot. "From there the road to Rosega is not difficult; and the Headman there will—if you give him this letter—provide you safe escort to Cettinje."

With the letter and the pocketbook clasped in her hands and her thanks all given, Rosamund still lingered.

The Abbot smiled inscrutably into her eyes until they fell, abashed at the thought that he could read the questions her lips dared not utter.

"I myself, my daughter, will convey the news of your departure to those of the community with whom you have been friendly. Now, farewell."

He raised his hands in prayerful benediction, and Rosamund, falling on her knees, received his blessing.

A gentle tapping on the panel of her door roused the girl at earliest daybreak. Starting from her bed she found that already her room was grey with the pale light of a new-born spring day. It was a very soft tapping, and for the moment she thought she must have dreamed the sound, until she remembered that her hour of freedom was come. Hastily dressing she unlatched her door. The Albanian, Hassan, with all semblance of his lay brotherhood put aside with his brown habit, stood outside. He had a cup full of milk and some bread in his hands, which he asked Rosamund to take quickly. "We both have to journey far to-day. We must start at once."

A few moments later she was crossing the cloistered courtyard. The air there was keen and damp, for the sodden melting snow still lay in the shady corners. The fawn with which she had played so often thrust a velvety nose from the ill-closed stable door as she passed. She patted it, and found it in her heart to be sorry to leave the little creature. She paused, too, by the chapel door, wondering if she should steal in and pray there for the last time. She had already raised her hand to push the door open when Hassan caught her by the cloak and hurried her on.

Outside the gloomy walls the day seemed lighter and the air dry and sweet. At the foot of the steps she had climbed so painfully many months ago the Albanian paused and hacked from a bush a stout staff.

"The way is rough. You will want it," he said in the bastard Italian he had picked up while he had been in the monastery.

Then he ran up the steps again and pulled the heavy door to with a crash.

Rosamund turned at the sound, and with parted lips and dewy eyes took silent leave of the place that had given her life, love, and home.

"Come to me soon, my dearest, come!" she whispered as she set her feet in the mountain path.

The snow had melted quite away from the rough track, and Rosamund, now that she faced a different view of her surroundings, was astonished to find how far the spring had really advanced. On either side of her the fresh grass was growing, and already the wild flowers were pushing their heads from among the tender green leaves. Down the mountain side on her right little silver streams slipped like snakes among the long grass. The pines were fast shedding their dead needles, which formed a fragrant carpet about their feet, and pale green spiky sprouts decorated the tip of every branch. Overhead the sky was a brilliant blue that grew deeper and clearer as the moments went by. Some shrill-voiced birds were singing high above her head and mingling their spring song with the feeble bleat of the baby lambs down in the meadows below.

The way wound so abruptly down the mountain side that in a few moments she had lost sight of the great grey building where she had passed so many months, and when she looked back it was only to find the pine forest clustering closely about her, and no trace of human habitation within sight or sound. The only being was the tall Albanian, who strode before her with heavy, sure steps in the loose stone path, and who as he walked looked now and again with eager eyes from side to side.

The solitude, save for the carolling of the birds and the silent, swinging figure of Hassan, was so complete, that Rosamund was unduly startled by suddenly catching sight of a figure crouched in the shelter of some low-growing bushes. Even as she turned astonished eyes in that direction, the man slipped out of sight so quickly and silently that she thought the appearance merely a trick of imagination.

Yet a vague sensation that stealthy footsteps and peering eyes were dogging her progress grew on her startled senses, and with a new feeling at her heart she hastened her pace down the ill-made path.

Perhaps it was the sound of her hurrying steps or the momentary flash of a scarlet fez from among a clump of pines that made the Albanian who walked before her suddenly pause.

As Rosamund, with throbbing heart and quick-drawn breath came up with him, he made the salutation, as of lifting his garment to his breast, his mouth, and his forehead, which she had seen in the mountain villages.

She saw at once that he was pale, and that every moment his fine, blue eyes stared to right and left. "I must leave you here," he said, hurriedly.

"Leave me here?" cried Rosamund. "The Abbot told me you would set me in the path for the village of Rosega."

He pointed with his staff down the mountain side, and she saw that the hand that carried it shook.

"There is only this path till you come to the great Cross, and then there is one road up the valley and another that goes down to Rosega. You cannot make a mistake; there are no other ways."

"And you—what will become of you?"

He glanced fearfully about him before he answered hurriedly: "They told me in the monastery that I must go when the spring came. I owe a debt of blood, and they do not wish me to pay it up there. I am going to make for the pass by a goat track, and so get down to Greece. Farewell."

In another second he plunged into a thicket, and a moment later even his footsteps crashing among the dried ferns and loose stones could be heard no longer.

Rosamund was determined to let not even the shadow of fear possess her. The day was too fair to admit any doubt of happiness or security. It was down hill to Rosega, where doubtless the people would remember her as having passed among them the previous autumn, and if now and again a pair of eyes peeped from among the bushes, or a heavily armed man slunk across her road, she could scarcely hope to have, on such a fair spring day, the whole teeming, sun-bathed mountain path to herself.

There *could* be nothing to fear.

She pushed back the hood from her head and let the sunshine play upon her face and hair. She tried once more to see if she could catch a glimpse of the monastery where Paul still was, and then she smiled to think that perhaps in another few hours his feet would tread where hers were now, and that he would hurry down the steep track to join her.

The birds sang on, and the sky grew bluer. At every fresh turn a thousand little streams came into view, rattling and tinkling in their self-made courses.   Every yard that she descended the bleating of the lambs and the lowing of the cows, turned after the long winter into the sweet, fresh pastures, sounded clearer and plainer, and Rosamund, full of thanks to God and gratitude to man that she had been preserved from an awful death and had lived safely and warmly through the past dreary months, thrust her strong staff into the loose stones before her, and with light feet almost ran down the mountain side.

She ran on with light in her eyes and a song on her lips.   Every pulse throbbed with the joy of motion and the passing of the sweet, soft air across her face.

She ran on until by degrees her lightly moving feet scarcely touched the ground in her swift flight, until the lilting song died on her white lips, and the blood ran icy cold through her veins.   For all unconsciously the knowledge came to her that she was being followed.

She never turned her head or looked from right to left, but the rustle of the bushes, the rattle of stones in the loose path, the short pant of heavily drawn breath, warned her keen senses that her footsteps were beset on all sides.

She ran on, till the whole vista of the smiling valley was stretched out before her unseeing eyes; ran till the track was flat and she knew she was near the cross roads. It was then that her foot slipped on a round stone, and she must have fallen prone in the path had not a strong hand gripped her by the arm.

"Well run! well run!" cried a mocking voice in her ears.

With a fierce energy born of a ghastly terror she tried to twist herself from the determined clutch.

"Let me go!" she cried, holding her head high and looking about her.

Before her lay the divided ways, one leading uphill to the monastery, one round the base of the low hill she remembered, towards the village, the third, which was barred by the sharp black shadow of the Black Cross, down to Rosega. But all this her eyes saw in a flash, for a moment later she was walled about with men and women, gaunt, fierce people who seemed to spring out of the earth.

It was a tall, black-browed man who held her in so close a grasp.

"Hold her, Agar!" cried the others. "Bring her to the village."

"That Nikleka should let her go again?" exclaimed Agar.

A woman, bent and hideous, thrust her way through the crowd and leered up in the girl's white face.

"What's that about Nikleka?" she screamed. "Agar is right; the Headman would only set the witch free."

The beldame's voice rose to a wild shriek as she raised her withered arms aloft.

"You've got the Sin of the Christian here—the Sin under which we've groaned and starved and died all the winter through.   Let the Punishment be here as well."

A wild yell answered the hag's words as the crowd closed in on the fainting girl.

CHAPTER XLVI

THE FLOOD

OVERNIGHT—the evening of the day on which Rosamund had left the monastery—the Abbot had sent for Paul and told him that as the term of his vows had expired he was free to leave the monastery.

"The signorina has already gone twelve hours," he had said. "It was to save scandal that I did not allow you to leave together, and it is to prevent undue comment among the brotherhood that I wish you to go in the morning without farewells or speech with any one."

The morning was a symphony of blue and gold. The sun was making a royal progress up the heavens as Paul sprang from his bed and made his final preparations for departure. At the last he caught up his strong oaken staff and heavy cloak, and from sheer habit thrust a knife and pair of long-barrelled pistols into his girdle. A moment later he was treading the polished floor of the quiet corridor and the stone staircase that led to the cloisters.

Over the well-worn flags he hurried to the iron-studded door which swung on chased hinges in the thick stone wall.

He stood upon the flight of rough steps, and with the joy of a free man inhaled deep breaths of the sweet morning air. He looked about him in all the delight and wonder with which a man regards a new world.

In the night a great snow field had slipped from the rocky side of the overhanging mountain. The scattered snow lay in patches and heaps everywhere, but the sun was fast reducing them to sparkling rivulets. Close by the edges of the track the hardy Alpine roses were putting forth green shining buds from their fantastically twisted branches.

In a hollow where the snow still lay, the tawny hairs of curled fern fronds had pushed valiantly through. Paul remembered that last May the ground about there was carpeted with dancing harebells. How beautiful it had all been then, and how beautiful it would all be again—when he and Rosamund were far away amid the rolling English grasslands.

As he set foot upon the ground and followed the path that ran beneath the outer wall of the monastery before beginning to descend, a rain of song floated down to him from the brilliant ether above. It was a lark, carolling its morning hymn. To Paul its notes sounded sweet and clear as a message from God. Jubilant he strode past the frowning walls till he rounded an angle and faced the rolling panorama of the valley and the further mountain range.

Save where a beetling crag cast a cold shadow, or a deep cleft marred the mountain side, all the lower slopes and undulating spurs were free from snow and looked in the morning sun as though spread with carpets of brilliant emerald green. Here and there were dotted groups of browsing cattle and white, heavy-fleeced sheep, at whose sides new-born lambs nestled and played.

Though he had every incentive to hurry, he was for the moment content to saunter down the first sharp dip in the path. As he went slowly on, his gaze remained riveted on the fair expanse of pasture land. He watched some women cross a field. They were calling the cows to be milked. He knew that in reality they were toil-worn, unwashed creatures, but to him—at that exquisite moment when the fulfilment of his own desires was so near attainment—they represented the sweetest ties of humanity and home. The tender thought that but a few hours before his love had gazed upon the same scene, set him dreaming for a while about her and of the life that was so soon to come to them together.

"How brave—how dear—she is," he murmured fondly to himself. "What other woman's love would have stood such trials and such temptations? Oh! Rosamund, my love, my heart, nothing that I can ever do can requite you for your staunch faith—your trust in me. From the hour in which I join you, I swear to devote my whole life to you and to your happiness. God send it may be soon! God send it may be—"

Suddenly a great crash split the air. With it came the cries of men and the booming thunder of swiftly running water. At the sound Paul gathered the heavy folds of his cloak about him and ran with sure, swift feet down the stony path. It twisted so erratically between high rocks and overhanging pines that in his impatience he fancied he had missed his way. But suddenly a sharp turn brought him again within full view of the ice dam and the prisoned lake behind it.

"The water flows! Thank God! The water flows," he cried.

The work of thirty-six days and nights had met with its reward at last. From the great, gaping mouth of the tunnel cut in the wall of ice a mighty river of thick, creamy snow water was pouring at fearful speed.

It foamed and roared as it struck the earth and tore

a course for itself through the mire and slush, fighting its way to its natural channel.   Blocks of dislodged ice, and masses of frozen snow were forced through the opening.   They shook the earth as they fell, but the people only waved gleeful hands as they stood and watched the waterfall.

The sight was grand and fascinating, but his heart urged his feet to leave the spot.   For a few moments the pathway overhung the valley, then the track took an easier gradient and bent its course round a small wood of hardy pine trees.   As he stepped within their shelter, the roaring of the liberated waters sank to a murmurous song, which harmonised with the twitter of the mating birds and the soft sighing of the western breezes in the waving branches, and helped to make love music in his ears.   Out of very joy he sang too.   Strains that breathed of love and nature—strains that he had thought never to sing again rose in his heart and poured from his lips. His feet and the sharp ring of his iron-shod staff beat time to the songs and kept him company until the swelling thunder of the torrent once more grew insistent and warned him that the pathway was bearing him again towards the face of the mountain and a view of the valley.

What a crowd there was about the waterfall.   Bent harridans and dotards waggled their palsied heads; half-naked brats splashed in the ooze; women, all cumbered with their flowing garments, heaped together a false bank for the foaming waters; the men lounged and laughed and exchanged greetings.

Suddenly a sound of music—a rolling, sonorous hymn floated up to him.   The populace knelt and with raised hands and fervent voices thanked Allah that the dreadful winter was passed and the danger which had threatened their lives and homesteads was averted.

As the people·rose to their feet again, Paul crossed himself and murmured "Amen!" then set out once more upon his way.

He was now half-way down the mountain of Argentalia, and the bleak monastery, hanging cold and grey on the cruel crag, looked from where he stood a mere rock among rocks. How sweetly different the scene was about him.

Long grasses and starry flowers peeped out shyly from the rough shelter of moss-grown boulders. The low bushes and saplings were tufted with bunches of bursting leaves. Glancing between the trees as he went, he saw a shepherd lad leading a flock of sheep up the slopes of a mountain on the further side of the valley to sweeter pastures.

The watercourse that meandered along the bottom of the valley was full, and the white, frothy waters shone like molten metal in the sun. All about his feet little streamlets sang blithe songs as they twisted like gleaming ribbons from shady spots where the snow lay wet and soft, out to the free, warm air of the mountain side. A butterfly, with gorgeous colouring, shining like cut gems, danced across Paul's path.

His eager steps brought him to a sheltered hollow low on the southern flank of the mountain. It was a favoured spot, where spring had fully come, and the tall, pale green fern sprang from a gaudy carpet of multi-coloured blossoms.

He pulled his cowl over his head, for the sun was hot, then flung himself upon the scented earth to rest a moment before surmounting the low hill which would lead him to the cross roads and the track to Rosega. Before him lay the sun-bathed panorama, backed by the great lake and the everlasting mountains. He was facing the waterfall now, and could see it very clearly, though the distance softened its mighty roar to his ears.

Suddenly he leaned forward with both elbows on his knees.

"I did not think they had made so wide a tunnel," he said to himself, with puckered brows. "It looks so large from here—as though the waters themselves had cut the ice away and widened the aperture."

As the words still lingered on his lips and in his brain the whole mountain trembled beneath him. With the hideous splitting sound, as of a riven creation, his horrified eyes saw the mighty wall of ice flung skywards in ten thousand pieces. Huge blocks of ice were tossed aloft like pebbles, and in their fall rent and ground one another with a sickening crash. It was as though a giant explosion had liberated the vast lake from its imprisonment.

The immense weight of water had burst the undermined ramparts of ice, which now, like a vast wall toppling to earth, fell in one terrific volume on the village.

As the awful mass of water struck the quivering ground, it uplifted fields and pastures like a gigantic plough. The tender green maize and the newly grown grass were torn up in sods that the water soaked instantly into pulp.

Amid the swirling waves the cottages of mud and laths melted and sank into the furious waters, as sand castles disappear at the first touch of a rising tide. With a ripping sound the wooden, white dome of the mosque was wrenched from its supporting walls, which in their turn were split to matchwood.

An orchard, hung with white blossoms and set like a fair bouquet amid the green, was crushed into nothingness, and only a branch of delicate bloom floating momentarily upon the dark bosom of the furious flood showed that it had ever existed. The grazing flocks and gambolling lambs were caught in the icy water and strangled out of life, and the quiet herds were swept like flies off the fields where they were browsing. In irresistible, rolling waves that thundered and foamed, the waters tore at the mountain's sides. Enormous boulders that for centuries had rested among the swards were torn from their beds and plunged headlong into the flood, leaving behind them in the grass-grown slopes gaping empty places that yawned like open, bleeding wounds.

Still the insatiable waves leapt on and up. A shepherd's hut here, a sheltered group of maize ricks there, were plucked away and tossed into the hideous broth. Higher the flood rose, louder it roared, hissing and boiling about a thick belt of lordly pine trees. Root and branch the waters dragged them from their mother earth and flung them hither and thither—mere slivers of splintered wood—in the awful chaos.

The great mass of water dashed its ice-strewn waves from side to side of the valley till the mountains rocked to their foundations. To Paul, paralysed at the fearful spectacle, the quivering of the earth and the wild chaos of the churning waters seemed heralds of complete dissolution.

"My God!" he cried at last, and scrambling to his feet. "The flood!—the flood!"

CHAPTER XLVII

THE PASSION OF ROSAMUND

MAD with sheer terror, unseeing, unthinking, with only the animal instinct of self-preservation hammering at his brain, Paul started to run. The track trended upwards again over the brow of the low hill beyond which lay the cross roads. The way was rough and the loose stones slipping from beneath his flying feet tripped him at every yard. But he was conscious of nothing but that he must run or die. A pandemonium of roaring water, a veritable hell of human cries pierced the shuddering air, but he ran on with never a backward look or a thought of helping any drowning creature.

At last he surmounted the hill. The path sloped gently downwards to where the cross roads, themselves elevated above the level of the valley, met. The flood, which was swirling like a millrace round the spur of the hill on which Paul stood, had not yet drawn the narrow tracks into its devouring embrace. So much and no more his wild eyes saw as he plunged headlong downhill, racing with death, until at the foot of the Black Cross he paused a moment for breath.

His heart beat like an iron hammer in his breast, the blood thundered louder than the rising waters in his ears. His eyes were strained to bursting. He pressed his hot palms over them.

"Paul! Paul!"

He hesitated and turned his pale face back over his

shoulder. Was it the sound of the waters, or the scream of some drowning woman, or the echoing cries of the frightened birds that seemed to shape his name?

"Paul! Paul!"

Weak and yet piercing, distant and yet at hand, his name throbbed on the air and rang in his ears.

"Paul!"

It was like a sigh, so mysterious that the hair rose on his head and the hot blood flowed back cold to his heart.

"Paul!"

The word was scarcely articulate, yet it crashed upon his senses with a voice of thunder.

It sounded like Rosamund's voice that called, and it was Rosamund's name he hurled again and again to the empty sky and the roaring waters and the ever-circling screaming birds, that, save himself, seemed the only living things in all that awful valley.

"Paul! Paul!"

The wailing cry tortured him.

"My love! My love! Where are you?" he gasped between the breaths that came like sobs from his heaving chest.

As he spoke, a long, rolling wave dashed madly against some jagged rocks that rose near his right hand. The waters broke with a roar and flung a cloud of spray high above the rocks and Paul and the Black Cross. He was brushing the icy drops from his eyes when he heard his name again:

"Paul!"

The sound came like the sigh of a departing spirit— from the clear air. He raised his haggard face and then gave a loud cry in which despair and love, rage and horror were commingled.

Far, far above him, with only the clear, blue sky for a background and her maiden purity for a garment, hung Rosamund Keith, lashed by rough thongs and ropes of leather to the gigantic Crucifix.

He clasped his hands before his aching eyes to shut out the dreadful vision, praying as he did so that when he looked again it might prove to be nothing more than a hideous dream.

But when he dropped his clenched fingers to his heart and raised his tortured gaze again the figure and the Cross were still there.

Across the gracious curves of her white body and the sweet fulness of her bosom her unbound hair waved like a gauzy veil, enhancing the silver fairness of her flesh. One long tendril whipped the brisk air and fluttered like a waving black ribbon out against the azure heavens. From throat to feet the spray from the dashing waves sparkled on her marble skin like glittering gems. Some of the drops hung on her pale cheeks and looked like tears.

In her passion she seemed unearthly, for the light of her eyes gleamed sombrely beneath her drooping white lids, and it was only when he saw the bow of her sad mouth part now and again in the unconscious uttering of his name that Paul realised that it was his beloved who hung martyred above him.

"God of Heaven! She is dying! They have crucified her!"

At last Paul's sleeping manhood woke in him; his virility and courage stirred at length.

With his knife between his teeth he leapt upon the stony mound, and with hands and knees clutched the rugged Cross. He first hastily hacked through the leather thongs that bound her feet, but the groan that parted

her white lips as the whole weight of her body swung
from her bruised wrists stabbed him to the heart.

"Courage! my love, courage!" he cried, as he painfully dragged himself higher and with frantic efforts
slashed at the cruel bonds.

The contact of his body, the sound of his voice
seemed to rouse in the girl some fearful memory. Her
great eyes, filled with an awful horror, opened wide, her
mouth parted in an effort to scream.

"Rosamund! 'Tis I! Paul!" he gasped, with chill
fear knocking at his heart, as he struggled to unloose
the knotted ropes.

The blinding spray from the tossing waves dashed
again in his face, the bitter drops stinging like the lash
of a whip.

He could hear the stones at the foot of the Crucifix
slipping into the ever-rising waters, he could feel the
great tree tremble and sway with every motion of his
body. Would the knife never sever the fastenings, or
must they die together?

With a final mighty effort he cut the last strand, and
the white wonder of Rosamund's body fell forward into
his arms.

"Paul!" she cried in a low voice, as she felt his
warm lips pressed against her cold cheek.

He saw now how the flood had swollen, and how like
a boiling rapid it came tearing between the jutting spurs
of the mountains. So high had the water risen that
already between the Cross and the slope of the grassy
hill down which he had run in his anxiety to escape, a
pool had formed. He knew that the next wave must
drag the fatal tree and all that surrounded it to the universal destruction on all sides.

Bracing himself for one last struggle, he put forth all

his strength, and with his love held against his heart, leapt the ever-widening gulf.   Then, with the water streaming from the edges of his cloak, his goatskin shoes sodden to a pulp, and the lifeless form of the girl he loved in his arms, he toiled up the steep rugged path, scaling rocks and fording streams, and only raising his eyes from her dear face to seek some safe, sun-warmed spot, where he might lay his burden down.

His head swam and his knees trembled under him before he found the refuge he sought.   It was a nook high up in the mountains, flower-carpeted, and hedged about with tall ferns and low, thick bushes.   From the rock that overhung it fell a tiny stream with a tinkle like the ringing of fairy bells.   Folding his cloak about Rosamund, and binding for greater warmth the long masses of her hair about her throat, he chafed the blood back to her clay-cold feet and poor bruised wrists.

She moaned, even at his tender touch, but the heavy lids still hung over her eyes, and her mouth was grey and drawn.   Almost in despair he filled his curved palms from the singing stream and dashed the water in her face.

"Paul!" had been her last cry and "Paul!" was her first on wakening.

"Dearest love, I am here.   Please God! you are safe!" he murmured, bending over her.

She smiled up at him, expressing all her love and her gratitude in one look of her radiant trust.

With reviving strength came confidence and courage, and while Paul pulled some broad, cool leaves and bound them with long grass about her wounded white wrists and slender feet, from sheer exhaustion she fell asleep. He kissed her as he folded her closer in the cloak.

He went a little way apart to seek a path which they might follow to shelter and safety.   Higher up the hill he turned and gazed down at the ruin that spread from end to end of the valley. He saw the waste of waters, surging to and fro, dashing high hungry waves over barren mountain slopes that less than an hour back had looked so green and peaceful. The turgid, foam-flecked surface of the flood was broken with the wreckage of a hundred farms and homesteads. Cattle and the women who had tended them, babes and their bearded fathers, ricks of maize, straw, and hay, fragments of houses and of the white mosque itself, tossed in one frightful chaos of destruction and death on the boiling waters; while now and then, as though the work were not yet done, mighty ice floes rolled by, crushing to pulp everything that came in their furious course.

Over all the terrible scene the sweet sun shone and birds, heavy in flight and cruel-beaked, wheeled and croaked. Sickened at last, he turned from the terrible sight, and made his way over the side of the mountain. As he climbed the brow of the hill the blue smoke of a camp fire met his sight and the welcome sound of voices struck his ears.

He hastened back to Rosamund, who had already wakened and was calling his name. At sight of Paul she struggled to her feet, but tottered weakly and stretched out her hands in a mute appeal for his support.

He hastened to her, and caught her in his arms.

"Dearest, come away from this place. I have found help and good people who will take us to safety and happiness."

She raised her dark eyes, swimming with love and tears to his face.

He stooped and kissed her on the mouth.

www.ingramcontent.com/pod-product-compliance
Lightning Source LLC
Chambersburg PA
CBHW031813270326
41932CB00008B/404